Learning Maya 7 | The Modeling & Animation Handbook

Alias | Learning Tools

ACKNOWLEDGEMENTS

Cover design:
Louis Fishauf

Cover image and interior book design:
Ian McFadyen

Production designer:
Diane Erlich

Editorial services:
Erica Fyvie

Technical Editor:
Cathy McGinnis

Additional technical review:
Marc Beaudoin, Rick Kogucki, Elliot Grossmann

DVD production:
Roark Andrade and Julio Lopez

Production Coordinator:
Lenni Rodrigues

Project Manager:
Carla Sharkey

Product Manager, Learning Tools and Training:
Danielle Lamothe

Director, Learning Tools and Training:
Michael Stamler

ABOUT *THE CHUBBCHUBBS!*

Sony Pictures Imageworks

The Academy Award® for best animated short film has a long and prestigious history that dates back to the 5th Academy Award ceremonies in 1932. Each year the competition is incredibly intense, and 2002 was no exception. How ironic, then, that the winner would have been a film created in-house at Sony Pictures Imageworks merely as a test of their animation pipeline. *"The ChubbChubbs!* was never even intended for release," explains Imageworks President, Tim Sarnoff. "When it was finished we showed it to people here at the studio and some of the executives in theatrical distribution decided it was worth showing to exhibitors. To our surprise people just kept responding enthusiastically."
The decision to test the Imageworks pipeline came about in the fall of 2001 when the company was looking into opening Sony Pictures Animation. While the two companies would share facilities and other resources, the mandate of animation would be geared more towards creating fully CG features while Imageworks would continue to focus on delivering high caliber visual effects. The best way to ascertain if the Imageworks effects pipeline could also support the production of full-length CG films was, of course, to try producing a complete CG film with it.

"We invited staff members to pitch their story ideas," recounts Sarnoff. "Jeff Wolverton, one of our animators pitched a story he called '*Attack of the ChubbChubbs*', and we chose it as the best candidate."

The story stars an awkward little alien, Meeper, with a kind heart and big dreams. As the "mop boy" of the intergalactic "Ale-E-Inn" bar he does have some difficulty getting the "respect" he deserves especially as he tries to warn the bar's patrons of an impending invasion by the fearsome ChubbChubbs.

FOREWARD

Doug Walker | President, Alias

As the President of Alias since 2001, I've had the privilege of watching the development of the 3D graphics industry from a unique perspective. I've been able to visit countless customer sites and watch the development of those customers' projects over time. While the nature of this collection of work may have varied greatly, they all shared one thing in common - their backbones were built on Alias technology. It's wonderful to see artists, designers, developers and others achieve incredible results and push the boundaries of what our software can do. It's even better to watch them get rewarded for it. And the rewards? They never stop.

I've been thrilled to watch Alias customers accept numerous accolades around the world and I'm proud of the role we've played in helping them get there. Because, ultimately, making Maya the world's most powerful 3D modeling and animation tool isn't just about selling software, it's about giving our customers what's necessary to be successful. It's about incorporating your feedback and continuously improving our tools to give you, the artist, the power you need to make your creative vision come alive. This ongoing process reaffirms our Corporate Vision – Alias | Imagination's Engine.

The book you hold in your hands is the result of one of the unique partnerships we have with our customers. "For more than a decade, Alias and Sony Pictures Imageworks have partnered with a common purpose - to use technology to create the most spectacular onscreen imagery," says Tim Sarnoff, President of Imageworks. "To continue surprising and surpassing the expectations of our audiences we need to constantly push ourselves. This challenge will never end for us - and that's why our partnership with Alias will continue to be critical to the success of Imageworks."

When we first approached Imageworks to see if they could contribute to this book, their enthusiasm was clear and they generously provided assets from their Academy Award-winning short film *The ChubbChubbs!* Within the pages of this book, you'll have the opportunity to model and animate production-quality characters like the awkward alien, Meeper, and the buxom singing Diva. By working with such characters you'll gain experience not only in modeling and animating in Maya, but in making the right decisions at each stage of the production pipeline. We also included a section on animating in Alias MotionBuilder to provide you with additional insight into the possibilities of opening up your pipeline to complementary technology.

In any art form, success isn't achieved by creativity alone. Hard work, dedication, long hours and sacrifice are all part of the recipe for success. Mastering your craft takes time and devotion. It isn't easy, but making your vision a reality is the most rewarding work of all. I'm confident this book can help you get there. We provide the engine, you provide the imagination - the possibilities are endless.

Doug Walker
President, Alias

This book would not have been possible without the generous help of Sony Pictures Imageworks. We would like to thank Camille Bingcang, Jerry Schmitz and Sande Scoredos for their tremendous contributions.

Primary author: Marc-André Guindon

Marc-André Guindon is the founder of Realities Studio (www.RealitiesStudio.com), a Montreal-based production facility. An advanced user of both Maya® and Alias® MotionBuilder® softwares, Marc-André and Realities have partnered with Alias on several projects, including *The Art of Maya*, *Learning Maya 6 | MEL® Fundamentals*, and the *Learning Maya 7* series. Realities Studio was also the driving force behind Pipeline Technique DVDs, such as *How to Integrate Quadrupeds into a Production Pipeline* and *Maya and MotionBuilder Pipeline*. Realities also created the Maya Quick Reference Sheets and contributed to *Creating Striking Graphics with Maya & Photoshop®* .

Marc-André has established complex pipelines and developed numerous plug-ins and tools for a variety of projects in both the film and games industries. His latest projects include the integration of motion capture for the Outlaw Game Series (*Outlaw Volleyball*, *Outlaw Golf 1* and *2* and *Outlaw Tennis*). He served as Technical Director on *XXX2, State of the Union* (Revolution Studios), *ScoobyDoo 2* (Warner Bros. Pictures), and *Dawn of the Dead* (Universal Pictures).

Marc-André is also an Maya MasterClass™ presenter. Marc-André continues to seek additional challenges for himself, Realities and his crew.

Contributing authors:

The following authors whose contributions have helped shape this book into what it is today:

Bill Dwelly, Lee Graft, Petre Gheorghian, Aref Hauer, Alan Harris, Cathy McGinnis, Cory Mogk, Rob Ormond, Chris Pawlik, Damon Riesberg.

A special thanks goes out to:

Carmela Bourassa, Steve Cimicata, Deion Green, John Gross, Dave Haapalehto, Rachael Jackson, Lorraine McAlpine, Brahm Nathans, James Christopher, Anthony Nehme, Paula Suitor, Jill Ramsay, Shai Hinitz.

We would like to thank Turbo Squid (www.turbosquid.com) for providing the bonus models included in this book's DVD-ROM. Thanks to Beau Perschall, Dan Lion and Brian Gaffney.

The film's director, Eric Armstrong, worked closely with Wolverton and the Imageworks storyboard department to hone the original story concept into a five minute piece. Meanwhile the film's producer, Jacquie Barnbrook was busy managing the project: finding artists who had time to devote to it, arranging sound and music production and keeping Armstrong – who was busy co-supervising the animation for *Stuart Little II* at the same time – on schedule.

Armstrong believes that, over the course of the project, there were probably about one hundred digital artists who had a hand in *The ChubbChubbs!* The reason for the large number is that animators were brought in as they became available, and left when another more official project came along. The maximum at any one given time were as many as fifteen Maya animators working on modeling, rigging and character/camera animation.

Imageworks has been using Maya for years in its visual effects pipeline. "We did a test a few years ago and found Maya to be the most flexible and powerful 3D package on the market," states Armstrong. "From that point on we've been using it for our modeling and animation needs."

Before winning the Oscar® for best animated short film, *The ChubbChubbs!* took first place at the Los Angeles International Short Film Festival, the London Effects and Animation Festival, and the Australia Effects and Animation Festival. Such a plethora of accolades is more than enough proof that the ChubbChubbs animation pipeline test has been – to put it mildly – a success, and that the Imageworks, Maya-centered pipeline is capable of producing animated features second to none.

Sony Pictures Imageworks also produced a second "made with Maya" film entitled *Early Bloomer* which was released in theaters in May 2003. The popular short stars an adorable but awkward tadpole trying to fit in with her mischievous friends. In September 2006, Imageworks expects to launch *Open Season*, Sony Pictures Entertainment's first fully animated feature length film from Sony Pictures Animation, featuring the voices of Martin Lawrence, Ashton Kutcher, Debra Messing and Gary Sinise.

Introduction

Project01

Project02

Project03

Project04

Project 05

Project 06

Project 07

Project 08

HOW TO USE THIS BOOK

How you use this book will depend on your experience with computer graphics and 3D animation. This book moves at a fast pace and is designed to help the intermediate level user improve their modeling and animation skills and understand how they relate to one another in a production pipeline. If this is your first experience with 3D software, we suggest that you begin with the *Learning Maya 7 | Foundation* book, as the prerequisite before proceeding through the lessons in this book. If you are already familiar with Maya or another 3D package, you can dive in and complete the lessons as written.

Updates to this book

In an effort to ensure your continued success through the lessons in this book, please visit our web site for the latest updates available: www.alias.com/learningtools_updates/

Windows® and Macintosh®

This book is written to cover Windows and Macintosh platforms. Graphics and text have been modified where applicable. You may notice that your screen varies slightly from the illustrations depending on the platform you are using.

Things to watch for:

Window focus may differ. For example, if you are on Windows, you have to click in the panels with your middle mouse button to make it active.

To select multiple attributes in Windows, use the Ctrl key. On Macintosh, use the Command key. To modify pivot position in Windows, use the Insert key. On Macintosh, use the Home key.

Alias packaging

This book can be used with either Maya Complete™, Maya Unlimited™, or Maya Personal Learning Edition, as the lessons included here focus on functionality shared among all 3 software packages.

As a bonus feature, this hands-on book will also introduce you to animation in Alias® MotionBuilder.®

These lessons can be completed with Alias MotionBuilder, or Alias MotionBuilder Personal Learning Edition software.

Learning Maya DVD-ROM

The Learning Maya DVD-ROM contains several resources to accelerate your learning experience including:

- Lesson support files

- Instructor-led overviews to guide you through the projects in the book.

- Interview with Alias Certified Instructor Cathy McGinnis

- Excerpt from the Sony Pictures Imageworks' short *The ChubbChubbs!*

- Turbo Squid 3D models – Value $460.00US

We recommend that you watch the instructor-led overviews before proceeding with the lessons in this book.

Because learning never stops, we've provided you with some great models from Turbo Squid for your use. Turbo Squid delivers innovative 3D models from artists around the planet. From automobiles to zebras, you're sure to find 3D models that fit your needs. To access these files, copy the *turbo_squid* folder from the DVD-ROM at the back of this book.

The following models are located in the Turbo-Squid folder of the DVD-ROM:

USMC Soldier model provided courtesy of Jan Absolin of Polygon Puppet. Copyright 2004.

Jill model provided courtesy of Newkat Studios. Copyright 2005.

Renault Alpine Rally car model provided courtesy of Jeff M. Garstecki (a.k.a. stecki). Copyright 2002.

Skyscraper and City Building models provided courtesy of Teinye Horsfall (a.k.a. giimann). Copyright 2003.

FBX Skyscraper and Real-Time Building models provided courtesy of Matt Thomas (a.k.a. ES3D). Copyright 2004-2005.

Installing lesson support files – before beginning the lessons in this book, you will need to install the lesson support files. Copy the project directories found in the *support_files* folder on the DVD disc to the *Maya\projects* directory on your computer. Launch Maya and set the project by going to File > Project > Set... and selecting the appropriate project.

Windows: *C:\Documents and Settings\username\My Documents\maya\projects*

Macintosh: *Macintosh HD:Users:username:Documents:maya:projects*

Please note: *Support files require Maya version 7*

Project One

Lessons

In Project One, you are going to model Meeper, a little alien, as a full polygonal character. This will give you the chance to explore more in-depth polygonal modeling.

You will start by revising the basics of polygon components. Then you will model Meeper's body using reference images. Once that is complete, you will model Meeper's head and attach it to the body.

These lessons offer you a good look at some of the key concepts and workflows for modeling in polygons.

Once the model is finalized, you will take a look into polygon texturing.

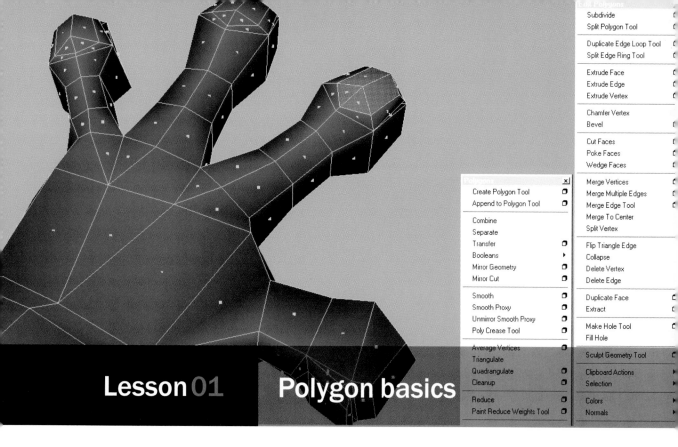

Lesson 01 — Polygon basics

Building polygonal surfaces in Maya is fast and easy. This lesson will cover the fundamental concepts of polygonal geometry and take you through the basic tools and techniques essential to building quality polygonal models.

In this lesson you will learn the following:

- The composition of a polygon;

- How to view polygonal surfaces and components;

- How to edit a simple polygonal model;

- How to diagnose polygon geometry problems.

What is a polygon?

The most basic definition of a polygon is a shape defined by its corners (vertices) and the straight lines between them (edges).

Maya uses polygons to create surfaces by filling in the space defined by the edges with a face. Three sets of edges and vertices form a triangular face, or *tri*. Four sets of edges and vertices form a quadrilateral face, or *quad*. Any number of edges and vertices beyond four form what is referred to in Maya as an *n-sided* face.

A single polygon face in Maya is sometimes referred to as a *polygon*.

POLY SHELLS VS. POLY OBJECTS

When several individual polygons are connected together sharing edges and vertices, we refer to this as a *polygon shell*. When connecting faces together, there is no limit to the number of faces and topology of these faces. Therefore, polygonal meshes can form just about any arbitrary shape desired and are not restricted by the rules that limit NURBS surfaces.

When several polygonal shells are combined together in one shape node residing under one transform node, we usually refer to this as a *polygon object*. The shells may appear to be singular objects but Maya now considers them as being one shape, or poly object, or mesh.

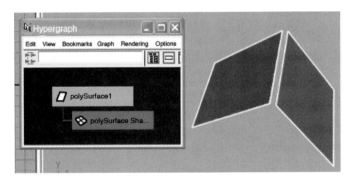

Two polygon shells in one polygon object

Creating a triangle, a quad and combining meshes

You are going to create two simple polygon objects, a triangle and a quad, using the *Create Polygon Tool*. You will then combine the two polygons to form one polygonal object, even though they will still be two separate polygon shells.

1 Create two simple polygons

- Switch to the **Modeling** menu set by pressing the **F3** key.

- Select **Polygons** → **Create Polygon** and in the *top* view place three points, then press the **Enter** key to finish the creation.

You have now created the first polygon.

- Repeat the above step, but this time placing four points to create a quad.

- Select **Window** → **Hypergraph**.

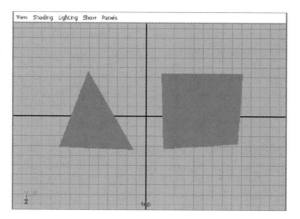

A triangle mesh and a quad mesh

You should see two objects: polysurface1 and polysurface2.

- Within the Hypergraph window, display the object's shape nodes by selecting **Options** → **Display** → **Shape Nodes**.

You should now see the two transform nodes and their respective shape nodes listed in the Hypergraph.

2   Combine the triangle and the quad

- Select *polySurface1* and *polySurface2*, then select **Polygons** → **Combine** in order to create a single polygon object out of the two polygon shells.

You will notice in the Hypergraph that a third new transform node and shape node has been created called polySurface3. If you select polySurface3, the two shells will be selected. You may notice that the original two transform/shape nodes still exist, connected by construction history. Maya will commonly leave nodes in the scene until you delete history on an object. If you wish to delete these nodes, select polySurface3 and **Edit** → **Delete By Type** → **History***.*

POLYGON COMPONENTS

Before you start modeling with polygons, it's a good idea to understand what components make up a polygon and how you can use these components to model in Maya. Some polygon components can be modified in order to directly affect the topology, or shape, of the geometry while other polygon components can be modified to affect how the polygon looks when rendered or shaded.

Vertices

The points that define the corners of a single polygon are called *vertices*, or singularly, a *vertex*. Vertices can be directly manipulated to change the topology of a polygon.

Edges

The lines connecting the vertices of a single polygon are called *edges*. Edges can be directly manipulated to change the topology of a polygon. The outside edges of a polygon shell are referred to as border edges.

Faces

The filled in area bounded by the vertices and edges of your polygon is called a *face*. Faces can be directly manipulated to change the topology of a polygon.

UVs

At the same location as the vertices on a polygon is another component called a *UV*. UVs are used to help apply textures to polygons. Textures exist in a 2D pixel based space with a set width and height. In order for Maya to understand how to apply a 2D texture to a 3D polygon, a 2D coordinate system, called *texture space,* is used. The UV at a given vertex is the 2D texture space position, or coordinate, for that vertex. The pixel at that position on the texture map will be located at that vertex.

UVs can be selected in the 3D space in Maya, but cannot be manipulated in 3D space. In order to directly manipulate UVs, you need to open the *UV Texture Editor*.

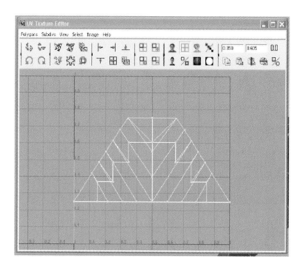

The UV Texture Editor window

Face normals

A polygon face can point in one of two directions. The component used to define the direction is called a *face normal*. Face normals cannot be directly manipulated, but they can be reversed if they are pointing in the wrong direction. Maya, by default, draws both sides of a polygon, but in technical terms polygons only have one facing direction represented by the normal direction. When using the Create Polygon Tool, the direction the polygon is created in will affect the initial face normal direction. When the polygon is created placing vertices in a clockwise direction, the normal will face away from you. When placing vertices in a counter-clockwise direction, the normal will face towards you.

Vertex normals

At each vertex, a third component exists called a *vertex normal*. The vertex normal is used to define how the polygon will look when shaded or rendered. When all vertex normals of shared faces point in the same direction, the transition from one face to another will appear smooth when shaded or rendered.

In this state, vertex normals are often referred to as *soft*. Alternatively, when all vertex normals of shared faces point in the same direction as the face normals, a sharp transition will appear between the faces. Vertex normals in this state are commonly referred to as *hard*.

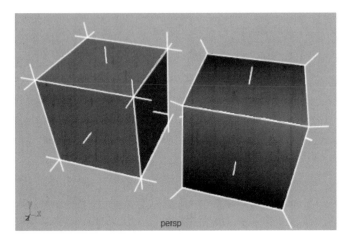

Soft and hard vertex normals

Tip: **RMB-click** *over a polygon object to easily select polygon components.*

Assessing and correcting polygon geometry

In this exercise, you will use the Custom Polygon Display window to assess different component aspects of a polygon object. You will also use selection constraints to select problematic components based on specific criteria. Once you have assessed the geometry, you will use several polygon editing tools to correct any problems.

1   Open the stair geometry file

- Select **File** → **Open** and select the *01-stairs.ma* file.

You should see a simple scene file with a set of stairs going up and down. This piece of geometry appears to be fine. You will now assess it to identify any hidden problems.

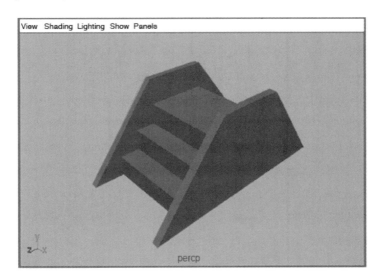

Simple stairs

2   Assess stairs with custom polygon display

- Select the stair geometry, then select **Display** → **Custom Polygon Display** → ❑, and set the following:

    Highlight Border Edges to **On**.

    Face Normals to **On**;

- Click **Apply and Close**.

Custom Polygon Display is an excellent tool for assessing polygon geometry. The polygon's border edges, which define the border of polygon shells, are now displayed three times thicker than regular edges, while the face normals appear as a line extending from the center of the face. The border edges show that the stairs are not one shell but two, and half of the face normals can now be seen to be pointing inward.

3   Correct the normals and merge the two shells

- **RMB-click** over the stair geometry and select **Face** component selection from the marking menu.

- Select the faces on the half of the stairs with the normals pointing inward and select **Edit Polygons** → **Normals** → **Reverse**.

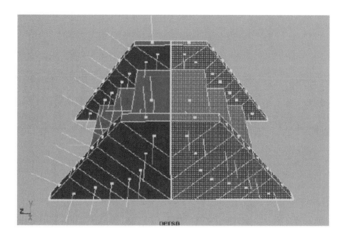

Normals to be reversed

- Select the vertices running down the center of the stair geometry and select **Edit Polygons** → **Merge Vertices**.

You will notice the border edge that was running down the middle of the stairs is now gone, indicating that there is currently only one polygon shell.

Note: *In this case, the normals of the stairs were reversed before trying to merge the vertices because vertices can only be performed on geometry that has normals pointing in the same direction.*

Alias
Tip: *Scene files get mysteriously filled with clutter, just like my house. It really helps to clean up regularly so that you're not tripping over unused locators or invalid NURBS curves. It eliminates some of the possible causes for problems later on, making it easier to troubleshoot the actual cause. And mom can be proud because you're always wearing clean data.*

Chris Carden | Technical Consultant

4   Floating vertices

When modeling with polygons, vertices that are no longer necessary can
be left behind accidentally. These floating vertices can present a problem
down the road so it is a good idea to keep an eye out for them and clean
them up. While it can be hard to locate these vertices visually, the Selection
Constraint Tool makes this task easy by allowing you to select polygon
objects and components based on different criteria.

- Select the stairs, switch to **Vertex** component selection mode and select
  all the vertices.

- Select **Edit Polygons** → **Selection** → **Selection Constraints** to open the
  Selection Constraints window with options related to vertex selection.

- In the **Constrain** section, select **All** and **Next**. Now open the **Geometry**
  section, and in the **Neighbors** section, set **Activate** to **On** and set the **min
  value** to **0** and the **max value** to **2**.

The floating vertices remaining on the stairs are now selected.

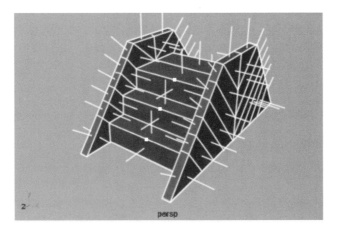

Floating vertices

Tip: *By setting the Selection Constraints to select vertices with a maximum
of two neighboring vertices, only the floating vertices, which always have
only two neighbors, will be selected.*

- With the vertices still selected, select **Edit Polygons** → **Delete Vertex**.

*The floating vertices are now deleted, or cleaned up, and the stairs are
finished. Now use the **Custom Polygon Display** to turn **Off** the display of the
border edges and face normals.*

IMPORTANT POLYGON CONSIDERATIONS

Planar and non-planar polygons

If all vertices of a polygon face reside on the same plane in world space, that face is considered *planar*. Because triangles always form a plane, triangular faces are always planar. If a face has four or more sides, and one or more of its vertices do not reside on the same plane, that face is considered *non-planar*. Whether a face is planar or not is important. A non-planar face may render improperly under certain circumstances and may not export correctly to a game engine.

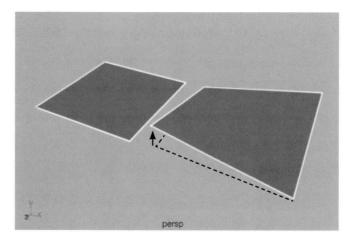

Planar and non-planar faces

Manifold and non-manifold geometry

While the arbitrary nature of polygonal surfaces provides tremendous freedom and flexibility when it comes to creating surface topology, it can also lead to invalid, or *non-manifold* geometry.

Manifold polygon geometry is standard polygon geometry that can be cut and unfolded. Non-manifold geometry is geometry that, due to the way the faces are connected, cannot be unfolded. The three types of non-manifold geometry are:

- *T-shaped* geometry - formed when three faces share a common edge.

- *Bowtie* geometry - formed when two faces share a vertex but not an edge.

- *Reversed normals* geometry - formed when two faces sharing an edge have opposing face normals.

Non-manifold geometry is considered invalid geometry because several modeling operations will not work with this type of geometry. Therefore, it is a good idea to avoid such geometry or clean up polygons with non-manifold geometry.

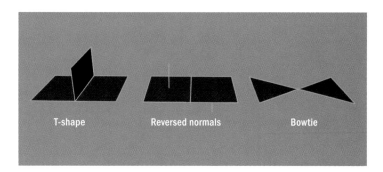

Types of non-manifold geometry

Lamina faces

Lamina faces are two faces that share all vertices and edges. The two faces are essentially laminated together and are considered incorrect geometry.

Polygon Cleanup

Polygon Cleanup is an excellent tool for dealing with non-planar faces, non-manifold geometry and lamina faces, as well as other unwanted polygon conditions. It is a good idea to perform a cleanup operation on your models when you are finished modeling to ensure the geometry is good. In the following lesson, Polygon Cleanup will be explored to correct problem geometry.

Conclusion

Understanding the anatomy of polygons before you start creating polygonal geometry in Maya can greatly assist diagnosis of your models. Knowing what you can do with polygon components can help you assess the best way to approach certain situations. Awareness of some of the problem conditions that can arise with polygons will help you quickly correct them. With this base knowledge, you are now ready to begin creating your own polygon objects.

In the next lesson, you will model Meeper's body.

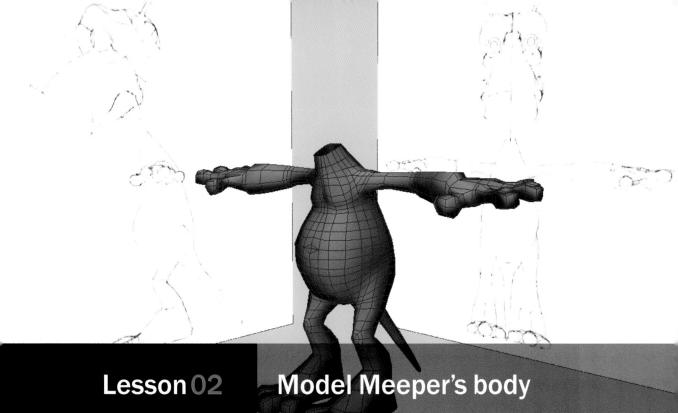

Lesson 02   Model Meeper's body

In this lesson, Maya polygonal tools and techniques will be applied to model the biped alien Meeper. You will model the torso, arms, legs and tail. The head of the character will be modeled separately in the next lesson.

In this lesson you will learn the following:

- How to model starting from a cube primitive;

- How to set up reference images with image planes;

- How to access polygonal components;

- How to edit the topology of a polygonal model;

- How to use several polygonal tools;

- How to create and work with edge loops;

- How to refine geometry in consideration of character muscles;

- How to mirror a model;

- How to smooth polygons to see the final result.

Character modeling and topology

It is important to plan before you begin modeling a character. This character will be broken down into three major areas:

Torso

The torso will be built from a primitive cube and extruded to add initial form.

Leg

One leg will extrude out from the torso and split to add detail. It will then later be mirrored.

Arm

One arm will be extruded from the torso in the same manner as the leg, and then mirrored.

Note: *When modeling characters, the two most important considerations when designing the flow of topology are (1) matching the shape of the character exactly, and (2) designing the topology so it will deform properly when animated. Typically, horizontal and vertical lines of topology will run through your entire character to define the overall shape, and loops of edges will be used to define areas of deformation, such as muscle mass. When creating characters with polygons, you want to define the shape with the least amount of detail as possible. If you end up with a mesh that has an unnecessarily large amount of detail, it can become very difficult to manage. Due to the linear nature of polygons, a polygon smooth operation can be used towards the end of the procedure to smooth the mesh for a more organic shape.*

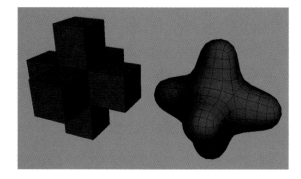

Smoothed object

Setting up Maya

You should copy the *Learning Maya* support files to your *Maya projects* directory. Support files are found in the *support_files* directory on the DVD-ROM included with this book.

The typical location of the *Maya projects* directory on your machine is:

Windows: *Drive:\Documents and Settings\username\My Documents\maya\projects*
Mac OS X: *Users/username/Library/Preferences/Alias/maya/projects*

Note: *To avoid the Cannot Save Workspace error, ensure that the support files are not read only after you copy them from the DVD-ROM.*

1   Set your new project

In order to follow this lesson, set your current project as *project1*.

- Go to the **File** menu and select **Project → Set...**

- Click on the folder named *project1* to select it.

- Click on the **OK** button.

This ensures that Maya is looking into the proper sub-directories when it opens up scene files or searches for images.

Image planes

To help create the character, image planes will be used for reference. Image planes are a great way to develop your model based on display images in the modeling windows.

1   Start a new scene

- File → **New Scene**.

Do not manipulate any of the cameras.

2   Create an image plane for the front camera

- Open the Hypershade window with **Window → Rendering Editors → Hypershade**.

- Display both the top and bottom tabs of the Work Area if they are not already displayed.

- Click on the **Cameras** tab to display all the cameras in the scene in the top panel.

- **MMB-drag** the *frontShape* camera down to the Work Area panel.

- In the **Create** column, select **Create All Nodes** from the drop-down list.

- Scroll down to the **Image Planes** tab and drag an *imagePlane* onto the camera named *frontShape* in the Work Area.

A connection menu will be displayed.

- Select the **Default** connection from the pop-up menu.

The new imagePlane is now connected to the camera.

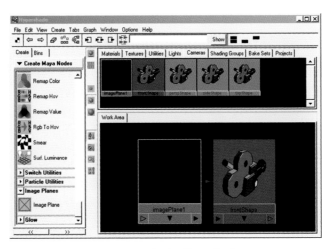

Image plane in the Hypershade

3   Add an image to the image plane

- **Double-click** on the *imagePlane1* node to open the Attribute Editor.

- Click on the folder beside the **Image Name** attribute and import the image called *meeperBodyFront.tif* from the *sourceImages* folder.

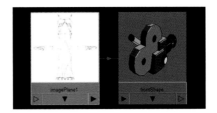

Image added to image plane

Note: *If the cameras were not moved before creating the image planes, the image should be properly aligned. If for some reason you have image planes that do not line up properly, they can be adjusted under* **Placement Extras** *in the Attribute Editor. Use the* **Center X, Y, and Z** *attributes to transform the image plane.* **Width** *and* **Height** *can be used to adjust the size. These attributes are also available in the Channel Box.*

4   Create an image for the side and top cameras

- Repeat steps 2 and 3 to bring in the image *meeperBodySide.tif* for the *side* camera and the image *meeperBodyTop.tif* for the *top* camera.

5   Move the image planes

- Under **Placement Extras**, set the *imagePlane1* **Center Z** attribute to **-20**.

- Set the *imagePlane2* **Center X** attribute to **-20**.

- Set the *imagePlane3* **Center Y** attribute to **-20**.

This will move the image planes off center and give you a clear view of your geometry in the Perspective panel.

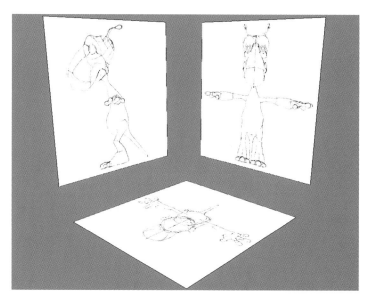

Image planes in Perspective view

Model the torso

Now that image planes have been created in the scene for reference, the model building can start. The torso will be modeled from a polygon cube. Initially, the torso shape will be blocked in and used to represent the overall general shape.

1 Create a polygon cube

- Make the front view active, select **Create → Polygon primitive → Cube → ❐**, and set the following:

  Subdivisions Along Width to **4**;

  Subdivisions Along Height to **1**;

  Subdivisions Along Depth to **3**.

- Move and scale the cube so it is placed at the base of the torso at the waist position, and is approximately the width and thickness of the torso.

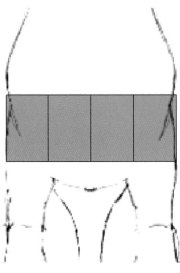

Initial cube

Note: *In your viewports, under* **Shading → Shade Options**, *you should set* **Wireframe on Shaded** *and* **X-ray** *modes to* **On**. *This setup will allow you to modify your geometry and see the image plane reference. It will also allow you to assess the flow of the polygon topology.*

- Move and scale the vertices of the *cube* to better represent the waist and pelvic regions of the character.

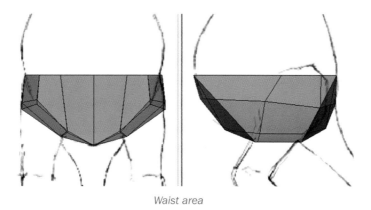

Waist area

Tip: *The most important adjustment you will make is moving the bottom row of vertices to facilitate the legs, which will join into the torso. Remember to make your adjustment in the front, side and top views.*

- Rename the cube to *torso*.

2   Extruding the torso

The next step is to create the initial overall shape for the rest of the torso. **Extrude Face** will be used for this step. Multiple extrusions will be used to define the shape at key points moving up the torso.

- Enable the **Polygons** → **Tool Options** → **Keep Faces Together** option before extruding.

- Select the faces at the top of the torso and then select **Edit Polygons** → **Extrude Face**.

- Extrude **six** times moving up the torso, defining a horizontal line of edges at the middle of the belly, the top of the belly, the bottom of the chest, the top of the chest, the base of the neck, and lastly, the middle of the neck.

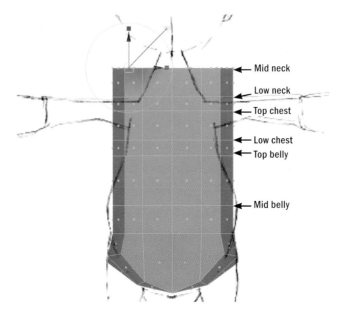

Mid neck
Low neck
Top chest
Low chest
Top belly
Mid belly

Extrude up the torso

▪ Move, rotate and scale the vertices in order to match the front and side profile shapes of the torso.

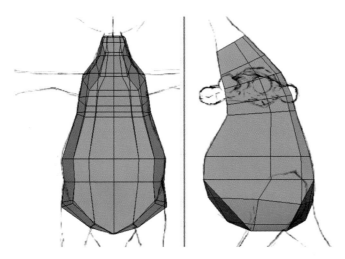

Torso adjustments

The base shape of the torso has now been established. You will notice that the overall form is still cubic in nature. In the next step, you will start adjusting rows of vertices to further round off the shape. You will also adjust rows of edges to better follow lines of topology.

3   Mirror the torso

A character is typically symmetrical across the center line of the torso. In order to ensure that you are working symmetrically, half the torso will be deleted and a mirror copy will be used to work with.

▪ Select and delete the faces on the right-hand side of the torso.

▪ Go to Object mode and with the half torso selected, select
Edit → **Duplicate** → ❑, and set the following:

Scale X to **-1**;

Geometry Type to **Instance**.

Any adjustments done to one side of the torso will simultaneously be done on the other side.

4   Backface culling

Currently, the front and back edges, faces and vertices are all visible in the viewports. This could be confusing when adjusting the topology. The following steps will hide any faces facing away from the camera.

▪ Select **Display** → **Custom Polygon Display** → ❑, and set the following:

Objects Affected to **All**;

Back Face Culling to **On**.

▪ Select the **Apply and Close** button.

Now only the front faces are visible in the view.

5   Shape the front and side of the torso

Move vertices to round off the original corner vertices from the cube.
Pull vertices back to form a more rounded shape. Also, adjust the vertices around the shoulders and neck to better define this area. Vertices can be adjusted to more accurately match the major topology lines of the torso.

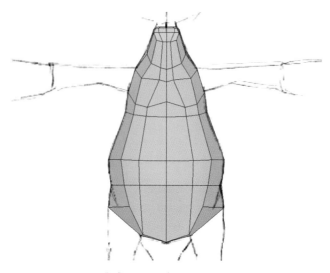

Refinements from the front

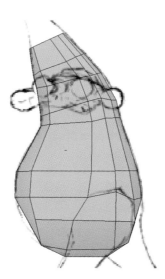

Refinements from the side

Note: You may notice that the image you are working with is not perfectly symmetrical. This is not a problem as long as you concentrate on just one half of the image.

6   Shape the back of the torso

Before more detail is added to the torso, the back needs to be shaped. Currently, the images being used do not help with the back shape. A new back image will now be employed for this next step.

- In the front view, select **Panels** → **Orthographic** → **New** → **Front**.

- Rename this camera *back*.

- In the back view, select **View** → **Predefined Bookmarks** → **Back**.

- With the back camera still selected, open the **Attribute Editor**.

- Open the **Environment** section and click the **Image Plane Create** button.

- Browse for a new image and load *meeperBodyBack.tif*.

- In the **Placement Extras** section, set **Center Z** attribute to **–20**.

- Hide the front camera while working on the back.

- Using the back camera, move vertices to refine the back of the torso.

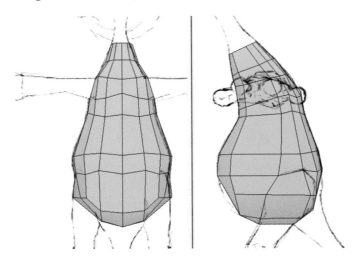

Refinements of the back

- Hide the back camera when you are finished with it and show the front.

7   Adding detail to the upper torso

The torso has been defined as best as possible with the current amount of topology. The next step will be to add detail to better define areas. The best way to do this is to work with things one area at a time. The first areas will be the shoulder and neck and then the upper back and chest.

- Select the faces at the top of the neck and delete them.

- Move the vertices at the top and bottom of the neck to properly form the shape of the neck opening. Make sure the vertices at the bottom of the neck follow the line along the shoulder muscle that runs up into the neck.

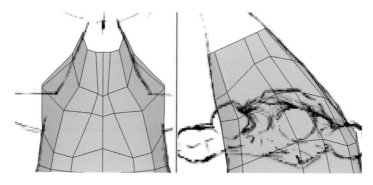

Neck refinements

- Use **Edit Polygons** → **Split Polygon Tool** to create a new row of edges to define the line that separates the top of the chest and the neck muscle. It will also separate the neck and shoulder.

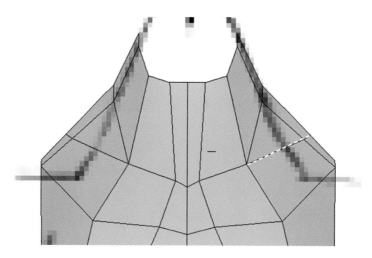

Shoulder split

Continue to move vertices to better define this new line of detail. The chest, shoulder and back do not have enough detail yet to begin defining the muscle mass.

- Split to create a new row of edges, starting from the center line of the chest, crossing under the shoulder, through the face that will be used to extrude the arm, and terminating at the center of the back.

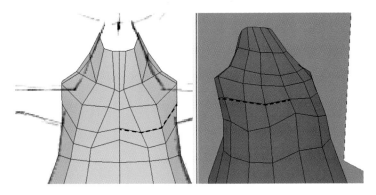

Chest split

- Use the newly added vertices to shape the chest.

Now that the initial shape of the shoulder area has been achieved, the next step is to add rows of edges to define the areas around the muscles. In the case of the upper torso, the two main areas to concentrate on are the chest and shoulders.

- Split the chest area as follows:

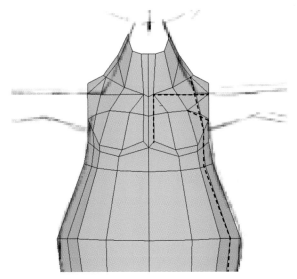

Splitting the chest

With the new edges added, some edges have become obsolete. You should remove those edges in order to keep your geometry clean and simple.

- Select the following edges:

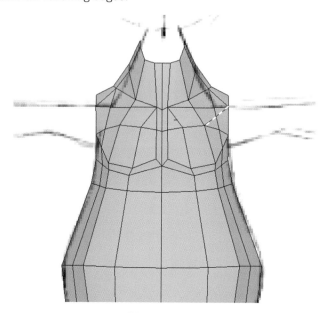

Edges to delete

- Delete the edges using **Edit Polygons** → **Delete Edge**.

Note: *You may notice that with each new split and adjustment, other slight adjustments are needed to keep the topology clean. You will always be going back and moving vertices in order to improve the shape. This is a natural and expected part of the workflow.*

8 Adding detail to the lower torso

You will now continue down the torso to the stomach and groin area and follow the same procedures that were used with the upper torso to define the areas of the lower torso.

- Select **Edit Polygons** → **Split Edge Ring Tool** .

This tool is used to create a continuous split across connected quads.

- **Click+drag** on one of the vertical edges in the middle of the belly area and release the mouse button to split a new edge ring.

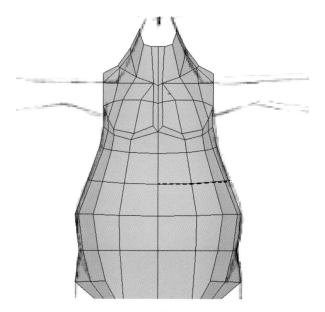

New edge ring

- Move vertices to refine the shape before continuing.

- Select the central belly vertex where the belly button should be, then select **Edit Polygons** → **Chamfer Vertex**.

When you chamfer a vertex, all the connecting edges to that vertex get split.

- Split and adjust the belly button to look as follows:

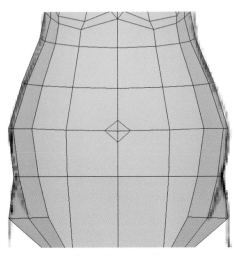

Split the stomach

- Split the groin area so that it looks as follows:

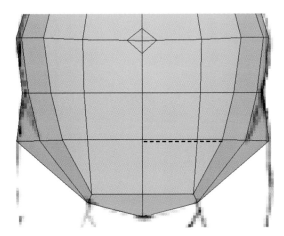

Refine the groin area

- Split a row of edges to refine the buttocks area, similar to what you did in the previous step.

- Adjust the vertices around the single face below the hips, which will be used for extrusion of the leg.

- Save your scene.

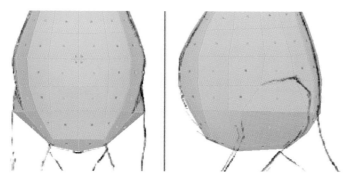

The groin area refined and the leg face

The initial work is now done for the torso. Additional splitting of edges and tweaking of vertices will be required once the arms and legs are added.

Tip: *If you would like to get a sense of the torso with more topology, you can use* **Polygons** → **Smooth** *to assess the model and then undo the Smooth before continuing.*

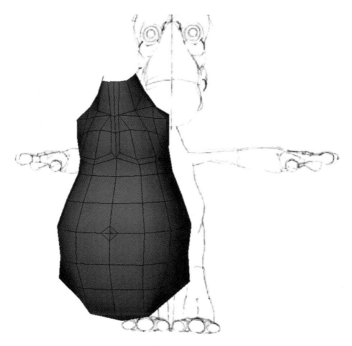

The torso

Model the leg

The leg of the character will be modeled in a very similar fashion as the torso. Extrusions will be used to establish the overall form and vertices will be moved to refine the shape.

1 Scene file

- Continue with your own scene.

Or

- Open the scene file *02-meeper body_02.ma*.

2 Extrude the leg

- Extrude the leg down **seven** times: to the middle of the upper leg, the top of the knee, the middle of the knee, below the knee, the middle of the lower leg, the top of the ankle and the bottom of the ankle.

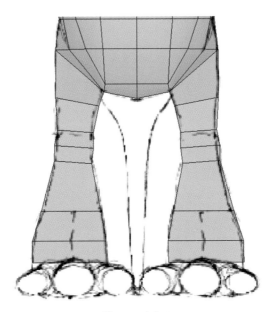

The rough legs

3 Shape the leg

- Move the leg vertices to define the shape of the leg, making sure that you keep the rows of vertices perpendicular to the leg. Try to avoid twisting the vertices as they run down the leg. The manipulator might have to be switched to **Global** to extract straight down.

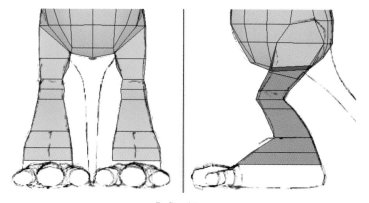

Refined legs

Tip: *To flatten a row of vertices, scale them on the axis that you want them to be flat on.*

Note: *Only a rough shape of the leg can be achieved with this amount of geometry.*

4   Split the leg

- Split the top of the leg as follows:

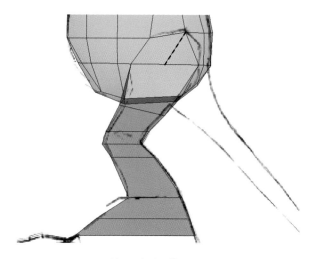

Upper leg split

- Select **Edit Polygons** → **Split Edge Ring Tool**.
- **Click+drag** on a horizontal leg line to add an edge line across the entire inside and outside of the leg.

Note: *By splitting the upper leg on its own, you prevented the Split Edge Ring Tool from continuing to split the edge up to the neck border.*

- Split the upper leg as follows in order to finalize the inside and outside split:

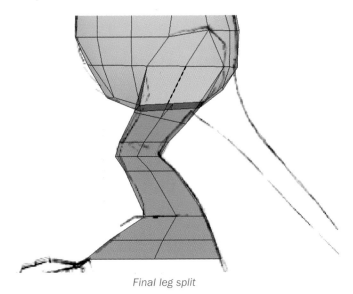

Final leg split

- Repeat the previous steps in order to split the front and back of the leg.
- Move the vertices to again refine the leg shape, round out the square edges and better define the knee area.

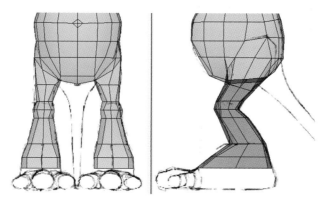

Refining the split leg

- Use the **Split Edge Ring Tool three** more times to split the leg.

- Now split horizontally **twice** through the thigh and **once** through the lower calf.

- Move vertices to continue refinement.

The calf and thigh muscles can now be defined to a degree.

The kneecap needs to be better defined. Once again, the same philosophy of adding in edges with the split polygon will be used.

- Split from the center of the kneecap so that **eight** edges now extend out radially from the center.

- Split a second loop of edges around the outside of the kneecap and move vertices to define the area better.

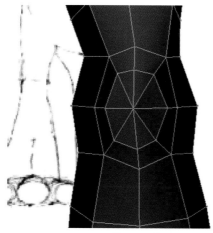

Knee split

The calf and lower leg should have enough topology to properly define the area without any more splitting. To define the bone ridge from the knee down to the ankle, tighten up the three center front rows of vertices. Spread out and define the muscle mass of the calf at the back of the leg and then tighten up the edges at the bottom of the calf to define the tendon at the back of the ankle.

5   Soften the model

- Select the entire object and select **Edit Polygons** → **Normals** → **Soften/Harden** → ☐.

- Click the **All Soft** button, then click the **Soft/Hard** button to execute the tool.

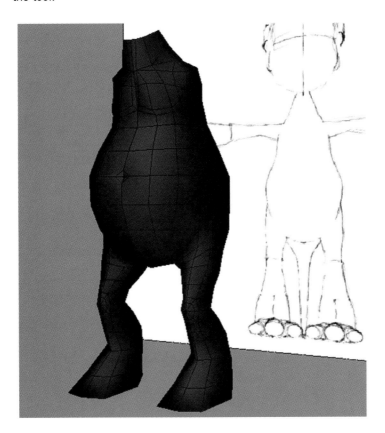

The soften model

- Save your work.

6   Extrude the foot

A series of extrusions will be used to define the shape of the foot.

- Select the faces at the bottom of the leg and extrude them down to the bottom of the foot.

- Move the vertices at the back of the foot to spread out the topology and form a rounded section at the heel.

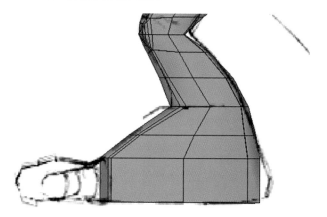

The foot

- Split the outside of the foot from the upper ankle down to the bottom of the foot twice, then continue under the foot up to the other side of the ankle.

These two additional splits will help define the sole of the foot.

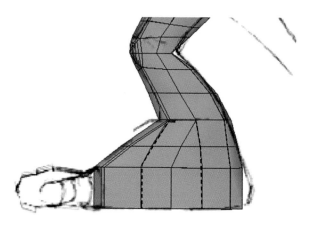

Split faces on the ankle

- Reconfigure the front portion of the foot in order to have three equal faces to use to extrude the toes.

Tip: *Split on both sides of the central edges, then delete the central edges using* **Edit Polygons** → **Delete Edge.**

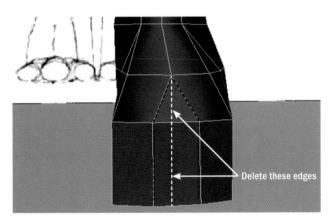

Delete these edges

Toe splits

- Turn **Off** the **Polygons** → **Tool Options** → **Keep Faces Together** option.

- Extrude all three toes **three** times, roughly shaping the toes as you are extruding.

Extrude the toes

- Move the toe and foot vertices to refine the shape even more.

7   Refine the sole of the foot

- Select **Edit Polygons** → **Split Edge Ring Tool**.

- **Click+drag** on a horizontal foot line to add an edge line across the entire foot, close to the sole.

- Refine the toe and foot sole vertices.

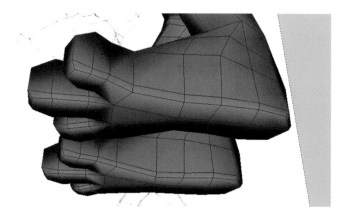

Foot sole refinement

- Save your work.

Model the arm

The arm of the character will be modeled in a similar fashion as the torso and leg. Extrusions will be used to establish the overall form and vertices will be moved to refine the shape.

1   Scene file

- Continue with your own scene.

Or

- Open the scene file *02-meeper body_02.ma*.

2   Subdivide the arm edges

Currently, the arm opening has six bordering edges. Ideally, the opening should have eight bordering edges. The top and bottom edges will be subdivided to facilitate this.

- Select the top and bottom edges on the arm opening faces and **Edit Polygons** → **Subdivide**.

Two new vertices will be added in the middle of these edges.

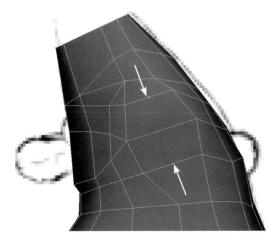

Subdivided edges

3 Extrude the arm

- Turn **On** the **Polygons** → **Tool Options** → **Keep Faces Together** option.

- Select the two faces at the arm opening and extrude them out **seven** times to the following locations: middle of upper arm, end of upper arm, middle of elbow, beginning of forearm, middle of forearm, beginning of wrist and end of wrist. Use the **Extrude Manipulator** to adjust the arm.

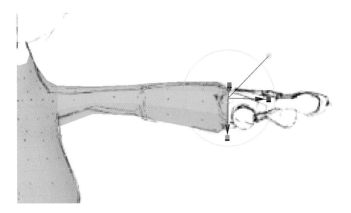

Extrude arm

Tip: *As you are extruding, you may want to switch the manipulator to global mode.*

4   Shape the arm

- Move vertices to shape the arm as best as possible with the current topology.

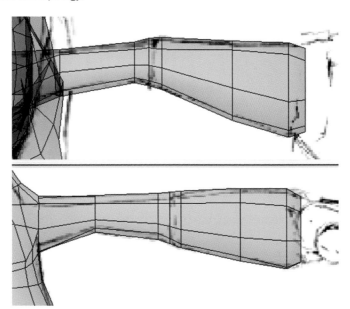

Refine arm

5   Split the upper arm

- Split the edges connecting the upper arm and the shoulder in order to continue the lines on the top of the arm and in the armpit.

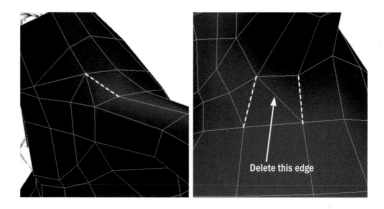

Arm splits

- Save your work.

6 Extrude the hand

You will start the hand by extruding the two faces at the end of the wrist.

- Extrude the two faces at the end of the wrist **twice** to form the hand.

- Move vertices as needed to form the hand shape. The vertex in the center of the palm can be pulled up slightly.

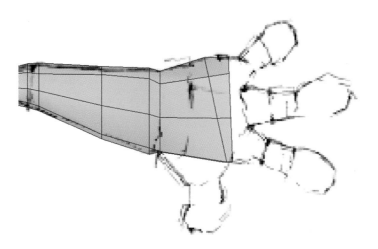

Extrude the hand

- Split the end of the hand **two** times (like the foot), to create the three faces that will be used to extrude fingers.

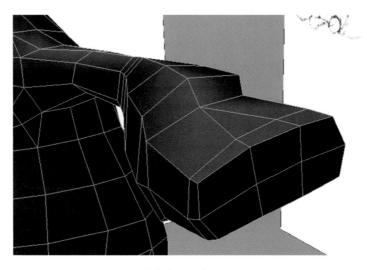

Split for the fingers

- Move the row of vertices at the bottom of the hand backwards and toward the palm slightly, and move the middle row of vertices down.

This will allow the fingers to be extruded with just the single faces and will round out the palm area to some extent.

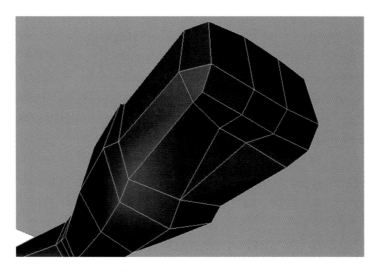

Move the bottom end vertices

- Extrude each finger **four** times.
- Move the vertices for each finger as you are extruding to shape them properly.

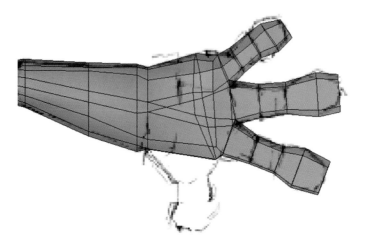

Extrude fingers

- Select the thumb side face, extrude it out **four** times and move the vertices to properly shape it.

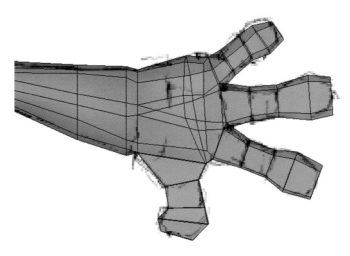

Extrude thumb

7   Refine the hand shape

Continue to split edges and move vertices on the hand until you are satisfied with the amount of detail. Concentrate on defining the overall structure of the hand and then refine areas, such as the knuckles and nails. You may need to delete some existing edges in order to maintain clean topological flow.

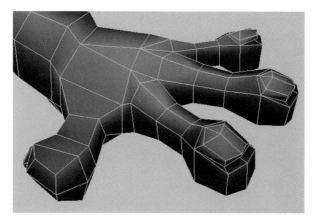

The refined hand

- Save the scene.

8   Preview the high resolution geometry

Smooth the geometry to see how the high resolution model will look. Be sure to undo the *polySmooth* before continuing with the lesson.

The smoothed model

Refine the whole body

The body has been built with some degree of refinement. At this stage, the flow of topology needs to be assessed and decisions need to be made about how to tie things together. The limbs could be integrated better into the flow of muscle mass.

You will notice the model has triangles and n-sided faces in several areas. Triangles can cause problems when deforming surfaces. Folds or spikes may appear in areas where you do not what them. Ideally, the model should follow a few rules: quads should be used as much as possible, especially in areas of high deformation; areas of deformation, such as muscles, should be isolated and defined using loops of edges; and loops of edges should be used to tie the whole model together where you can.

Following are some areas where you will find these loops:

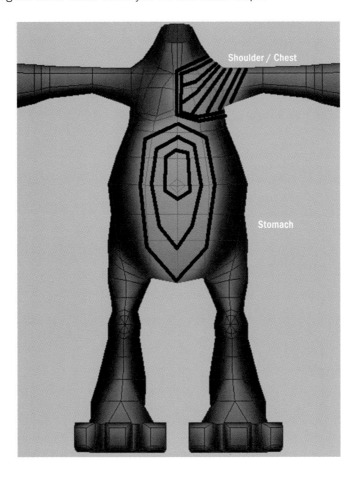

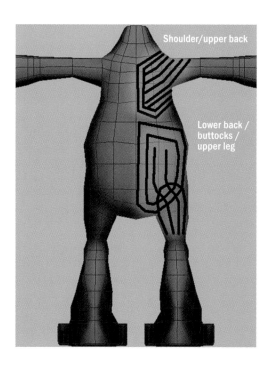

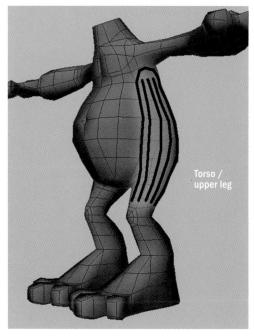

Areas of connected topology

The chest, shoulder and shoulderblade

1 Scene file

- Continue with your own scene.

Or

- Open the scene file *02-meeper body_03.ma*.

2 Refine the chest, shoulder and upper back

The chest, shoulder and upper back need to be tied together. Currently, this area has been modeled and shaped to define the overall contour. This is a good start. The same techniques for splitting, moving, and deleting edges and vertices followed thus far will be used.

- Split from the front of the arm and chest area and around the outside of the shoulder to the back. Also, split the front of the neck.

These split lines will help create a better deformation of the shoulder and neck.

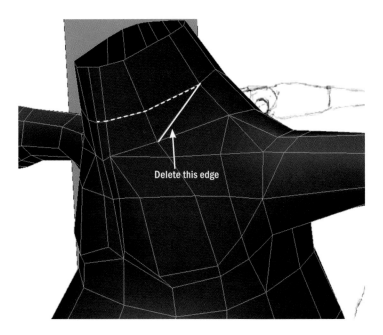

New splits

- Delete unwanted edges.

- Repeat the split and delete process to add a row of edges to the chest shape and muscle mass until it looks like this:

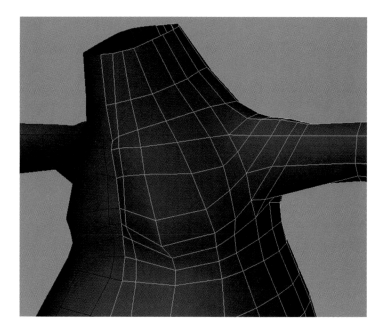

Clean chest splits

Note: *In some cases, you will need to further define an area before cleaning it up. Even though it is preferrable to always define quads, sometimes you will have to define triangles where several edges meet.*

- Reorganize the upper back so that it looks like the following:

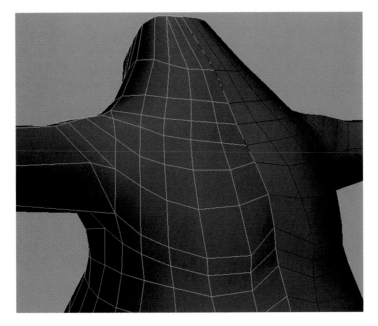

The back

You should now have a sense of the process of redirecting the flow of topology.

At this time, you will notice the topology flows nicely from the chest, over the shoulder and through the back. Triangles exist in some areas and this is fine as long as the overall topology consists of quads and flows nicely. This exact same approach will be used for the rest of the body in key areas discussed later.

3   Clean up

- With the geometry selected, select **Edit Polygons** → **Normals** → **Soften/ Harden** to soften any hard edges.

- Select **Edit** → **Delete All by Type** → **History** to delete all the construction history in the scene.

- Save your work.

The torso and leg

The upper part of the leg needs to be connected to the side of the torso, as well as loop around the inside of the leg (going up into the groin area and buttocks at the back). The transitional area between the leg and torso requires a lot of work as the topology is sparse right now.

1   Scene file

- Continue with your own scene.

Or

- Open the scene file *02-meeper body_04.ma*.

2   Refine the areas

Using all the tools and techniques discussed earlier, refine the side of the torso flowing into the upper leg, the inside of the leg into the groin and the back of the leg into the buttocks.

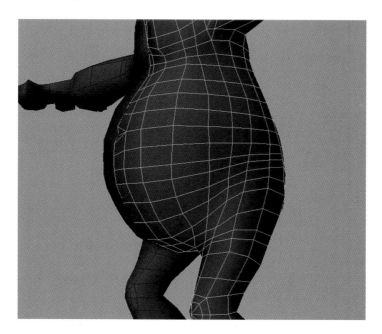

The side of the torso

3   Clean up

- With the geometry selected, select **Edit Polygons** → **Normals** → **Soften/ Harden** to soften any hard edges.

- Select **Edit** → **Delete All by Type** → **History** to delete all the construction history in the scene.

- Save your work.

Mirror geometry

At this point, the body has been developed as far as it will be in this lesson. This does not mean it cannot be refined further. If you wish, continue to use the principles you've learned in this chapter to further develop and refine the body. Focus on greater muscle definition and further refinement of the hand and foot.

1   Scene file

- Continue with your own scene.

Or

- Open the scene file *02-meeper body_05.ma*.

2   Delete the instance

- Select the right half of the body and delete it.

3   Snap the central vertices

- In the *front* view, select all the vertical central vertices.

- **Double-click** on the **Move Tool** to open its options.

- In the tool options, make sure the **Retain Component Spacing** option is turned **Off**.

- Still in the front view, hold down **x** to snap to grid and **click+drag** on the **X-axis** in order to snap all the vertices in a perfect vertical line.

Doing so will close any gaps upon mirroring of the geometry.

4   Mirror the geometry

- Ensure that all the construction history on the remaining body piece is deleted.

- Select the half body, then select **Polygons** → **Mirror Geometry** → ❑, and set the following:

    Mirror Direction to **-X**;

    Merge With The Original to **On**;

    Merge Vertices to **On**.

- Click on the **Mirror** button.

The tail

You will now extrude Meeper's tail and refine the surrounding area. Having waited for the body to be mirrored before modeling the tail will greatly simplify its extrusion.

1   Extrude

- Using all the tools and techniques discussed earlier, extrude Meeper's tail from the rear four faces like the following:

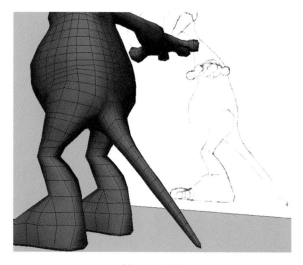

Meeper's tail

Tip: *Make sure to equally space the tail extrusions. Doing so will greatly improve the model's deformation.*

Finalize the model

1   Smooth the model

The chest, shoulder and back topology is now complete.

- Use the **Edit Polygons** → **Sculpt Polygon Tool** to smooth out areas of the model by setting the operation to **Smooth**.

2   Clean up

- With the geometry selected, select **Edit Polygons** → **Normals** → **Soften/Harden** to soften any hard edges.

- Select **Edit** → **Delete All by Type** → **History** to delete all the construction history in the scene.

3   Smooth the body (optional)

- Select the body, then select **Polygons** → **Smooth** → ❑, and set the following:

  Subdivision Method to **Linear**;

  Push Strength to **0.2**.

The **Push Strength** *attribute was increased slightly to maintain muscle definition. If desired, experiment by increasing the* **Push Strength** *and consider increasing the divisions per edge to* **2***.*

Tip: *If you would like to refine topology in some areas, undo the smooth and continue refining the low resolution model. Be aware that you will need to deal with vertices on both sides of the body to maintain symmetry.*

4   Save your work

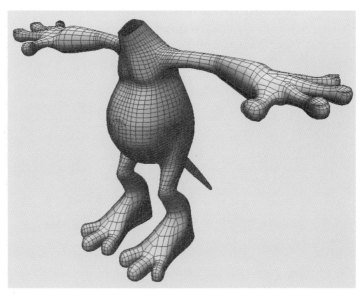

The smoothed body

Note: *The final scene file is named 02-meeper body_06.ma.*

Conclusion

In this lesson, you learned how to model starting from a simple cube to create Meeper's refined polygon body. By using image planes, the body could be accurately achieved. Splitting polygons to create loops of edges to define key areas was covered, as well as using extrusions to create limbs. Polygon smooth was discussed as an option to provide the final overall level of detail.

In the next lesson, you will model Meeper's head.

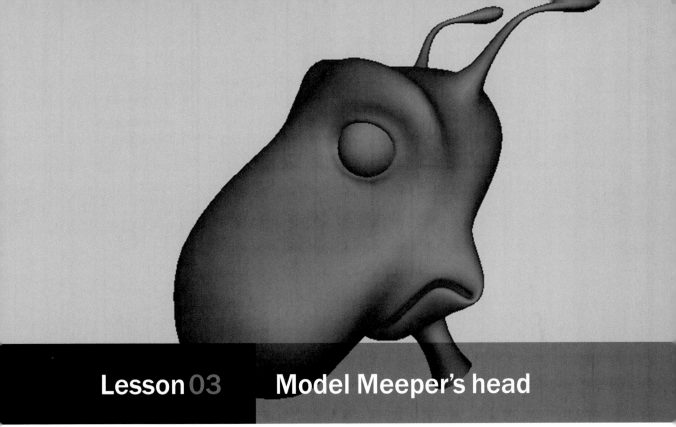

Lesson 03   Model Meeper's head

Now that Meeper's body has been modeled, this lesson will use the same technique to model his head.

In this lesson you will learn the following:

- How to model starting from a cube primitive;

- How to set up reference images with image planes;

- How to edit the topology of a polygonal model;

- How to use several polygonal tools;

- How to refine geometry when considering facial muscles;

- How to use selection constraints to identify problem areas;

- How to mirror a model;

- How to smooth polygons to see the final result.

Creating a basic polygon head shape

The workflow for modeling a head is very similar to the body, however, the head is a much more complex area and if the proportions and topological flow are not handled correctly, the head will texture and deform improperly.

1   Import image planes

Using the same technique as in the previous lesson, create three image planes for the head with the images *meeperHeadFront.tif*, *meeperHeadSide.tif* and *meeperHeadTop.tif*.

- Adjust the image plane center attributes as needed to align them properly.

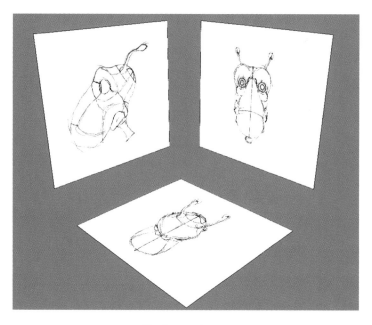

The image planes

> **Note:** *Based on the concept images, it would be easier to start modeling the head using a polygonal sphere, but since this lesson is about how to generate geometry, you will start from a cube.*

2   Create a cube

A polygon cube will be used initially to create the overall shape of the head.

- Select **Create → Polygon Primitives → Cube → ❑**.

Set the following:

Subdivisions Along Width to **4**;

Subdivisions Along Height to **3**;

Subdivisions Along Depth to **2**.

- Scale the cube so it fits around the bounding area of the head, based on the image planes.

- Rename the cube *head*.

3 Create the instanced copy

- Delete the faces at the bottom of the head.

- Delete the faces on the right half of the head and use **Duplicate** with an **X Scale** of **-1** and **Instance** option set to **On** to create the mirror half.

- Hide the backfaces of the head by selecting **Display** → **Component Display** → **Backfaces** with the *head* selected.

4 Work on the basic shape

- Move and scale vertices in the different views to round off the square edges and define the head shape more accurately.

Tip: *Remember to avoid moving the central vertices of the head away from the center line to prevent a gap from being created between the object and the instance.*

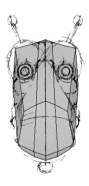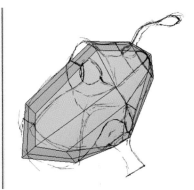

Basic head shape

- Select the border edges around the neck and extrude them **three** times using **Edit Polygons** → **Extrude Edges**.

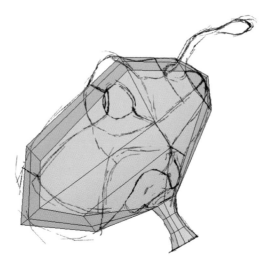

Neck extrusion

- Split the head from the forehead to the cheekbone.
- Move the vertices to refine the brow line.

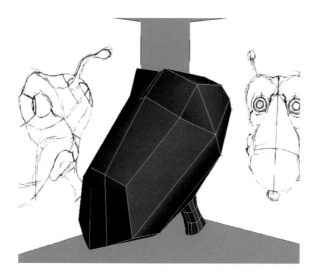

Eyebrow line

- Split again from the top of the nose down through the mouth, as well as the side of the nose as follows:

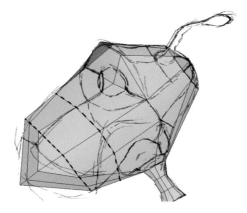

Split the mouth area

5 Refine the basic shape

- Split again from the chin to the lower back of the head.

- Continue to move vertices to refine the shape of the head.

Tip: *Focus on rounding and tightening up the brow and mouth areas.*

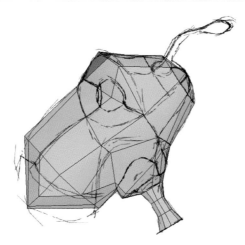

Some more refinement

Edge loops

Edge loops are rows of edges that form looping topology. They are very good for defining areas of muscle, as well as allowing for refinement in specific areas without having to continue your edge splitting across the whole object.

1   Split edges to create nose edge loops

All the horizontal lines forming Meeper's nose should meet radially at the tip. Also, all the vertical lines forming the nose should be edge loops.

- Select the two vertices on the tip of the nose that are not part of a vertical edge loop.

- Hold **v** down to Snap to Point and snap the vertices to the tip vertex.

- Switch to Object mode and merge the vertices using **Edit Polygons** → **Merge Vertices**.

Single vertex nose tip

- From the *side* view, use the **Edit Polygons** → **Cut Faces Tool** to add **three** edge loops to the front of the nose.

▪ Move the vertices so that the nose looks as follows:

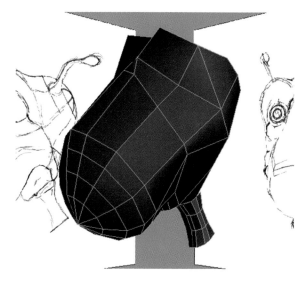

New nose topology

2 Split edges to create eye edge loops

▪ Split the eye area as follows to create the eye edge loops:

Eye edge loops

- Delete the edges forming an X in the middle of the eye socket.

- Split from the middle of the face between the eyebrow, down under the mouth, connecting into the neck.

- Split from the tip of the nose to the back of the head, through the eye socket.

Eye splits

- Move the vertices to refine the outside of the eye, the eye socket and brow area.

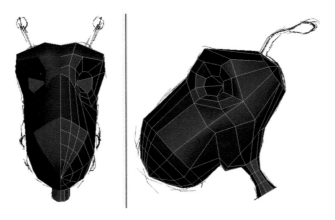

Refined eye socket

3   Back of the head

Now that the eye socket has been established, refine the topology for the back of the head.

- Repeat **step 1** in order to have a single vertex at the tip of the head.

- Make sure to create vertical edge loops and split any n-sided polygons.

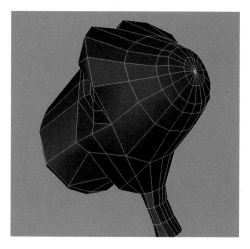

Back of the head topology

4   Define the jaw line

- Split the mouth area as follows in order to create more definition:

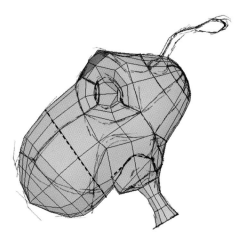

Splits to refine the jaw

> **Note:** *You will not be able to split edges across polygons that don't share edges. You will need to stop the split and continue with a second split.*

- Refine the mouth shape by moving out the newly created vertices according to the image planes.

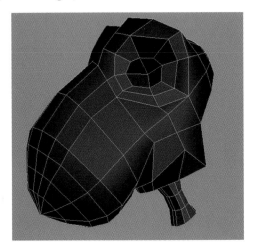

Refined mouth shape

5 Refine the lips

- Split faces to create edge loops around the mouth area.

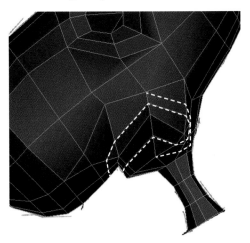

Lips edge loops

Take some time to readjust the whole shape to match the image planes more closely.

6 Clean up

- With the head selected, select **Edit Polygons** → **Normals** → **Soften/Harden**.

- Select **Edit** → **Delete All by Type** → **History**.

7 Save your work

Extruding the antenna

In this step, you will extrude the antenna along a curve. You will then refine its connection to the back of the head.

1 Scene file

- Continue with your own scene.

Or

- Open the scene file *03-meeper head_01.ma*.

2 Create the path curve

- Select **Create** → **EP Curve Tool** → ❒.

- Make sure the **Curve Degree** option is set to **3 Cubic**, then press the **Close** button.

- From the *side* view, draw the antenna using **five** curve points following the reference image.

- From the other views, place the curve appropriately.

3 Create the antenna

- Select the curve, then **RMB-click** on the head and select **Face** from the context menu located on the next page.

- Select **two** faces on the top of the cranium to use in the extrusion process.

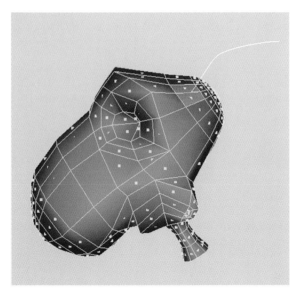

Antenna selection

- Select **Edit Polygons** → **Extrude Face**.

Note: *The Extrude Face tool is using the selected curve as an extrusion path by default.*

- In the Channel Box, set the following:

    Local Scale X to **2**;

    Local Scale Y to **2**;

    Offset to **3.5**;

    Divisions to **8**;

    Taper to **0.5**;

    Smoothing Angle to **180**.

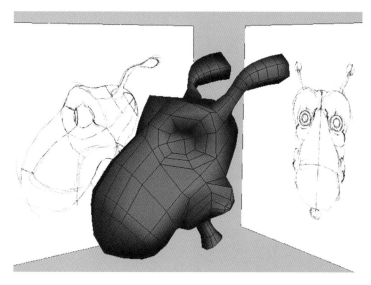

Extruded antennae

- Round up the new vertices to define a better shape.

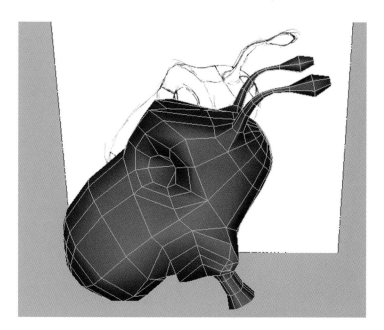

Refined antennae

4   Delete the curve

- Select **Edit** → **Delete All by Type** → **History**.

- Delete the curve used for the extrusion.

5   Save your work

Adding the eyes

Now you will define the eyes. Again, edge loops will be used and the resulting vertices will be adjusted.

1   Scene file

- Continue with your own scene.

Or

- Open the scene file *03-meeper head_02.ma*.

2   Refine the eyelid

- Select the **four** faces in the eyeball area.

- Extrude the eyelid faces **twice**, scaling them down and moving them in slightly each time.

Refined eyelid

3 Shape around the eyeball

In order to refine the eyelid shape, a sphere should be created as the eyeball.

- Select **Create** → **NURBS Primitives** → **Sphere**.

- Place the *sphere* where the eyeball should be.

- Rotate the *sphere* by **90 degrees** on the **X-axis** and increase its scaling slightly.

- Rename the *sphere* to *eyeball*.

- Assign the eyeball to a new layer and set the layer to be a template layer.

This will allow you to view the sphere and work the eyelid without accidentally selecting and moving the sphere. You will notice that the eyelid requires adjustment in order to properly follow the eyeball.

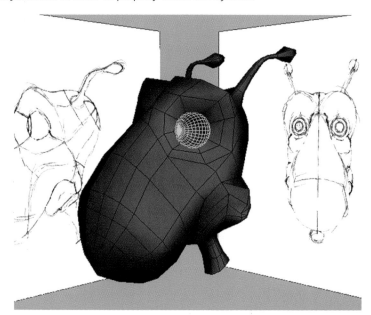

The template eyeball

Tip: *If the wireframe of the eyeball is not dense enough, select the eyeball through the Outliner and press **3** on your keyboard to set its smoothness to its highest.*

4 Shape around the eyeball

- Move the eyelid vertices to properly follow the eyeball surface.

 Tip: *The inner eyelid vertices should be barely visible when the eyeball is shaded.*

- Round up the eyelid and adjust the surrounding vertices.
- Use the **Edge Loop Tool** to add another line of edges around the eyelid and carve it in.
- Split the eyebrow in order to get more definition.

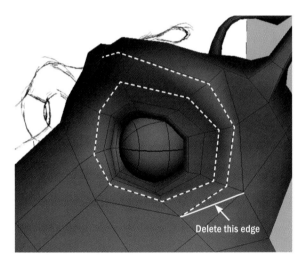

Delete this edge

The refined eyelid

5 Save your work

Refining the mouth

In this step, you will refine the mouth area and create the inner mouth.

1 Scene file

- Continue with your own scene.

Or

- Open the scene file *03-meeper head_03.ma*.

2 Fix upper lip topology

- Split and delete edges to fix the topology of the upper lip as follows:

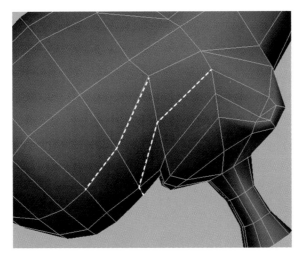

Split the upper lip

Doing so will significantly improve and simplify the lips' refinement.

3 Add an edge loop to the lips area

- Split an edge loop to define the lips tightly around the upcoming mouth opening.

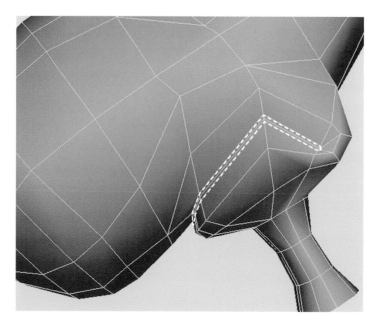

Split the inner lips

▪ Split a second edge loop around the lips and round up the lips.

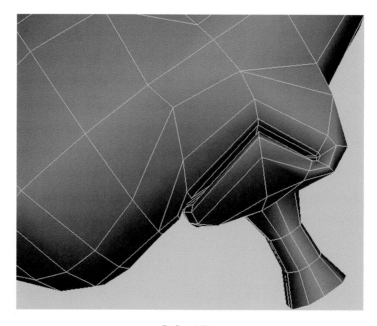

Refined lips

4   Create the mouth opening

- Select all the edges in the center of the lips' line.

- Scale the edges inside the head to form the mouth opening and inner mouth.

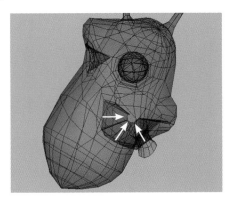

The edges scaled inside the head

5   Refine the inner mouth

Refining the inner mouth can be quite challenging since you may have to work in wireframe. Visualizing the 3D surface through a wireframe tangle requires a very good understanding of your geometry. The best way to work on the inner mouth is to reverse the head's normals and hide the backfaces. Doing so will allow you to see the inside of the head.

- Select the head, then select **Edit Polygons** → **Normals** → **Reverse**.

- If the backfaces are visible, hide them by selecting **Display** → **Component Display** → **Backfaces**.

- Refine the inner mouth to achieve a better shape as follows:

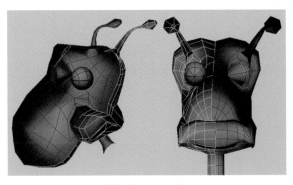

The inner mouth

- When you are done, select the *head* and select **Edit Polygons** →
  Normals → **Reverse**.

6   Refine the general head shape

This is a good time to refine the overall shape of the head. A smooth can
also be applied to assess the head, if you are going to ultimately use a
higher resolution model.

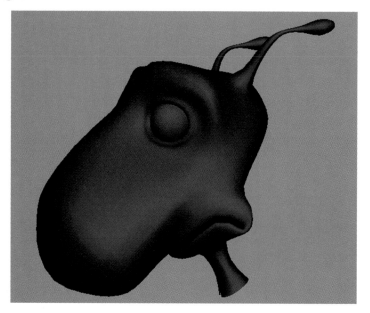

The previewed head

Tip: *Make sure to undo the polygon smooth before continuing with the lesson.*

7   Clean up

- With the head selected, select **Edit Polygons** → **Normals** → **Soften/Harden**.
- Select **Edit** → **Delete All by Type** → **History**.

8   Save your work

Refining and fixing the whole head

The structure of the head is done, however, undesirable topology exists in several areas. Triangles and five-sided faces are evident in areas where they should not exist. Selection constraints can be used to help you identify the problem areas. As well, the nose, top of the head and mouth could use another level of refinement.

1   Scene file

- Continue with your own scene.

Or

- Open the scene file *03-meeper head_04.ma*.

2   Assess and clean up

- Press **F11** to switch to face components.

- Open the **Edit Polygons** → **Selection** → **Selection Constraints...**, and set the following:

> **Order** to **Nsided**;
>
> **Constrain** to **All and Next**.

Any five-sided or greater face on the head gets selected. Assess which faces need correcting. This same procedure can be used to select triangles to minimize them.

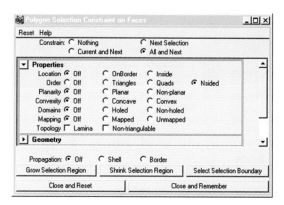

The Polygon Selection Constraint on faces window

- When closing the **Polygon Selection Constraint** window, use the **Close and Reset** button in order to reset the Selection Mode.

- Split the n-sided polygons in order to clean up the head topology.

Note: *If you recheck your model with the Selection Constraints, you will see the five-sided faces are no longer there.*

- Continue the clean up work, but this time to minimize triangles.

3   Final adjustment

Refine the whole head shape. Concentrate on defining the lip line, the cheekbone and the brow line. Work less with the image planes and more in 3D views to achieve a nice looking model from all angles.

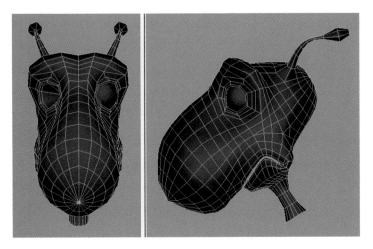

The final head topology

4   Save your work

Wrapping things up

At this point, two different approaches can be taken to complete the head. Following the current lines of topology, you can continue to add detail and the head can be sculpted to its final shape or the mesh can be smoothed. If you choose to smooth the mesh, you will need to delete the left half of the head and mirror the geometry to create a single mesh and then smooth. Experiment with smoothing options until you are satisfied with the results. If you choose to continue adding detail manually, you will need to mirror the head at the end of your work.

1 Scene file

- Continue with your own scene.

Or

- Open the scene file *03-meeper head_05.ma*.

2 Delete the instance

- Select the right half of the head and delete it.

3 Snap the central vertices

- In the *front* view, select all the vertical central vertices.

- **Double-click** on the **Move Tool** to open its options.

- In the tool options, make sure the **Retain Component Spacing** option is turned **Off**.

- Still in the *front* view, hold down **x** to snap to grid and **click+drag** on the **X-axis** in order to snap all the vertices in a perfect vertical line.

Doing so will close any gaps upon the mirroring of the geometry.

4 Mirror the geometry

- Ensure that all the construction history on the remaining head piece is deleted.

- Select the half head, then select **Polygons** → **Mirror Geometry** → □, and set the following:

> **Mirror Direction** to **-X**;
>
> **Merge With The Original** to **On**;
>
> **Merge Vertices** to **On**.

- Click on the **Mirror** button.

5 Smooth the model

- Select **Edit Polygons** → **Sculpt Polygon Tool** to smooth out areas of the model by setting the operation to **Smooth**.

Tip: *You can paint equally on both sides of the head by turning **On** the **Reflection** option against the **X-axis** under the **Stroke** section. Also, you can select vertices on which you want to paint. Lastly, you can click the **Flood** button to smooth the selection all at once.*

6 Clean up

- With the head selected, select **Edit Polygons** → **Normals** → **Soften/Harden**.

- Select **Edit** → **Delete All by Type** → **History**.

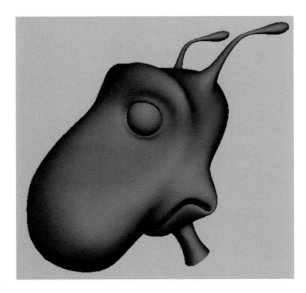

Smoothed head

7 Duplicate the eye

- Remove the eye layer.

- Reset the duplicate options and duplicate the eye on the other side of the head.

- Parent the eyes to the head.

8 Save your work

Combining the body and the head

Meeper's body and head can now be combined. This is an easy procedure with only one main consideration: the number of edges at the neck openings need to match up.

1   Import the body

- With the file from the last step or with *03-meeper head_06.ma*, select **File** → **Import** and select *02-meeper body_06.ma*.

- Scale and move the head until it matches the opening at the top of the *body*.

Note: *A small gap can be left between the two pieces.*

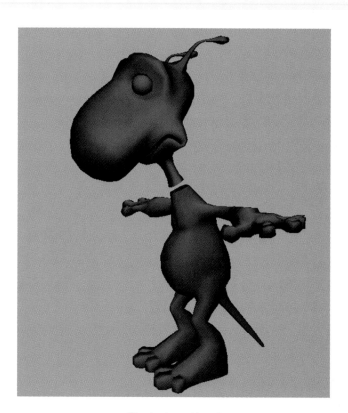

The body and head

2 Match the vertices

The head has 18 vertices at the neck opening and the body has 22. Four vertices on the body opening will be merged to match the opening of the neck.

- On the body, select the **three** vertices at the front of the neck and select **Edit Polygons** → **Merge Vertices** to merge them.

Tip: *You may need to increase the* **Distance** *value in the* **Merge Vertices** *options.*

- Repeat the previous step **twice** to merge two vertices on each side of the body's neck opening.

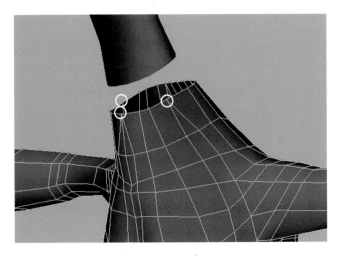

Merged body vertices

3 Attach the pieces

Now that the two openings have the correct number of vertices, the head vertices can be snapped to the body to flow nicely into each other.

- With the **Move Tool** active, hold down **v** to Snap to Point and snap each head vertex to its correspondent body vertex.

Neck and body together

- Select the body and the head and then select **Polygons** → **Combine**.

The body and head are now one piece.

- Select Meeper and then select **Edit Polygons** → **Merge Vertices**.

The neck vertices are now merged together.

4   Finalize Meeper

You may wish to adjust the neck vertices somewhat and add an edge loop, but remember that you need to adjust both sides at once to maintain symmetry. You can also use the Sculpt Polygon Tool to even out the neck.

5   Clean up

- Rename the geometry *meeper*.

- With *meeper* selected, select **Edit Polygons** → **Normals** → **Soften/Harden**.

- Select **Edit** → **Delete All by Type** → **History**.

- Delete any obsolete nodes in the Outliner.

- Delete the image planes from the Hypershade.

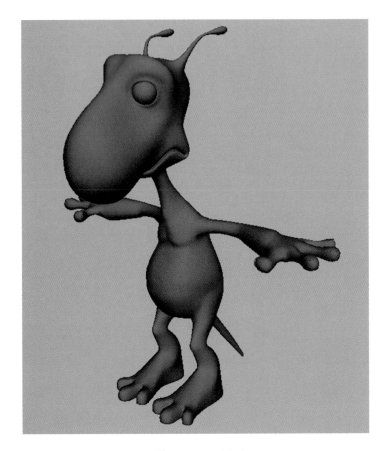

Meeper completed

6   Save your work

Note: *The final scene is called 03-meeper complete.ma.*

Conclusion

Congratulations – you have now modeled an entire character! In the process, you learned how to model using several polygonal tools. You also learned where to split edges to create edge loops around key areas of the face. Doing so greatly helps when it comes time to deform the model.

In the next lesson, you will texture Meeper using several polygonal texturing tools.

Lesson 04   Polygon texturing

*UVs determine how textures
appear on the surface.
While NURBS surfaces have
predictable UVs, polygonal
surfaces, due to the arbitrary
nature of their topology, do
not. Before texturing a poly
surface, its UVs must be
properly set up.*

*In this lesson, you will texture
Meeper's geometry.*

In this lesson you will learn the following:

- Basic workflow for texturing polygonal surfaces;

- How to project UVs;

- How to cut and sew UVs;

- How to unfold UVs;

- How to organize UVs in the 0-1 UV space;

- How to export a UV snapshot;

- How to create a simple PSD network.

Texturing polygonal surfaces

In this exercise, you will set up the UVs for Meeper from the previous lesson.

> **Note:** *Throughout this lesson, your results may vary from the images shown here.*

1   Open Meeper's scene file

- Open the scene from the previous lesson called *03-meeper complete.ma*.

- Save the scene as *04-meeperTexture_01.ma*.

2   Switch to the Perspective view/Texture Editor layout

- From the menu bar at the top of the *Perspective* view, select **Panels → Saved Layouts → Persp/UV Texture Editor**.

3   Check the UVs for the poly head

- Select *Meeper*'s geometry and check the layout of its UVs in the **UV Texture Editor** window.

As they are right now, the UVs will not provide good coordinates for applying a texture.

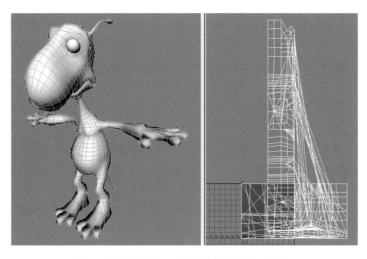

Meeper's UVs displayed in the UV Texture Editor

4   Assign a new material to the head

- **RMB-click** on the geometry and select **Materials** → **Assign New Material** → **Lambert** from the context menu.

Doing so will automatically create a new lambert material, assign it to the geometry and open its Attribute Editor.

5   Assign a checker texture to the Color channel

- In the Attribute Editor, click on the **Map** button for the **Color** channel.

*Doing so will display the **Create Render Node** window, which allows you to create and map a texture to the selected attribute.*

- Click on the **Checker** texture in the **Create Render Node** window.

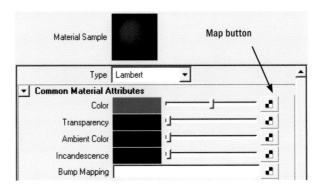

Map button for Color channel

6   Switch to shaded with texture

- Hit the **6** key on your keyboard to enable hardware texturing.

The checker texture should now appear on Meeper, and due to the poor UV layout, the checker looks irregular.

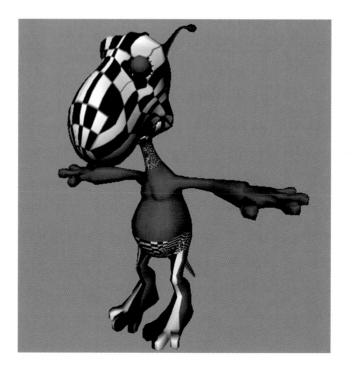

Irregular texture placement due to poor UVs

7 Change the checker's Repeat values

- In the Attribute Editor, select the *place2dTexture* tab.

- Change both **Repeat U** and **V** values to **20**.

8 Increase the display quality of the texture

- In the Attribute Editor with the new *lambert2* shader selected, open the **Hardware Texturing** section and change **Texture Resolution** to **Highest (256x256)**.

Doing so will display the texture more accurately in the viewport.

9 Turn off the texture display in the UV Texture Editor

- In the UV Texture Editor menu bar, select **Image** → **Display Image** to toggle the display of the checker texture **Off**.

10 Apply a planar projection to the body

- Select the body, then select **Polygon UVs** → **Planar Mapping** → ❑.

- In the **Planar Mapping** options, make sure **Fit to Bounding Box** is turned **On** and the **Mapping Direction** is set to **Z-axis**.

Doing so will rearrange the surface's UVs by projecting new UV coordinates on the Z direction.

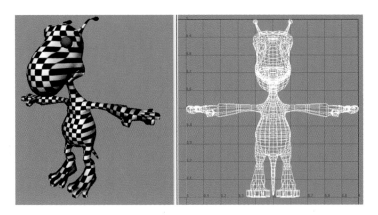

Meeper's UVs using Planar Mapping

11 Save your work

Cut the UVs

In order for the UVs to be properly unfolded, you must first cut the UVs into UV shells, which will define the different parts of the body, such as the head, arms and legs. The shells should be able to lay relatively flat when unfolded without overlapping, much like a cloth pattern is laid flat for a piece of clothing prior to sewing.

The location of the UV cuts requires some planning to obtain the best unfolded result. The better the UV cuts, the better the correlation between the original polygons and their corresponding UV mesh. In addition, you should anticipate that the polygon edge cuts will result in texture mismatches along those edges and plan their locations on the model accordingly so they are less visible. For example, you can make edge cuts under the arms or on the back of the legs of a character.

1   Display UV borders

▪ Select **Display** → **Custom Polygon Display** → ❑.

▪ In the option window, turn **On** the **Highlight Texture Borders** checkbox.

This option will display UV borders with a thicker line so that they can be easily distinguished.

2   Cut the neck UVs

▪ Select the horizontal edge ring at the base of the head where it meets with the neck.

▪ Select **Polygon UVs** → **Cut UVs**.

By cutting the UVs at the neck, the UVs are now divided into two distinct shells: the head UV shell and the body UV shell.

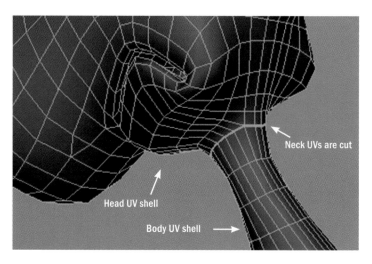

Cut UVs at the base of the head

3   Separate the shells in the Texture Editor

▪ In the Texture Editor, with the *Meeper* UVs visible, **RMB-click** and select **UV** from the context menu.

▪ **Click+drag** to select a few UVs that are part of the head.

▪ Choose **Select** → **Shell**.

All the UVs from the head shell are selected.

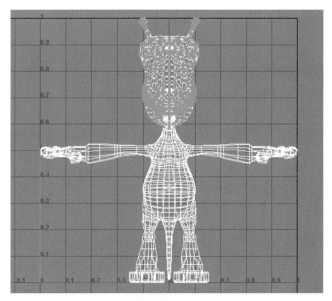

Head UV shell

- Activate the **Move Tool** by pressing **w** on your keyboard.

- Translate the head shell next to the body.

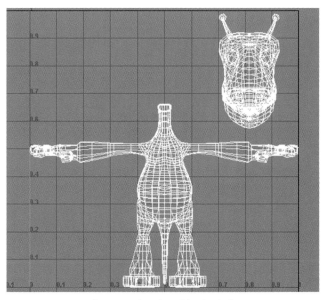

Separate head and body shells

4   Cut the head UVs

In order to be able to unfold the head UVs, the head shell must be cut again a couple of times. In this step, you will create UV shells for the left and right side of the head, the inner mouth and the antennae.

- From the *front* view, select the vertical edges in the middle of Meeper's face.

Tip: To make the process faster, you can select only one edge and then select **Edit Polygons** → **Selection** → **Select Contiguous Edges** to help select a contiguous edge line.

- Select **Polygon UVs** → **Cut UVs**.

The left and right side of the head are now separate in two UV shells.

- Select the edge rings at the bottom of both antennae.
- Select **Polygon UVs** → **Cut UVs**.
- Select the edge loop located in the inner mouth, just behind the lips.
- Select **Polygon UVs** → **Cut UVs**.

Note: Cutting the UVs in the mouth rather than outside the mouth will help hide the seam created by the head and mouth textures meeting along that cut.

5   Separate the UV shells

- In the **Texture Editor**, separate each individual shell by selecting a single UV component, then using **Select** → **Shell**.

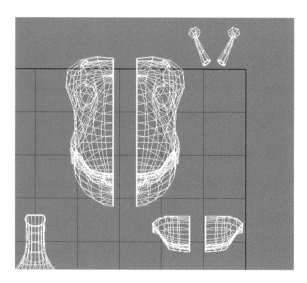

Separate head shells

6   Sew the inner mouth UV shells

The inner mouth shells do not need to be separate, so they will be
sewn together.

- In the **Texture Editor**, **RMB-click** and select **Edge** from the context menu.

- Select the edges along the vertical center line on one of the inner
  mouth shells.

*Notice that the same edges are also being selected on the other side of the
inner mouth shell.*

- Select **Polygons** → **Move and Sew UVs**.

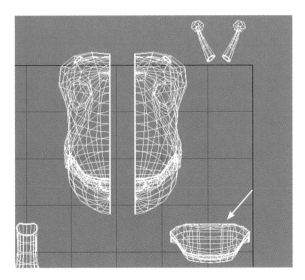

The inner mouth shell

7 Cut the antennae

In order to unfold the antennae correctly, their UVs must be split along the antenna's tube.

- Select the edges underneath the antennae, from their base up to the tip.
- Select **Polygon UVs** → **Cut UVs**.

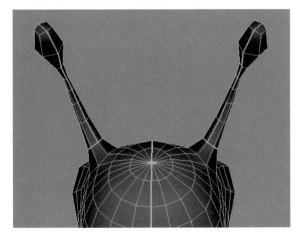

Cut the antennae

8 Save your work

Unfold the head

The *Unfold UVs* function lets you unwrap the UVs for a polygonal object while it attempts to ensure that the UVs do not overlap. Unfold UVs helps to minimize the distortion of texture maps on organic polygon meshes by optimizing the position of the UV coordinates so they more closely reflect the original polygon mesh.

1   Scene file

- Continue with your own scene.

Or

- Open the scene file *04-meeperTexture_02.ma*.

2   Unfold UVs

- Select the **UVs** from one half of Meeper's face.

- From the **Texture Editor**, select **Polygons** → **Unfold UVs** → ❐.

*The **Unfold UVs** options are displayed.*

- Make sure to select **Edit** → **Reset Settings**, then click the **Apply** button.

The command will automatically unfold the UV shell as follows:

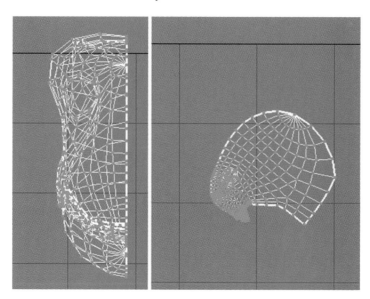

The unfolded face

Tip: *Unfold UVs will unfold only the selected UVs. If no UVs are selected, the command will unfold all the UVs on the selected objects.*

3   Unfold UVs with pinning

In the last step, the Unfold command moved and scaled the UV shell. To prevent that from happening, you can deselect some UVs so the Unfold solver considers them as pinned in location.

- Undo the previous **Unfold** command.

- Select the **UVs** from one half of *Meeper*'s face.

- Deselect the **UVs** at the tip of both the nose and the cranium so they stay in that position.

- Select **Polygons** → **Unfold UVs.**

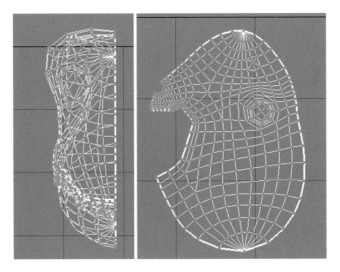

The unfolded face using pin unselected

4   Repeat for the other half of the head

- Repeat the previous step to unfold the other half of the head.

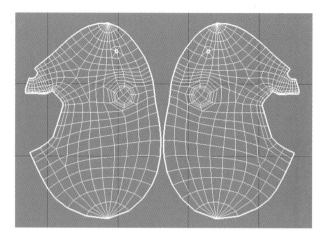

Properly unfolded head

5 Sew the face shells together

To avoid having a texture seam in the middle of the face, the two head shells can be sewed together starting at the tip of the nose up to the tip of the cranium.

- Select the border edges from the tip of the nose up to the tip of the cranium on *Meeper*'s face shells.

- Select **Polygons** → **Sew UVs**.

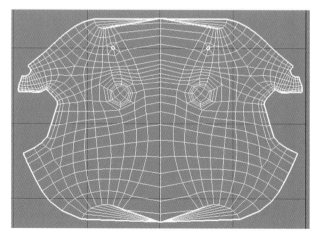

Head UVs sewed together

6 Unfold the head shell again

You can make the head UV shell better by unfolding a second time, specifying pinned UVs.

- Select all the UVs of the new united head shell.

- Deselect UVs intended for pinning such as the tip of the nose, the tip of the cranium and the corners of the upper lip on each side of the head.

- Select **Polygons** → **Unfold UVs**.

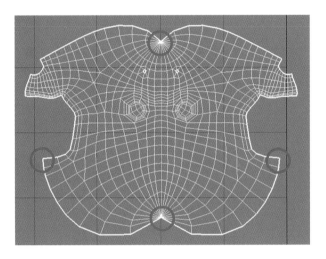

Unfolded head with pinned UVs

Tip: *You can sew more UVs to get as few visible seams as possible. For instance, you could sew the edges from the tip of the nose to the upper lip. Keep in mind that sewing too many edges can cause texture stretching.*

7 Repeat for the other head shells

- Repeat the previous steps to unfold the remaining head shells.

Tip: *You can move the UVs intended for pinning around for the Unfold solver to generate different results.*

- Tweak the resulting UVs as desired.

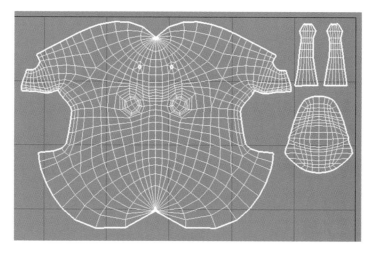

Final head UVs

Now that the head UVs have been properly unfolded, they are in much better shape for supporting textures.

Head with textures

Cut and unfold the rest of the body

Now that you have more experience unfolding polygonal geometry, you can unfold the rest of the body. The following steps are similar to what you have done with the head, but there are areas where the unfolding will be somewhat more difficult, such as the fingers and toes.

1 Scene file

- Continue with your own scene.

Or

- Open the scene file *04-meeperTexture_03.ma*.

2 Unfold the arms

The arm UVs should be cut at the shoulder and the wrist. The UV cut along the arm should be located underneath the arm, starting in the shoulder pit, going to the wrist. The hands will be in separate UV shells.

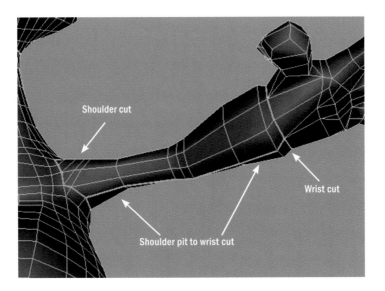

The arm cuts

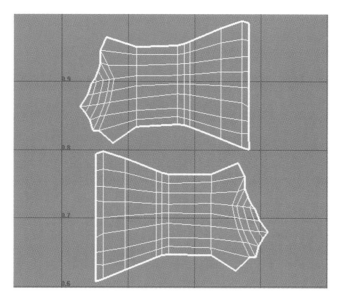

The arm UV shells

3 Unfold the hands

The hands are a little trickier since they cannot be unfolded as easily. The simplest way to unfold them is to cut the hand in half horizontally. You will then have a top and bottom UV shell for each hand.

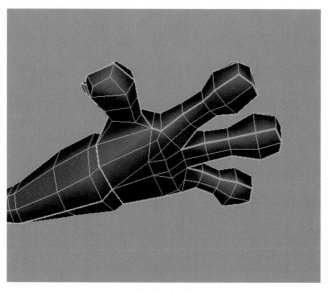

The hand cuts

You should now select each shell's faces and assign planar mapping in the **Y-axis**. Once that is done, it is easier to unfold the shells using pinning on the wrist and fingers.

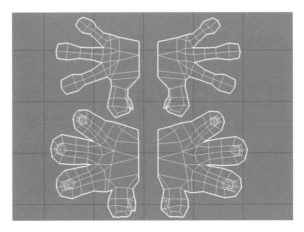

The hand UV shells

Tip: *At certain times it might be easier and more logical to fix the UVs manually instead of always using the Unfold command.*

4   Unfold the legs

The legs are similar to the arms and hands and should be cut nearly the same way.

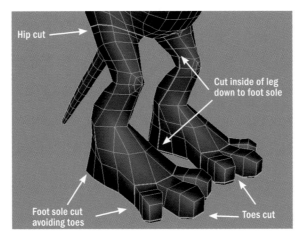

The leg cuts

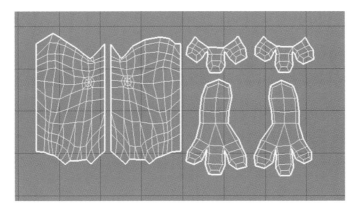

The hand UV shells

5   Unfold the tail

The tail is very similar to the antennae, due to its tube shape.
Do a UV cut near the buttocks and another one along the tail to the tip.

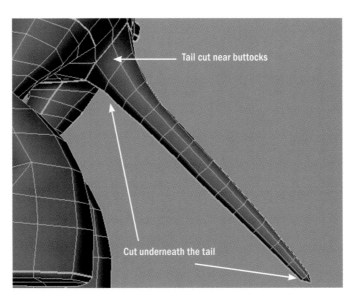

The tail cuts

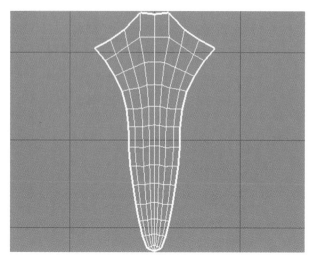

The tail UV shell

6 Unfold the body

The simplest solution for unfolding the body is to cut vertically in the middle of the back. Two additional cuts can be made to simplify the unfold process by dividing the front from the back.

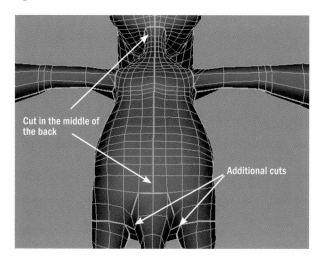

The body cuts

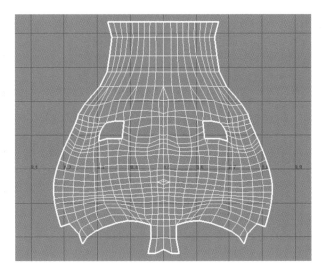

The body UV shell

7   Save your work

The 0-1 UV space

Now that the entire character's UVs have been unfolded, you must place all the shells into the 0-1 UV space. The 0-1 UV space is visible in the Texture Editor and is defined by the upper right quadrant of the grid.

When you load a texture, Maya will normalize it to be in the 0-1 space, thus making it square, regardless of its width and height.

If you use one big texture map for your entire character, it is better to place the character's UV shells in the 0-1 space to lose as little as possible of the texture map. On the other hand, if you use multiple texture maps for your character (for instance, one map for the head, one for the body and one for the arms and legs), you can place the UV shells into different quadrants to avoid having a tangle of UV shells in the same quadrant.

Note: *With texture wrapping, it is possible to use other quadrants besides the upper right one. Texture wrapping repeats the texture beyond the 0-1 UV space.*

1   Scene file

- Continue with your own scene.

Or

- Open the scene file *04-meeperTexture_04.ma*.

2   Place all the shells in the 0-1 UV space

For this lesson, you will use a single texture map, thus placing all the UV shells in the same quadrant.

 Tip: *At the top of the Texture Editor there are buttons to flip and rotate the selected UVs.*

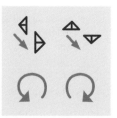

The toolbar buttons to flip and mirror UVs

- Place the shells to optimize usage of the 0-1 UV space.

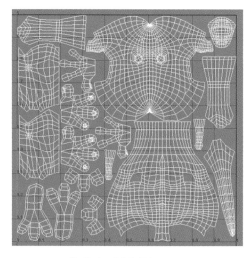

Optimized 0-1 UV space

3   Export UVs to paint the texture

- From the Texture Editor panel, select **Polygons** → **UV Snapshot**...

- In the **UV Snapshot** options, browse for the current project *sourceImages* folder, and name the output image *outUV*.

- Set the following:

    > **Size X** and **Y** to **512**;

    > **Image Format** to **TIFF**.

- Click the **OK** buton.

The UV snapshot image outUV.tif will be saved out to the sourceImage folder.

- Open the UV snapshot image in a paint program to paint the character's texture map. When you are done painting the texture, map a file texture instead of the checker and load your new texture.

4   Using a PSD (Photoshop) texture

As an alternative to the UV snapshot, you can use Photoshop (PSD) file textures.

- Press **F5** to change the current menu set to **Rendering**.

- Select *Meeper*'s geometry, then select **Texturing** → **Create PSD Network**.

Doing so will display the options of the PSD network.

- In the **Attribute** section, select the *color* channel and click the **>** button.

This will place the color channel in the PSD file.

- Click the **Create** button.

There is now a PSD file in the sourceImages folder.

- Open the PSD image in Photoshop to paint the character's texture map. When you are done painting the texture, select **Texturing** → **Update PSD Networks** to reload the PSD textures.

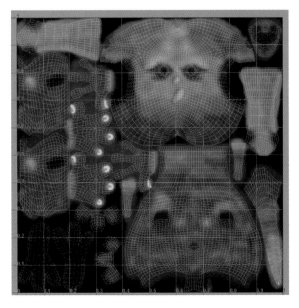

Texture map

Meeper with textures

Note: *The eyes were textured using a ramp. Open scene file 04-meeperTexture_ 05.ma to see the final results.*

Conclusion

You just textured a complete character! You learned about polygonal UV mapping tools such as Planar Mapping, cut, sew and u.nfold UVs. You also learned about 0-1 UV space, which is very important for any texturing task. Lastly, you exported a UV snapshot and created a PSD shading network.

In the next project, you will model a similar character, but this time using NURBS.

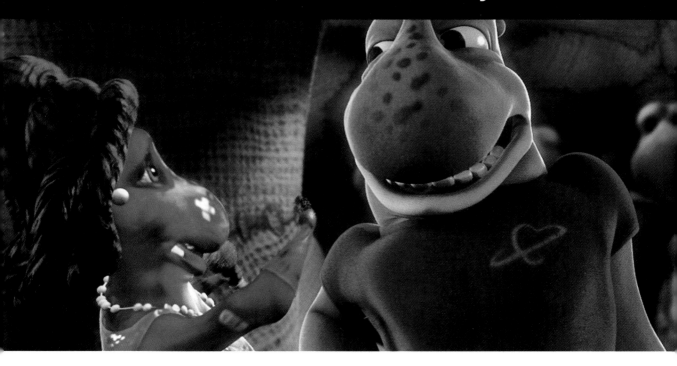

Project Two

Lessons

In Project Two, you are going to model Meeper's coworker, the cabaret singer, Diva. She will be modeled as a full NURBS character. This will give you a chance to explore more in-depth NURBS modeling.

You will start by revising the basics of NURBS components. Then you will model the singer's body using reference images. Once that is complete, you will model Diva's head and attach it to her body. Lastly, you will model all of her accessories, such as jewels, clothing and hair.

These lessons offer you a good look at some of the key concepts and workflows for modeling in NURBS.

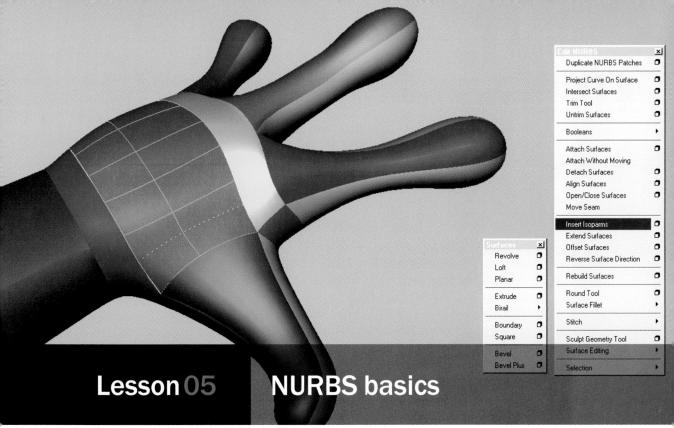

Lesson 05   NURBS basics

Edit NURBS

Duplicate NURBS Patches

Project Curve On Surface
Intersect Surfaces
Trim Tool
Untrim Surfaces

Booleans

Attach Surfaces
Attach Without Moving
Detach Surfaces
Align Surfaces
Open/Close Surfaces
Move Seam

Insert Isoparms
Extend Surfaces
Offset Surfaces
Reverse Surface Direction

Rebuild Surfaces

Round Tool
Surface Fillet

Stitch

Sculpt Geometry Tool
Surface Editing

Selection

Surfaces

Revolve
Loft
Planar

Extrude
Birail

Boundary
Square

Bevel
Bevel Plus

NURBS modeling is a fast and easy way to produce smoothly contoured shapes. NURBS modeling tools and techniques are well suited to both organic shapes, such as people, and industrial designs, such as cars.

In this lesson you will learn the following:

- The relationship between NURBS curves and surfaces;

- The anatomy of NURBS curves and surfaces;

- Curve and surface degree;

- Parameterization;

- Curve direction;

- Continuity;

- Curve quality;

- Open, closed, and periodic geometry;

- Normals.

WHAT IS NURBS GEOMETRY?

NURBS stands for Non-Uniform Rational B-Spline, and it is a method for producing freeform 3D curves and surfaces in Maya. NURBS curves, and the surfaces produced from those curves, are easy to work with and can achieve almost any shape.

Relationship between NURBS curves and surfaces

Essentially, a NURBS surface can be considered a grid of NURBS curves. As a result, most aspects of NURBS curves, such as degree, parameterization, direction, and form, behave the same way with surfaces as they do with curves. Surfaces simply have an additional parametric direction.

CURVES

Anatomy of a NURBS curve

Every NURBS curve is made up of:

- Control vertices (CVs), which lie off the curve and define its shape;

- Hulls, which connect sequential CVs as a visual and selection aid;

- Edit points (EPs), which lie on the curve and mark the beginning and end of curve spans;

- Spans, which are the individual sections within a curve as defined by edit points.

Degree

Curves in Maya can be drawn in first, second, third, fifth, or seventh degree. The higher the degree of the curve, the more complex a single span can be. The *degree of a curve* refers to the largest exponent value used in the polynomial equation that defines the shape of a span within the curve.

A single span first degree curve will be a simple straight line, and will only be able to cross any given axis once. A first degree curve with more than one span will look like a jagged line.

A single span second degree curve will be a parabola, and will be able to cross any given axis twice.

Single span third degree curves are often described as *simple S's,* meaning they look like the letter S. Single span third degree curves can cross any given axis three times.

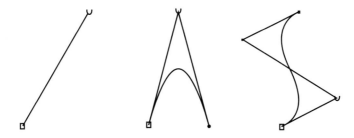

First, second and third degree single span curves

When creating curves you must always place one CV greater than the degree type before the first span will be created. So, to create a first degree curve you would have to place two CVs, to create a second degree curve you would have to place three CVs, and to create a third degree curve you would have to place four CVs.

This project will focus on first and third degree NURBS geometry.

Parameterization

Parameterization, also known as *knot spacing*, refers to how Maya distributes value along the length of a curve. There are two types of parameterization in Maya: *uniform* and *chord length*.

Uniform parameterization distributes value evenly, per span, through the curve regardless of the actual length of the span. For example, a uniformly parameterized curve with 3 spans will have parametric values from 0 to 3, with the value at each edit point being 0, 1, 2, or 3. As a result, curves with uniform knot spacing have very predictable values.

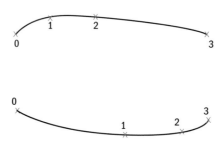

Two uniform curves and their parametric values at EPs

Since the parametric value within each span is equal, regardless of the span's length, the overall distribution of value in curves with spans of greatly different sizes can be uneven. This can lead to texturing problems in surfaces created from these curves.

Lofted surface with texture

Tip: *While it's not essential, a good rule is to try and keep the spans in your curves roughly the same length.*

Chord length parameterization distributes value through the curve according to the physical distance between the edit points. As a result, parametric value is distributed evenly throughout the entire length of the curve.

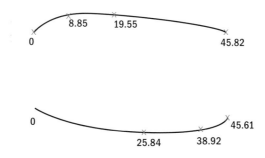

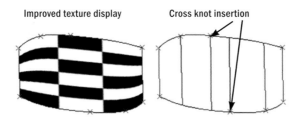

Two chord length curves and their values at the EPs

While chord length knot spacing can solve some texturing problems, the unpredictable value within the curve can lead to surface problems, such as *cross knot insertion*.

Diagram of lofted surface, with and without texture

While chord length parameterization has its uses, most modelers opt for the predictability of uniform parameterization when creating curves.

Curve direction

All NURBS curves have a U direction. The curve's U direction simply refers to the direction along the curve in which its parametric value increases. The direction of a curve is clearly indicated by the first two CVs of the curve. The CV at the beginning of the curve looks like a little square, while the second CV is indicated by a U.

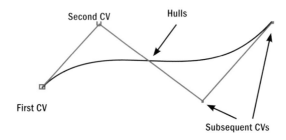

Curve with CVs and hulls displayed

Continuity

Continuity refers to the physical relationship at the intersection between two NURBS curves or surfaces. There are several levels of continuity in Maya. For the purposes of this project, we will examine the two most important levels of continuity:

- Positional continuity (or G0);
- Tangent continuity (or G1).

Positional continuity means that two curves simply intersect at their ends. If surfaces were produced from two curves with *G0* continuity there would be no gaps between the surfaces, but there would be a visible seam at the intersection point. In other words, the two surfaces would look like one continuous surface with a corner.

G0 continuity is achieved simply by having the first or last CV of one curve on top of the first or last CV of another curve.

G0 curves and surfaces

Tangent continuity means that two curves intersect at their ends with the tangent of each curve matching at the intersection point. The tangency of a curve is the direction that a curve is pointing at any given point along the curve. Surfaces produced from curves with *G1* continuity will have no gaps at the point of intersection, and show no visible seam. In other words, the two surfaces would look like one perfectly smooth continuous surface.

G1 continuity is achieved first by achieving G0 continuity, then by having the neighboring CVs on the curves line up. In short, four CVs in a row equals tangent continuity.

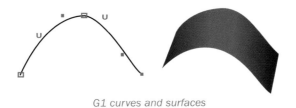

G1 curves and surfaces

G1 continuity is essential to seamless NURBS patch models.

Quality curves

Since NURBS surfaces are often created from one or more NURBS curves, it is essential that those curves be well constructed.

- Opposing curves should have the same parameterization.

- Parameterization should be consistent between curves.

- Appropriate continuity should be achieved between curves and surfaces.

Open, closed and periodic geometry

NURBS geometry can exist in three forms: *open*, *closed* and *periodic*.

Open curves or surfaces typically have their start and end edit points at different locations, creating a curve that looks open. However, if you were to place the first edit point on top of the last edit point so that the curve looped back on itself, it would still be considered open geometry because the edit points could still be moved away from each other.

Closed curves or surfaces are always loops because their start and end edit points lie on top of each other and are seamed together. If you select the first edit point on a closed curve and move it, the last edit point will go with it. Moving the first or last edit point of a closed curve may result in loss of G1 continuity at the seam.

Periodic curves or surfaces are also loops with a seam, but they have two unseen spans that extend past and overlap the first and last visible spans. The overlapping spans maintain G1 continuity at the seam when edit points are moved.

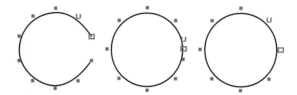

Open, closed and periodic curves

SURFACES

Anatomy of a NURBS surface

Every NURBS surface is made up of:

- Control vertices (CVs), which lie off the surface and define its shape;

- Hulls, which connect sequential CVs in the surface's U and V directions;

- Isoparms, which lie on the surface, denoting consistent parametric value and defining surface spans (or patches);

- Spans, which are the individual sections defined by the isoparms.

U and V surface direction

Like NURBS curves, NURBS surfaces have directions of increasing parametric value. A surface's U and V directions will affect the orientation of a texture applied to the surface. It will also determine which direction the surface's normal faces.

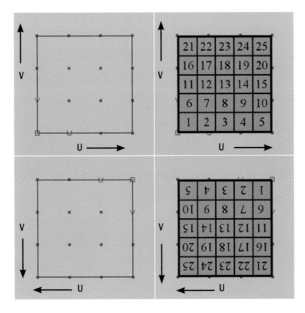

U and V surface direction and texture orientation

Degree

Like NURBS curves, surfaces can be first, second, third, fifth, or seventh degree. However, NURBS surfaces can be different degrees in their U and V directions. For example, a cylinder could be more geometrically economical by making it first degree along its length where it's straight, and third degree around its circumference.

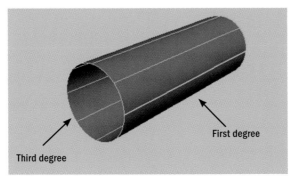

First and third degree cylinder

Normals

Like polygonal surfaces, NURBS surfaces have normals that are perpendicular to the surface. The U and V directions of a NURBS surface will determine which direction the normals face on the surface.

Commonly referred to as the *right-hand rule*, the relationship between U and V directions and a surface's normals can be predicted using your thumb, index finger and middle finger. Using your right hand, simply point your thumb in the U direction of the surface and your index finger in the V direction. Then point your middle finger so that it's perpendicular to your index finger. Your middle finger will now indicate the normal direction of the surface.

Note: *Reversing the U or V direction of a surface will cause the normal to face in the other direction.*

Changing surface direction

The increase in either U or V parametric value can be reversed so that it runs in the other direction. Or, the U and V directions can be swapped when necessary to reverse surface normals, reorient textures, or correct rigid body penetration problems.

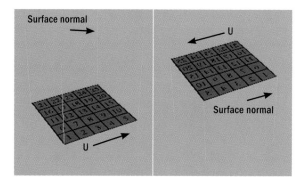

Surface normal reversed because the U direction reversed

Isoparms

Isoparms are the flow lines that run through NURBS surfaces in both the U and V direction, defining the surface's shape according to the CVs. In the same way that edit points on a curve define its spans, isoparms on a surface define its patches.

In mathematical terms, isoparms indicate lines of consistent parametric value in the U or V direction of a surface. As a result of this flow of consistent value, isoparms can be used to break, or *detach*, a single NURBS surface into two separate surfaces.

Curves on surface

Like isoparms, a *curve on surface* is a line that appears on a NURBS surface. Unlike isoparms, they do not indicate a line of consistent parametric value, rather they define an arbitrary boundary in the UV coordinates of the surface.

Curves on surface can be created by drawing directly on a *live* NURBS surface, by projecting an existing NURBS curve on to a surface, or by intersecting one NURBS surface with another.

Curves on surface are typically used to cut away, or *trim*, unwanted sections of a NURBS surface.

Trimming NURBS surfaces

While NURBS surfaces are extremely flexible and capable of achieving almost any shape, they are ultimately four-sided patches, and, as such, they have certain limitations. To overcome these limitations, NURBS surfaces can be trimmed to cut away unwanted sections. If you were modeling a surface that needed to have openings in it, such as the air vents in a bicycle helmet, you would trim those holes out.

While trimming surfaces is well suited for industrial design, it is inappropriate for models that need to deform because the trimmed boundaries will tear apart during deformation, showing gaps in the model.

Conclusion

In this lesson, you learned about the various principles of NURBS geometry, including curve and surface degree, parameterization, curve direction and quality, and changing curve and surface direction.

In the next lesson, you will apply these principles to build Diva's body using NURBS patches.

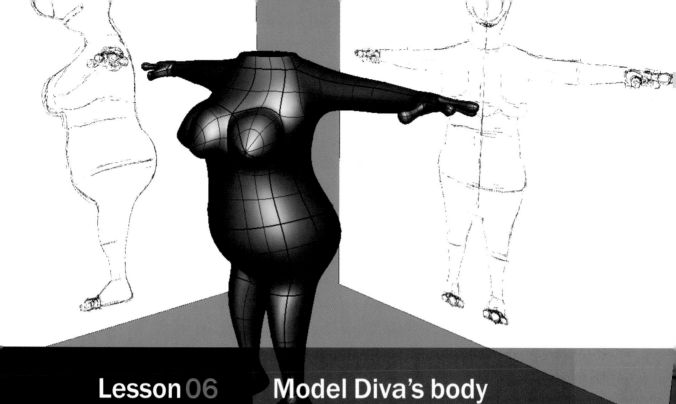

Lesson 06   Model Diva's body

*In this lesson you will build
Diva's body out of NURBS
patches using an organic
modeling technique commonly
referred to as socking. Organic
NURBS modeling relies more
on strategy and technique
rather than complex tools.*

In this lesson you will learn the following:

- How to build a custom NURBS patch modeling tool shelf;

- How to sock a simple example;

- How to block out a character using NURBS primitives;

- How to refine existing geometry;

- How to sock body parts to each other;

- How to redirect the flow of topology;

- How to show and reverse normals;

- How to mirror geometry.

Custom shelf

NURBS patch modeling relies on the effective implementation of a few tools and techniques. To speed up your workflow, you will create a custom tool shelf and fill it with the tools most commonly used during NURBS patch modeling.

1 Scene file

- Select **File** → **New**.

2 Create a new shelf

- Select **Window** → **Settings/Preferences** → **Shelves**.

- In the displayed window, select the **Shelves** tab, then click on the **New Shelf** button.

- Rename the new shelf *PatchModeling*.

- Click the **Save All Shelves** button.

There is now a new shelf displayed in the shelves of the main interface.

 Tip: *If the shelves are not displayed in the main interface, select* **Display** → **UI Elements** → **Shelf.**

3 Add the Move Normal Tool to the shelf

- Hold **Ctrl+Shift** and select **Modify** → **Transformation Tools** → **Move Normal.**

The **Move Normal Tool** *will appear on your custom tool shelf.*

 Note: *The* **Move Normal Tool** *allows you to move CVs along a surface's U or V direction, or along the surface's normal. The* **Move Normal Tool** *is useful for moving CVs to readjust the flow of a surface's isoparms while maintaining the original shape.*

4 Attach Surfaces options

- Select **Edit NURBS** → **Attach Surfaces** → ❐.

- Reset the settings.

- Set the following options:

    Attach Method to **Blend**;

    Blend Bias to **0.5**;

    Insert Knot to **Off**;

    Keep Original to **Off**.

- Select **Edit** → **Save Settings**.

- Click the **Close** button.

5 Add Attach Surfaces to your shelf

Now that the options for the **Attach Surfaces Tool** are set properly for your needs, you will add the tool to your new shelf.

- Hold **Ctrl+Shift** and select **Edit NURBS** → **Attach Surfaces**.

The **Attach Surfaces Tool** *will appear on your custom tool shelf.*

Note: *The* **Attach Surfaces Tool** *joins two separate NURBS surfaces into one surface.*

6 Rebuild Surfaces options

- Select **Edit NURBS** → **Rebuild Surfaces** → ❐.

- Reset the settings.

- Set the following options:

    Rebuild Type to **Uniform**;

    Parameter Range to **0 to #Spans**;

    Keep CVs to **On**.

- Select **Edit** → **Save Settings**.

- Click the **Close** button.

7   Add Rebuild Surfaces to your shelf

- Hold **Ctrl+Shift** and select **Edit NURBS** → **Rebuild Surfaces**.

The **Rebuild Surfaces** *command will appear on your custom tool shelf.*

Note: *The* **Rebuild Surfaces** *command recreates a NURBS surface with good parameterization.*

8   Add Detach Surface to your shelf

- Hold **Ctrl+Shift** and select **Edit NURBS** → **Detach Surface**.

The **Detach Surface** *command will appear on your custom tool shelf.*

Note: *The* **Detach Surface** *command splits a NURBS surface at the selected isoparm(s).*

9   Add Insert Isoparm to your shelf

- Hold **Ctrl+Shift** and select **Edit NURBS** → **Insert Isoparm**.

The **Insert Isoparm** *command will appear on your custom tool shelf.*

Note: *The* **Insert Isoparm** *command allows you to add an isoparm defined on the surface.*

10   Rebuild Curves options

- Select **Edit Curves** → **Rebuild Curves** → ❑.
- Reset the settings.
- Set the following options:

    Rebuild Type to **Uniform**;

    Parameter Range to **0 to #Spans**;

    Keep CVs to **On**.

- Select **Edit** → **Save Settings**.
- Click the **Close** button.

11 Add Rebuild Curves to your shelf

- Hold **Ctrl+Shift** and select **Edit Curves** → **Rebuild Curves**.

Note: *The* **Rebuild Curves** *command works just like* **Rebuild Surfaces** *except that it works on curves.*

12 Add the Rebuild Surfaces option window to your shelf

- Hold **Ctrl+Shift** and select **Edit NURBS** → **Rebuild Surfaces** → ❑.

When you press this shelf button, the **Rebuild Surfaces** *option window will be displayed.*

13 Add a Rebuild Curves option window to your shelf

- Hold **Ctrl+Shift** and select **Edit Curve** → **Rebuild Curves** → ❑.

When you press this shelf button, the **Rebuild Curves** *option window will be displayed.*

14 Global Stitch options

- Select **Edit NURBS** → **Stitch** → **Global Stitch** → ❑.
- Reset the settings.
- Set the following options:

  Stitch Corners to **Closest Knot**;

  Stitch Edges to **Match Params**;

  Stitch Smoothness to **Normals**;

  Max Separation to **0.1**;

  Modification Resistance to **10.0**;

  Sampling Density to **1**;

  Keep Original to **Off**.

- Select **Edit** → **Save Settings**.
- Click the **Close** button.

15 Add the Global Stitch Tool to your shelf

- Hold **Ctrl+Shift** and select **Edit NURBS** → **Stitch** → **Global Stitch**.

Note: The **Global Stitch Tool** *sews multiple NURBS surfaces together to make them appear to be in one piece.*

16 Label the shelf icons

- Select **Window** → **Settings/Preferences** → **Shelves**.

- Select the **Shelf Contents** tab.

- Highlight the *Rebuild Surface Option Box* item.

- Set the **Icon Name** to **Opt**.

- Highlight the *Rebuild Curve Option Box* item.

- Set the **Icon Name** to **Opt**.

- Click the **Save All Shelves** button.

Doing so will save your shelf preferences on disk for your next Maya session.

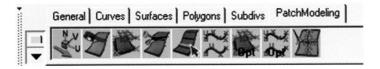

The new custom shelf

Tip: *You can also save your preferences by selecting* **File** → **Save Preferences**.

Socking

Complex shapes, like shoulders, can be difficult to achieve if not approached properly. One of the principle techniques used in NURBS patch modeling is commonly referred to as *socking*. Socking is the practice of repeatedly attaching, detaching, and rebuilding NURBS patches to create an integrated network of patches that appear to be seamless. Socking will be discussed later in this lesson when you sock the arm to the torso.

Note: *NURBS patches are always four-sided, but borders of CVs can be all at the same location, thus giving the impression of three or two-sided surfaces.*

1   Create two primitive NURBS surfaces

In a new scene, you will use half a sphere and a cylinder to represent a simplified version of a shoulder and arm.

- Select **Create → NURBS Primitives → Sphere.**

- **RMB-click** on the sphere and select **Isoparm.**

- Select the vertical isoparm that appears thicker than the other ones.

This specific isoparm indicates the UV start and end of the surface.

- Detach the *sphere* by clicking on the appropriate shelf button.

Even if it doesn't look like you detached the surface, you just opened the sphere along that isoparm.

- Select the vertical opposite isoparm.

- Detach the *sphere* again by clicking on the appropriate shelf button.

The sphere is now split into two parts.

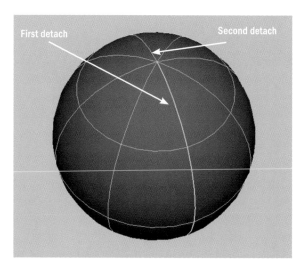

Isoparms used to detach the sphere

- Delete the right half of the detached sphere.

- Select the remaining half, then select **Edit → Delete by Type → History.**

- Select **Create → NURBS Primitives → Cylinder.**

- Move and rotate the *cylinder* as follows:

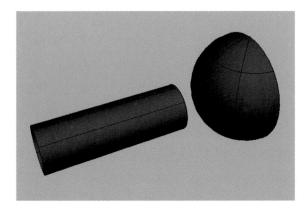

Simple arm and shoulder

 Tip: *Change the view's shading mode to display **Wireframe on Shaded** to always see the isoparms, even when the surfaces are not selected.*

Because of the layout of each surface's topology, it will be impossible to create a smooth transition between them by simply attaching. To solve this problem, you will detach both surfaces into multiple pieces, then strategically re-attach them to each other.

2 Rebuild the sphere

During the socking process, pieces from the sphere will be attached to corresponding surfaces in the cylinder. As a result, the way that each piece is broken up will have a tremendous impact on the final transition between the two surfaces. To facilitate the transition of the topology from the cylinder to the sphere, the sphere will be rebuilt to have more spans.

- Select the *sphere*, then click on the **Rebuild Surfaces Opt** from the shelf, and set the following:

    Keep CVs to **Off**;

    Number of Spans to **8** in both **U** and **V**.

- Click the **Rebuild** button.

The sphere now has more spans to work with.

3   Detach the sphere at an isoparm

- **RMB-click** on the sphere and select **Isoparms**.

- Drag a selection box to select the following **4** isoparms:

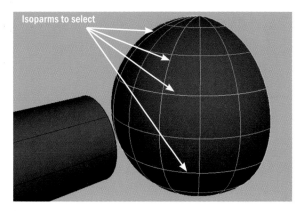

Simple arm and shoulder

Tip: *Clicking on an isoparm will select it and highlight it yellow. If you* **click+drag** *on an isoparm, the selection becomes a dotted yellow line, which means you are defining a new isoparm. By selecting isoparms using the selection box, you are guaranteed to select only existing isoparms and not define new ones.*

- Click on the **Detach Surface** shelf icon.

- You will need to continue detaching the *sphere* until it has been divided up into **9** pieces.

4   Delete the center surface

- Select the surface at the center of the nine patches and delete it.

5   Rebuild the cylinder

- Rebuild the cylinder to have **8** spans in **U** and **V**.

6   Detach the cylinder into four slices

- Select the four isoparms on the cylinder that flow into the corners created by the missing surface on the sphere.

- Detach the cylinder.

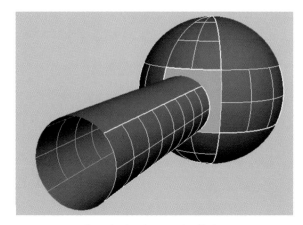

Detached sphere and cylinder

7   Attach the cylinder surfaces to the sphere surfaces

- Select the top surface on both the sphere and the cylinder.

- Click on the **Attach Surfaces** shelf icon.

- Click on the **Rebuild Surfaces Tool** to rebuild the surfaces.

Note: *You should generally rebuild a surface with the* **Keep CVs** *option after you attach it. Rebuilding with Keep CVs forces the CVs to hold their position, allowing the surface to maintain its shape while the parameterization of the surface is cleaned up.*

8   Repeat for the other surfaces

- Repeat the process outlined above to attach each of the remaining cylinder surfaces.

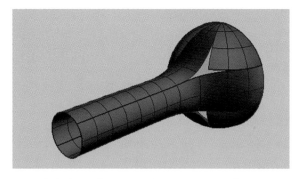

Cylinder surfaces attached to sphere surfaces

9   Detach where you just attached

- Select the isoparm nearest the point where the attachment occurred and detach there.

10   Narrow the gap at the top right corner

Attaching the cylinder and sphere surfaces begins the transition between the two, but there are still big gaps at the corners. To correct this, you will now attach, rebuild and detach the corners.

- Select the top right surface in the sphere, then **Shift-select** the adjacent surface below it.

- Attach the two surfaces.

- Rebuild the new surface.

- Select the isoparm where the attach just occurred and detach there.

- Select the second surface from the last operation, then **Shift-select** the surface below it.

- Attach, rebuild and detach the surface.

- Repeat this process until you have attached, rebuilt, and detached all of the surfaces in the corner of the sphere and cylinder.

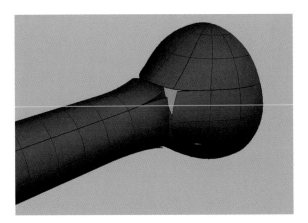

The current patches

11 Deleting the history

Each of the commands outlined above will generate a construction history node for the surfaces. In order to keep your scene clean, you should delete the construction history to delete unnecessary history nodes.

- Select all of the surfaces, then select **Edit** → **Delete by Type** → **History**.

12 Apply a Global Stitch

- Select all of the surfaces and click on the **Global Stitch** button on your shelf.

Note: *It is possible that the Global Stitch doesn't entirely close the surfaces because the gaps can be too wide. The following step will solve this issue.*

13 Adjust the Max Separation value

If there are still gaps between your surfaces, you may need to adjust your **Max Separation** value.

- Select one of the surfaces just stitched.

- Select *GlobalStitch1* in the **Inputs** section of the Channel Box.

- Increase the **Max Separation** value in small increments until the gaps disappear.

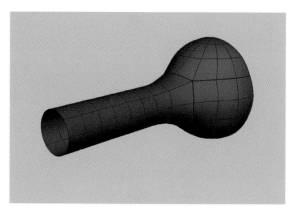

Cylinder and sphere surfaces, once they have been stitched together

Note: *You can delete the history to remove the **Global Stitch** from the models' construction history, but the stitch will ensure that gaps never appear between patches as they are moving or deforming.*

The torso

The first step in building a NURBS patch body is to block out the character with NURBS primitives, such as cylinders and spheres. You will begin modeling Diva by opening a scene file that already has image planes set up.

1 Scene file

- Open the file called *06-divaBody_01.ma*.

Diva's front, side, top and back reference image planes have already been set up in this scene.

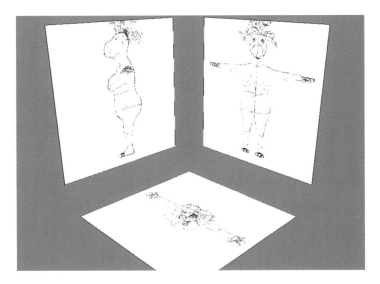

The reference images

Note: *To see the back reference image, simply select the back camera and make it visible.*

2 Create a default NURBS cylinder

- Select **Create** → **NURBS Primitives** → **Cylinder** → ❏.

- In the NURBS cylinder options, select **Edit** → **Reset Settings**.

- Click the **Create** button.

3 Transform the cylinder

- Using the *front* and *side* reference images, move and scale the cylinder so that it roughly matches the proportions of Diva's torso.

Tip: You can use **View Compass** to quickly change between views.

The Perspective View Compass

4 Increase the number of spans in the U direction

- Select the *cylinder*'s construction history node in the **Inputs** section of the Channel Box.

- Increase the **Spans** value to **4**.

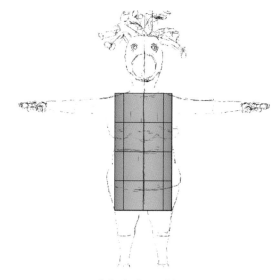

Cylinder in position

Shaping the torso

You are about to start editing the torso cylinder by manipulating CVs and hulls directly. In addition to the shape of the surface, the flow of topology will also be adjusted.

1   Delete history from the cylinder

Since changing values associated with the construction history will cause unpredictable results if components are manipulated, you should delete the cylinder's construction history.

- With the cylinder highlighted, select **Edit** → **Delete by Type** → **History**.

2   Shape the cylinder

- **RMB-click** on the cylinder and select **Hulls**.

- One at a time, select each of the hulls running horizontally across the cylinder. Move and scale them until the cylinder matches the image plane as closely as possible with the existing geometry.

Tip: *Remember to work in the front and side views.*

Note: *It is important to keep the number of spans in your NURBS surfaces to a minimum during the geometry blocking process. Keeping your geometry light makes it easier to work with. You should always try to achieve as much shape in the surface as possible with the existing CVs before adding more.*

3   Use the Move Normal Tool to adjust the flow of geometry

Once you are satisfied with the shape of the torso, you should adjust the flow of topology by using the **Move Normal Tool** to move CVs. This tool will allow you to move CVs along the surface, minimizing changes to the shape of the surface.

- **RMB-click** on the cylinder and select **Control Vertex**.

- Select the CV at the front center of the cylinder.

- Change to the **Move Normal Tool** by clicking on its shelf button.

- Move the CV along the surface's **U** direction by **click+dragging** on the manipulator's U handle.

- Continue adjusting CVs until you are satisfied with the flow of the surface's isoparms.

> **Note:** *Good topological flow makes sculpting your surface easier and ensures that your model will deform properly when it is bound. Whenever possible, it is a good idea to establish good topological flow early in the model when the geometry is light. That way, as you increase the number of spans in a surface, the topology is maintained.*

4   Delete one half of the cylinder

- **RMB-click** on the *cylinder* and select **Isoparm.**

- Select the isoparm at the front center of the cylinder.

- Detach the surface.

- Select the isoparm at the back center of the torso and detach again.

The cylinder should now be divided into two pieces.

- Delete the left piece.

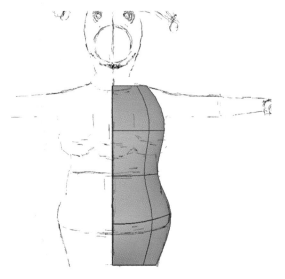

The torso starting to take shape

> **Note:** *Later on, you will mirror the geometry on the right side of the character. Doing so will save you a lot of modeling work.*

5   Save your work

  ▪ Save the scene as *06-divaBody_02.ma*.

The arm

Now you will create Diva's arm using the same technique employed to create the torso.

1   Scene file

  ▪ Continue with your own scene.

  Or

  ▪ Open the scene called *06-divaBody_02.ma*.

2   Create a NURBS cylinder aligned with the X-axis

  ▪ Select **Create** → **NURBS Primitives** → **Cylinder** → ☐, and set the following:

     Axis to **X**;

     Number of Spans to **2**.

  ▪ Click the **Create** button.

3   Move and scale the cylinder

  ▪ Using the *front* and *top* views, move and scale the cylinder to match the arm in the image plane.

4   Adjust the shape

  ▪ Adjust the shape of the cylinder by manipulating its hulls and CVs.

5   Create a NURBS sphere for the deltoid

You will now create a NURBS sphere to define the character's deltoid and shoulder.

  ▪ Select **Create** → **NURBS Primitives** → **Sphere**.

  ▪ Using the *front* and *top* views, translate, rotate and scale the sphere to match Diva's deltoid and shoulder areas.

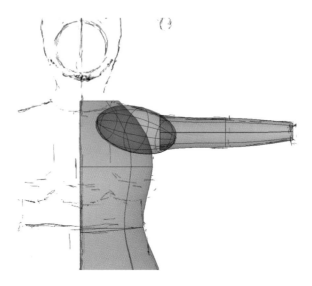

Primitive arm and shoulder

Creating the leg

1 Create a NURBS cylinder

- Create a default NURBS cylinder aligned with the **Y-axis**.

2 Move the cylinder into position

- Translate the cylinder to the knee in the *front* image plane.

- Scale the cylinder up on **Y** to the approximate length of the leg from the crotch to the ankle.

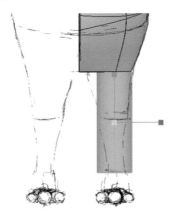

Place the primitive leg cylinder

3 Scale the CVs to match the image plane

- Manipulate the cylinder's hulls and CVs to shape the cylinder-like Diva's leg in the reference image.

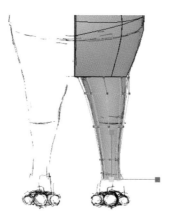

Initial shape of leg

Tip: *Don't forget to use the front and side views.*

Creating the breasts

1 Primitive breast

- Create a NURBS sphere with the poles on the **Z-axis**.

- Move and scale the *sphere* into the middle breast position.

2 Duplicate the breast

- With the sphere selected, press **Ctrl+d** to duplicate it.

- Move and rotate the duplicated sphere so that it aligns with the torso.

3 Detach the middle sphere

Since this specific character has a middle breast, you can split the sphere in half in order to mirror the other half later in this lesson.

- Detach the middle sphere by selecting the appropriate isoparm and detaching it using your shelf button.

- Delete the half on the right side of the character.

- Rebuild the remaining half.

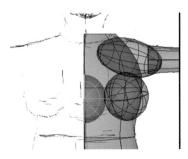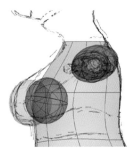

Placement of the breasts' sphere

4   Deform the breast using a lattice

Deformers, such as lattices, are excellent modeling tools since they generally change the shape of a surface more smoothly and gradually than could be achieved by simply pulling CVs.

- With the *left* sphere selected, select **Deform** → **Create Lattice** → ❑ from the **Animation** menu set.
- Reset the options, then set all three **Number of Divisions** options to **4**.
- Click the **Create** button.

5   Tweak the lattice points

- **RMB-click** on the lattice and select **Lattice Points**.
- Select the front **16** lattice points.
- Scale down and move the lattice points on the **Y-axis** to refine the shape of the front of the sphere.
- If necessary, scale and move the next row of lattice points to further refine the breast.

6   Delete history from the breast

Once a surface has been shaped to your satisfaction with a deformer (such as a lattice), the deformer should be deleted by removing the history from the surface.

- Select the sphere affected by the lattice, then select **Edit** → **Delete By Type** → **History**.

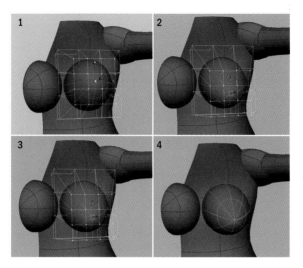

Deformation of breast using a lattice

Note: *Simply deleting a deformer from a surface will result in the surface snapping back to its original, undeformed shape.*

7 Do the same lattice deformation for the middle breast

- Repeat the previous steps to shape the middle breast sphere.

Tip: *Try to avoid moving the central lattice points and CVs from the X-axis. Not moving them will simplify the mirroring of the surface.*

8 Save your work

- Save the scene as *06-divaBody_03.ma*.

Refining the torso

Now that all the pieces are in place you will refine the surfaces' shapes before socking the arm, leg and breast to the torso.

1 Scene file

- Continue with your own scene.

Or

- Open the scene called *06-divaBody_03.ma*.

2 Increase the torso's number of spans

- With the torso selected, click on the **Rebuild Surfaces Opt** shelf button.

- Reset the settings.

- Set the following options:

> **Rebuild type** to **Uniform**;
>
> **Parameter Range** to **0 to # Spans**;
>
> **Direction** to **U**;
>
> **Number of Spans U** to **9**.

- Click the **Rebuild** button.

- Use the **Rebuild Surfaces Opt** shelf button again and rebuild the torso to have **6** spans in the **V** direction.

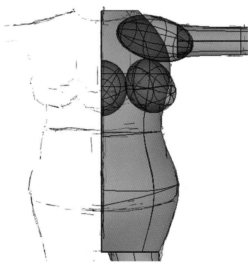

Refinement of torso

Note: *As you build your character, it is a good idea to refine the character as a whole.*

Refining the deltoid

You will now refine the shape of the deltoid by using a lattice.

1   Apply a lattice to the deltoid sphere

- Select **Deform** → **Create Lattice** → ❑, and reset the options.

- Click the **Create** button.

- Set the number of **T Divisions** to **5**.

2   Shape the deltoid

- Move lattice points to refine the deltoid into a muscular teardrop shape.

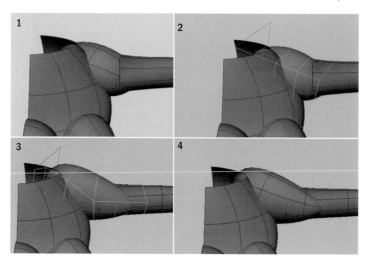

Deltoid deformed by lattice

3   Remove the lattice by deleting history

- Select the *deltoid sphere* and select **Edit** → **Delete By Type** → **History**.

4   Save your work

- Save the scene as *06-divaBody_04.ma*.

Attach the arm and deltoid

You will now join the deltoid to the arm by doing a series of strategic attaches and detaches.

1 Scene file

- Continue with your own scene.

Or

- Open the scene called *06-divaBody_04.ma*.

2 Detach the deltoid and arm

- Detach a vertical isoparm in the middle of the upper arm.

- Delete the part of the upper arm that is inside the deltoid sphere.

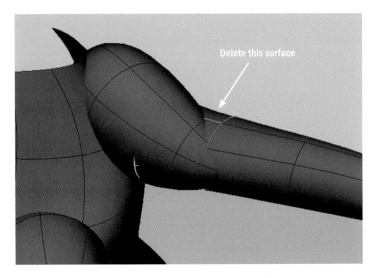

Detach and delete the upper arm surface

- Detach the deltoid sphere into three horizontal slices using the isoparms at the bottom, front and back of the sphere.

Doing so will leave you with a top section made of four spans, and two smaller surfaces of two spans each in the armpit area.

- Drag and select new vertical isoparms on the three deltoid surfaces created above.

Select convenient places to detach in order to get the best possible transition from the deltoid to the arm.

- Detach each of the three surfaces.

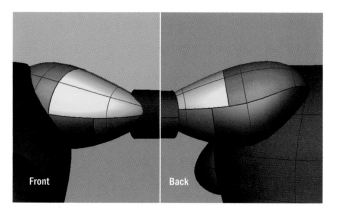

Front   Back

Detach the deltoid

Note: *In order to make it easier to see the patches, colored shaders are assigned to the different pieces.*

- Delete the unnecessary parts, as shown in the following image:

Detach the deltoid

- Rebuild the remaining surfaces of the deltoid.

- Select three horizontal isoparms in the arm cylinder nearest the detachment point for the deltoid, then detach the new slices.

You should define three surfaces that match the deltoid surfaces, which is one top surface made of four spans and two smaller surfaces of two spans each under the arm.

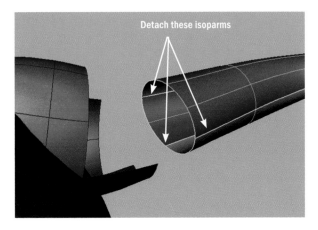

Arm isoparms to detach

3   Attach the arm to the deltoid

- Select the upper deltoid surface and then **Shift-select** the *upper arm surface*.

- Attach and rebuild the new surface.

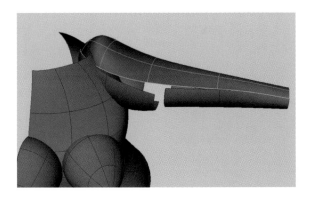

Upper deltoid and arm surfaces attached

Note: *When attaching surfaces, both surfaces must either have the same number of spans or the number of spans must be multiples of each other. If not, cross knot insertion will occur, resulting in poorly parameterized surfaces.*

4 Blend Bias value

When attaching surfaces, the Attach Tool blends between the two original surfaces in the attachment area. Adjusting the **Blend Bias** value controls which surface's shape exerts more influence over the shape of the new attached surface.

- Select the *attachSurface1* created in the previous step.

- In the **Input** section of the Channel Box, adjust the **Blend Bias** of the attachment by changing the value between **0** and **1**.

Or

- Highlight the **Blend Bias** attribute and **MMB+drag** in the view to invoke the virtual slider.

5 Attach the remaining surfaces of the deltoid and arm

- Repeat **step 3** for the remaining arm surfaces.

Lesson 06

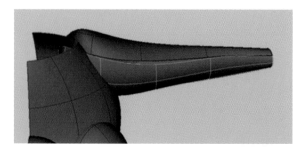

Arm surfaces attached

Note: *If rebuilding your surfaces with* **Keep CVs** *set to* **On** *results in a poorly parameterized surface, then one or both of the surfaces probably have poor parameterization. Try to undo the attach operation, then rebuild each surface before attaching.*

6   Close the surface

- Attach the three arm slices together.

Note: *If your surfaces attach at edges other than the ones you intended, you will have to indicate where you want the attach to occur on each surface. Do this by picking an isoparm near the edge where you want the attachment to occur.*

Tip: *Make sure the last attachment is made on the isoparms underneath the arm. This will help hide the seam of the geometry and texture.*

- Select the surface and check its characteristic in the Attribute Editor.

You will see that the surface is still open in **V**.

- Select **Edit NURBS → Open/Close Surface → ❒**.
- Reset the settings and set the following:

    Surface Direction to **V**;

    Shape to **Blend**.

- Press the **Open/Close** button.

The surface should now be closed appropriately.

Refining the shape of the arm

Now that the arm and deltoid are in one piece, the arm's shape will be refined slightly to develop the elbow area.

1 Blinn material

When modeling, using a blinn material is very useful since its specular highlights will make it easier to judge subtle contouring in the surfaces.

- Select all NURBS surfaces.

- Press **F5** to change to the **Rendering** menu set, then select **Lighting/ Shading** → **Assign New Material** → **Blinn**.

The new blinn material will be assigned to all selected surfaces and the Attribute Editor will display the material's attributes.

- Rename the material to *bodyBlinn*.

2 Insert an isoparm near the elbow

Doing so will help deformation purposes in the elbow area.

3 Rebuild with Keep CVs set to On

4 Move CVs

- Move the CVs to refine the elbow geometry.

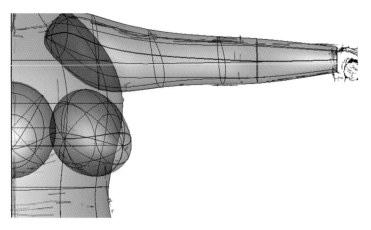

Refinement of elbow

5 Save your work

- Save the scene as *06-divaBody_05.ma*.

The process of blocking out your character is generally the longest phase of the NURBS body. At the end of this phase you should have a series of independent NURBS surfaces with the correct proportions, and essentially the proper shape for your character.

In the next phase you will begin socking the pieces together to create an integrated series of patches.

Sock the arm to the torso

1   Scene file

- Continue with your own scene.

Or

- Open the scene called *06-divaBody_05.ma*.

Note: *When socking, it is important to plan ahead when detaching the pieces to be socked. You should always consider how the two surfaces will flow into each other when they are attached. Generally, the isoparms should flow together in corners. The number of spans on the surfaces is not an important consideration because the surfaces can easily be rebuilt prior to attaching.*

2   Detach the deltoid and rib cage

- Detach the deltoid vertically.

- Detach the arm horizontally into four sections of two spans each.

Doing so will allow you to attach the arm to the torso.

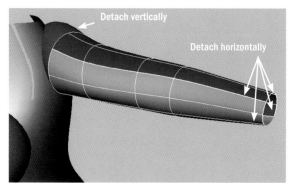

Detach deltoid and arm

- Delete the unnecessary part of the deltoid.

- Repeat to break the upper torso into **nine** pieces.

You will have to insert an isoparm at the neck. The four pieces corresponding to the arm surfaces should have two spans each.

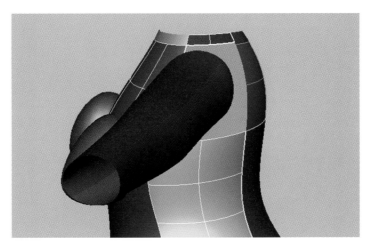

Detach the torso

- Delete the unnecessary part of the torso.

3   Rebuild where necessary

- Rebuild detached surfaces so that it has the same number of isoparms as the surface it is about to be attached to.

Tip: *If one surface has three spans, and the other has two, you should rebuild the surface with the lower number of spans to match the surface with the larger number of spans. Otherwise you are likely to lose detail when the denser surface is rebuilt.*

Tip: *Remember that surfaces with spans that are evenly divisible don't need to be rebuilt before attaching.*

4   Narrow the gaps between the deltoid and torso surfaces

- Working your way around the shoulder, attach, rebuild, and detach the surfaces of the deltoid and torso to narrow the gaps between them.

5   Apply a Global Stitch

- Once you have attached all around the shoulder, select all of the surfaces and click on the **Global Stitch** button on your tool shelf.

6   Adjust the Max Distance value

Chances are there will still be gaps between some of your surfaces after the stitch is applied. If necessary, select the *globalStitch* node in the **Inputs** section of the **Channel Box** and increase the **Max Separation** value until the gaps close.

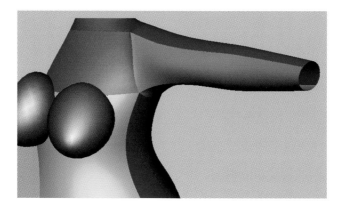

Arm socked to the torso

Note: *In some cases you will find that increasing the* **Max Separation** *value starts stitching unwanted vertices together before it closes all of the holes. If this happens, there are two things you can do. First, lower the* **Max Separation** *value until the unwanted stitching is corrected, then select just the surfaces with the gap. Apply a new Global Stitch to them, and adjust the* **Max Separation** *value for this stitching. Second, you could undo the Global Stitch, then try narrowing the gap further by repeating the attach, detach, rebuild process in the area with the excessive gap. Following that, apply the Global Stitch.*

7   Save your work

- Save the scene as *06-divaBody_06.ma*.

Socking the breasts

Socking the breast to the torso uses the same techniques employed for the arm, but there are extra considerations with the breast since it must flow smoothly into the torso, the armpit and the other breast of the character.

1   Scene file

- Continue with your own scene.

Or

- Open the scene called *06-divaBody_06.ma*.

2   Prepare for socking

- Detach the rear section of the left breast as indicated in image 1 on the following page, and delete the piece you don't need.

- Detach the torso at the rib cage in **nine** pieces as shown in image 2 on the following page.

- Delete the unnecessary piece behind the breast.

- Detach the breast on median isoparms in **four** pieces that correspond with the pieces at the rib cage.

- Rebuild all new surfaces with **Keep CVs**.

3   Attach the left breast surfaces to the torso

- Attach the corresponding pieces of the breast to the torso, as shown in image 3 on the following page.

- If necessary, adjust the **Blend Bias** of the attach nodes or use the **Move Normal Tool** to refine the shape of the attached surface.

4   Detach the middle breast vertically

You need to sock the middle breast with the left breast.

- Detach and rebuild the middle breast following the same principle as the left breast, as shown in image 4 on the following page.

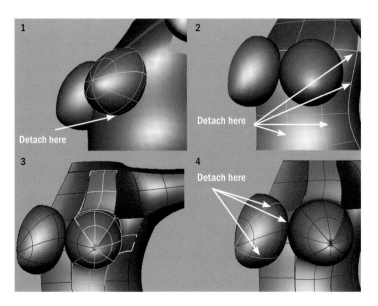

Torso and breasts detached and attached together

5 Delete the backside of the middle breast

6 Attach the left and middle breasts

- Attach the two breast surfaces and **rebuild**.

- Attach and rebuild the remaining breast slices to the corresponding torso surface.

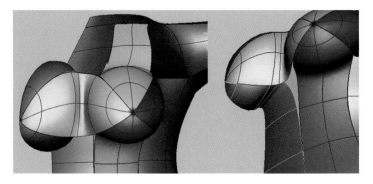

Breast slices attached

7   Detach the surface between the two breasts

- Detach and rebuild the central breast surface.

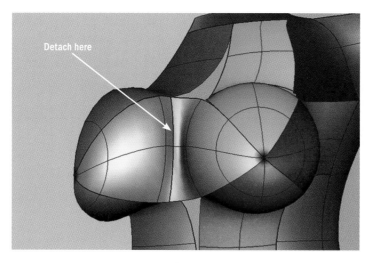

Breast surfaces detached

8   Detach the two slices that come from the torso to the upper part of the two breasts

- Detach and rebuild the **four** resulting surfaces.

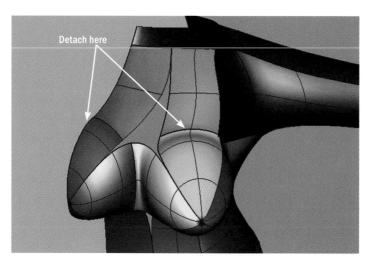

Upper slices' surfaces detached

9   Attach the upper breast surfaces

- Attach and rebuild each of the breast surfaces to the in-between breasts' surfaces.

- Attach and rebuild the **three** torso pieces above the breasts.

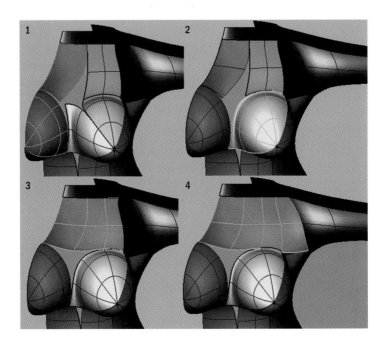

Working the upper breast patches

10   Delete history

Since you repeatedly attached, detached and rebuilt surfaces, unwanted history will build up. It is a good idea to periodically delete history from the scene.

- Select **Edit → Delete All By Type → History**.

11   Detach the lower breasts

- Detach and rebuild the lower breasts' surfaces from the rib cage.

12   Attach each breast

- Attach the breast surfaces together.

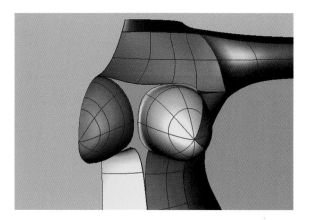

Each breast surface attached

13 Split the breasts

- Detach and rebuild each breast surface in order to get them ready to be attached as one.

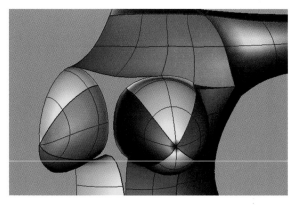

Breast patches

14 Update the lower neck parameterization

- Make sure the lower neck has the same amount of isoparms as the upper chest part by rebuilding it to **4** spans in **U** and **1** span in **V**.

- Attach and rebuild the chest to the lower neck.

- Detach where it was attached, then rebuild the two surfaces.

Doing so will update the parameterization of the lower neck isoparms.

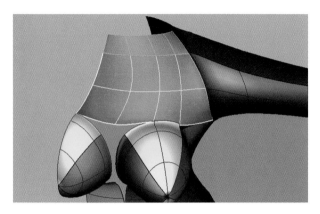

Lower neck updated

15 Detach the upper torso

- Detach and rebuild the torso surface in **three** pieces corresponding to the breast patches.

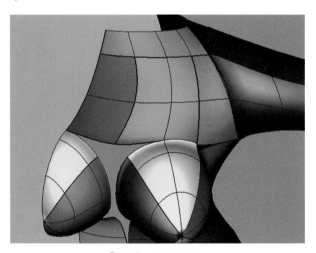

Detach upper torso

16 Attach the two middle breast patches

- Attach and rebuild the two breast surfaces together.

17 Attach the breast patches with torso surfaces

- Attach and rebuild the remaining breast surfaces to the torso.

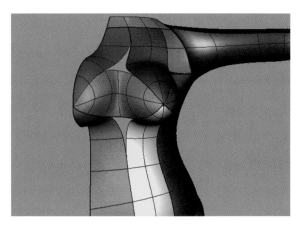

Attached breasts' surfaces to torso

18 Pull CVs to adjust the shape, if necessary

19 Detach in patches

- Detach and rebuild the surfaces just attached in patches in order to get ready for the Global Stitch.

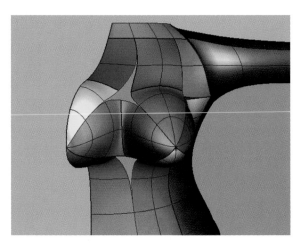

Detach in patches

20 Global Stitch

- Sock the surfaces together with a **Global Stitch**.

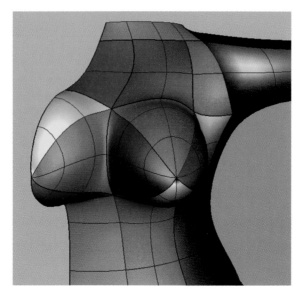

Breasts and torso socked together

21 Save your work

- Save the scene as *06-divaBody_07.ma*.

Flow of topology

When building the leg, buttock and torso intersection of your character, it is essential that the topology flows well to ensure good deformation once the character is bound. In this section, you will redirect the flow of the back of the leg into the buttock to maintain the shape of the buttock. You will also redirect the flow of the torso surface in the crotch area so that it can be connected to the leg.

Reshaping the groin

The groin area of the character hasn't been manipulated since the early blocking stage. You will now re-create the lower abdominal surface to a shape that will work better when it is time to sock everything together.

1   Scene file

- Continue with your own scene.

Or

- Open the scene called *06-divaBody_07.ma*.

2   Reshape the groin area

- Select the two bottom rows of CVs in the groin area.

- Move the CVs until the belly isoparms align with the vertical isoparms of the leg.

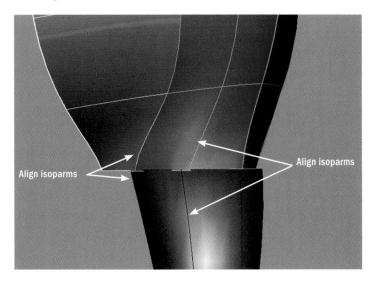

Scaled CVs to fit with leg isoparm

Beginning the buttock

When building the buttock, it is obvious that the topology must flow well into the upper leg, lower back and hip, but it is equally important for the buttock's topology to flow between the legs and into the groin at the front.

1 • Detach the torso

- Detach all the patches forming the lower torso at the fourth isoparm starting from the bottom.

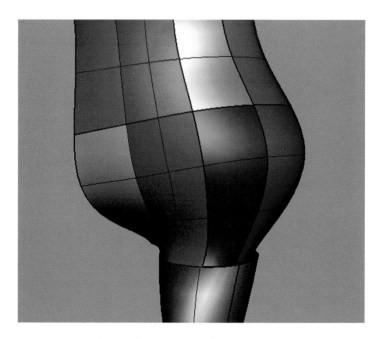

Detach the torso at the fourth isoparms

2 Split leg in slices corresponding to the torso divisions

- Detach the leg to fit the torso patches, making sure to leave a three span surface for the inner leg.

Detach the leg

3 Loft between the legs

- Select the isoparm at the bottom of the buttock surface, then **Shift-select** the isoparm at the groin.

- Select **Surfaces** → **Loft**.

This will create a NURBS patch in-between the two selected isoparms as seen in the following image.

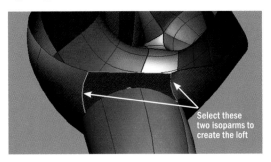

Select these two isoparms to create the loft

Surface lofted from buttock to groin

- Move the CVs on the new lofted surface to better fit the leg geometry.

4 Attach the loft to the leg

- Attach the loft surface to the corresponding leg surface.

- Detach where you just attached.

The loft surface is now aligned with the leg and has a matching amount of spans.

Attach lofted surface to the leg

5 Align the surfaces

- Continue to attach, rebuild and detach surfaces to reduce the gaps between the different surfaces.

6   Stitch the surfaces together

- Select **Edit** → **Delete All By Type** → **History**.

- Select all of the surfaces, then apply a **Global Stitch**.

- Adjust the **Max Separation** value as necessary.

7   Refine the geometry

When a patch model is stitched together, you can use the **Sculpt Geometry Tool** to refine the shape of the geometry further.

- Select all the patches that you wish to sculpt.

- Select **Edit NURBS** → **Sculpt Geometry Tool**.

- Sculpt the surfaces.

*The **Global Stitch** applied in the previous step will make sure to keep the patches together as you sculpt the model.*

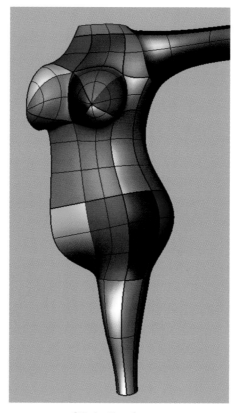

Stitch all surfaces

8   Save your work

- Save the scene as *06-divaBody_08.ma*.

NURBS hands and feet

Building NURBS hands and feet uses the same techniques that have been explored throughout this lesson.

1   Scene file

- Continue with your own scene.

Or

- Open the scene called *06-divaBody_08.ma*.

2   Import basic hand and foot

- Select **File** → **Import**.

- Select the scene called *06-divaHandFoot.ma*.

Note: *The basic structures of Diva's hand and foot have already been created in this scene to speed things up.*

3   Detach the knuckles area

- Insert an isoparm and detach the knuckles area.

Doing so will give more definition to the knuckles.

4   Prepare the fingers for socking

- Detach each of the fingers at the corners into **four** slices.

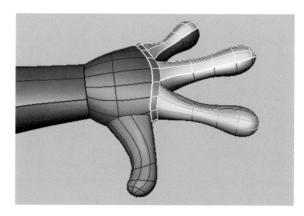

Detach fingers and knuckles

5   Attach, rebuild and detach the fingers

- Attach the surfaces between the fingers to each other.

Tip: *Don't forget to pick the isoparms directly if the surfaces don't attach as you expect.*

- Rebuild the surfaces.
- Detach the surfaces at the isoparm where the attach was done.

6   Stitch the fingers and knuckles

- Use a **Global Stitch** to sock the finger and knuckle surfaces to each other.

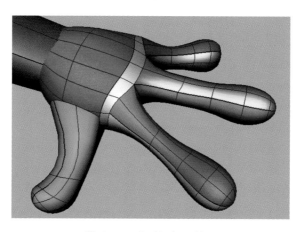

Fingers socked to knuckles

Socking the thumb

Socking the thumb is similar to socking the fingers, except you are working with a much larger transition area.

1   Detach the thumb

- Detach the thumb in **four** matching slices with the palm.

2   Detach the hand surfaces

- Insert an isoparm near the wrist.

- Detach the back of the hand and the palm where the thumb should meet the hand.

Tip: *You might want to define new isoparms.*

- Delete unnecessary surfaces.

3   Rebuild the hand surfaces

- Rebuild the detached surfaces and make sure to have the appropriate number of spans to accomodate the thumb.

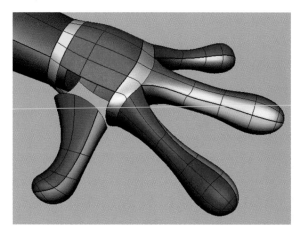

Hand and thumb detached appropriately

4   Loft between the thumb and hand

The thumb needs to be socked to the rest of the hand. If you attach the thumb to the existing hand surfaces, the resulting surfaces may be difficult to work with. You will now create lofted surfaces between the thumb and hand to compensate for this.

▪ Select an edge isoparm on the top thumb surface, then **Shift-select** the adjacent edge isoparm on the top hand surface.

▪ Loft between the two selected isoparms.

▪ Repeat for the bottom sections between the thumb and hand.

▪ Attach the front and back sections of the thumb to the hand.

5   Attach the thumb and the lofted surfaces

▪ Attach the thumb surfaces to their corresponding lofted surfaces.

▪ Reshape the surfaces pulling CVs.

6   Stitch the hand

▪ Select all of the forearm and hand surfaces.

▪ Apply a **Global Stitch**.

▪ Adjust the **Max Distance** value, if necessary.

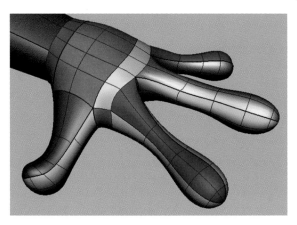

Lofted surfaces between thumb and hand

7   Attach the hand to the arm

▪ Insert isoparms at the wrist location on the arm.

▪ Attach the hand to the arm.

Note: *You might have to propagate new isoparms along the arm.*

8   Repeat for the foot

9   Save your work

- Save the scene as *06-divaBody_09.ma*.

Final touches

1   Scene file

- Continue with your own scene.

Or

- Open the scene called *06-divaBody_09.ma*.

2   Assign a blinn

- Select all the patches.

- Select **Lighting/Shading** → **Assign New Material** → **Blinn**.

3   Reverse normals

- Select all the patches.

- Select **Display** → **NURBS Components** → **Normals**.

Alias
Tip: *My biggest tip to a new user would be: "Learn MEL". At least learn how to pick out the pieces you want from the output in the script editor window. Then learn how to write a simple script which loops through multiple items in a selection list and does something useful. This will save you untold amounts of time. You should also know that holding Ctrl+Shift+Alt and selecting a menu item creates a button on the Shelf for you. Once you've learned that, you can take the time to learn how to create customized marking menus and hotkeys.*

Tim Fowler | Software Engineer, Product Development

Note: *NURBS normals only display in shaded mode.*

- Select patches that the normals seem to be pointing at inwardly.

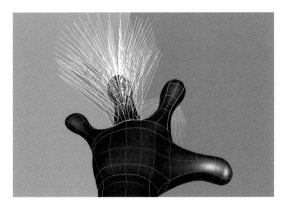

Normals direction

- Select **Edit NURBS** → **Reverse Surface Direction** → ❏.
- Set the options to reverse either in **U** or **V**, then click the **Apply** button.
- Repeat until there are no more reversed surfaces on the entire character.
- Turn **Off** the normals' display.

4 Mirror and stitch

- Select all the patches and group them.
- Duplicate the group and set **Scale X** to **-1**.
- **Attach** the center surfaces two by two.
- Apply a **Global Stitch** on all the surfaces.

5 Clean up

- Select all the patches.
- Select **Modify** → **Center Pivot**.
- Select **Modify** → **Freeze Transformations**.
- Select **Edit** → **Delete All By Type** → **History**.
- Select **File** → **Optimize Scene Size**.

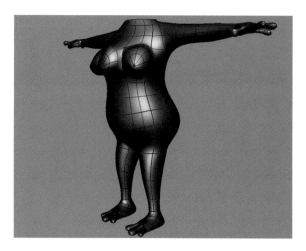

The Diva body

Note: *You will be adding clothes in Lesson 8.*

6 Save your work

- The final scene is called *06-divaBody_10.ma*.

Conclusion

In this lesson you learned how to create a custom NURBS tool shelf, how to block out a character with primitives, how to sock geometry together and how to redirect topology. The character modeled here was quite simple and without any muscular definition, but in order to create more complex characters, you will need to perfect your skills by progressively increasing the level of difficulty.

In the next lesson you will expand what you have learned so far by creating a NURBS head. Instead of starting with primitive surfaces, you will begin by building a network of NURBS curves that will be used to generate the patches.

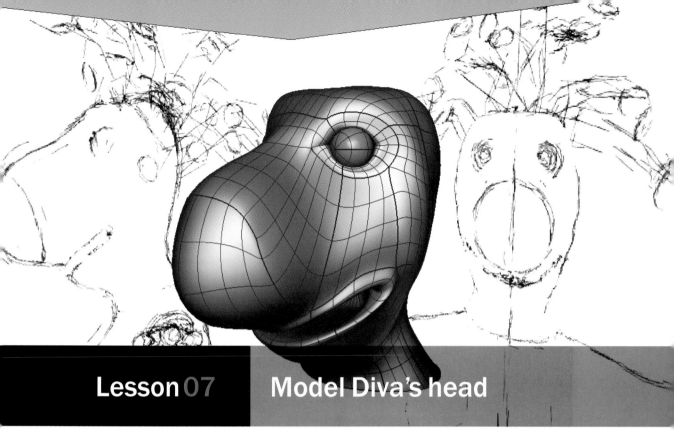

Lesson 07 Model Diva's head

In this lesson, you will build Diva's head to attach to the NURBS body built in the previous lesson. First, a network of NURBS curves will be created for the framework of the head. A series of NURBS patches will then be produced from those curves. Finally, the surfaces will be socked together.

In this lesson you will learn the following:

- How to continue modeling from an existing model;

- How to create a network of curves;

- How to cut curves;

- How to clean up curves to ensure good surfaces;

- How to produce surfaces from curves;

- How to model eyelids using Make Live.

Create profile curves

The first step in creating the NURBS head will be to create a network of curves that will serve as the basis for the final surfaces. You will attempt to have the profile curves follow the natural structure of facial muscles. As a result, the surfaces created from these curves will have good topologies and will help deform them correctly.

1   Scene file

- Open the scene file *07-divaHead_01.ma*.

Note: *This scene already has image planes set up for reference. There is also the modeled neck piece from the previous lesson from which you will start modeling.*

2   Duplicate the border curve from the neck surface

Since the head needs to conform to the body, you will start by duplicating the curve from the isoparms at the top of the neck patch from the existing body.

- **RMB-click** and select **Isoparm** on each of the surfaces of the neck.

- Select the top most isoparms forming the neck opening.

- Select **Edit Curves** → **Duplicate Surface Curves**.

- **RMB-click** on the the original neck surfaces and select **Actions** → **Template**.

3   Rebuild the curves

Even though the curves have been duplicated from surfaces with good parameterization, it is recommended to rebuild them anyway.

- Select all the curves and rebuild them with **Rebuild Curves** with **Keep CVs** to **On**.

4   Delete the neck geometry

- Delete the neck surfaces since they are no longer required.

5   Draw the first profile curve

The **EP Curve Tool** lets you draw freeform NURBS curves by placing edit points.

- Select **Create** → **EP Curve Tool** → ❑.

- Click the **Reset Tool** button.

- From the *side* view, hold down **c** to snap to curve, then **click+drag** to the back of the neck curve.

The first curve point will be created at the very back of the duplicated neck curve.

- Continue placing curve points to draw a curve matching the profile of the head in the image plane.

- Finish the curve at the throat by pressing **c** to snap the last curve point to the front of the neck curve.

- Switch to Component mode and adjust the curve by pulling CVs, if necessary.

Tip: *When drawing the profile curve, try to keep it simple. Use as few CVs as possible while still conforming to the basic shape of the head. Also, try to keep the CVs evenly spaced.*

6   Draw the next profile curve

You will now draw the curve defining the side of the head.

- While working in the *front* view, use curve snapping to place the first CV of the new curve at the top of the profile curve you just drew.

- Continue placing curve points to draw the front profile of the head.

- Snap the last curve point at the chin location on the first profile curve.

- Pull CVs as necessary to adjust the shape of the curve.

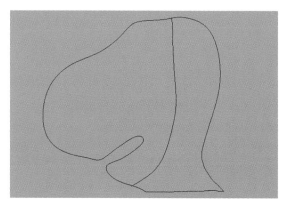

Profile curves drawn in the front and side views

7   Implied tangency

The following steps will ensure that the second profile curve's tangency is set across the X-axis. Giving a curve implied tangency across the axis of symmetry helps to ensure that the surfaces built from this curve will be tangent with their mirrored counterparts.

- **RMB-click** on the second profile curve and select **Curve Point**.

- **Click+drag** a curve point on the curve and drag it to the top of the head.

- Selecting **Edit Curves** → **Curve Editing Tool**.

*The **Curve Editing Tool** is a powerful tool for manipulating the shape of curves. In this case, you will use the **Curve Editing Tool** to impose implied tangency across the X-axis.*

- Click on the tool's **red** tangent manipulator handle to snap the curve's tangency to the **X-axis**.

Doing so puts the last two CVs of a curve in a straight line.

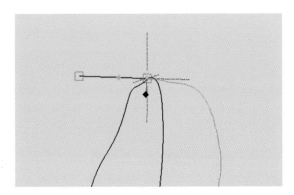

The tangency aligned on the X-axis

- Repeat for the other end of the curve.

Creating curves for the eyes

You will now create two curves that will be used as the inner and outer boundaries of the eye. A surface will then be lofted between these two curves, creating a surface with radial topology ideal for eye deformations.

1   Draw the inner eye curve

- Using the **EP Curve Tool**, draw a curve for the inner boundary of the eye.

- Snap the end curve point to the beginning curve point to make a closed circle.

- Pull CVs as necessary to adjust shape.

Note: *The EP Curve Tool is being used rather than the CV Curve Tool because the CV Curve Tool places CVs that lie off the curve, while the EP Curve Tool places edit points that lie directly on the curve. Drawing the curve directly makes it easier to draw following the reference images.*

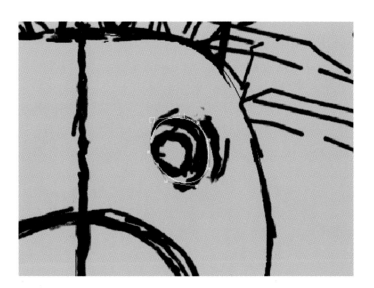

Inner eye curve drawn in front view

2   Close the inner eye curve

Even though the curve appears to form a closed loop because there are no visible gaps, the loop can easily be broken by moving either the first or last CV of the curve. This will make editing the shape of the curve without opening the loop difficult.

You will now close the curve, which will correct this problem. Closing the curve will prevent the loop from opening because it will connect the first and last CVs so that they always move together.

- Select the inner eye curve.

- Select **Edit Curves** → **Open/Close Curves** → ❐.

- Reset the options.

- Set the **Blend** option to **On**, and make sure that **Keep Originals** is turned **Off**.

- Click the **Open/Close** button.

3   Move the curve into position

- Center the curve's pivot by selecting **Modify** → **Center Pivot**.

- In the *side* view, move the inner eye curve along the **Z-axis** so that it lines up with the eye in the image plane.

4   Adjust the curve's shape

- Pull CVs to refine the shape of the inner eye curve, so that it looks good in all the different views.

Inner eye curve in front and side views

> **Note:** *Since the reference images in image planes rarely line up perfectly, you will have to make judgment calls when trying to conform the shape of a curve or surface to front and side images.*

5 Duplicate the inner eye curve

6 Scale the duplicated curve up

- Scale the duplicated curve up to match the outer boundary of the eye area, generally defined by the eye socket.

7 Adjust the shape of the curve

- Pull CVs on the curve to match the image plane.

Note: *The curves you create make up the basic framework of the head. Look at the curves in the Perspective view as you create them and try to picture your model. If the curves seem incorrect, adjust their shape.*

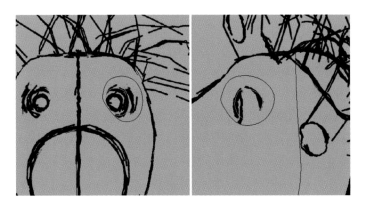

Outer eye curve adjusted in front and side view

8 Connect the outer eye curve to the front profile curve

The **EP Curve Tool** is ideal for situations where you want to draw a curve between two existing objects.

- Press **c** to snap to curve, then place a first curve point at the corner of the outer eye curve.

- Draw a second curve point at the center of the front profile curve.

This curve forms part of the upper boundary for the base of the ear, so the second edit point should line up with the upper base of the ear in the side view.

9 Create another connecting curve

- Starting at a point just below the first connecting curve, draw a second EP curve from the outer eye curve to the front profile curve.

The second edit point of the curve should line up with the cheekbone.

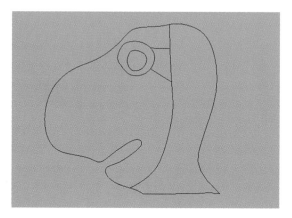

Establishing radial curves, starting from the eye

10 Adjust the shape of the curves

- Pull CVs on each of the connecting curves to adjust their shape.

Creating curves for the mouth

You will now create curves for the character's mouth. Once again, inner and outer curves will be used as the basis for a radial surface.

1 Draw the boundary for the lips

- Using **EP Curve Tool**, draw a curve to match the outline of the lips.

- Make sure to snap the first and last points of the curve to the side profile curve.

2 Adjust the curve's shape

- Pull CVs in the side view to conform the shape of the curve to the mouth in the image plane.

> **Tip:** *Remember that the image planes are only helpful to a point, and that you must use your own judgment to shape the curves in 3D space for best results.*

3 Draw an outer boundary for the mouth

- Draw a second mouth curve just below the nose, snapping it to the side profile curve.

4 Adjust the curve's shape

- Pull CVs to adjust the shape of the outer lips curve.

5 Rebuild the second mouth curve

You will now rebuild the second mouth curve to match the number of spans of the first mouth curve.

- Select the outer mouth curve, then **Shift-select** the inner mouth curve.

- Click the **Rebuild Curve Opt** button on your tool shelf.

- Set the **Rebuild Type** to **Match Knots**.

This option will make sure the parameterization of the two selected curves match together. Doing so will ensure better surfaces when the curves are lofted together.

- Click the **Rebuild** button.

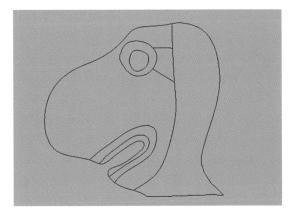

Mouth curves from front and side views

6   Detach the side profile curve to open the inside of the mouth

You will now open the inside of the mouth.

- **RMB-click** on the side profile curve and select **Edit Point**.

- Select the edit point closest to the center of the inside of the mouth.

- Detach the curve by selecting **Edit Curves** → **Detach Curve**.

7   Draw the remaining profile curves

From this point, you will continue drawing the network of profile curves. Remember to follow the structure of facial muscles. Also, remember that since these curves will be used to generate surfaces, they should always define a four-sided border.

- Draw the remaining profile curves.

- Use the illustrations below as a guide for creating the rest of the profile curves.

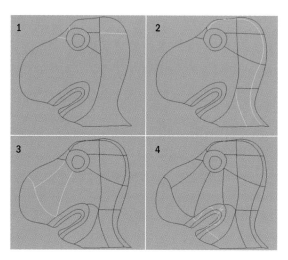

Development of profile curves

 Tip: *The vertical curves connecting to the base neck curves should be snapped to edit points in order to facilitate the attachment of the head on the body.*

8 Save your work

- Save your scene as *07-divaHead_02.ma*.

Rebuilding a curve network

You now have a network of interconnected curves, but many of those curves, like the front and side profile curves, are connected to multiple curves and stretch well beyond the area of any one surface patch. As a result, the parameterization of these curves within any one patch is going to be unpredictable, which could result in poor surfaces. To ensure the best possible surfaces from your curves, you will break the curves into individual pieces with each piece representing only the area of the surface it bounds. The curves will then be rebuilt to the appropriate number of spans.

1 Open an existing scene file

Before rebuilding the curve network for your head, you will try rebuilding a simple curve network.

- Open scene file *07-curveNetwork_01.ma*.

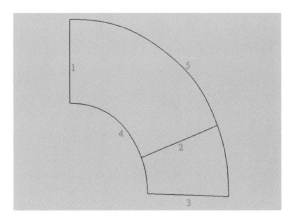

Simple curve network

2 Create a square surface in the upper section

- Select curves **1**, **5**, **2** and **4** in that order.

- Selecting **Surfaces → Square**.

A square surface is created in the area not limited by the selected curves.

3 Create a square surface in the lower section

- Repeat the process above to create a square surface in the lower section bounded by curves **2**, **5**, **3** and **4**.

> **Note:** *The topology of both surfaces is very uneven, with isoparms at odd intervals. This is known as cross knot insertion, and it is a result of surfaces being created from curves with mismatched topology.*

4   Display the edit points for all curves

- Select all of the curves, then switch to Component mode and display their **Edit Points**.

Note that the edit points are unevenly spaced on the curves. They indicate the beginning and end of a curve's spans. One isoparm in defined on the surface for each corresponding edit point on a curve.

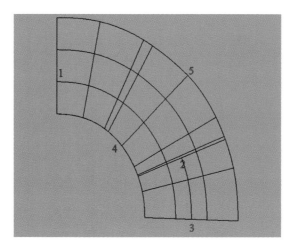

Poor surfaces resulting from poorly parameterized curves

5   Delete the surfaces created earlier

6   Cut the curves

The **Cut Curves Tool** detaches curves wherever they touch other curves.

- Select all of the curves, then select **Edit Curves** → **Cut Curves** → ❏.

- Reset the options, then set **In 3D Only** to **On**.

- Click the **Cut** button.

7 Rebuild the curves

The curves have been cut into sections representative of the surfaces they will create, but their topology is still very poor. You will now rebuild the curves to correct that.

- Select the larger piece of what used to be curve **4** and curve **5**.

- Rebuild it to **4** spans.

- Select **Edit Curves** → **Rebuild Curve** → ❐.

- Reset the options and make sure **Number of Spans** is set to **4**.

- Rebuild the smaller pieces of curves **4** and **5** to have **2** spans each.

- Rebuild curves **1**, **2**, and **3** to have **1** span each.

Note: *The number of spans a curve is rebuilt to should be based on how much detail will be required in a given surface, as well as general consistency with the neighboring curves.*

8 Create new square surfaces

- Create square surfaces in the areas bounded by the curves.

Now that the curve network's topology has been corrected, with the curves on each end of a boundary having the same number of spans, you should get much better results from the square operation.

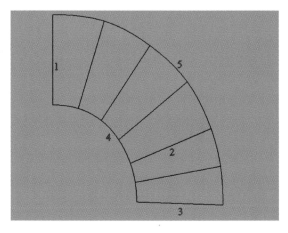

Good surfaces from rebuilt curves

Rebuilding the head's curve network

You will now use what you have just learned to rebuild the profile curves of Diva's head.

1   Scene file

- Continue with your own scene.

Or

- Open the scene called *07-divaHead_02.ma*.

2   Loft the eye surface

- Select the inner and outer eye curves and **Loft** a surface between them.

- Increase the loft's **Sections Span** value to **2**.

> **Note:** *The surface is being lofted now because the eye curves will soon be cut into pieces, making lofting more difficult.*

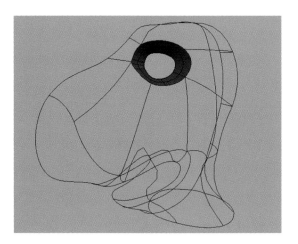

Lofted eye surface

3 Adjust the loft's shape

- Use the **Move Normal Tool** to make minor changes to the shape of the lofted surface as necessary to refine its shape.

4   Cut the mouth curves

- Select the first profile curves that you drew and the two curves defining the outside and the inside of the lips.

- Select **Edit Curves** → **Cut Curves** → □.

- Make sure **In 3D Only** is selected.

- Click the **Cut** button.

This will detach the curves where they intersect.

Note: *Just like when detaching isoparms on surfaces, you might have to repeat the operation in order to cut the curves at every intersection point.*

5   Detach the mouth curves

- Use **Edit Curves** → **Cut Curves** to cut the two lips' curves where they intersect with radial curves.

6   Rebuild the mouth curves

After being cut, the curves will have poor parameterization, so they should be rebuilt.

- Rebuild all the vertical lips' curves that define the profile of the lips to **2** spans.

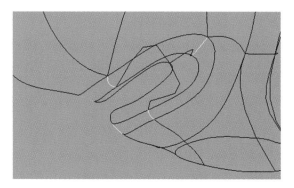

Rebuild the lips' profile curves

- Rebuild the other curves defining the lips and inner mouth to have **4** spans each.

7 Implied tangency

- Pull CVs to refine the inner mouth shape.

- Use the **Curve Editing Tool** to give the inner mouth curve implied tangency across the **X-axis**.

8 Birail the upper lips

You will now use the **Birail 2 Tool** to birail the lips.

- Select **Surfaces** → **Birail** → **Birail 2 Tool**.

In the Help Line, the tool will prompt you to select two profile curves.

- Select the upper lip's inner curve as the first profile curve, then select the upper lip's outer curve as the second profile curve.

In the Help Line, the tool will prompt you to select two rail curves.

- Select the upper curve defining the outline of the mouth and the inner mouth curve as the rail curves.

9 Repeat the birail operation

- Birail the rest of the lips.

- Tweak the new surfaces CVs to achieve good shapes.

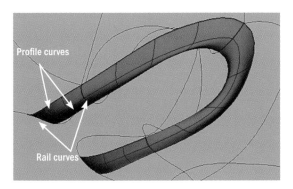

The lips' surfaces

10 Delete history from the curves

- Select **Edit** → **Delete All By Type** → **History**.

11 Cut the rest of the head's curves

- Select all of the curves.

Tip: *Turn off the surface selection mask to ease the curve selection process.*

- Select **Edit Curves** → **Cut Curves**.

Tip: *If curves don't intersect, they will not be cut. Use snap to curve on edit points to fix this.*

- Make sure all the curves are properly cut by selecting them. Repeat if necessary.

12 Rebuild curves

You will now rebuild the curves to correct their topology. Remember that curves on opposite sides of a boundary must have the same number of spans, that the number of spans should reflect the amount of geometry required in the surface to be built from the curve, and that the physical size of spans should be roughly consistent.

- Select the following curves:

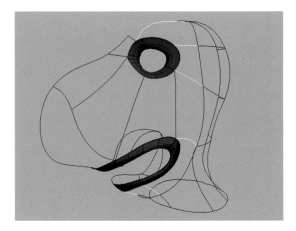

Opposing curves to be rebuilt

- Rebuild the curves to **4** spans.
- Continue selecting and rebuilding opposing curves on the head.

> **Tip:** Rebuild the curves with a low number of spans when they represent a fairly small area on the head. Rebuild the curves with a higher number of spans when they represent a large area on the head. The amount of spans you are using directly influences the amount of definition you will have on the final head.

13 Rebuild the remaining curves

- Repeat the previous step on all curves not already rebuilt.

> **Note:** The amount of spans on the base neck curves is important for attaching the head to the body. Rebuild the base neck curves to your need with a multiplier number of spans. For instance, if a curve has 2 spans, you can rebuild it to 4, 8, 12, etc.

> **Note:** The number of spans is visible in the Attribute Editor under **NURBS Curve History**.

14 Clean up

- Group all the curves together and rename the group *curvesGroup*.

- Create a new layer and name it *curvesLayer*.

- Select all of the curves and add them to the *curvesLayer*.

15 Save your work

- Save your scene as *07-divaHead_03.ma*.

Creating the surfaces

Creating the curve network for the head is by far the hardest and most time-consuming part of the process. You will now begin the relatively easy task of producing surfaces from the curves.

1 Scene file

- Continue with your own scene.

Or

- Open the scene called *07-divaHead_03.ma*.

2 Build the surfaces

You can now use any surface tools to create the head geometry. Following are some guidelines:

- Use **Birail 2** with **four** curves to create nice round surfaces.

- Use **Square** with **four** curves to create more flat surfaces.

- Use **Boundary** to create surfaces from **three** curves.

You will most likely use this surface tool for the top of the head and inside the mouth, where only three curves are available.

Tip: You may want to turn **NURBS surfaces** off in the **Show** menu of your working view. This will help you see the curves better.

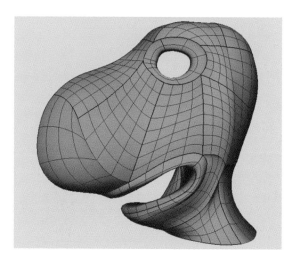

Initial square surfaces

Creating eyelids

It is important for the eyelid and eyeball surfaces to maintain a close relationship, so you will use an eyeball surface to help you create the eyelids themselves.

1   Create an eyeball

- Select **Create** → **NURBS Primitives** → **Sphere**.

- Rotate the sphere by **90 degrees** on the **X-axis**.

- Move the sphere into position using the reference images.

- Assign a **phong** material and map it with a **Ramp**.

- Tweak the *ramp* to define the iris of Diva's eye.

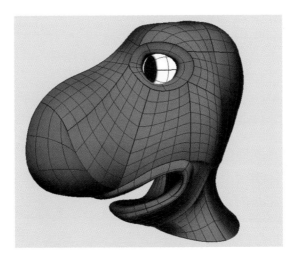

Diva's eyeball

2   Hide the curves

For the next few steps you will be working with the eye surface and a curve duplicated from it, so you will hide all curves on the *curvesLayer* to prevent confusion.

- Hide the *curvesLayer*.

3   Conform the lofted eye surface to the surrounding geometry

Currently, the surface which was originally lofted at the eye does not match the surrounding surfaces' topology. You will now re-loft the eye surface to correct that.

- **RMB**-click on the eye loft surface and select **Isoparm**.

- **Click+drag** an isoparm so that it aligns with any isoparm of a surrounding surface.

- Hold down the **Shift** key and **click+drag** another isoparm so that it lines up with the next isoparm.

Tip: *Make sure to select them in order.*

- Continue holding down the **Shift** key and selecting new isoparms until you have placed an isoparm to match the position of every isoparm on the surrounding surfaces.

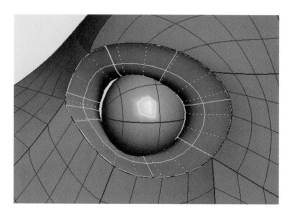

The selected isoparms

- Select **Surfaces** → **Loft** → ❑.

- Reset the options, then turn **On** the **Close** option.

- Click the **Loft** button.

- Select the original surface and delete it.

By lofting the surface this way you should now have a radial surface around the eye that matches the topology of the surrounding surfaces. This will be essential later when you sock everything together.

4   Make the eyeball Live

- Turn **On** the **Live** mode for the *eyeball*.

5   Snap the eyelid CVs to the Live eyeball

- Select each CV on the new loft surface and, one at a time, move them just a little.

Since the eyeball is Live, the CVs will snap onto it.

- Turn **Off** the **Live** mode of the *eyeball*.

- Tweak the second row of CVs closest to the eyeball to form a rounded eyelid.

Tip: *You can use the arrows on your keyboard to change the selected CV.*

6   Insert isoparms

- Insert an isoparm in the eyelid area to create more definition.

7   Tweak the shape of the eyelid

- Tweak the CVs to refine the eyelid.

- Try pinching the eye corners.

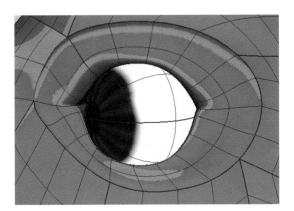

Refined eyelid

8   Save your work

- Save your scene as *07-divaHead_04.ma*.

Socking the patches

Now that every piece of the head is created, you can start socking them together.

1   Scene file

- Continue with your own scene.

Or

- Open the scene called *07-divaHead_04.ma*.

2   Attach surfaces

- Select the two surfaces at the forehead and attach them.

- Rebuild with **Keep CVs** set to **On** after every attach.

- Continue attaching surfaces until there is one long strip around the face.

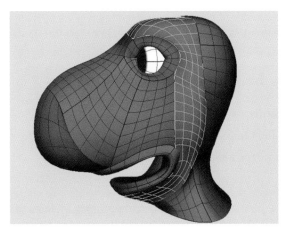

Attached strip

3   Detach surfaces

- Select each of the isoparms where you just attached and detach them.

4   Attach in other directions

- Using your own discretion, attach, rebuild and detach the rest of the surfaces of the head until they have all been done.

5 Stitch the head

Once all the surfaces have been attached, rebuilt, and detached at least once, the head surfaces should be fairly smooth. As you would expect, there are small gaps in the patch corners, but you will fix that by applying a **Global Stitch** to the head.

- Select **Edit** → **Delete All By Type** → **History**.

- Select all of the surfaces.

- Apply a **Global Stitch**.

- If necessary, adjust the **Max Separation** attribute of the Global Stitch node.

Refine the head

Now that the basic structure of the head is complete, you should refine details and the corners of the eyes. Do this by rebuilding surfaces when necessary to increase the number of spans in a surface, as well as by pulling CVs. Also, duplicate and mirror the head and attach the center parts together.

Import the body

1 Sock the body

- Select **File** → **Import**.

- Import the scene file called *06-divaBody_10.ma*.

- Sock the head to the body.

- Select the head and neck surfaces, then apply a **Global Stitch**.

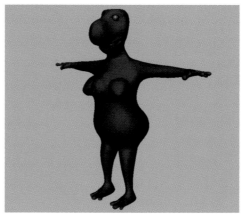

Finished head and body

2 Reverse normals

- Select all the patches.

- Select **Display** → **NURBS Components** → **Normals**.

- Select patches that the normals seem to be pointing at inwardly.

- Select **Edit NURBS** → **Reverse Surface Direction**.

- Repeat until there are no more reversed surfaces on the entire head.

- Turn **Off** the normals display.

3 Save your work

- Save the scene as *07-divaFull_05.ma*.

Conclusion

Building a NURBS patch character is a relatively easy task in terms of tools, but it requires lots of visualization experience in order to be perfect.

In this lesson, you learned how to use a curve network to build a patch head. A few basic rules were discussed to simplify the process, such as ensuring that your curves match the facial structure of your character, and that the curve network has clean and predictable topology.

In the next lesson, you will add accessories such as clothes, jewelry and hair to Diva.

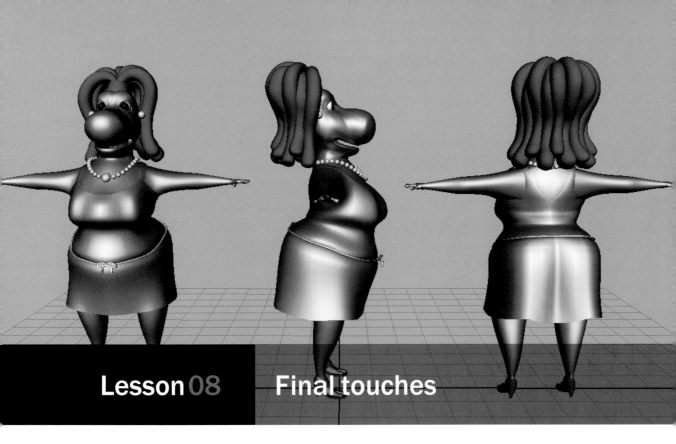

Lesson 08   Final touches

In this lesson, you will first ensure the Diva has good proportions. You will then add NURBS accessories such as jewelry, hair and clothing.

In this lesson you will learn the following:

- How to modify proportions using a lattice deformer;

- How to continue modeling over existing geometry;

- How to close a curve and move its seam;

- How to convert Maya Paint Effects to NURBS;

- How to use motion paths and animation snapshots;

- How to extrude geometry;

Proportions

Before adding details to the Diva model, you must make sure that she has accurate proportions. The transition from 2D concept drawings to a 3D world often creates deformed geometry.

In the following exercise, you will use a lattice to deform the entire model to adjust Diva's proportions.

1 Scene file

- Open the scene file from the last lesson called *07-divaFull_05.ma*.

2 Clean up the scene

- Delete the image planes used to model the basics of Diva.

Tip: *The easiest way to do this is by selecting the* **Cameras** *tab in the Hypershade, then deleting the imagePlane nodes.*

3 Lattice deformer

Your goal here is to create a lattice deformer with enough definition to change the global proportions of the character. Once this is done, you will create another lattice box with even more definition to refine smaller parts of the body.

- Select all of Diva's surfaces.

- Select **Deform** → **Create Lattice**.

- In the **Inputs** section of the **Channel Box**, set the lattice shape attributes as follows:

> **S Division** to **9**;
>
> **T Division** to **13**;
>
> **U Division** to **5**.

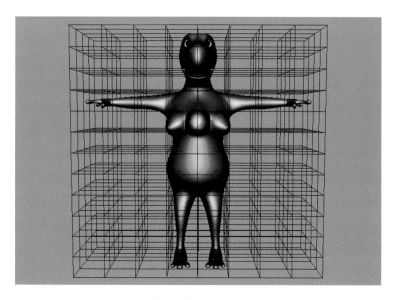

The lattice deformer

Tip: *In order to prevent the separation of patches, it is preferable to do one big lattice rather than a localized smaller lattice. If you do create a smaller lattice, be careful not to move points too close to the border edges.*

- **RMB-click** on the lattice and select **Lattice Point**.

4   Change Diva's proportions

You can now start modifying Diva's proportions. Following are some guidelines:

- Enlarge the entire waist area to give her a more feminine cartoon look.

- Flatten her nose and move her head backwards to counterbalance her prominent chest.

- Reduce the size of her hands and feet by half.

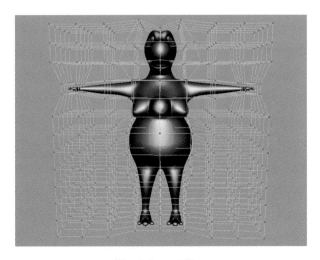

The deformed Diva

5   Continue tweaking the geometry

Before you continue deforming the geometry by creating a new lattice, you must first delete the existing one by deleting the history.

- Select **Edit** → **Delete All By Type** → **History**.

- Select all of Diva's surfaces.

- Select **Deform** → **Create Lattice**.

- This time, add more definition to the lattice in order to localize deformations.

Tip: *It might be easier to deform only one half of the model and then mirror the other half. Doing so will ensure that the model is symmetrical.*

6   Recreate the eyeball

If you deformed the eyeballs, recreate new ones and tweak the eyelids.

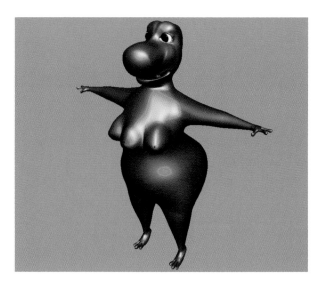

The new proportions

7   Save your work

- Save the scene as *08-divaAccessories_01.ma*.

Model clothes

You will now dress up Diva with a skirt, top and waist belt. You will be using primitives, existing geometry and curve extrusions in order to model the outfit.

1   Scene file

- Continue with your own scene.

Or

- Open the scene called *08-divaAccessories_01.ma*.

2   Detach the hips' surfaces

- Detach the hips' surfaces at the second isoparm from the bottom.

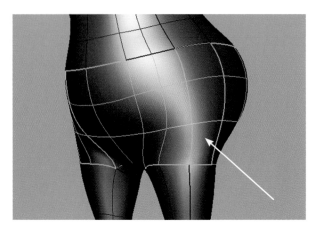

The isoparms detach to create the skirt

3 Model the skirt

- Select **Edit** → **Delete All By Type** → **History**.

Doing so will remove any unwanted history.

- Select the top sections of the detached surfaces.

- Switch to Component mode and scale CVs and hulls to create the skirt as follows:

The basic skirt

Tip: *You may want to hide the legs while you work on the skirt.*

4   Break the tangency

- Select the CVs on both sides of the hips' cut.

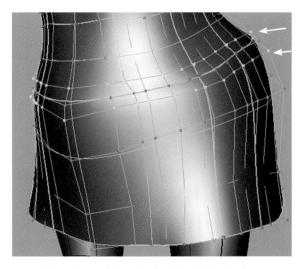

The selected CVs on both sides of the hips' cut

- Scale the vertices up to create a groove for the belt.

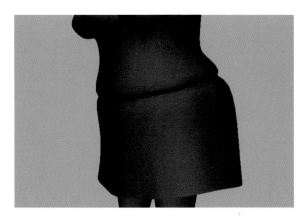

The groove for the belt

5   Duplicate belt curves

- Select a horizontal row of isoparms in the groove all around the belly.

- Select **Edit Curves** → **Duplicate Surface Curves**.

- Scale all the new curves up in order to move them outside the geometry.

6   Attach all the curves together

- Select **two** adjacent curves, then select **Edit Curves** → **Attach Curves** → ❏.

- In the option window, set **Keep Originals** to **Off**.

- Click the **Attach** button.

- Repeat the above step to attach all the curves together.

Tip: *If a curve attaches in the wrong direction, set the* **Reverse1** *attribute in the construction history to* **On**.

7   Adjust the CVs

8   Close the belt curve and move the seam

- Select the *belt* curve.

- Select **Edit Curves** → **Open/Close Curves**.

- **RMB-click** on the curve and select **Curve Point**.

- Define a curve point at the front center of the belt curve.

- Select **Edit Curves** → **Move Seam**.

Doing so will place the seam of the curve behind the bow tie that you will create in the next step.

9   Make a bow

- Select **Create** → **EP Curve**.❏

- Draw a bow in the front view.

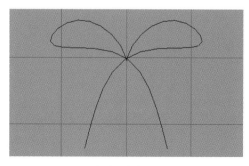

A simple bow

> **Tip:** *If you used two curves to make the bow,* **Attach** *the curves with the* **Method** *option set to* **Connect**.

- Delete the history on the bow.

10 Place the bow on the curve

- Using Snap to Curve, place the bow in front of the belt curve created earlier.
- Adjust CVs.

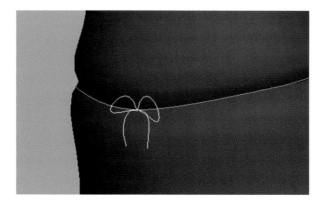

The bow in place

11 Create the belt geometry

You will now use Maya Paint Effects to quickly create the belt geometry.

- Press **F5** to go in the **Rendering** menu set.
- Select **Paint Effects** → **Get Brush**.
- In the **Visor** window, open the *Fibers* directory and select the *wickerTubeProc.mel*.
- Close the Visor.
- Press **q** to exit the **Paint Effects Tool**, then select both the *belt* and the *bow* curves.
- Select **Paint Effects** → **Curve Utilities** → **Attach Brush to Curves**.
- With both strokes selected, select **Modify** → **Convert** → **Paint Effects to NURBS**.

12 Tweak the geometry

Using a Paint Effects stroke allowed you to generate the geometry quickly, but it might not be perfect. You will now take some time to adjust it.

- From the Outliner, select the two strokes created in the previous step.

- In the **Channel Box**, in the **Inputs** section, highlight the *wickerTube* node.

- Change the **Global Scale** to **5.0**.

- Select **Edit** → **Delete All By Type** → **History**.

- Delete the *strokes* and *curves* from the Outliner.

- Detach and attach the geometry to remove any bad segments.

- Scale the CVs at the end of the bow to close it.

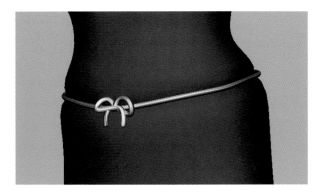

The belt and bow geometry

13 Save your work

- Save the scene as *08-divaAccessories_02.ma*.

Upper section of the dress

You will now continue building the dress by using the existing geometry.

1 Scene file

- Continue with your own scene.

Or

- Open the scene called *08-divaAccessories_02.ma*.

2 Create a cylinder

- Create a primitive NURBS cylinder.

- Set its number of **Sections** to **12** and its number of **Spans** to **3**.

- Place it over the breasts and start editing its shape.

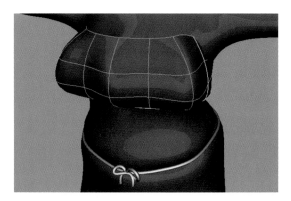

The upper dress section

- Detach the cylinder in half if you don't want to edit both sides at the same time.

3 Sock the cylinder

- Detach and rebuild the cylinder to accommodate the belly surfaces.

- Attach the cylinder to the belly surfaces in order to create a nice surface.

- Tweak the cylinder to refine its shape.

Make sure to move one span up in order to create the strap in the next step.

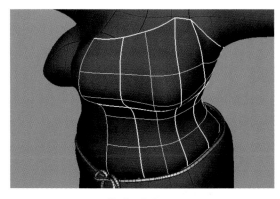

Refined shape

Tip: *Reduce the size of the breasts, if needed.*

4   Shoulder strap

- Select the isoparm to be used for the strap, then select
  Edit Curves → Duplicate Surface Curve.

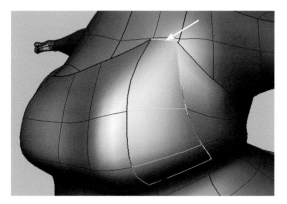

The isoparm to be used to model the shoulder strap

- Move the new curve next to the clavicle.

- Duplicate the new curve **three** more times, moving one on top
  of the shoulder, on top of the shoulderblade and in the middle of the
  back respectively.

- Select the front strap isoparm, **Shift-select** the duplicated curves in order,
  then **Shift-select** the back isoparm.

- Select **Surfaces → Loft**.

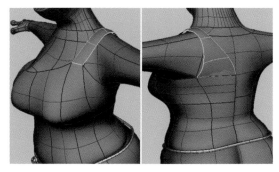

The shoulder strap

Tip: *Refine the strap placement by moving the curves. Also, leave a space between the shoulder and the strap, which will help with later deformations.*

5 Mirror

In order to simplify your work, you will mirror the upper dress on the other side of the character.

- Select **Edit** → **Delete All By Type** → **History**.

- Delete the obsolete body surfaces.

- Select all the surfaces to be mirrored.

- Press **Ctrl+d** to duplicate, then **Ctrl+g** to group the surfaces.

- Set the **Scale X** of the new group to **-1**.

- Attach the center surfaces together.

6 Global Stitch

- Apply a **Global Stitch** on the entire upper dress surfaces.

- Apply a **Global Stitch** on the chest surfaces.

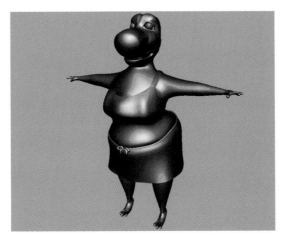

The final dress

7 Save your work

- Save the scene as *08-divaAccessories_03.ma*.

Jewelry

You will now create a pearl necklace and earrings from basic primitives.

1   Scene file

- Continue with your own scene.

Or

- Open the scene called *08-divaAccessories_03.ma*.

2   Create earrings

- Create a primitive NURBS sphere.

- Move and scale it to Diva's ear position.

- Duplicate and move the earring on the other side.

3   Create the necklace curve

- Create a primitive NURBS circle.

- Move and scale it to fit Diva's neck.

- Adjust the CVs as needed, and make sure to leave a good space between the curve and Diva's geometry.

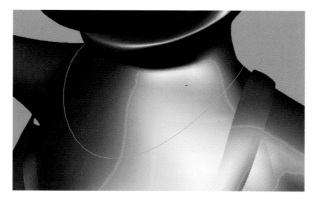

The necklace curve

4   Use a motion path to create the pearls

- Set the Time Slider to go from **1** to **200**.

- Duplicate the earring sphere created earlier, and set its **Scale** to **0.2** in all axes.

- Select the sphere, then **Shift-select** the necklace.

- In the **Animation** menu set, select **Animate** → **Motion Paths** → **Attach to Motion Path**.

- In the **Channel Box**, change the **Front Twist** value of the *motionPath1* node to bank the sphere so that it flows along the curve.

- With the sphere selected, select **Animate** → **Create Animation Snapshot** → ❐.

- In the option window, set **Time Range** to **Time Slider** and **Increment** to **6**.

- Press the **Snapshot** button.

Pearls will be duplicated along the path curve.

The finished necklace

- Delete the original *sphere* and *necklace curve*.

- Tweak the necklace as desired.

Hair

You will create Diva's hair with curves and then extrude hair geometry.

1   Draw a hair curve

- From the *side* view, draw a curve to generate Diva's dreads.

The hair curve

- From the Perspective view, duplicate, rotate and offset the hair curves on Diva's cranium.

2   Create the profile curve

- Create a NURBS circle.

- Scale the NURBS circle down.

3   Extrude geometry

You will now use the NURBS circle as the profile curve for extrusion along the hair curves.

- Select the *profile circle*, then **Shift-select** one *hair* curve.

- Select **Surfaces** → **Extrude** → ☐.

- In the option window, set the following:

> **Style** to **Tube**;
>
> **Result Position** to **At Path**;
>
> **Pivot** to **Component**;
>
> **Orientation** to **Profile Normal**;
>
> **Output Geometry** to **Nurbs**.

- Click on the **Extrude** button.

The circle has been extruded along the hair curve.

• Repeat the last steps to extrude all the other hair.

Note: *Do not translate the NURBS circle, as this will result in an offset of the geometry on the hair curves.*

4 Tweak the hair geometry

• If needed, scale the circle to change the diameter of the hair tubes.

• If needed, move the circle CVs to change the shape of the hair.

5 Refine the geometry

• Select **Edit → Delete All By Type → History**.

• Delete the *hair* and *circle curves*, as they are no longer required.

• Refine the geometry by closing the end of the hair tubes and randomly scaling the diameter of the hair.

• Insert isoparms as needed or rebuild the surfaces with more isoparms.

The hair geometry

6 Add a hair band

• Create a primitive NURBS cylinder.

• Transform it to hide the base of the hair where is connects with the head.

High heels

In order to give even more detail to the model, create high heels as shown in the image below:

The high heels

Clean up

Take some time to clean up the scene and organize all the nodes into hierarchies. It is also a good idea to place the objects onto layers.

1   Organize nodes into groups

2   Create a layer for Diva

3   Rename the objects with the Quick Rename option of the Entry Field

4   Delete the history

5   Optimize scene size

6   Save your work

- The final scene for this lesson is called *08-divaAccessories_04.ma*.

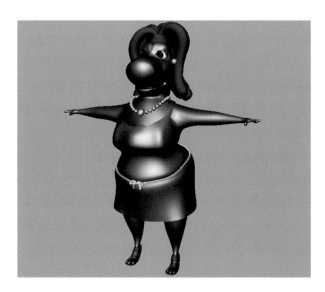

The finished Diva model

Conclusion

In this lesson, you used other techniques to generate geometry, such as the animation snapshot, Maya Paint Effects and extrusion. Being aware of different tools and techniques to create surfaces will help you solve different modeling issues.

In the next lesson, you will learn about various NURBS tasks, such as conversion, tessellation and texturing.

Render View

File View Render IPR Options Display Help

Maya Software

IPR: 0MB

ize: 640 480 zoom: 1.000   (Maya Software)
Render Time: 0:04   Camera: persp

Lesson 09   NURBS tasks

In this lesson, you will examine a number of general tasks related to modeling with NURBS, such as conversion, tessellation and texturing.

In this lesson you will learn the following:

- How to convert NURBS surfaces to polygonal surfaces;

- How to display and reverse normals;

- How to deal with the tessellation of NURBS surfaces;

- How to use 3D textures when working with NURBS patch models;

- How to create texture reference objects.

Converting NURBS to polygons

Depending on the specific needs of your production, you will often need to convert NURBS surfaces into a polygonal mesh. The following exercise shows the workflow of converting NURBS to polygons.

1 Create a new scene file

2 Create a primitive NURBS sphere

3 Convert the NURBS sphere to polygons

- With the *sphere* selected, select **Modify** → **Convert** → **NURBS to Polygons** → ❑, and set the following:

  Type to **Quads**;

  Tessellation Method to **General**.

- Under **Initial Tessellation Controls**, set the following:

  U Type to **Per Span # of Iso Params**;

  Number U to **1**;

  V Type to **Per Span # of Iso Params**;

  Number V to **1**.

- Click the **Tessellate** button.

The polygonal version of the sphere is created.

4 Move the poly sphere to the side

- Translate the poly sphere to the side of the original NURBS sphere.

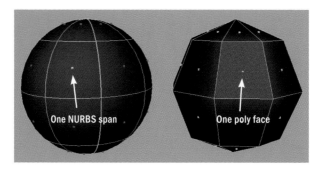

NURBS sphere and converted poly sphere

5   Evaluate the conversion

Using the current tessellation, the polygonal sphere was converted with one quad (four-sided face) for every span in the original sphere. As a result, the poly sphere appears multifaceted. Unlike NURBS surfaces, whose tessellation can be adjusted at render time, what you see is what you get with polygons, so you will need to determine on a case by case basis how precisely the sphere should be converted.

6   Delete the poly sphere

7   Convert with a higher tessellation setting

- With the NURBS sphere selected, select **Modify** → **Convert** → **NURBS to Polygons** → ❒, and set the following:

    Number U and **V** to **3**.

- Click the **Tessellate** button.

A polygonal version of the sphere, which is much closer to the original sphere, is created.

8   Move the poly sphere to the side

- Translate the poly sphere to the side of the original NURBS sphere.

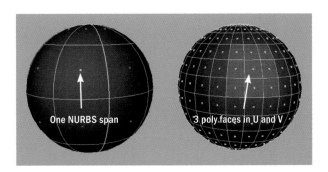

NURBS sphere and higher resolution poly sphere

9   Evaluate the conversion

This time, the conversion created three faces in the U and V direction for each span on the original sphere, resulting in a polygonal sphere which appears less faceted.

Dealing with border edges

A common workflow is to build a model out of multiple NURBS patches, taking advantage of sophisticated NURBS modeling techniques, then converting those patches into a single polygonal mesh before binding or texturing. In order to do this, the NURBS patches must be converted into individual polygonal surfaces, which are then combined into a single poly mesh.

Before converting a multi patch NURBS model, you will take a quick look at the issues associated with combining multiple polygonal surfaces into a single mesh.

1 Open an existing scene file

- Open the scene file *09-simpleExample_01.ma*.

2 Combine the two polygonal surfaces

- Select the **two** polygonal surfaces, then select **Polygons** → **Combine**.

The polygonal surfaces are now combined into single poly mesh, with two distinct poly shells.

3 Display the mesh's border edges

- With the poly mesh selected, select **Display** → **Custom Polygon Display** → ❐, and set the following:

    Highlight Border Edges to **On**;

    Highlight Texture Borders to **Off**;

    Border Width to **3**.

- Click on the **Apply and Close** button.

Visually thicker edges appear around the poly mesh faces that have edges not shared by any other face.

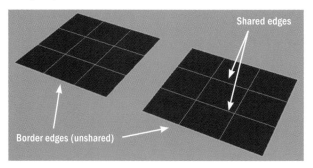

Border edges displayed on poly mesh

4 Delete the poly mesh

5 Make layer2 visible

Layer2 contains two separate, single span NURBS surfaces with G1 continuity.

6 Convert the two NURBS planes to polygons

- Using the same tessellation settings as set earlier, convert the two NURBS planes to polygons.

7 Delete the NURBS surfaces

8 Combine the poly surfaces

- Select the two polygon surfaces and combine them into a single poly mesh.

9 Display the mesh's border edges

- Display the polygon border edges like you did in the previous example.

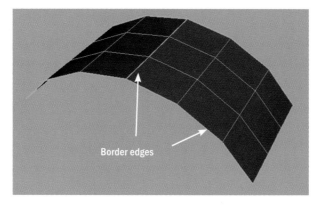

Border edges displayed on poly mesh

Note: *Like the previous example, border edges appear wherever there are edges that do not share a face. In the previous example it was easy to see that the border edges didn't share faces. However, in this case the edges in the center of the mesh appear to share faces on each side, when in fact they don't.*

10 Select one vertex on an internal border edge

- **RMB-click** on the mesh and select **Vertex**.

- Select a single central vertex by clicking once directly on it.

11 Translate the selected vertex

- Move the selected vertex on the **Y-axis**.

You will notice that there are in fact two vertices at that location and that you have selected only one of them. Like the previous example, combining the two poly surfaces may have made them into a single poly mesh, but the individual vertices are unaffected. The vertices must be merged to eliminate the border edge.

The vertex moved down

- Undo the previous move.

12 Select all of the mesh's vertices

- Select all of the mesh's vertices.

- Select **Edit Polygons** → **Merge Vertices** → ❐.

- Reset the options, and click the **Merge Vertex** button.

13 Adjust the Distance value

Even if the vertices are right on top of each other they might not actually merge with such a low **Distance** setting, so the border edge will remain.

If this is the case, do the following:

- Select the surface and in the **Inputs** section of the **Channel Box**, increase the *polyMergeVert1* **Distance** attribute in small increments until the border edge disappears.

Merged vertices

Note: *Be careful to increase the* **Distance** *value in small increments or you may end up merging vertices that you don't want to merge.*

Dealing with flipped normals

Depending on how it was built, a network of NURBS patches may have surface normals that do not all face in the same direction. In this case, merging the surface's vertices will not be enough to eliminate internal border edges because the normals must all face in the same direction.

1 Delete the poly surface from the last example

2 Display layer3

- Make *layer3* visible.

This layer has two pairs of NURBS surfaces.

3 Display the surface normals

- Select the **four** NURBS surfaces, then select **Display** → **NURBS Components** → **Normals**.

One pair of surfaces has normals facing the same direction, while the other pair has normals facing in opposite directions.

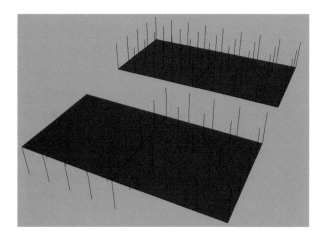

Surface normals

4 Convert the surfaces to polygons

- Convert the **four** NURBS surfaces to polygons.

- Delete the original NURBS surfaces.

5 Combine the surfaces

- Select one pair of surfaces and combine them.

- Select the other pair of surfaces and combine them.

6 Display the border edges and normals

- Display the border edges for both poly meshes.

Both meshes should have border edges where the center vertices need to be merged.

- Also, select the polygonal normals by selecting **Display → Polygon Components → Normals**.

7 Merge the vertices

- Merge the vertices for both meshes.

The internal border edges disappear on the surface with consistent normals, but not the other mesh with flipped normals.

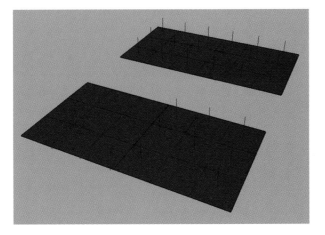

Border edge still visible on mesh with flipped normals

8   Reverse the surface normals

- **RMB-click** on the surface with incorrect normals and select **Face**.

- Select the faces with the reversed normals.

- Select **Edit Polygons** → **Normals** → **Reverse**.

Reversing the surface normals will eliminate the border edge.

Note: *The border edge was merged because of the polyMergeVert1 construction history node.*

Converting a NURBS patch model

You will now use the above techniques to convert a NURBS patch model into polygons.

1   Open an existing scene file

- Open the scene file *09-simpleExample_02.ma*.

2   Convert the NURBS patches to polygons

- Select all of the NURBS patches.

- Select **Modify** → **Convert** → **NURBS to Polygons** → ❐, and set the following:

    Number U to **1**;

    Number V to **1**.

Note: *You can use the* **Attach Multiple Output Meshes** *option to automatically combine and merge the resulting surfaces.*

- Click the **Tessellate** button.

3   Delete the original NURBS surfaces

4   Display the normals for the new poly surfaces

- Select all of the poly surfaces and select **Display** → **Polygon Components** → **Long Normals**.

Most of the poly surfaces have normals that are facing out, but some of them are facing in. You could correct that now by reversing the normals for selected surfaces, but you will correct all of the normals later in a single operation.

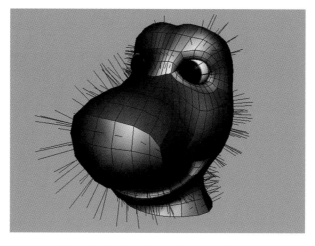

Normals displayed on polygonal surfaces

5 Combine the poly surfaces into a single mesh

- Select all of the converted poly surfaces and combine them into a single poly mesh.

6 Display the border edges

7 Merge the vertices

- Select **Edit Polygons** → **Merge Vertices**.

Some of the border edges will remain. Any faces with normals that are facing in the opposite direction from their neighbor will create a border edge.

8 Conform the normals

You will now conform the surface's normals so they are all facing in the same direction.

- Select the mesh and select **Edit Polygons** → **Normals** → **Conform**.

The tool will determine how many faces have normals facing out, and how many have normals facing in, and reverse the normals of the faces in the minority. With the normals corrected, the border edges should disappear.

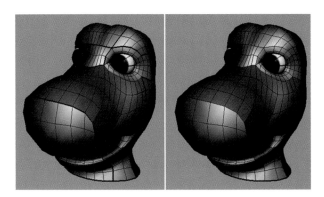

Conform normals will remove remaining border edges

9 Make sure the normals are facing out

Since the Conform command reverses the normals of the fewer number of faces, it will not necessarily leave the normals facing in the appropriate direction. Generally speaking, it's best for normals to point outward.

- If the faces of your mesh are currently facing in, select the mesh and then select **Edit Polygons** → **Normals** → **Reverse**.

10 Soften the normals

Even after merging the vertices and correcting the mesh's normals, you may find that seams appear on areas of your mesh when you render. These seams are caused by *hard* normals from one face to the next. Normals must be softened to eliminate these seams in your render.

- Select the poly mesh, then select **Edit Polygons** → **Normals** → **Harden/Soften** → ▢.

- Click on the **All Soft (180)** button, then click the **Soft/Hard** button.

11 Render the poly mesh

- Click on the **Render Current Frame** button to render the scene into the Render View window.

Rendered poly head

Tip: *You can assign a poly smooth to the head geometry to further refine it even more.*

Tessellating NURBS surfaces

Tessellation is the process of dividing a NURBS surface up into triangles, either as part of a conversion to a polygon surface, or so that it can be rendered.

Note: *NURBS surfaces are always converted to polygons before rendering.*

Polygonal surfaces are pre-tessellated because they are already made up of triangles (four-sided faces are ultimately divided into two triangles). That's why polygonal surfaces tend to look faceted when rendered, unless the mesh is quite dense. NURBS surfaces, on the other hand, are tessellated at render time, so the apparent roundness of a NURBS surface can always be adjusted.

In this exercise you will adjust the tessellation of NURBS surfaces to refine how they appear when they are rendered.

1 Open an existing scene file

- Open the scene file *09-simpleExample_03.ma*.

2 Render the head

- Frame the eye area of Diva's head in the view.

- Render the scene.

The rendered image will reveal some problems where the patches meet together.

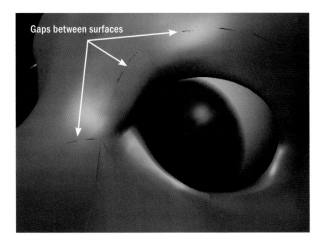

Visible problems in the render

3 Display render tessellation

- Select all the surfaces.

- Select **Window** → **General Editors** → **Attribute Spread Sheet**.

- Under the **Tessellation** tab, click on the **Display Render Tessellation** column header, then set the attributes to **1** and hit **Enter** to set them to **On**.

The surfaces should now appear according to how they will be tessellated during the render. The same gap that is visible in the software render should now be visible in the view.

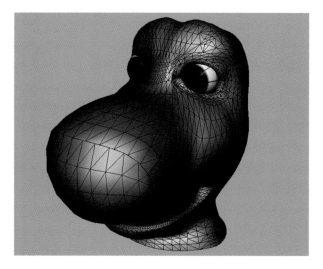

The displayed render tessellation

4 Improve the tessellation

There are many tessellation settings that you can change on the surfaces to improve the rendered images, but perhaps the simplest one to use at this time is **Smooth Edge**. This option increases the number of triangles only along the boundary of an object. This lets you smooth the edges or prevent cracks between shared curves of adjacent surfaces without tessellating across the entire object.

- With all the surfaces still selected and with the **Attribute Spread Sheet** opened, set the **Smooth Edge** column to **On**.

- Render the scene.

The gap between the surface should now be gone.

The gaps are now closed

Note: *You can also increase the* **U** *and* **V Division Factors** *of the surfaces, but doing so will increase render time. Be judicious when setting your tessellation values. Only increase the tessellation until the surface renders acceptably.*

Tweak the Diva model

Using what you have just learned, you will now fix the normals and tessellation on the Diva model created in the last lesson.

1 Open an existing scene file

▪ Open the scene file *08-divaAccessories_04.ma*.

2 Freeze transformations

If some models were mirrored and not frozen, when you freeze transformations the normals might get reversed. Thus, you need to freeze all the geometry before pursuing.

▪ Select all the surfaces, then select **Modify** → **Freeze Transformations**.

3 Normals

- Select all the surfaces, then select **Display** → **NURBS Components** → **Normals**.

- Reverse the direction of any surface in which the normals point inside the body by selecting the surface and choosing **Edit Nurbs** → **Reverse Surface Direction** → ❑.

- To hide the normals, select the object and then select **Display** → **NURBS Components** → **Normals**.

4 Tessellation

- Select all the surfaces.

- Select **Window** → **General Editors** → **Attribute Spread Sheet**.

- Under the **Tessellation** tab, click on the **Smooth Edge** column and set it to **On**.

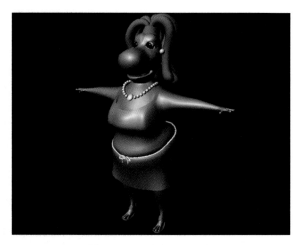

Diva now renders correctly

5 Save your work

- Save your scene as *09-divaNormals_01.ma*.

Texturing NURBS surfaces

While NURBS surfaces' inherent UVs generally makes texturing them easy, applying a texture to a series of NURBS patches can be a little more difficult. In this exercise you will use a projected texture to place a texture across multiple NURBS patches.

1 Scene file

- Continue with your own scene.

Or

- Open the scene called *09-divaNormals_01.ma*.

2 Switch view layout

- Select **Panels** → **Saved layouts** → **Hypershade/Render/Persp**.

3 Display the top and bottom tabs in the Hypershade

- Click on the **Show Top and Bottom Tabs** button in the Hypershade.

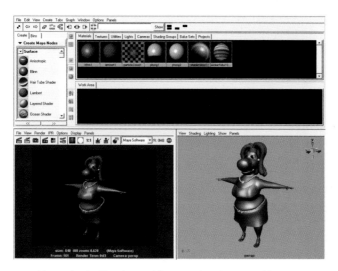

Hypershade, Render and Perspective view panel layout

4 Pearl shader

The spheres used to create the jewelry are fairly simple to texture, so you will begin with them.

- Create a phong material and assign it to all the jewelry (if it doesn't already exist).

- Map a marble texture into its **Color** and tweak it so it looks like the following:

Pearl shader

Using a 3D texture simplifies the task of texturing NURBS since you don't have to bother about UVs.

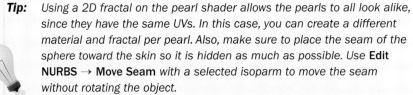

Tip: *Using a 2D fractal on the pearl shader allows the pearls to all look alike, since they have the same UVs. In this case, you can create a different material and fractal per pearl. Also, make sure to place the seam of the sphere toward the skin so it is hidden as much as possible. Use* **Edit NURBS → Move Seam** *with a selected isoparm to move the seam without rotating the object.*

5   Eye shader

- Create another phong material and assign it to the eyes (if it doesn't already exist).

- Map a Ramp into its **Color** and tweak it so it looks like the following:

Eye shader

6   Belt shader

- Tweak the belt material that was created from the Maya Paint Effects stroke.

7   Hair shader

- Create a Ramp shader and assign it to the hair.

- Tweak the *rampShader* to your needs.

- Create a phong material with the same color as the hair and assign it to the hair band.

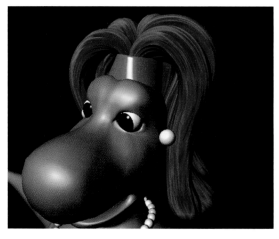

Hair shader

- Assign the same shader from the hair band onto the high heels.

High heels shader

8 Gloves shader

In order to simplify the glove texturing, you will modify the geometry slightly to cut the arm surfaces in the middle of the forearm.

- Detach both forearms and move CVs to break the continuity of the surface.

- Make sure to parent and rename the new geometry correctly in Diva's hierarchy.

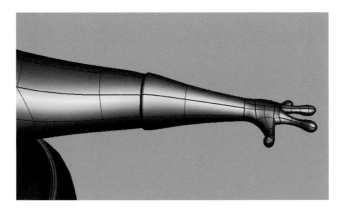

The detached glove surfaces

- Assign the same shader from the hair band and shoes onto the gloves.

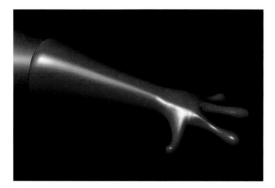

Gloves shader

9 Skin shader

- Create a blinn material and assign it to all the skin surfaces.

- Map a Solid Fractal texture to the **Color** attribute.

- Change the texture color to appear blue with very subtle variations.

- Change the blinn material's **Eccentricity** to a higher value.

Doing so will enlarge the specular highlight, simulating sub-surface light scattering.

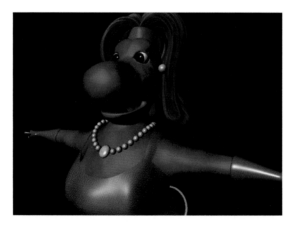

Skin shader

10 Dress shader

- Create an anisotropic material and assign it to all the dress surfaces.

- Change the color of the material to the same color as the shoes and gloves.

- Set the Angle attribute to **90**.

- Map a 3D leather texture in the **Specular Color** of the anisotropic shader.

- Set the following for the leather texture:

  Cell Color to **white**;

  Crease Color to **black**;

  Cell Size to **1.0**;

  Density to **0.5**;

  Spottyness to **0.6**;

  Randomness to **0.85**;

  Threshold to **0.85**.

- Set the **Alpha Gain** to **0.2** under the **Color Balance** section.

Note: *You changed the Alpha Gain attribute because you will map it to the glow of the shader.*

- Open the **Attribute Editor** for the anisotropic material and open the **Special Effect** section.

- **MMB-drag** the leather texture onto the **Glow Intensity** attribute under **Special Effects** in the Attribute Editor.

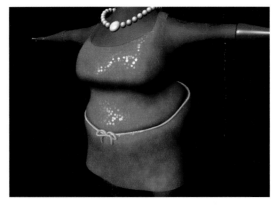

Dress shader

11 Save your work

- Save your scene as *09-divaTextures_01.ma.*

Texture reference object

In order to keep the 3D textures from sliding on the geometry when animating Diva, you will have to create *Texture Reference Objects*. Texture reference objects are duplicates of the original surfaces and keep all the texturing information.

1 Scene file

- Continue with your own scene.

Or

- Open the scene called *09-divaTextures_01.ma*.

2 Create Texture Reference Objects

If you followed the steps of the previous exercise, you now have 3D textures on the dress, the skin and the pearls. Those are the objects for which you will need to create texture reference objects.

- From the Hypershade, **RMB-click** on the skin material and choose **Select Objects With Material**.

- In order to be able to modify them all at the same time, group the skin surfaces together.

- Rename the group *skinGroup*.

- With *skinGroup* selected, go to the **Rendering** menu set and select **Texturing → Create Texture Reference Object**.

A templated duplicate of skinGroup is created and now serves as a texture reference object.

- Repeat the previous steps to create texture reference objects for any other surface using 3D texture, such as the dress and jewelry.

3 Texture objects layer

- Create a new layer and rename it *txtRefLayer*.

- Group all the texture reference objects and the *place3dTexture* nodes together.

- Select all the texture reference objects from the Outliner and add them to the *txtRefLayer*.

- Make the layer reference invisible.

4 Clean up

- Make sure everything is organized into hierarchies and named appropriately.

- Select **Edit → Delete All By Type → History**.

- Select **File → Optimize Scene Size**.

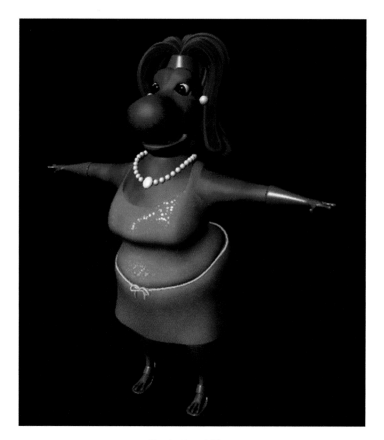

The textured Diva

5 Save your work

- Save your scene as *09-divaTextures_02.ma*.

Conclusion

Congratulations, you have now finished the Diva model! In this lesson, you learned about generic workflow when using NURBS surfaces. You also learned about surface normals and tessellation, which will greatly improve NURBS rendering quality. Other lessons learned include how to convert NURBS into polygons, which gives you the freedom of either pursuing with NURBS or polygons for the rest of the character pipeline. Lastly, you textured Diva using 2D and 3D textures, and added texture reference objects to prevent the 3D textures from sliding when the surfaces move or deform.

In the next project, you will learn about subdivision surfaces modeling.

Project Three

Lessons

In Project Three, you will use subdivision surfaces to model various objects used by the characters. Working through the lessons will allow you to explore more in-depth subdivision modeling.

You will start by revising the basics of subdivision components. Then you will model a stool and a microphone. These objects will be used by the characters in upcoming lessons in this book.

Get ready to learn some of the key concepts and workflows for modeling in subdivision surfaces!

Texture	▶
Full Crease Edge/Vertex	
Partial Crease Edge/Vertex	
Uncrease Edge/Vertex	
Mirror	◻
Attach	◻
Match Topology	
Clean Topology	
Collapse Hierarchy	◻
Standard Mode	
Polygon Proxy Mode	
Sculpt Geometry Tool	◻
Convert Selection to Faces	
Convert Selection to Edges	
Convert Selection to Vertices	
Convert Selection to UVs	
Refine Selected Components	
Select Coarser Components	
Expand Selected Components	
Component Display Level	▶
Component Display Filter	▶

Lesson 10 Subdivision basics

Subdivision surface modeling combines the convenience of poly modeling's arbitrary topology with the rendering quality of NURBS surfaces.

In this lesson you will learn the following:

- The anatomy of subdivision surfaces;

- The advantages of subdivision surfaces;

- The meaning of hierarchical components;

- The differences between Standard Mode and Polygon Proxy Mode;

- A basic subdivision workflow.

WHAT ARE SUBDIVISION SURFACES?

Subdivision surfaces (or SubDs) are a combination of some of the best features of both NURBS and polygon surfaces. Subdivision surfaces get their name from the ability to add geometry to localized areas of the surface where greater detail is needed, without affecting the rest of the surface. This ability to add detail just where you need it makes SubDs an excellent choice for complex organic shapes.

SubD surfaces compared to polygons and NURBS

Like polygons, SubDs allow arbitrary topology. This means that you are not restricted by the limitations of a single four-sided patch, or the difficulties presented by a series of four-sided patches, like you are with NURBS modeling.

Like NURBS, SubDs are not pre-tessellated, so they render smoothly. While the arbitrary topology of polygons makes them easy to model with, the fact that polygons are pre-tessellated means that they tend to appear faceted when rendered.

ANATOMY OF SUBD SURFACES

Hierarchical components

The ability to edit components on different levels of a hierarchy is integral to the idea of working with localized subdivisions of detail. This hierarchical approach to components means that edits applied to a coarse level of the hierarchy affect components on refined levels in the same area. As a result, you can make adjustments on a refined component level to alter fine details (such as the shape of the corner of an eye), and then edit components on a coarser level to change the overall shape of the surface. The fine details will follow along.

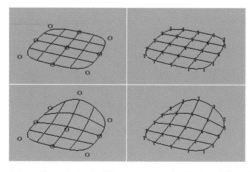

Level 1 vertices following the movement of a level 0 vertex

> **Note:** *You can change the display type of SubD vertices between numbers or points in the* **General Preferences***, under the category* **Subdivs***.*

Standard Mode vs. Polygon Proxy Mode

SubDs can be manipulated in two different modes, *Standard Mode* and *Polygon Proxy Mode*, which you can switch between at any time.

In Standard Mode, you work directly with the hierarchical components of the SubD surface itself. Standard Mode is generally used for adjusting the details of a SubD surface.

Switching to Polygon Proxy Mode creates a temporary polygon proxy surface that matches the level 0 components of the actual SubD surface. Polygon Proxy Mode is mostly used for adjusting the overall shape of a SubD surface. Most of the Maya suite of poly editing tools can be used while in Polygon Proxy Mode.

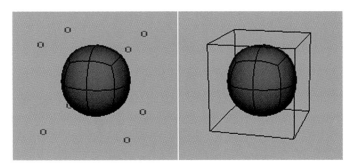

Standard Mode and Polygon Proxy Mode

SubD components

Unlike NURBS or polygonal surfaces where the nature of components is constant, SubD components are associated with the SubD surface itself, or the poly proxy object.

While working in Standard Mode you can select and edit vertices, edges, and faces at any given level of the component hierarchy. While working in Polygon Proxy Mode, selecting or editing vertices, edges, or faces is limited to the level 0 components of the SubD surface.

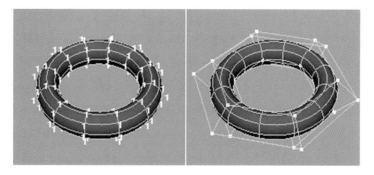

Vertices of level 1 in Standard Mode and level 0 in Polygon Proxy Mode

BASIC SUBD WORKFLOWS

Achieving basic shape while in Polygon Proxy Mode

Probably the most popular SubD modeling technique is working in Polygon Proxy Mode to achieve the basic shape of your model, then switching to Standard Mode while working with surface details.

This technique has the advantage of poly modeling's large suite of tools to create the basic shape, and Standard Mode's hierarchical components to create detail only where necessary.

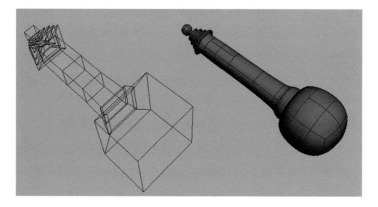

Basic shape achieved in Polygon Proxy Mode, with detail created in Standard Mode

Refining SubDs

Refining is the process of adding detail to a surface by increasing the level of components in a given area of the surface, thus increasing the number of points available in that area.

To refine a SubD surface, select a component on the surface in the area where you want to refine the detail, then **RMB-click** on the surface and select **Refine** from the contextual menu.

Level 1 vertices refined to level 2

Switching between levels

Switching between levels allows you access to the components associated with a given level of the hierarchy. To switch between levels of the component hierarchy, display the surface's compunctions, **RMB-click** on the surface, then select **Display Level** → **#**.

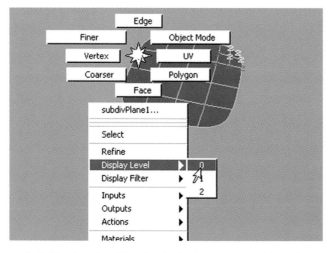

Switching from level 2 to level 0 in the component hierarchy

Creasing SubD surfaces

SubD surfaces can be creased to sharpen corners. *Full creases* move the surface to the selected edge or vertex, creating a hard or sharp corner. *Partial creases* move the surface closer to the edge or vertex than it originally was without moving it all the way to the edge or vertex. This has the effect of creating a sharper inflection in the shape of the surface without creating a visible edge.

Creases are indicated by dotted edges in the poly proxy object.

Creases can be removed after they are created by selecting the creased edge, then selecting **Subdiv Surfaces** → **Uncrease Edge/Vertex**.

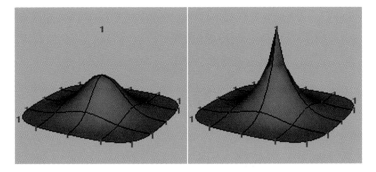

Full crease applied to center vertex

Cleaning up SubDs

Once points are added to a surface by refining, they cannot be removed unless you use the *Clean Topology* command. This will remove added points that have not been edited, and therefore, are not necessary to define detail in the surface.

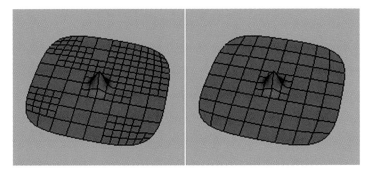

Unnecessary components deleted by Clean Topology

SubDs smoothness

Just like NURBS surfaces, you can specify the smoothness of SubDs in the viewport by pressing **1**, **2** or **3** on your keyboard.

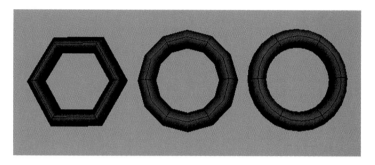

SubD smoothness

Conclusion

Subdivision surfaces are an excellent choice for models that require varying levels of detail. Now that you are familiar with the principles and basic workflows of SubDs, you will apply these ideas and techniques in the next lessons to model a SubD microphone and a SubD stool.

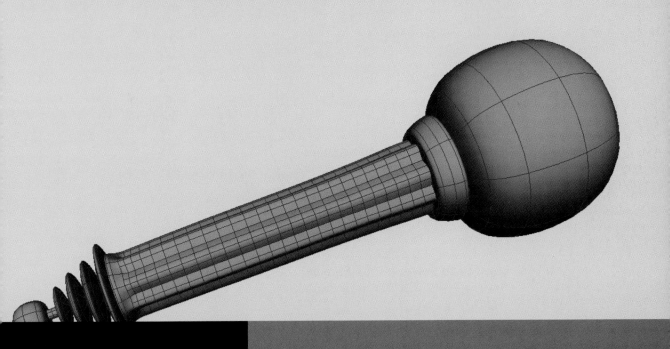

In this lesson, you will model a subdivision surface microphone. Doing so will allow you to gain experience using SubD surfaces.

In this lesson you will learn the following:

- How to define a shape using Polygon Proxy Mode;

- How to switch between Standard Mode and Polygon Proxy Mode;

- How to define creases;

- How to refine hierarchical components;

- How to convert component selection;

- How to clean SubD topology.

Define a shape in Polygon Proxy Mode

The first step in building the microphone is creating the basic shape while in Polygon Proxy Mode.

1 Create a SubD primitive sphere

- Create a SubD sphere by selecting **Create** → **Subdiv Primitives** → **Sphere**.

- With the sphere still selected, hit the **3** key to increase the sphere's display resolution.

- Rename the *sphere* to *microphone*.

2 Switch to Polygon Proxy Mode

- **RMB-click** on the sphere and select **Polygon** from the radial menu to switch to Polygon Proxy Mode.

A temporary polygonal object is displayed, which represents level 0 of the SubD surface's hierarchical components.

Note: *You can also access the* **Polygon Proxy Mode** *through the* **Subdiv Surfaces** *menu.*

3 Display the poly object's faces

- **RMB-click** on the sphere and select **Face** from the radial menu, or press **F11**.

The faces of the temporary polygon object are displayed.

4 Extrude face to create the handle

- Select a face on the side of the poly object.

- Select **Edit Polygons** → **Extrude Face** and extrude it along its local **Z-axis** twice to create the handle of the microphone.

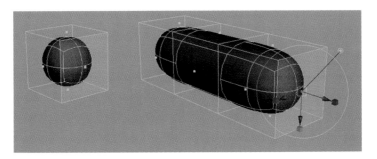

Face of SubD sphere extruded to create handle

5 Extrude to create a border

- Extrude the face three more times to create a border at the tip of the handle.

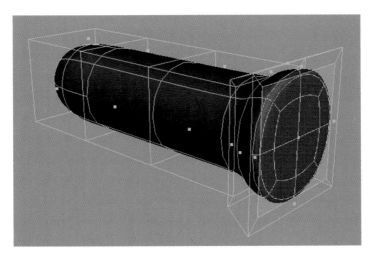

End of handle extruded twice

6 Extrude the ball of the microphone

- Extrude two more times to create the ball of the microphone.

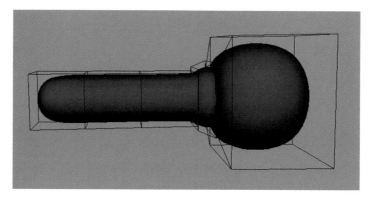

Ball of microphone extruded

7   Extrude the antenna of the microphone

- Extrude several more times in order to create a futuristic antenna as follows:

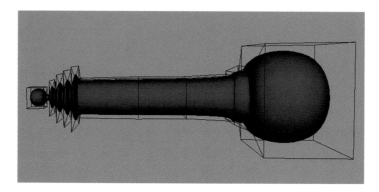

The completed shape

Tip: **RMB-click** *on the microphone and select* **Vertices** *from the context menu to refine the shape of the microphone, just like you would do with a polygonal object.*

8   Save your work

Working in Standard Mode

Now that the basic shape of the microphone has been achieved, you will switch to Standard Mode and create the surface's details with hierarchical components.

1 Continue with your own scene

2 Switch to Standard Mode

- **RMB-click** on the *microphone* and select **Standard** from the context menu.

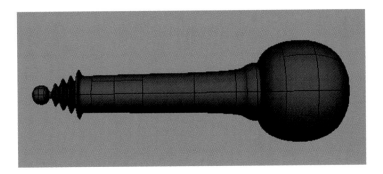

Microphone in Standard Mode

3 Display the vertices in the microphone's handle

- **RMB-click** on the *microphone* and select **Vertex** from the context menu.

Level 0 vertices of the SubD surface are displayed.

4 View a finer level of the component hierarchy

You are going to pull vertices in the handle to create ridges, but editing the level 0 vertices will cause too broad a change of shape. You will now view a finer level of the component hierarchy to see if it will provide enough detail.

- **RMB-click** on the *microphone* and select **Display Level → 1** from the radial menu.

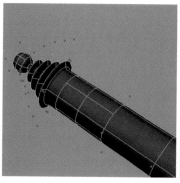

Areas covered by level 0 and level 1 vertices

Note: You can also select **Display Finer** or **Display Coarser** from the context menu.

5   Expand the level 1 components

Currently, there are not that many level 1 vertices. Before attempting to refine the existing level 1 components to level 2, you will expand them so that the entire handle area is covered with level 1 vertices.

- Select the current level 1 vertices and select **Subdiv Surfaces → Expand Selected Components**.

- Select the level 1 vertices again and expand them again until the entire handle is covered with level 1 vertices.

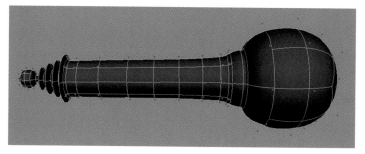

Level 1 vertices expanded to cover the handle

Note: As an alternative to expanding the existing level 1 vertices, the level 0 vertices could have been refined. You will see how to refine vertices in the next step.

6 Refine the components in the handle

Even at the finer level of the hierarchy, the amount of vertices present will not provide enough detail to define the shape required. You will now refine the components in the handle so that there are more vertices to work with.

- Select all of the level 1 vertices in the handle, then **RMB-click** and select **Refine Selected** from the context menu.

There should now be level 2 vertices in the handle area of the surface.

Level 1 vertices refined to level 2

7 Use the Move Normal Tool to push the vertices into the handle

- Select every other row of level 2 vertices running along the length of the microphone handle.

- Select **Modify → Transformation Tools → Move Normal Tool**, in order to push the selected vertices into the handle to create ridges in the surface.

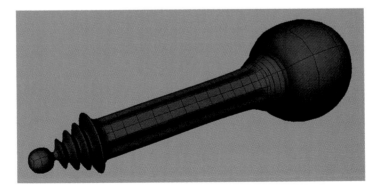

Ridges defined with level 2 vertices using the Move Normal Tool

8   Convert selection to edges

- With the vertices still selected, select **Subdiv Surfaces** → **Convert Selection to Edges**.

- Deselect the ring of edges from an Orthographic view in order to keep only the edge line located at the bottom of the ridges.

9   Add a Full Crease to the edge of each ridge

- With the level 2 edges still selected, select **Subdiv Surfaces** → **Full Crease Edge/Vertex**.

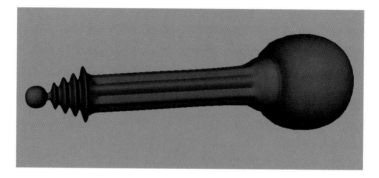

Full Crease applied to the ridges

10 Crease the edges on the extremity of the handle

- **RMB-click** on the *microphone* and select **Display Coarser** until the level 0 edges are displayed.

- Select the level 0 edges at the extremity of the handle and apply a Full Crease to them.

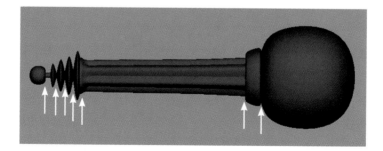

Full Crease applied to level 0 edges

Note: *Full crease edges are displayed with dotted lines in the viewport.*

11 Experiment with vertices

- Adjust the shape of the mirophone by refining and moving vertices.

12 Clean the geometry

During the SubD modeling process, vertices are often created that end up being unnecessary to express the shape of the surface. While you can't directly delete these vertices, you can use Clean Topology to remove them automatically.

- Select the SubD object, then select **Subdiv Surfaces** → **Clean Topology**.

Any unnecessary components on the surface will be deleted.

13 Save your work

Conclusion

You are now more familiar with the SubD's hierarchical components. You learned how to create a basic shape using Polygon Proxy Mode and how to refine and display various levels of detail. Lastly, you creased components and cleaned up topology.

In the next lesson, you will use more polygonal tools to create a SubD stool.

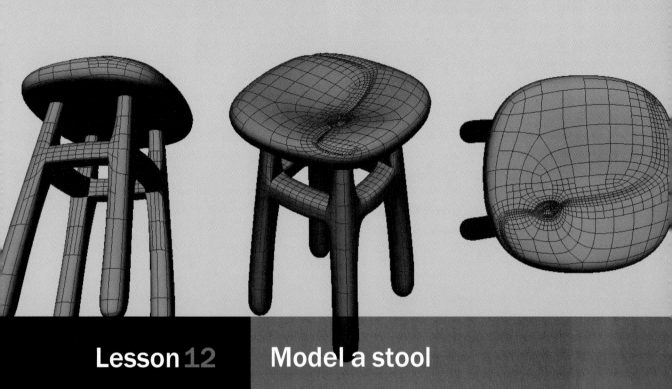

Lesson 12   Model a stool

In this lesson, you will use SubDs to build a stool in Polygon Proxy Mode. Some of the techniques used here will be similar to the ones used to mirror Meeper in Project 2.

In this lesson you will learn the following:

- How to build your model in Polygon Proxy Mode;

- How to use poly modeling techniques with a SubD object;

- How to mirror and attach SubD surfaces;

- How to refine selected components.

Creating the basic shape

In this lesson you will build a SubD wooden stool by switching back and forth between Standard Mode and Polygon Proxy Mode. The first step will be creating a subdivision surface sphere, then switching to Polygon Proxy Mode to achieve the basic shape of the stool.

1 Open a new file

2 Create a SubD sphere

- Select **Create** → **Subdiv Primitives** → **Sphere**.

- With the *sphere* selected, hit the **3** key to increase the sphere's display resolution.

- Rename the *sphere* to *stool*.

3 Switch to Polygon Proxy Mode

- **RMB-click** on the stool and select **Polygon** from the context menu to create a temporary polygonal object that matches the level 0 vertices of the SubD sphere.

4 Cut the poly object in half

You will take advantage of the stool's symmetry and build only half of it, using an instanced duplicate to stand in for the other side of the stool.

- Select the poly object, then select **Edit Polygons** → **Cut faces Tool** → ❑, and set the following:

    Cut Direction to **Cut Along YZ-plane**;

    Delete the cut faces to **On**.

- Click the **Cut** button.

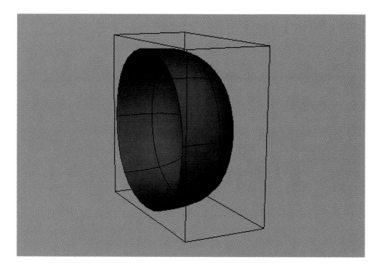

Delete half the model

5   Create an instanced duplicate

- Select the poly object and select **Edit** → **Duplicate** → **❒**.

- Set the **Scale X** to **-1** and **Geometry type** to **Instance**.

- Click the **Duplicate** button.

Note: *When you merge the two pieces together at the end of this lesson, the seam across the mirror axis will disapear.*

6   Shape the poly object

- Scale the vertices on the poly object to create the seat of the stool.

- Split the bottom faces in half on the poly object.

- Turn **Off** the **Polygons** → **Tool Options** → **Keep Faces Together**.

- Extrude the new faces in order to get four distinct quads to extrude the stool legs as follows:

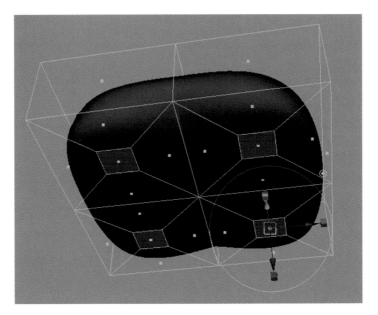

Quads for leg extrusions

Note: *Avoid changing the topology, such as subdividing a face, in areas where you've edited components in Standard Mode. Changing the topology can alter the surface in unexpected ways. This is not a problem for edits to level 0 components.*

7 Extrude the stool legs

- Extrude the polygonal faces **four** times in order to create the appropriate topology for the legs.

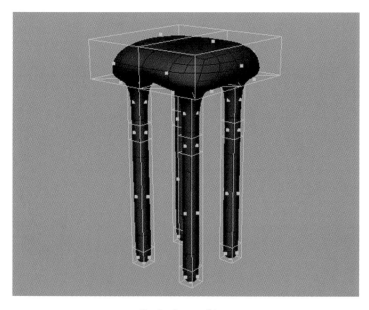

Basic shape of legs

8   Refine the stool legs

- Widen the new leg vertices in order to refine the stool's shape.

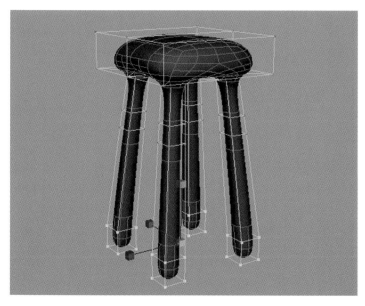

Refine the stool legs

Continuing the structure

Now that the stool legs have been extracted, you can crease the junction between the legs and the seat. You can also add vertical bars to style the model.

1 Switch to Standard Mode

- **RMB-click** over the stool object and select **Standard** from the context menu.

2 Make edges full creased

- **RMB-click** over the stool object and select **Edge** from the context menu.

- Select the edges connecting the legs to the seat.

- Select **Subdiv Surfaces** → **Full Crease Edge/Vertex**.

Leg creases

3 Switch back to Polygon Proxy Mode

- **RMB-click** over the *stool* object and select **Polygon** from the context menu.

4 Extrude the bars

- Select the inside faces of the stool and extrude the horizontal bars. Leave a gap where the extrusions meet.

5 Delete the obsolete faces

- With the faces still selected, press the **Delete** key on your keyboard.

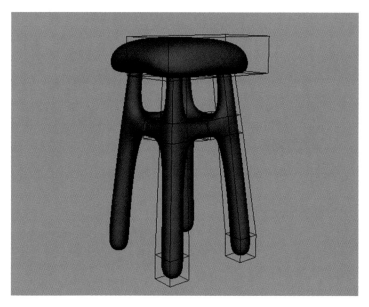

Horizontal bars

6   Merge vertices

- **Edit Polygons** → **Merge Vertices** the central vertices two by two in order to unite the horizontal bar.

> **Note:** Upon the first merge, you will get a message saying that some vertices are nonmanifold. This is normal since the merge command caused polygonal faces to be connected by only one vertex. The problem will be solved upon the second merge command.

7   Snap vertices

Since you cannot merge the vertices to the mirrored instance, the remaining vertices will simply be snapped to the X-axis.

- From the *side* view, select the bar vertices to be snapped.

- Press **w** to make the **Move Tool** active.

- Hold down **x** to **Snap to Grid**, then **click+drag** the **red** manipulator arrow.

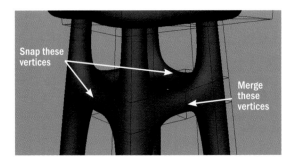

The merged and snapped vertices

8 Switch to Standard Mode

- **RMB-click** over the stool object and select **Standard** from the context menu.

9 Make edges full creased

- **RMB-click** over the stool object and select **Edge** from the context menu.
- Select the edges connecting the bars to the legs.
- Select **Subdiv Surfaces** → **Full Crease Edge/Vertex**.

Bar creases

10 Adjust the proportions of the stool

- Work the shape and proportions of the stool.
- Split the seat in order to carve the top faces in.
- Use **Subdiv Surfaces** → **Partial Crease Edge/Vertex** on the horizontal edges of the bars to make them more square.

Current stool view

11 Save your work

Refine the stool

Now that the basic shape and proportions of the stool have been achieved, you will mirror and attach the geometry to create the final geometry. Once that is done, you will experiment with the refinement of SubDs to create wood grain on the seat.

1 Delete instanced duplicate

- Select the instanced duplicate of the left half of the stool and delete it.

2 Mirror the SubD surface

- Making sure that you are in Standard Mode, select the SubD surface, then select **Subdiv Surfaces → MIrror → ❐**.

- Reset the window, then set **Mirror** to **X**.

- Click the **Mirror** button.

3 Attach the two SubD surfaces

- Select both SubD surfaces, then select **Subdiv Surfaces → Attach → ❑**.

- Reset the options, then set **Keep Originals** to **Off**.

- Click the **Attach** button.

- Increase the display resolution after attaching the two SubD surfaces, if necessary.

4 Merge the central vertices

- **RMB-click** over the stool object and select **Polygon** from the context menu.

- Select the central vertices on the seat and the horizontal bars.

- Select **Edit Polygons → Merge Vertices**.

5 Split to get details on the seat

- Select **Edit Polygons → Split Polygon Tool → ❑**.

- In the tool options, turn **Off** the options **Snap to Edges** and **Snap to Magnets**.

Doing so will allow you to define split points in the face itself and not only on edges.

- Split the top faces to create a wood knot as follows:

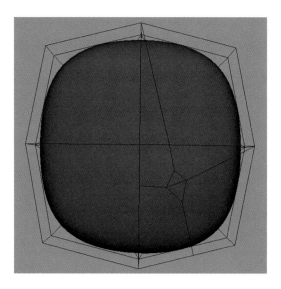

Wood knot split

Tip: *If you get an error message saying that the surface computation failed, it is because you have defined invalid geometry. In order for the geometry to be valid, you must define only triangles or quads.*

6   Refine the SubD surface

- **RMB-click** over the stool object and select **Standard** from the context menu.

- **RMB-click** over the *stool* object and select **Vertex** from the context menu.

- **RMB-click** over the stool object and select **Display Level** → **2** from the context menu.

- Select the SubD vertices that would form a nice wood knot groove.

- **RMB-click** on the surface and select **Refine Selected**.

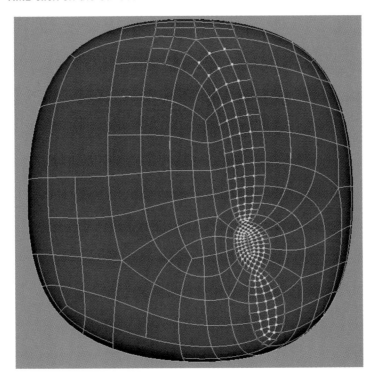

Refined surface

Lesson 12

7 Create the groove

- Select and move down vertices to create the groove.

- Convert the selection to edges using **Subdiv Surfaces** → **Convert Selection to Edges**.

- Deselect the edges that are not meant to be part of the groove.

Tip: *You can use the* **Lasso Tool** *while holding down* **Ctrl** *in order to deselect multiple edges at once.*

- Select **Subdiv Surfaces** → **Full Crease Edge/Vertex**.

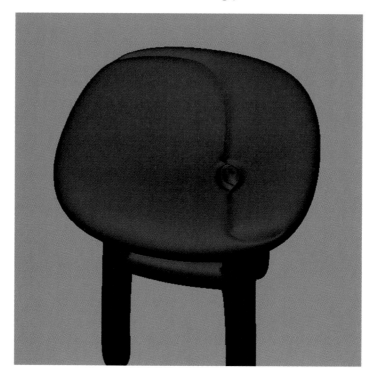

Wood knot groove

Tip: *Wood grain or less apparent grooves can be achieved more easily by using bump mapping or displacement mapping in the stool shader.*

Cleaning up geometry

Once you are satisfied with the model, it is a good idea to clean up the geometry. Cleaning up the geometry will get rid of any unnecessary hierarchical components that you created during the refinement of other components, or by Maya when components were edited.

1   Clean up the SubD surface

- Select the stool, then select **Subdiv Surfaces** → **Clean Topology**.

2   Save your work

Final stool

Conclusion

In addition to combining some of the best features of NURBS and Polygon Proxy Modeling, subdivision surface modeling offers the flexibility of hierarchical components.

In the next lesson, you will learn about converting SubDs and texturing them.

Lesson 13

Subdivision tasks

In this lesson, you will examine
a number of general tasks
related to modeling with
subdivision surfaces (SubDs).

In this lesson you will learn the following:

- How to convert polygons to SubDs;

- How to convert SubDs to polygons;

- How to map SubD UVs;

- How to assign a ramp;

- How to assign a 3D texture;

- How to assign shaders to portions of a
  SubD model;

- How to tweak SubD UVs.

Converting polygons to SubDs

In order to create a high resolution model, it is possible to convert polygon surfaces to subdivision surfaces. While this process is generally problem free, you may encounter two typical issues: the first one is an insufficient Maximum Base Mesh Faces setting in the Convert Polygon to Subdiv option window, and the second issue is to have nonmanifold geometry.

The following exercise explains both of these issues.

1 Open an existing scene file

- Open the scene file *13-polyToSubD.ma*.

The scene contains a modified version of Meeper built in Lesson 4.

2 Convert the polygon mesh to SubDs

- Select Meeper's geometry, then select **Modify → Convert → Polygons to Subdiv**.

Note: *An error message should appear informing you that the conversion failed, and that details can be found in the Script Editor.*

3 Open the Script Editor

- Click on the **Script Editor** button at the lower right-hand corner of the interface to open the Script Editor window.

The Script Editor states that the conversion failed because the resulting surface would have more base mesh faces than the maximum allowed by the conversion settings.

- Take note of the number of base mesh faces the resulting surface would have.

4 Increase the Maximum Base Mesh Faces value and convert

- With the mesh still selected, select **Modify → Convert → Polygons to Subdiv → ❑**.

- Increase the **Maximum Base Mesh Faces** to a value higher than the value listed in the Script Editor, such as **3000**.

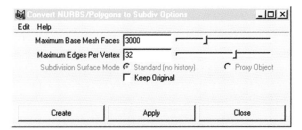

Convert Polygons to Subdiv options

This new setting value will fix the first issue that you may encounter when converting polygons to SubDs.

5 Convert the mesh to SubDs

▪ Click on the **Create** button.

Note: *Once again, an error message should appear informing you that the conversion failed, and that details can be found in the Script Editor.*

6 Open the Script Editor

The Script Editor states that the conversion failed because one or more edges is nonmanifold. The surface will have to be cleaned up to correct the nonmanifold geometry.

7 Clean up the polygonal mesh

▪ Select the poly mesh, then select **Polygons → Cleanup → □**, and set the following:

▪ Under **General Options**:

   Operation to **Select and Cleanup**.

▪ Under **Other**:

   Nonmanifold Geometry to **On**.

Tip: *If you don't want the tool to automatically clean up the geometry, set the* **Operation** *option to* **Select Geometry.** *Doing so will allow you to frame the problematic geometry and correct it manually.*

- Click the **Cleanup** button.

The tool will correct the nonmanifold geometry.

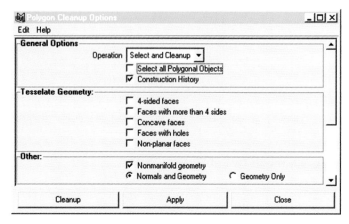

Polygon Cleanup Options window

Note: *The nonmanifold geometry was located in Meeper's mouth and was an extracted T-shaped polygon. The **Cleanup Tool** has simply separated the polygons from the mouth geometry.*

8 Convert the poly mesh to SubDs

- With the mesh still selected, select **Modify → Convert → Polygons to Subdiv**.

The conversion is successful.

The converted geometry

Converting SubDs to polygons

It is not uncommon to take advantage of workflows that are unique to subdivision modeling, such as hierarchical components, then convert the SubD surface to polygons for texturing and binding. How you choose to convert from SubDs to polygons will depend on your requirements at the time.

1   Open an existing scene file

- Open the scene file *13-subDToPoly.ma*.

2   Check the number of component levels

- **RMB-click** on the SubD *stool* and check the number of display levels it has.

Note: *The stool should have display levels from 0 to 4.*

3   Convert SubDs to polygons

- Select the stool, then select **Modify** → **Convert** → **Subdiv To Polygons** → ❐, and set the following:

    Tessellation Method to **Vertices**;

    Level to **0**.

- Click the **Apply** button.

The stool will be converted into a polygonal mesh that reflects the level 0 components of the SubD surface.

Polygonal surface after converting the Level 0 faces

4 Undo the conversion

5 Convert at higher settings

- In the **Convert** options, set the **Level** option to **1** and click the **Apply** button again.

Once again, the SubD surface is converted to a poly surface, this time reflecting the level 1 vertices. The resulting surface is a more accurate representation of the original SubD surface, but the poly mesh is denser.

- Undo the conversion, then repeat the conversion at **Level 4**.

Converting at level 4 creates a perfectly faithful reproduction, but it also creates an extremely dense mesh.

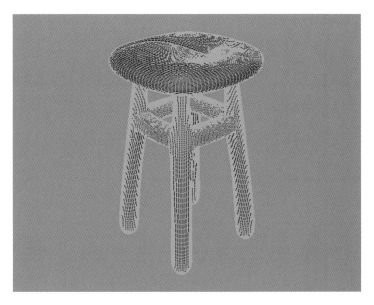

Polygonal surface after converting the level 4 faces

Note: *When converting from one surface type to another you will often have to strike a balance between accuracy in the resulting surface and density of the geometry.*

Texturing SubD surfaces

Texturing SubDs is much the same as texturing polygonal surfaces, although there are less tools for SubD texturing than the ones available for polygons.

In this exercise, you will apply a texture to the SubD stool built in Lesson 12.

1   Open a scene file from previous lesson

- Open the scene file *12-stool.ma*.

2 Map the color channel of the phong material with a ramp

- **RMB-click** on the *stool* and select **Material** → **Assign New Material** → **Phong** from the context menu.

The Attribute Editor for the new phong material will be displayed.

- Map the **Color** channel with a ramp.

Note: *Make sure that* **Normal** *is selected at the top of the* **2D Textures** *section of the Create Render Node window.*

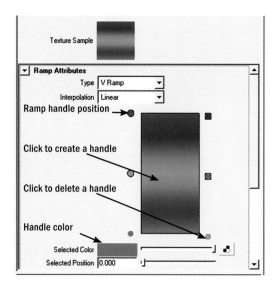

Ramp texture

3 Set up the Ramp's colors

- Delete the **green** handle by clicking on its small box with the **x** on the right side of the ramp.
- Click on the **red** handle at the bottom of the ramp to select it.

The handle's color and position are loaded in the lower portion of the ramp attributes.

- Click on the **Selected Color** swatch in order to define a new color.
- Select a dark brown color in the displayed **Color Chooser** window.
- Change the blue handle at the top of the ramp to a lighter brown.

4 Move the handle position in the ramp

- Move the ramp handles closer together by **click+dragging** them.

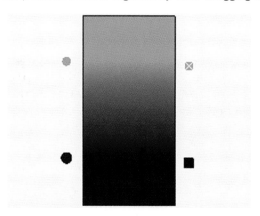

Ramp handles moved toward the middle

- Close the Attribute Editor.

5 Display the stool's UVs in the UV Texture Editor

- Select the *stool*, then switch to the **Persp/UV Texture Editor** saved layout.

The polygonal surface UVs are in poor shape for texturing.

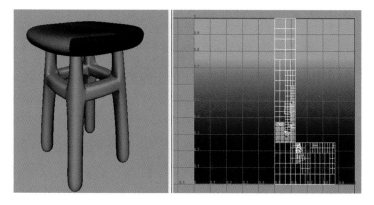

UVs viewed in the Texture Editor

6   Map the subdivision surface's UVs

- Select all the stool's **Level 0** faces.

- Select **Subdiv Surfaces** → **Texture** → **Planar Mapping** → ☐.

- Set **Mapping Direction** to X-axis.

- Click the **Project** button.

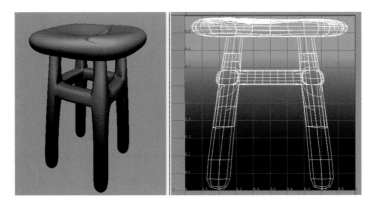

Corrected UVs

7   Map a wood texture

- Open the Attribute Editor for *ramp1* created earlier.

- Scroll down to the **Color Balance** section.

- Click on the **Map** button for the **Color Gain** attribute.

- In the **Create Render Node** window, select **Wood** from the **3D Textures** section.

Doing so will create a 3D wood texture that will appear within the ramp texture, providing a nice gradient effect. It will also create a 3D placement box, which can be used to place the texture in the scene.

- Press **6** in the Perspective view to enable Hardware Texturing.

Note: *You will only see a texture preview in the viewport. You will need to render the stool in order to see the result of the wood on the geometry.*

The 3D placement box

8 Tweak the wood texture

- In the Attribute Editor for *wood1*, set the following to tweak the look of the wood grain:

  Layer Size to **0.2**;

  Amplitude X to **0.5**;

  Amplitude Y to **0.5**;

  Ripples to **5, 0, 0**.

9 Test render

- Go to the **Create** menu and add some lights to the scene.

- Test render the stool to view the result of the wood grain on the geometry.

The rendered stool

> **Tip:**   *You should parent the wood 3D placement box to the geometry. If you don't, when you move the stool the 3D texture will slide on the geometry.*

10 Save your work

Texturing the SubD microphone

You will now texture the SubD microphone modeled in Lesson 11. Instead of applying the same shader on the entire object as in the previous example, you will assign different shaders to the microphone.

1   Open a scene file from previous lesson

- Open the scene file *11-microphone.ma*.

2   Planar mapping

- **RMB-click** over the microphone and select **Face** from the context menu.

- **RMB-click** over the microphone and select **Display Lever** → **0** from the context menu.

- Select all the faces defining the ball of the microphone.

- Select **Subdiv Surfaces** → **Texture** → **Planar Mapping** → ❑.

- In the option window, set **Mapping Direction** to **X-axis**, then click the **Project** button.

3 Assign a phong and a texture

- Press **F5** to display the **Rendering** menu set.

- With the same faces selected from the previous step, select **Lighting/ Shading** → **Assign New Material** → **Blinn**.

- Through the Attribute Editor, map a cloth texture to the new *blinn*'s Color channel.

- Select the *cloth*'s *place2dTexture* tab, then set **Repeat UV** to **20** and **20**.

4 Tweak the UVs

- Select **Window** → **UV Texture Editor** and tweak the UVs to look like this:

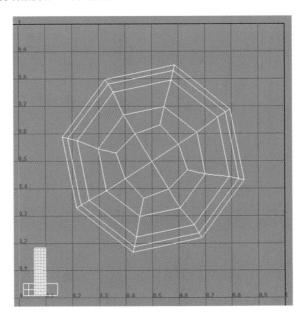

The microphone UVs

> **Note:** The rest of the microphone geometry will not have textures assigned, so you don't need to unfold them.

5   Create and assign the remaining shaders

- Select the faces of the border between the ball and the handle of the *microphone*.

- **Shift-select** the faces of the antenna at the tip of the handle.

- Select **Lighting/Shading** → **Assign New Material** → **Blinn**.

- Tweak the new blinn's attributes.

- Select the faces of the handle of the *microphone*.

- Select **Lighting/Shading** → **Assign New Material** → **Lambert**.

- Tweak the new lambert's attributes.

Final microphone render

> **Note:** In the render above, a glow was added to the antenna's blinn and the cloth texture was used for bump mapping.

6   Save your work

Conclusion

You are now able to convert polygons to SubDs or SubDs to polygons. Doing so will allow you to decide whether you want to work with SubDs or polygons. You also learned about SubD UV mapping and texturing.

In the next project, you will set up a character rig for Meeper.

Lessons

In Project Four, you will create a character rig for Meeper from Project One. You will start by revising the basics of character rigging nodes, such as bones, IKs, locators and constraints. You will then build a complete rig. By the end of this project, you will have a full rig ready to be bound to Meeper.

Lesson 14   Skeleton

To begin, you are going to set up Meeper's skeleton, which will help you prepare him for movements as well as provide a framework for applying deformations. This is done by drawing a series of joint nodes to build a skeleton chain.

To create the greatest flexibility for animating, you will set up the character's skeleton by combining several techniques.

In this lesson you will learn the following:

- How to use layers and templating;

- How to freeze transformations;

- How to use the Joint Tool;

- How to traverse a hierarchy;

- How to create, move and parent joints;

- How to use the Move Pivot Tool;

- How to assume preferred angle;

- How to quickly rename nodes;

- How to rename nodes using MEL;

- How to mirror joints.

Layers

The Layer Editor is a good tool for organizing the various parts of a character. It provides an easy way to separate all the parts of Meeper – geometry, skeletons, IK, etc. into logical groups. In the Layer Editor, you can hide, show, template and reference selected layers to speed up interactivity by reducing the visible and modifiable elements in the scene.

Element visibility

The more elements you can hide in your scene, the quicker you can interact with it. Layers can greatly accelerate the process of hiding and showing scene elements.

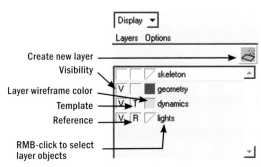

The Layer Editor

Element selection

It can be difficult to select objects and groups of objects efficiently in the interface. Layers offer various options in order to make the selection of objects easier.

Template elements

By templating layers, you still see a transparent representation of their elements, but they cannot be selected.

Reference elements

By referencing layers, you see their elements, but they cannot be selected. This enables you to view your scene normally, but you cannot select or modify referenced objects. A referenced object will also allow you to snap points to its wireframe.

Selecting and displaying only the elements of the scene you are working on is crucial to successfully operating in a scene.

Layers can also be used to logically break down your scene. You can make your background elements one layer and your foreground elements another layer. You can also create render layers that will render separately as compositing passes. By using this feature, you can render elements such as characters, background and effects separately.

Prepare Meeper's geometry

You are going to use Meeper's body to help position the skeleton properly. You will first prepare the geometry for rigging. Once you begin creating the skeleton, you don't want to accidentally modify Meeper, so you will create a layer just for the geometry, allowing you to template it.

1 Open Meeper's geometry file

- Open the file called *14-meeperGeometry.ma* from the *support_files* directory.

2 Group, move and freeze the geometry

- Select all of Meeper's geometry and press **Ctrl+g** to group them together.

The group will allow you to move the geometry pieces more easily.

- Rename the group to *geoGroup*.

- Make sure that Meeper's geometry is facing the **2-axis**.

- Move the geometry in the **Y-axis** to place the feet on the grid.

- Still with *geoGroup* selected, select **Modify** → **Freeze Transformations**.

All the geometry is now frozen, meaning that their transform attributes are reset to their default values with the objects in the current position.

Note: *Freezing transformations makes it easier to reset the geometry to its original position if needed later in production.*

3 Naming, history and clean up

- Open the Outliner and make sure all nodes are properly named.

- Select **Edit** → **Delete All by Type** → **History**.

This will delete any unwanted construction history.

Tip: *Make sure you don't have a Smooth applied on Meeper before deleting the history.*

- Select **File** → **Optimize Scene Size**.

This will remove any unused nodes in the scene.

4 Create a new layer for Meeper's geometry

- Press the **Create a New Layer** button in the Layer Editor.

A new layer will appear in the Layer Editor.

Tip: *If the Layer Editor is not visible, enable the **Channel Box/Layer Editor** button under **Display** → **UI Elements**.*

- **Double-click** on the *layer1* to open the **Edit Layer** window.
- Name the layer *geometryLayer,* then click on the **Save** button to confirm the changes.
- Through the Outliner, select *geoGroup* node.
- **RMB-click** on the *geometryLayer* and select **Add Selected Objects.**

The selected objects are now a part of the geometryLayer.

Note: *You can see the layer's connection in the **Inputs** section of the Channel Box for the selected elements.*

5 Template the layer

- Click on the middle box next to the *geometryLayer* to display a **T**, which means the layer is templated.

You can now see Meeper's geometry in wireframe. The geometry is also not selectable through the viewports.

Note: *The geometry can still be selected through editors such as the Outliner or the Hypergraph.*

6 Save your work

Drawing the skeleton

In Maya, a skeleton chain is made up of *joints* that are visually connected by *bones*. A skeleton chain creates a continuous hierarchy of joint nodes that are parented to each other. The top node of the hierarchy is known as the *root* joint. The joints and bones help you visualize the character's hierarchy in the 3D views but will not appear in renders.

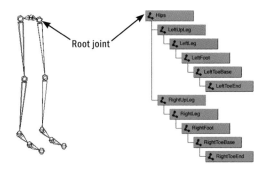

Joints and bones in the viewport and Hypergraph

Joint hierarchies let you group or bind geometry. You can then animate the joints, which in turn, animates the geometry. When you transform the joints you will most often use rotation. If you look at your own joints you will see that they all rotate. Generally, joints don't translate or scale unless you want to add some squash and stretch to a character's limbs.

When you rotate a joint, all the joints below it are carried along with the rotation. This behavior is called forward kinematics and is consistent with how all hierarchies work in Maya. In Lesson 16, you will learn how to use inverse kinematics to make it easier to animate joint rotations.

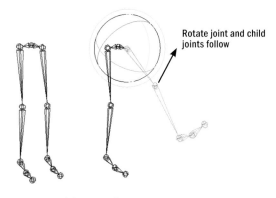

Joints rotations

Tip: *Use the up, down, left and right arrow keys to traverse through a hierarchy.*

The leg joints

Using the geometry as a guide, you will begin by creating Meeper's left leg skeleton. You will then mirror the joints to create the right leg skeleton. Later in this lesson you will build the upper body, which will be connected by the *Hips* joint.

1 Scene file

- Continue with your own scene.

Or

- Open the scene file *14-meeperSkeleton_01.ma*.

2 Draw the left leg

- From the *side* view, frame Meeper's legs.

- Press **F2** to display the **Animation** menu set, then select **Skeleton** → **Joint Tool** → ❐.

- In the option window, set the following:

    Orientation to **None**.

Note: *Joint orientation will be discussed in the next lesson.*

- Starting at the hip, place **five** joints for the leg, as shown in the image at the top of the next page.

- Rename the joints to *LeftUpLeg*, *LeftLeg*, *LeftFoot*, *LeftToeBase* and *LeftToeEnd*.

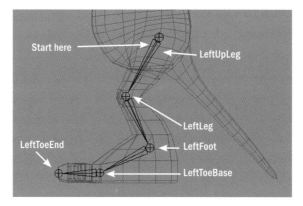

Left leg joints

Tip: *Always make sure to draw the knee in a bent position. This will make it easier to apply an IK solver to the chain.*

3 Move the joint chain to Meeper's left side

The *LeftUpLeg* joint is now the *root* node of the leg's joint chain hierarchy. If you pick this node you can move the whole chain at once.

- From the *front* view, select the *LeftUpLeg* joint and move it along the **X-axis** so it aligns with the position of Meeper's left hip bone.

- Still in the *front* view, move the *LeftLeg* joint and *LeftFoot* joint along the **X-axis** so it aligns with the position of Meeper's left knee and ankle.

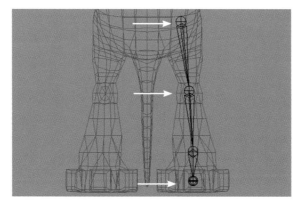

Moving the joint chain into Meeper's left leg

4 Mirror the leg to create the right leg

- Select the *LeftUpLeg* joint.

- Select **Skeleton** → **Mirror Joint** → ❑.

- In the options, set the following:

    Mirror Across to **YZ**.

- Press the **Mirror** button.

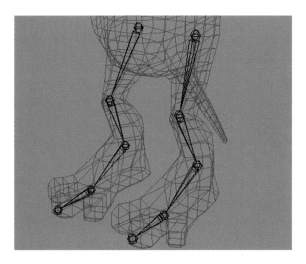

Mirrored leg

5   Rename the right leg

It is important to take the time to name your objects so they are easy
to find and select.

- Rename the right leg joints to *RightUpLeg*, *RightLeg*, *RightFoot*,
  RightToeBase and *RightToeEnd*.

Tip: *This type of task is perfect for using MEL scripting to rename all the joints
automatically. Execute the following MEL command to rename the currently
selected node's Left for Right:*

```
for($each in `ls -sl`) rename $each `substitute "Left"
$each "Right"`;
```

6   Save your work

The spine joints

You will now create another skeleton hierarchy for Meeper's pelvis, spine, neck and head. The hierarchy will start from the hips, which will be the root of the skeleton. The root joint is important since it represents the parent of the hierarchy. Using the hips as the root, the upper body and the legs will branch off from this node. You can then move the whole skeleton hierarchy by simply moving the root.

1   Scene file

- Continue with your own scene.

Or

- Open the scene file *14-meeperSkeleton_02.ma*.

2   Pelvis joint

- Select **Skeleton → Joint Tool → ❐**.

- In the options, set **Orientation** to **XYZ**.

*By creating the joints with **Orientation** set to **XYZ** and the **Second Axis World Orientation** set to +y, the X-axis of the joint will always point towards the child joint and the Y-axis will point in the world positive Y-axis direction. You set the orientation to XYZ so that the local rotation axis of the joints will be aligned in the direction of the spine. This topic will be covered in more detail in the next lesson and throughout the book.*

- From the *side* view, **click+drag** the pelvis bone just above the hip joint.

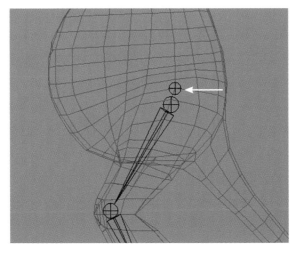

First joint

Tip: While placing joints, you can use the **MMB** to modify the placement of the last created joint. When using the **Move Tool** on a joint hierarchy, all the child joints will move accordingly. Press the **Insert** key to toggle the **Move Pivot Tool**, which will move only the selected joint and not its children.

3 Spine joints

▪ Draw equally spaced joints until you reach between Meeper's shoulders.

Tip: Try to follow the shape of Meeper's back to create a joint chain similar to the spine under his skin.

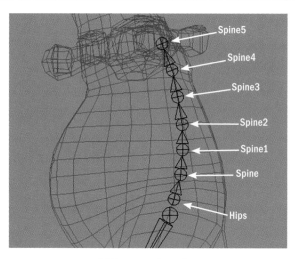

Joint names for spine

▪ Press **Enter** on your keyboard to complete the joint chain.

▪ Rename the joints according to the illustration above.

4 Neck and head joints

▪ Press **y** to activate the **Joint Tool**.

▪ Click on the last joint between Meeper's shoulders to highlight it.

Doing so will specify that the Joint Tool should continue drawing from that joint.

- Draw the neck and head joints as follows:

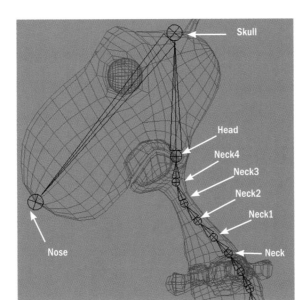

Skull

Head

Neck4

Neck3

Neck2

Neck1

Nose

Neck

Joint names for neck and head

Tip: *There are no strict rules about how many joints are needed to create the upper body spine; it really depends on how you want to animate the motion in the back. You could use an IK Spline for the back to simplify the control of such a large number of joints. Here are some guidelines for determining the number of joints to use in a typical biped character: spine (3 - 10 joints), neck (1 - 5 joints).*

- Rename the joints according to the illustration above.

5 Save your work

Parenting skeletons

You now have three separate skeleton hierarchies: one for each leg and the spine. To make them one hierarchy, you need to parent the legs to the root joint.

There are several rigging approaches to the hip/spine relationship. The method you use depends on what the animation requires and how much control you need. For Meeper, you will create a setup that provides natural lower body motion and easy control.

1   Scene file

- Continue with your own scene.

Or

- Open the scene file *14-meeperSkeleton_03.ma*.

2   Add a single joint

- Press y to activate the **Joint Tool**.
- Click on the *Hips* joint to highlight it.
- Hold down **v** to Snap to Point and draw a single joint over the *Hips*.
- Press **Enter** to confirm the joint creation.

If you open the Outliner, you will see that you have just created a single joint, which is a child of the Hips. Both legs will be parented to this new joint.

- Rename the new joint *HipsOverride*.

3   Parent the legs to the override

- Open the Outliner.
- Select the *LeftUpLeg* joint, then hold the **Ctrl** key to select the *RightUpLeg*.
- Hold **Ctrl** again and select the *HipsOverride* joint.
- Select **Edit** → **Parent** or press the **p** key.

Note: The HipsOverride was selected last since it has to be the parent of the two legs. You could have also used the Outliner to parent these joints by **MMB+dragging** the child node onto the intended parent.

4   Test the lower body

- Rotate each leg to see how it reacts.
- Rotate the *Hips* and *HipsOverride* to see how they react.

Note: You will notice that the HipsOverride bone gives you an independent control of the hips rotation.

- When you are finished testing the lower body rotations, select the *Hips* joint, then select **Skeleton** → **Assume Preferred Angle**.

Tip: *You can also select the **Assume Preferred Angle** command by **RMB-clicking** in the viewport when a bone is selected.*

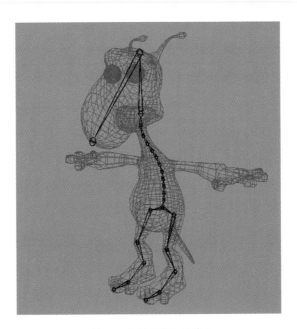

Meeper's skeleton so far

5 Save your work

The arm joints

You will now create Meeper's arms and hands using the character's geometry to aid the joint placement.

In this exercise, you will learn about an arm technique that will set up special skinning characteristics in the forearm area. You will do this by creating a roll joint between the elbow and the wrist. When you later skin Meeper, this extra forearm joint will cause the forearm to twist when the wrist rotates, just like a human arm.

When you create the roll bone, it is important to ensure that the forearm joints are created in a straight line.

1   Scene file

- Continue with your own scene.

Or

- Open the scene file *14-meeperSkeleton_04.ma*.

2   Left arm joints

- Select the **Skeleton** → **Joint Tool**.

- From the *Perspective* view, click on the *last spine* joint to highlight it.

> **Tip:**   *If you don't know which spine joint is the last one, click on any spine joint,*
> *then use the **Up** and **Down** arrows to walk in the hierarchy to find the*
> *appropriate joint.*

- In the *top* view, place one joint at each of the following articulations:
  clavicle, the shoulder, the elbow, the middle of the forearm and the wrist.
  Hold down the **Shift** key as you place the *roll bone* and *wrist* joints to make
  sure they are in a straight line with the elbow.

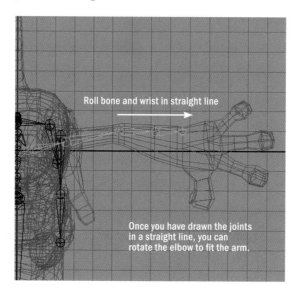

Arm joints

- **Rename** the joints *LeftShoulder, LeftArm, LeftForeArm, LeftForeArmRoll*
  and *LeftHand*.

3   Place the arm joints

- Still from the *top* view, rotate and scale the *LeftForeArm* joints to achieve proper alignment with Meeper's forearm. You can also scale the *LeftForeArmRoll* to reach Meeper's wrist.

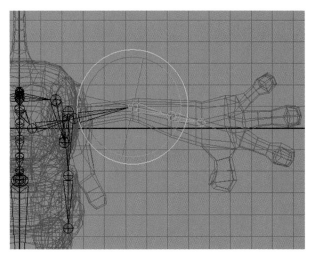

Arm joints aligned in top view

- Select the *LeftShoulder* joint.

- Press the **w** key to enter the **Move Tool**, then press the **Insert** key (**Home** on Mac), to enter the **Move Pivot Tool**.

- From the *front* view, translate the *LeftShoulder* joint down so that it is closer to the center of the chest.

Note: *Since you will be reorienting the joints in the next lesson, it is okay to translate the specified joints.*

- Press the **down** arrow to change the selection to the *LeftArm* joint.

- Press the **Insert** key (**Home** on Mac) again, to toggle back to the **Move Tool**.

- Translate, rotate and scale the *LeftArm* joint up to fit Meeper's arm.

Note: *Make sure to keep the arm joints in a straight line in the front view.*

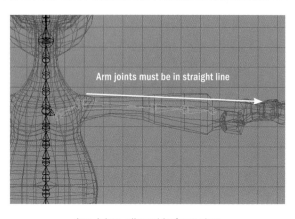

Arm joints aligned in front view

4 Left hand joints

- Select the **Skeleton** → **Joint Tool**.
- Click on the *LeftHand* joint to highlight it.
- In the *top* view, place the following index joints:

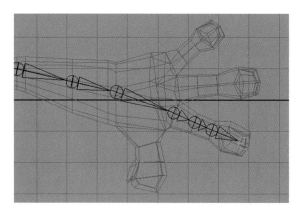

The index joints

- Press the **up** arrow **four** times to put the selection on the *LeftHand* joint.
- Repeat the previous two steps to create the rest of the fingers.

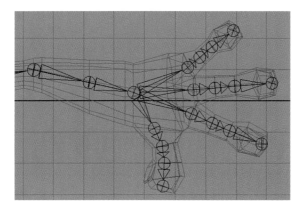

All fingers created

- Press **Enter** to exit the **Joint Tool**.

5 Place the fingers

- Place the fingers in Meeper's geometry by translating and rotating the first joint of each finger. Only rotate the other finger joints.

6 Rename the fingers

- Select the first index joint.

- Select **Edit → Select Hierarchy**.

- Locate the **Field Entry** at the top right of the main interface and change its setting to **Quick Rename**.

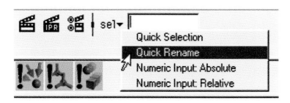

The Field Entry

- Type *LeftHandIndex* in the **Field Entry,** then hit **Enter**.

The selected joints will be renamed as follows:

  LeftHandIndex1, LeftHandIndex2, LeftHandIndex3, LeftHandIndex4.

- Repeat the previous steps to select and rename the middle fingers to *LeftHandMiddle*.

- Repeat the previous steps to select and rename all the ring fingers to *LeftHandRing*.

- Repeat the previous steps to select and rename the thumbs to *LeftHandThumb*.

7 Mirror the arm joints

- Select the *LeftShoulder* joint and mirror it by selecting **Skeleton** → **Mirror Joint** → □.

- In the options, set the following:

  Mirror Across to **YZ**;

  Search For to *Left*;

  Replace With to *Right*.

- Press the **Mirror** button.

Meeper's right arm skeleton is created.

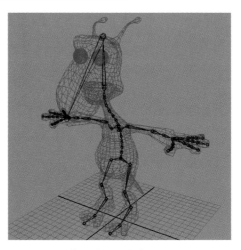

Completed skeleton

Note: *Make sure the right arm is named properly.*

8 Save your work

- The final scene for this lesson is called *14-meeperSkeleton_05.ma*.

Conclusion

This lesson introduced the use of joints for building skeletal structures. Joints are objects specially designed to live in hierarchies and maintain the parent-child relationship. They also contain special attributes to control their orientation, which is important for character animation. These joints, as you will see in the next lesson, can be animated using controls such as inverse kinematics and Set Driven Key.

In the next lesson, you will learn the importance of knowing how joints operate with respect to their orientation, specifically their local rotation orientation.

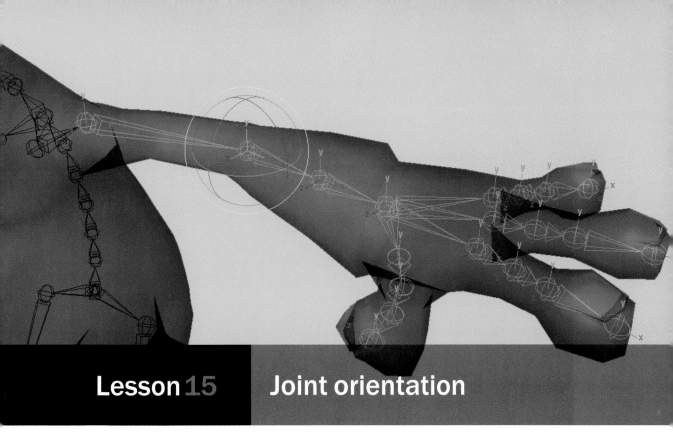

Lesson 15 Joint orientation

In this lesson, you will learn about the local rotation axis and how to tweak axes on the Meeper skeleton from the last lesson. Having the proper local rotation axis for each joint is crucial when setting up and animating a character.

In this lesson you will learn the following:

- What a local rotation axis is;

- How to use Auto Joint Orient;

- How to freeze joint transformations;

- How to reorient a joint local rotation axis;

- When to worry about local rotation axes;

- How to verify and correct a joint's local rotation axis;

- How to mirror and rename at the same time;

- How to set and assume preferred angles;

- How to test joint motions.

Joint orientation

Each joint has a *Local Rotation Axis* that defines how the joint will react to transformations. For most parts of a character, the default orientation is fine. When setting up more complex situations, it is important to make sure that all the joints' axes of rotation are aimed in a consistent manner.

By using *Auto Joint Orient*, you ensure that all local rotation axes of new joints are aligned with the bones that follow. This will help control the joints' transformations when using forward kinematics.

Following are some simple examples that explain the basics of local rotation axes.

1   Open a new scene

2   Orientation turned Off

- Select **Skeleton** → **Joint Tool** → ❑ and set the following:

    Auto Joint Orient to **None**;

    Second Axis World Orientation to **None**.

- In the *front* view, draw joints in an **S** pattern.

You will see that the round joint icons are all aligned like the world axis.

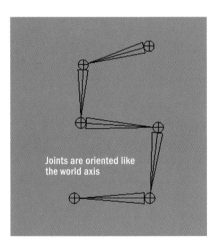

Joint orientation set to none

3 Auto Joint Orient turned On

- Select **Skeleton** → **Joint Tool** → ❐, and set the following:

  Auto Joint Orient to **XYZ**;

  Second Axis World Orientation to **None**.

- In the *front* view, draw joints in an **S** pattern.

The joint icons are all aligned with the first bone that follows. Only the last joint in the chain is aligned with the world axis because there is no child bone to align to.

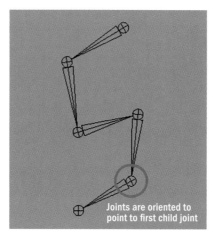

Joint orientation set to XYZ

4 Draw joints with World Axis Orient turned On

- Select **Skeleton** → **Joint Tool** → ❐, and set the options back to default values as follows:

  Auto Joint Orient to **XYZ**;

  Second Axis World Orientation to **+Y**.

- In the *front* view, draw joints in an **S** pattern.

As with the last skeleton, the joint icons are all aligned with the bone that follows them. The only difference is the Y-axis, which has been aligned to the world positive Y-axis. The only way you can see the difference is by either rotating the joints or displaying their local rotation axes.

5   Display the joint axes

- Select the fourth joint in all three of the hierarchies.

- Press **F8** to switch to Component mode.

- Enable the **?** mask button in the Status Line.

This will display the local rotation axes of the selected hierarchies.

The first skeleton has its axes aligned with world space. The second skeleton has its X-axis pointing down the bone. The third skeleton has its X-axis pointing down the bone and it's Y-axis pointing in the world positive Y direction.

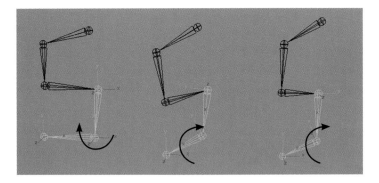

Displayed local rotation axes

> **Note:** *Local rotation axes are aligned according to the right-hand rule. For example, if you select an orientation of XYZ, the positive X-axis points into the joint's bone and towards the joint's first child joint, the Y-axis points at right angles to the X-axis and Z-axis, and the Z-axis points sideways from the joint and its bone.*

6   Rotate joints around the X-axis

- Go back to Object mode, then click on the **Rotate X** channel in the Channel Box to highlight it.

- **MMB+drag** in the view to invoke the virtual slider and change the **Rotate X** value interactively.

The second and third skeletons rotate nicely around the bone while the first skeleton is rotating in world space with no relation to the bone at all.

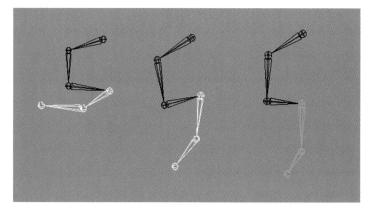

Joints rotated around their local X-axes

- Press the **z** key to **undo** the rotations.

Joint edits and joint orientation

In the last lesson, you repositioned joints using several techniques, such as translating, rotating and scaling joint pivot. Some of these techniques can offset the local rotation axis from its child bone, which could be problematic when animating. Following is a review of the four techniques and their effect on the local rotation axis:

Rotating joints

When rotating a joint, its local rotation axis is not affected, but the bone's rotation values change. Attempting to keep zero rotation values makes it easy to reset joints' rotations. This issue can be resolved by freezing transformations on the joints.

Rotating joints

Scaling joints

From all the techniques described here, scaling a bone is the most unobjectionable, but will alter the default scaling values which could be avoided. This issue can also be resolved by freezing transformations.

Scaling joints

Translating joints

When translating a joint, the parent joint's local rotation axis will offset from pointing to its child bone and can create inappropriate rotations when animating. This issue can be resolved either by manually tweaking or automatically reorienting the local rotation axis.

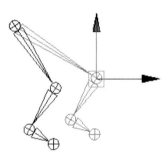

Translating joints

Translating joint pivots

When translating a joint pivot, both the parent and the translated joints' local rotation axes will offset from pointing to its child bone and can create inappropriate rotations when animating. This issue can be resolved either by manually tweaking or automatically reorienting the local rotation axis.

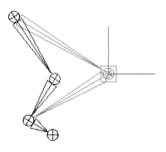

Translating joint pivots

Reorient local rotation axes

When you use the Joint Tool with Auto Joint Orient set to XYZ, the tool forces the X-axis to point down to the bone toward the first child joint. If the joints' placements are adjusted, you might need to also adjust their local rotation axes so they will correctly point down the bone. One solution is to simply reorient the joints, as if they were just drawn.

1   Translating joints

- Select and translate the joints of the second S-shaped skeleton created earlier to create a clear offset on their local rotation axes.

- Select the *root* joint, then select **Skeleton → Orient Joint → ❑.**

- Set the options as follows:

    Orientation to **XYZ;**

    Second Axis World Orientation to **+Y;**

    Orient Child Joints to **On;**

- Click the **Orient** button.

    Notice that all joints of the selected hierarchy now have proper default rotation axes.

Note: *If you notice that some joints are not properly aligned, you might have to fix the flipped local rotation axis manually. You will learn how to do this in the next exercise.*

It is important to note what happens in the Attribute Editor when the joint orientation is changed:

Rotation doesn't change.

Joint Orient changes so that the **Rotate** attributes don't have to change.

Editing local rotation axes

In addition to making sure that one axis always points down the bone, you also want to make sure that the other axes relate to the skeleton in the same way.

1   Selecting local rotation axis component

- Select the root joint of the last S-shaped skeleton created earlier.

- Press **F8** to switch to Component mode, and make sure the **?** selection mask button is enabled.

All the local rotation axes of the selected joints are displayed. Notice the orientation in which the Z-axes are pointing. Some are pointing in one direction while others are pointing in the opposite direction.

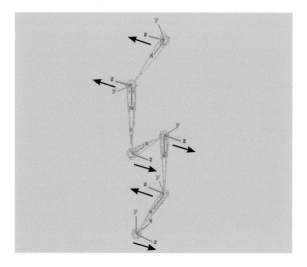

Joints rotated around X-axis.

2   The problem

- Go back to Object mode.

- With the root joint still selected, choose **Edit → Select Hierarchy**.

- Rotate the bones on their **Z-axis**.

Notice how the bones rotate unexpectedly since they are not all rotating in the same direction. This is the problem you want to fix.

- Undo the rotations.

3   Rotate the joint axes interactively

- Go back to Component mode.

- Select one of the local rotation axes pointing in the opposite direction to the root.

- Rotate the axis by about **180 degrees** on its **X-axis**.

Tip: *Make sure the* **Rotate Tool** *option is set to* **Local.** *When dragging an axis, an indicator in the middle of the* **Rotate Tool** *will show the rotation angle.*

4   Rotating the joint axes using a script

You can also rotate the axes more accurately by entering a simple MEL script in the Command Line. Because the joints were created with **Auto Orient** set to **XYZ**, if an axis is flipped, it needs to be rotated by **180 degrees** on the **X-axis**.

- Select the remaining local rotation axis pointing in the opposite direction to the root.

- In the Command Line, enter the following command:

```
rotate -r -os 180 0 0
```

Note: *Don't worry about the last joint. Its local axis is not oriented towards anything and does not affect how the skeleton works.*

Note: *The* **Second Axis World Orientation** *option available when creating or reorienting joints will eliminate the need to worry about flipped secondary axes in most cases.*

Freeze joint transformations

When you use the Rotate Tool or Scale Tool to alter the placement of a joint, it is good to reset the rotation and scale attributes to their default values at the rigging stage. This will allow the skeleton to be quickly reset into its default position.

1   Freezing joints

- Select, rotate and scale the joints of the last S-shaped skeleton created earlier to change their values in the Channel Box.

- Select **Modify → Freeze Transformations**.

Notice the altered rotation and scale values in the Channel Box are reset back to their default values with the joint chain still in the current position.

Lesson 15

Note: *The translation values of joints cannot be reset to their default values or else they would be moved at their parent position. Another way of resetting joints is to recreate a complete skeleton, using Snap to Point.*

When to worry about local rotation axes

To determine the proper axis for your joints, you need to understand what you are going to do with the joints. The following options explore some of the possibilities discussed throughout the rest of the book. You may want to return to this list when you are more familiar with the options available.

Forward kinematics (FK)

For FK, it is important for joints to be able to rotate correctly, local to their direction. How a joint rotates is directly linked to the orientation of its local rotation axis. This is very apparent when animating fingers and you will be looking at this in more detail later in this lesson.

Expressions and Set Driven Keys

If an expression is created to rotate multiple joints simultaneously around a specific axis, you want the joints to rotate in a consistent direction. If one of the axes is flipped, the task of writing an expression is much more difficult.

Inverse kinematics (IK)

The differences are not as apparent when an IK goes through the joints. In many cases, joints will only need to rotate around the proper axis, and having the local rotation axis set before adding IK will help, especially when you intend to allow blending between IK and FK.

Constraints

With constraints, any rotation results will depend on whether the objects involved in the constraint have similar orientation.

Correcting Meeper's skeleton

Next, you will correct Meeper's local rotation axes. With all the joint orientations set correctly, you will not have to worry about them anymore.

1   Open an existing scene file

- Open the scene file from the last lesson called *14-meeperSkeleton_05.ma.*

2   Delete right side joints

At this time, you need to bother only with one half of Meeper's skeleton. There is no need to correct all of the left arm and then all of the right arm. The Mirror Joint command will take care of this for you.

- Select the *RightShoulder* and the *RightUpLeg* joints.

- Press **Delete** on your keyboard.

3   Reset the skeleton

Since you used several techniques in the last lesson to place your joints in Meeper's geometry, it is a good idea to reorient all the local rotation axes of each joint.

- Select the *Hips,* then select **Skeleton → Orient Joints**.

Doing so will reorient all the local rotation axes to XYZ.

- Select the *Hips,* then select **Modify → Freeze Transformations**.

This will reset any non-default values on the joints.

4   Display the local rotation axes

- Select the *Hips* joint, then press **F8** to switch to Component mode.

- Make sure the **?** selection mask button is enabled.

5   Verify the joint alignment

When looking at Meeper from the front, all the vertical joints, such as the pelvis, spine, head and leg, should have their Z-axes pointing to the same side. All horizontal joints, such as the arm and hand, should have their Y-axes pointing to the same side.

- Locate, select and rotate the problematic local rotation axes around their **X-axis**.

Tip: *The Hips and HipsOverride local rotation axes should be oriented like the world axis. This will greatly simplify the animation tasks on the pelvis.*

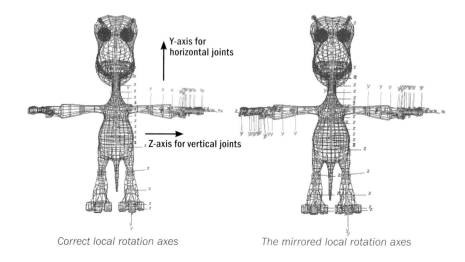

Y-axis for
horizontal joints

Z-axis for vertical joints

Correct local rotation axes   *The mirrored local rotation axes*

6   Mirror the joints

- Go back to Object mode.

- Select the *LeftShoulder* joint.

- Select **Skeleton** → **Mirror Joints** → ❏.

- In the options window, set **Search For:** to *Left* and **Replace With:** to *Right*.

Doing so will automatically rename the joints correctly.

- Click **Apply** to leave the option window open.

- Select the *LeftUpLeg* joint.

- Select **Skeleton** → **Mirror Joints**.

Note: *If you look at the mirrored joints local rotation axes, you will notice that their X-axes and Y-axes are pointing in opposite directions. This is the desired effect and will make animation tasks easier.*

7   Set the preferred angle

- Select the *Hips* joint.

- Select **Skeleton → Set Preferred Angle**.

The skeleton's current pose will be kept in memory as the preferred angle and can be recalled at any time using the **Assume Preferred Angle** *command.*

8   Test rotations

Take some time to test orientation by selecting multiple joints simultaneously. For instance, select the shoulders on both arms and notice the effect of the mirrored local rotation axis. When you are done, select the *Hips* joint, then **RMB-click** and select **Assume Preferred Angle**.

9   Save your work

- The final scene is called *15-meeperOrientation_01.ma*.

Conclusion

Creating joints, orienting them appropriately and naming them correctly is the trademark of a good rigger. Understanding why Maya assigns orientation based on child joint orientation can help predict where a *flip* of local rotation orientation may occur.

There are many tricks to setting up joints quickly including snapping, parenting, and duplicating. Riggers can usually speed up repetitive tasks by using MEL macros, commands and scripts.

In the next lesson, you will learn about the basics of inverse kinematics.

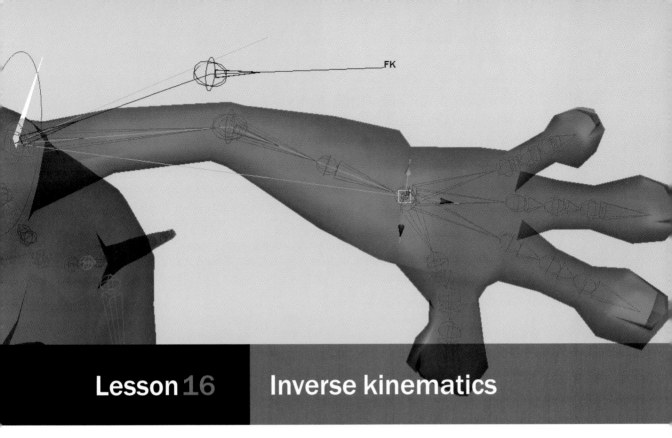

Lesson 16   Inverse kinematics

In this lesson, you will learn about inverse kinematics (IK). You will see that IK can provide control over a joint chain that would be very difficult to achieve using forward kinematics (FK).

In this lesson you will learn the following:

- The difference between IK and FK;

- The different IK solvers found in Maya;

- How to set up single chain IK solvers;

- How to set up rotate plane IK solvers;

- How to use the preferred angle;

- How to change the IK stickiness and priority;

- Important IK attributes;

- How to use the pole vector and twist attributes;

- How to animate IK handles and joints;

- How to use IK/FK blending.

Forward vs. inverse kinematics

In the last lesson, you used *forward kinematics* (FK) by rotating joints manually. While FK is very powerful, it has some limitations when it comes to animating a complex setup such as a character. Since all of the animation is accomplished using the rotation of joints, if you rotate a parent joint in the hierarchy, all of its children also get moved. For instance, if you were to rotate a character's foot so that it plants on the ground, any movement in the pelvis area would move the foot out of place.

Inverse kinematics (IK) solves this problem by controlling a series of joints using an IK handle. Moving either the handle or a parent joint evokes the IK solver, which calculates the appropriate joint rotations to achieve the desired pose.

Maya contains three main IK solvers:

Single chain IK solver

This solver provides IK in its simplest form. By moving the IK handle, the chain will update so that the joints lie along a plane relative to the IK handle's rotation. The single chain IK solver will be used with Meeper's reverse foot setup.

Rotate plane IK solver

This solver gives you more control and is the most commonly used IK solver. You can use the IK handle so that the joints lie along a plane and then you can rotate the plane using a twist attribute or by moving a pole vector handle. The rotate plane IK solver will be used to rig Meeper's arms and legs.

Spline IK solver

This solver lets you control the joint rotations using a spline curve. You can either move the chain along the curve or update the shape of the curve using its CVs. The spline IK solver will be used to control Meeper's spine.

Forward kinematics example

The following example shows a simple leg being controlled by FK:

1   Create the leg joints

- In the *side* view panel, draw **three** joints representing a leg.

- In front of the leg, place two cubes as follows:

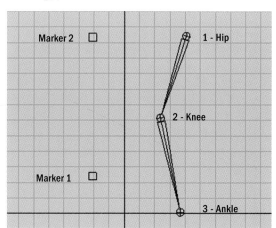

Leg joints and positioning markers

These will help you visualize what is happening as you work with the joints.

2 Rotate the joints

- Rotate the *hip* and *knee* joints so that the *ankle* joint is positioned at *marker1*.

With FK, you must rotate the joints into place to position the ankle.

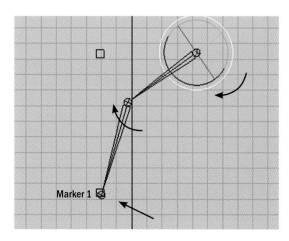

Positioned leg

3 Move the hip joint

- Move the *hip* joint forward to place it on *marker2*.

You will see how the knee and ankle joints also move. Now the ankle joint is no longer on the first marker. You would have to rotate the joints back to return the ankle into its previous position.

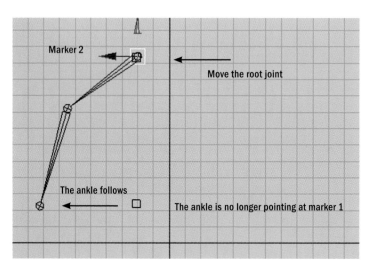

Moving the hip joint

Inverse kinematics example

The following example shows a simple leg being controlled by IK:

1 Single Chain IK handle

- Undo the previous moves to get back to the original leg position.

- Select **Skeleton** → **IK Handle Tool** → ◻.

- In the option window, set the following:

  Current Solver to **ikSCsolver**;

  Sticky to **On**.

Note: *The **Sticky** option will be explained later in this lesson.*

- Press the **Close** button.

- Click on the *hip* joint to establish the root of the solver.

- Click on the *ankle* joint to place the IK handle.

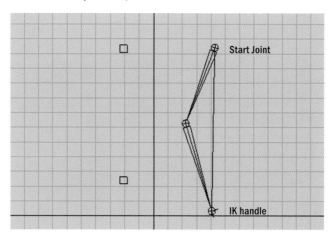

The IK handle

2   Move the IK handle

- Move the IK handle so that it's placed on *marker1*.

Notice how the knee and hip joints rotate to achieve the proper pose.

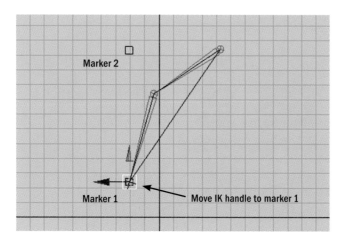

Moved IK handle

3   Move the hip

- Select the *hip* joint.

- Translate the *hip* joint to place it on *marker2*.

The IK handle keeps the ankle joint on the first marker as you move the hip joint forward. The ankle will pull away from the IK handle if you pull the hip too far.

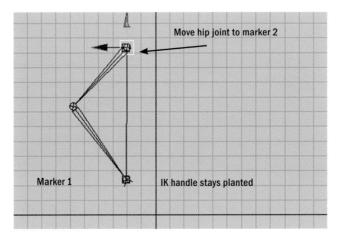

Moved hip joint

Preferred angle

The IK solver will use a joint's preferred angle to establish the direction a joint should bend. It can be thought of as a default bend direction. For example, if you create a straight up and down leg joint, run IK through that joint and try to manipulate it, the solver will not be able to bend the joint. By setting the preferred angle, the solver has a guideline to follow.

1   Create straight leg joints

- In a new scene, draw three joints in a straight line, holding down **x** to Snap to Grid.

2   Add a Single Chain IK handle

- Select **Skeleton → IK Handle Tool**.

- Select the *hip* joint as the root and then the *ankle* joint to place the IK handle.

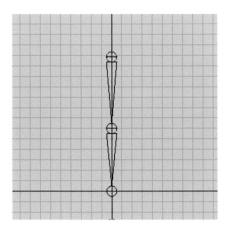

New leg joints

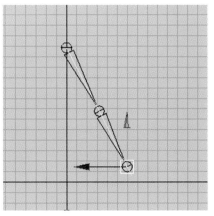

Moved IK handle

3   Move the IK handle

- Move the IK handle to affect the chain.

Notice the knee does not bend. This is because there is no bend in the bones on either side of the knee. Therefore, the solver is not able to figure out which direction to bend.

4   Undo

- Undo the last move on the IK handle to return the chain to its original position.

- Delete the IK handle.

5   Set the preferred angle

- Select the *knee* joint.

- Rotate the *knee* to bend the leg.

- With the *knee* still selected, select **Skeleton** → **Set Preferred Angle** → ❐.

- In the option window, turn **Selected Joint** to **On**.

- Press the **Set** button.

- Rotate the *knee* joint back to **0**.

Lesson 16

6 Add another IK handle

- Press the **y** key or select **Skeleton** → **IK Handle Tool.**

- Select the *hip* joint as the root and then the *ankle* joint to place the IK handle.

7 Move the IK handle

- Move the IK handle to affect the chain.

Now the knee should be bending since the preferred angle tells the solver in which direction to bend.

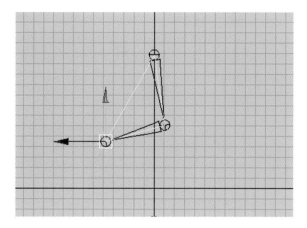

Moved IK handle

Stickiness

In the previous examples, you turned on IK's stickiness in order to plant the IK handle in one place. Without this, an IK handle will move when you move the root joint of a chain and this might not be what you expect. For instance, with stickiness on, a foot will stay planted on the ground and not move if you move the character's hips. The foot would move if stickiness was set to off.

Note: *As soon as a keyframe is set on the IK handle, the IK's behavior will change, just like if stickiness is turned on.*

1   Turning on or off stickiness after its creation

- Select the IK handle.

- Open the Attribute Editor.

- Under **IK Handle Attributes**, set **Stickiness** to **Sticky**.

IK priority

IK priority is the order in which IK solvers are evaluated. A solver with a priority of **1** is evaluated before a solver with a priority of **10**. This is important to keep in mind as you build up the controls for a character. For instance, an IK solver in the hand or fingers should be evaluated after the IK solver in the arm. The joints in the finger are lower in the skeleton hierarchy as they depend on the joints in the arm for their placement.

Note: *If it seems that an IK chain is not updating properly in the interactive display or you notice differences between your interactive and final renderings, you should check the IK priority of the solvers.*

1   Changing an IK handle's priority on creation

- Select **Skeleton** → **IK Handle Tool** → □.

- In the option window, set the **Priority** option to the desired value.

2   Changing an IK handle's priority

- Select an IK handle.

- Open the Attribute Editor.

- Open the **IK Handle Attributes** section and set the **Priority** attribute to the desired value.

Tip: *You can change multiple IK handles' priority by selecting the IK handles and typing the following MEL command:* `ikHandle -edit -autoPriority;`

The **autoPriority** *flag will automatically prioritize the selected IK handles based on their position in the hierarchy.*

Rotate plane IK solver

So far, you have only used the single chain IK solver. This type of IK lets you easily control the bending of a joint chain, but it doesn't give you good control over the orientation of the chain. For instance, if you set up a Single Chain IK on a character's knees, you could not easily spread the knees outward.

The rotate plane IK solver enables you to specify the orientation of the joint chain, using a *twist* attribute or *pole vector* attributes. These attributes will define the rotate plane vector, which runs between the start joint and the end effector. The rotate plane acts as the goal for all joint rotations. By default, the IK handle will manipulate the joint chain so that it follows the default rotate plane. You can then rotate the plane by either editing a twist attribute or by moving a pole vector handle.

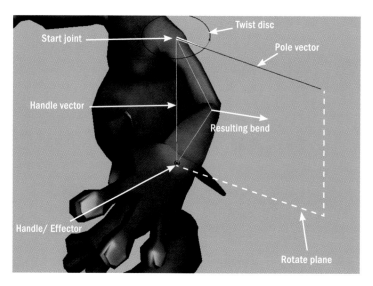

Diagram of rotate plane IK

The following example shows an arm being controlled by the rotate plane IK solver:

1 Create arm joints

- In a new scene, draw three joints as shown here:

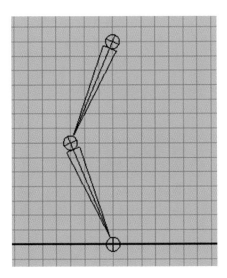 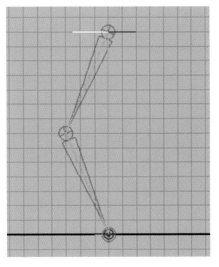

New joints   *Rotate plane IK handle*

2 Add a rotate plane IK handle

- Select **Skeleton** → **IK Handle Tool** → ❑.

- In the option window, set the **Current Solver** to **ikRPsolver**.

- Click on the *shoulder* joint to set the start joint of the IK handle.

- Click on the *wrist* joint to place the IK handle.

3 Move the IK handle

- Move the IK handle.

The IK handle appears to be working in a similar manner to the single chain IK solver. Basic IK handle manipulation is the same for both solvers.

Lesson 16

4   Control the handle's pole vector

- Select the **Show Manipulator Tool**.

A series of manipulators appears to let you control the IK handle's pole vector and twist attributes.

- In the *Perspective* view, **click+drag** on the pole vector's handle to rotate the IK solver's plane.

This lets you control the joint chain orientation solution.

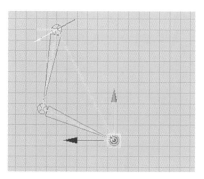

Moving the IK handle

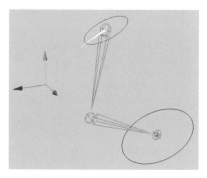

5   Manipulate the twist disc

- With the **Show Manipulator Tool** still enabled, **click+drag** the twist disc to alter the IK solution away from the rotate plane.

The twist attribute can be considered an offset from the plane defined by the pole vector.

Pole vector manipulator

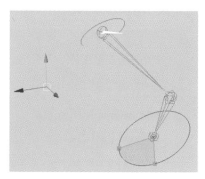

IK handle's twist attribute modified

Pole vectors

Sometimes when manipulating IK handles, the solver can flip the joint solution by 180 degrees. Flipping occurs when the end effector is moved past the plane's pole vector axis. To solve a flip issue, you need to move the pole vector handle out of the way. You may need to set keys on the pole vector handle in order to control flipping during a motion.

To give you easy access to the pole vector, you can constrain it to an object. By doing so, you don't have to use the Show Manipulator Tool in order to edit the pole vector location. You will be using pole vector constraints in the next two lessons.

IK/FK blending

While IK animation of a skeleton chain is an excellent way to control goal-oriented actions like a foot planting on the ground or a hand picking something up, simple actions like an arm swinging as a character walks are typically easier to accomplish with FK animation. For this reason, IK/FK blending makes it easy to seamlessly switch between IK and FK control of a skeleton chain.

In this exercise, you will animate a skeleton chain using IK, switch to FK animation for a few poses, then switch back to IK animation.

1   Open the scene file

- Open the scene file *16-IkFkBlending.ma*.

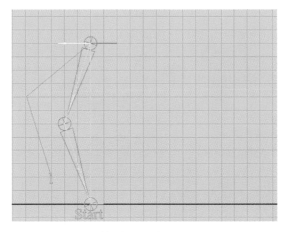

16-IkFkBlending.ma

2   Turn On Ik Fk Control attribute

- Select the IK handle and open its Attribute Editor.

- In the **IK Solver Attributes** section of the ikHandle1 tab, turn **On** the **Ik Fk Control** attribute.

This attribute tells the solver that you want to use the Ik/Fk blending functionality.

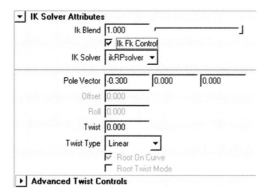

Ik Fk Control attribute turned On

3   Animate the IK

- Make sure that you're at frame **1** on the **Time Slider**.

- Select the IK handle and **keyframe** it by hitting the **s** key.

- Advance to frame **10**.

- Move the IK handle to the first marked position.

- Set a **keyframe**.

- Advance to frame **20**.

- Move the IK handle to the second marked position and set a keyframe.

- Advance to frame **30**.

- Move the IK handle to the third marked position and set a keyframe.

Note: *When switching between IK and FK, the affected joints change to orange in IK and green in FK when nothing is selected. If the IK handle is selected, you will see three distinct joint chains, one for the IK, one for the FK, and another one for the result of the blending.*

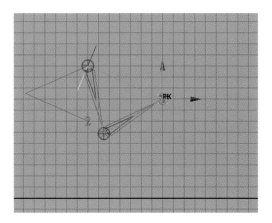

Current position of IK handle

4   Switch from IK to FK

You will now switch from IK to FK control of the arm between frames **30** and **40**.

Note: *When blending from IK to FK animation, you must set keys for both the skeleton joints and the IK handle during the transition period.*

- Make sure that you are still at frame **30**.
- Select the shoulder and elbow joints in the arm and keyframe them.

Note: *Setting keys for the joints at the same frame that you stopped using IK is necessary to define the transition range for the blend from IK to FK.*

- Advance to frame **40**.
- Select the IK handle again.
- Find the **Ik Blend** attribute in the **Channel Box**.
- Set its value to **0**.
- Set a keyframe for the IK handle.

By keying the IK Blend value at 0 at frame 40, you are specifying that you want to control the arm using FK at that frame.

5   Animate the arm using FK

- While still at frame **40**, pose the arm in the fourth marked position by rotating the joints.

- Set a keyframe for both the *shoulder* and *elbow* joints.

- Advance to frame **50**.

- Pose the arm in the fifth marked position by rotating the joints.

- Keyframe both joints again.

- Advance to frame **60**.

- Pose the arm in the sixth marked position by rotating the joints.

- Keyframe both joints again.

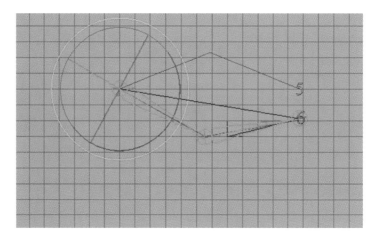

Joints rotated to position

6   Switch back from FK to IK

Now that you are finished animating the arm using FK animation, you will switch back to IK control.

- Select the IK handle.

> **Note:** The IK handle should still be where you left it at frame **30** when you changed its IK Blend value to **0**.

- Set another keyframe for the IK handle at frame **60**. This is the last frame you set keys directly on the joint rotations.

- Advance to frame **70**.

- Set the IK handle's **Ik Blend** value back to **1**.

The arm is now controllable with the IK handle.

- Move the IK handle to the seventh marked position and set a keyframe for it.

- Advance to frame **80**.

- Move the IK handle back to the original start position and set a keyframe.

- Play the animation.

The skeleton chain should achieve each position, animating seamlessly between IK and FK as it goes.

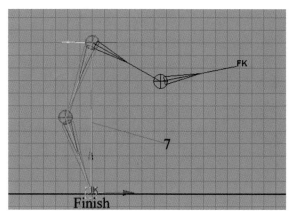

IK handle moved back to its first position

Note: Maya will display the position of the FK joints so you know where they are when you want to blend back to FK.

IK/FK blending in the Graph Editor

When you switch between IK and FK and vice versa, the Graph Editor can display the animation curves of an IK handle and its joints partly as solid lines and partly as dotted lines.

That allows you to see the animation curve of an IK handle as a solid line when IK is *on* and as a dotted line when IK is *off*. In other words, the solid lines show where the joint chain gets its animation from.

This functionality of the Graph Editor is enabled only when you use the **Set IK/FK Key** command.

1 Select the IK handle

- Select the IK handle and go to frame **30**.

2 Open the Graph Editor

- Display the IK handle's animation curves by selecting **Window** → **Animation Editors** → **Graph Editor**.

- Select **View** → **Frame All** or press the **a** hotkey.

Notice the curves appear normal.

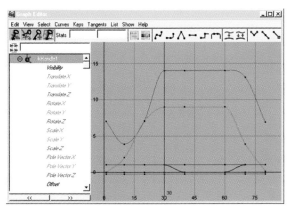

IK handle's normal animation curves

3 Set IK/FK Key

- Still with the IK handle selected, select **Animate** → **IK/FK Keys** → **Set IK/FK Key**.

The Graph Editor now displays the curves with dotted lines where the IK handle does not control the joint chain.

Project Four

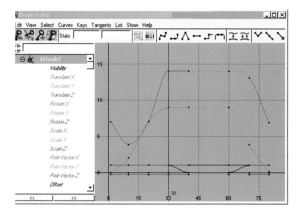

IK handle's dotted animation curves

The **Set IK/FK Key** menu item sets keys on all the current IK handle's keyable attributes and all the joints in its IK chain. When you use Set IK/FK Key, Maya performs additional operations to ensure a smooth transition between IK and FK.

When you want to key IK and FK animation on the same joint chain, you can use this menu item instead of setting a traditional keyframe. It is recommended that you use Set IK/FK Key when animating a joint chain with both forward and inverse kinematics.

Note: Keys that are bordered by a solid curve on one side and a dotted curve on the other should be edited with caution, since adjustments will likely cause the skeleton chain to pop as the IK and FK may no longer match.

Conclusion

In this lesson, you learned about both the single chain and rotate plane IK solvers. The rotate plane solver is well suited for working situations where more control is needed, like for arms and legs, and it is a superset of the single chain solver. The rotate plane solver contains attributes that add a further level of control for the animator, and help prevent inappropriate solutions such as those that result in flipping or illogical rotations.

IK animation of joint hierarchies requires understanding of the different types of IK solvers available in Maya and their benefits and limitations. Some animators will prefer to use FK for some situations and IK for others.

In the next lesson, you will implement IKs on Meeper's lower body.

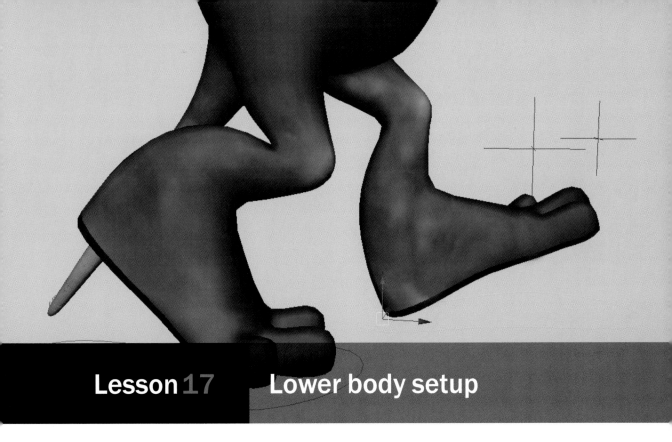

Lesson 17   Lower body setup

In this lesson, you will set up
Meeper's lower body. You will
start by creating IKs, which
will then be parented into a
separate skeleton chain used
for manipulating the foot. You
will also create pole vectors
to offer more control over the
leg placement. The goal of this
setup is to create a simple
control mechanism for driving
the action of the legs and feet.

In this lesson you will learn the following:

- How to set up IK on Meeper's legs;

- How to build a reverse foot setup;

- How to parent IK handles in a hierarchy;

- How to drive the reverse foot setup with
  a manipulator;

- How to add attributes and set limits;

- How to add pole vectors.

Adding IK to Meeper's legs

The first thing to know when creating an IK chain is that you should never create a single IK handle on joints you intend to animate on their own. The joints in an IK chain should always be moving all together, unless using IK/FK blending. For instance, if you have a single IK chain starting from the hip going down to the toes, the IK will prevent you from animating the ankle and toes.

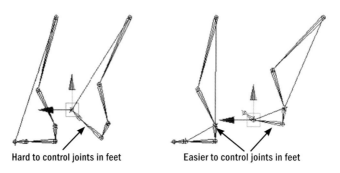

Hard to control joints in feet   Easier to control joints in feet

Different IK chains

In this lesson, you will create a more complex setup using several IK chains to control the different parts of the leg. One chain will work from the hip to the ankle and two more will define Meeper's foot. The three IK handles will be part of a more complex hierarchy, which will allow you to achieve a nice heel-to-toe motion.

Create the IK handles

You will now set up Meeper's controls using one rotate plane IK solver for the leg and two single chain IK solvers for the foot.

1 Open the scene

- Open the scene file *15-meeperOrientation_01.ma*.

2 Hide Meeper's right leg

In order to not confuse the left and right leg, you will temporarily hide the right leg.

- Select the *RightUpLeg* joint.

- Select **Display → Hide → Hide Selection** or press the **Ctrl+h** hotkey.

3 Set up a RotatePlane IK

- Select **Skeleton** → **IK Handle Tool** → ❐.

- In the option window, set **Current Solver** to **ikRPsolver**.

- Select the *LeftUpLeg* to establish the start joint of the IK chain and then the *LeftFoot* to establish the end effector of the IK chain.

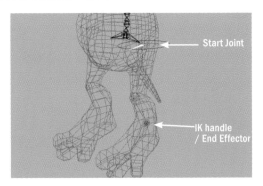

IK added to the leg

- Rename the IK handle to *leftLegIK*.

4 Set up single chain IKs

- Select **Skeleton** → **IK Handle Tool** → ❐.

- In the option window, set **Current Solver** to **ikSCsolver**.

- Click on the *LeftFoot* joint and the *LeftToeBase* joint to create your next IK chain.

- Create the last IK chain starting from the *LeftToeBase* joint to the *LeftToeEnd* joint.

- Rename the IK handles to *leftAnkleIK* and *leftToeIK*.

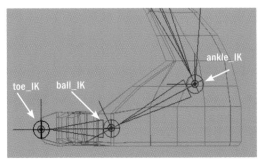

Foot IK handles

Create the reverse foot

You will now create the skeleton chain that will control the IK handles. The reverse foot skeleton will allow you to use simple joint rotations to control the character's foot. Just like any other joint, it is important to set their local orientations properly.

1   Draw the joints

- Select **Skeleton** → **Joint Tool** → ❑, and set **Orientation** to **XYZ**.

- From the *side* view, hold down the **v** key to **Snap to Point**, then **click+drag** the first joint in order to snap it to the existing LeftToesBase joint.

- **MMB-click** to show the **Move Tool** without exiting the Joint Tool.

- **MMB-drag** the newly created joint at the base of Meeper's heel.

> **Note:** *The reason you used the Snap to Point and **MMB-dragging** is that it created the new joint in line with the foot joints, rather than snapping the joint on the world grid.*

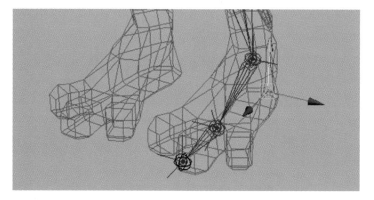

The new joint is aligned with the ankle

- Still in the *side* view, hold down **Shift** to place another joint in a straight line on the tip of the toe geometry.

- Using **Snap to Point**, place **two** new joints, one on the *LeftToeBase* and one on the *LeftAnkle*.

- Rename the reverse joints as follows:

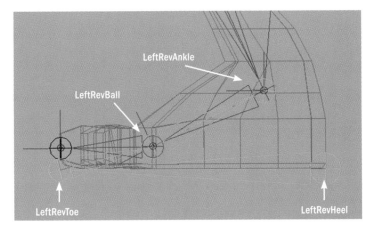

The reverse joints

Note: *The joint LeftRevToe could be snapped onto the LeftToeEnd joint, but having it placed at the very tip of the sole will give proper toe rotation.*

2 Check the local rotation axes

- Select the *LeftRevHeel*, then press **F8** to switch to Component mode and enable the **?** selection mask button.

- Make sure to align all **Z-axes** on the local rotation axes in the same direction.

3 Parent the IK handles

You will now parent each IK handle to its respective joint in the inverse foot. Doing so will allow you to control the IK handles' position by rotating the reverse foot joints.

- Through the Outliner, select an IK handle and **Ctrl-select** the correspondent joint in the inverse foot, then press the **p** hotkey to parent them.

- The final hierarchy should look like this in the Outliner:

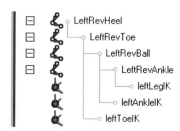

The appropriate hierarchy

- Test the rotation of the different reverse joints to see their effect on the leg IKs.

4   Save your work

Create a manipulator

One of your goals in setting up Meeper is to create a system of puppet-like controls that will be easy to identify and select, and provide logical centralized controls for all aspects of Meeper's behavior.

While the reverse joint chain could be used as the main foot object for Meeper's left leg, in order to keep the selection process consistent, and ultimately easier, the reverse foot will be parented to an easy-to-select curve.

1   Scene file

- Continue with your own scene.

Or

- Open the scene file *17-meeperLegSetup_01.ma*.

2   Create a manipulator for Meeper's foot

- Select **Create** → **NURBS Primitive** → **Circle**.

- Rename it *leftFootManip*.

- **RMB-click** on the curve and select **Control Vertex**.

- Move the CVs to match the following illustration:

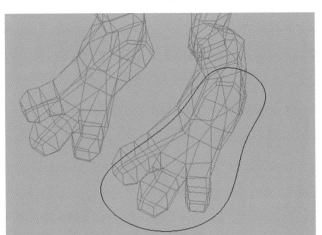

Left foot manipulator

3 Move the pivot to the invMain joint

- Back in Object mode, select the *leftFootManip*.

- Press **w** to invoke the **Move Tool**, then press **Insert** on your keyboard.

The manipulator will change to the **Move Pivot Tool***.*

- Press the **v** key to **Snap to Point**, then **MMB-drag** the pivot on the
  LeftRevHeel joint.

The pivot will snap to the LeftRevHeel joint.

- Press the **Insert** key again to switch back to the **Move Tool**.

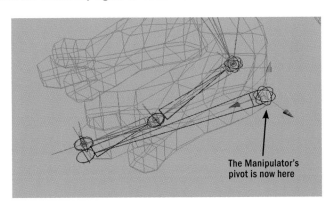

The Manipulator's
pivot is now here

Manipulator's new pivot position

Lesson 17

4   Freeze the transformations

Now that *leftFootManip* is well placed, it's a good idea to freeze its transformations, which will make it easy for an animator to reset its position.

▪ Select *leftFootManip,* then select **Modify** → **Freeze Transformations**.

5   Parent the reverse chain to the manipulator

▪ Select the *LeftRevHeel* joint, then **Shift-select** the *leftFootManip*, and press **p** to parent them.

Adding custom attributes

For the *leftFootManip* to be an effective control object, it should provide control for all aspects of Meeper's foot and leg. To this end, you will now add a series of custom attributes to the *leftFootManip* object.

1   Add a custom attribute

▪ Select the *leftFootManip* node.

▪ Select **Modify** → **Add Attribute...**

▪ In the **Add Attribute** window, set the following:

    Attribute Name to **heelRotX;**

    Data Type to **Float**.

▪ Click **Add**.

A new attribute appears in the Channel Box called Heel Rot X. At this time, the attribute is not connected to anything, but you will use the Connection Editor later on to make it functional.

Note: *Minimum and maximum values could be added at this time, but since you don't know what your minimum and maximum values will be, attribute limits will be set later.*

> **Note:** *The Channel Box can show attributes in three different ways: Nice, Long and Short. If the attribute translateX was displayed in the Nice setting, it would look like Translate X. In the Long setting, it would look like translateX and the Short setting would display it as tx. You can change these settings within the Channel Box by selecting* **Channels** → **Channel Names**.

2   Add additional attributes

As long as the **Add** button is pressed in the **Add Attribute** window, the window will remain open. Pressing the **OK** button will add an attribute and close the window.

- Add the following attributes to the *leftFootManip*:

  > *heelRotY*;
  >
  > *heelRotZ*;
  >
  > *ballRot*;
  >
  > *toeRotX*;
  >
  > *toeRotY*;
  >
  > *toeRotZ*.

3   Lock and hide channels

Now that you have added a series of custom attributes to the manipulator, it's a good idea to lock, and make non-keyable, any attributes that should not be used by the animator.

- Select *leftFootManip*.

- In the Channel Box, highlight the **Scale X, Y, Z** and **Visibility** attributes.

- **RMB-click** in the Channel Box and select **Lock and Hide Selected** from the contextual menu.

These attributes are now locked and therefore can't be changed accidentally. They have also been made non-keyable, which removes them from the Channel Box.

> **Note:** *In general, you should lock and make non-keyable all attributes on your control object that you don't want the animator to be changing. This will simplify the animator's work and also make character sets creation much easier.*

Connecting custom attributes

Now that you have defined a custom manipulator with attributes, it is time to connect those attributes to their corresponding channels on Meeper's foot.

1   Connect the first attribute

- Open the Connection Editor by selecting **Window** → **General Editors** → **Connection Editor**.

- Select *leftFootManip* and click the **Reload Left** button, then select the *LeftRevHeel* joint and click the **Reload Right** button.

- In the left column, select the *Heel Rot X* attribute and in the right column, open the **Rotate** section and select the *Rotate X* attribute.

The two attributes are now connected with a direct relationship. Changing the value of leftFootManip Heel Rot X will also change the value of LeftRevHeel Rotate X.

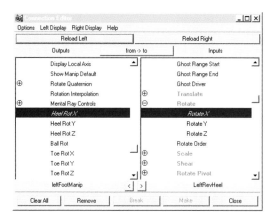

Heel Rot X connected to Rotate X

2 Connect the rest of the custom attributes

Use the Connection Editor to connect the rest of the custom attributes:

> *Heel Rot Y* to *leftRevHeel Rotate Y*;
>
> *Heel Rot Z* to *leftRevHeel Rotate Z*;
>
> *Ball Rot* to *leftRevBall Rotate Z*;
>
> *Toe Rot X* to *leftRevToe Rotate X*;
>
> *Toe Rot Y* to *leftRevToe Rotate Y*;
>
> *Toe Rot Z* to *leftRevToe Rotate Z*.

3 Test the connections

At this point, it is a good idea to make sure that the connections are made properly, and the foot is behaving the way you expect.

- Select *leftFootManip* and try translating and rotating it to test the basic leg motion.

- Undo the last transformations, or simply enter values of **0** for all of *leftFootManip*'s attributes.

- Test each of the custom attributes in the Channel Box by highlighting them, then **MMB-dragging** in the viewport to invoke the virtual slider.

You should notice that some of them behave properly within a certain range of values, but cause unwanted actions outside of that range.

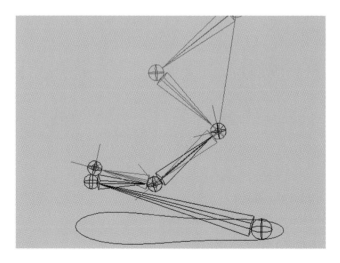

Testing the foot's behavior

Adding limits

In order to control the internal actions of the foot, it is necessary to add limits to *leftFootManip*'s attributes.

> **Note:** *It would also be possible to set limits on the rotations of the joints themselves, but that would result in the joints stopping at a given value while the custom attributes continue to change. Setting limits on the manipulator's attributes will give more predictable results.*

1   Range of motion

- Select *leftFootManip*.

- Highlight the *Ball Rot* attribute in the Channel Box.

- **MMB-drag** in the viewport to invoke the virtual slider.

The foot acts properly as long as the Ball Rot value is less or equal to **10**, *but when it goes above* **10** *the foot bends inappropriately.*

- Reset *Ball Rot* back to **0**.

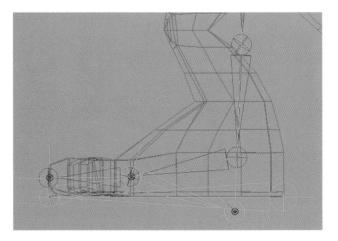

Ball rotate outside of acceptable range

2   Set a minimum limit

- Select **Modify → Edit Attribute...**

- In the **Edit Attribute** window, select *ballRot*.

- Check **Has Maximum** to **On** and set the maximum value to **10**.

3 Set limits for the other attributes

- Test each of the other custom attributes and set limits accordingly.

- Set limits as follows:

Heel Rot X	Min **-90**, Max **90**;
Heel Rot Y	Min **-90**, Max **90**;
Heel Rot Z	Min **-45**, Max **45**;
Ball Rot	Max **10**;
Toe Rot X	Min **-90**, Max **90**;
Toe Rot Y	Min **-90**, Max **90**;
Toe Rot Z	Min **-45**, Max **45**.

4 Save your work

Final touches

Now that you have a good control system for Meeper's foot, it's time to finalize the setup.

1 Scene file

- Continue with your own scene.

Or

- Open the scene file *17-meeperLegSetup_02.ma*.

2 IK/FK blend

If you intend to use IK/FK blending, add the following to your foot manipulator:

- Select the *leftFootManip* node.

- Select **Modify** → **Add Attribute...**

Lesson 17

- In the **Add Attribute** window, set the following:

  Attribute Name to ikFkBlend;

  Data Type to **Float**;

  Minimum to 0;

  Maximum to 1;

  Default to 1.

- Click **OK**.

- Through the Connection Editor, connect this new attribute to the *Ik Blend* attributes of all three IK handles of Meeper's leg.

- Under the section **IK Solver Attributes** in the Attribute Editor, turn **On** the **Ik Fk Control** checkbox for all three IK handles.

3   Lock and hide unnecessary attributes and objects

To prevent bad manipulation of the reverse foot setup, it is recommended to lock and hide all the attributes and objects that are not intended for animation.

- Select the *LeftRevHeel* joint.

- Set its **Visibility** attribute to **Off**.

- Highlight all the attributes visible in the Channel Box, then **RMB-click** and select **Lock and Hide Selected**.

Tip: *For proper locking, you should repeat the last step for all the objects and attributes in the reverse foot setup, but for simplicity reasons, you will only lock and hide the LeftRevHeel joint. You can also use the* **Window → General Editor → Channel Control** *to lock and hide attributes.*

Repeat for Meeper's right leg

Now that the left leg is set up, unhide the right leg and repeat the lesson. Following are some tips to speed up the process.

Note: *This is a good example of a task that could be automated using MEL scripting.*

1 Duplicate and mirror the left foot setup

- Select the *leftFootManip* and duplicate it.

- Press **Ctrl+g** to group the setup and set its **Scale X** attribute to **-1**.

Doing so will mirror the foot setup for the other leg.

2 Freeze transformations

- Unparent the new *LeftRevHeel* from its temporary manipulator.

These temporary bones are unfortunately not usable in the new setup. You will use them later to create new joints using Snap to Point.

- Select **Window** → **General Editor** → **Channel Control** to unlock the *leftFootManip1* scaling attributes.

- Unparent the new *leftFootManip1* from its temporary group.

- With the *leftFootManip1* selected, select **Modify** → **Freeze Transformations**.

This will reset the new manipulator's attributes to their default.

- Rename *leftFootManip1* to *rightFootManip*.

3 Create the new reverse joint chain

- Unhide the new *LeftRevHeel*.

> **Tip:** Use the **Window** → **General Editor** → **Channel Control** to unlock the *visibility attribute.*

- Select **Skeleton** → **Joint Tool**.

- Hold down **v** to **Snap to Point**, then create a new reverse foot joint chain for the right foot.

- Rename the new joint chain accordingly.

- Parent the new *RightRevHeel* to the new *RightFootManip*.

4 Clean up

- From the Outliner, delete all unnecessary nodes.

5   Rebuild the setup

- Create all the right leg IK handles.

- Parent the IK handles accordingly.

- Connect all the custom attributes.

- Double check custom attributes' limits to see if they require any changes.

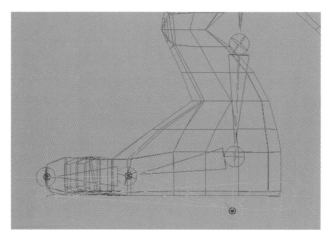

Meeper's right foot setup

Pole vectors

In order to have fully functional legs, the last thing to add are pole vector objects. Doing so will give maximum control to the animator for any leg manipulations.

1   Create locators

- Select **Create** → **Locator**.

- Hold down **v** to **Snap to Point** and move the locator onto Meeper's knee.

- Press **Ctrl+d** to duplicate the locator and snap it to the other knee.

- Select both locators and move them in front of the knees on the Z-positive axis.

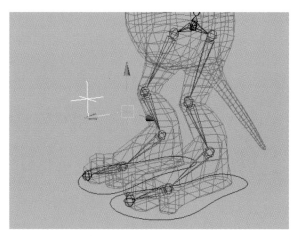

The locators

- Rename the locators to *leftPoleVector* and *rightPoleVector*.

2 Add the pole vector constraints

- In the Outliner, select the *leftPoleVector*, then **Ctrl-select** the *leftLegIK*.

- Select **Constrain** → **Pole Vector**.

If the left leg moves when you create the pole vector constraint, you can translate the locator on the X-axis in order to keep the skeleton as close as possible to its default position.

- Repeat for the other leg.

3 Freeze transformations

- Select both the *leftPoleVector* and *rightPoleVector*.

- Select **Modify** → **Freeze Transformations**.

4 Lock and hide attributes

- With both the *leftPoleVector* and *rightPoleVector* locator selected, highlight all the Rotate, Scale and Visibility attributes in the Channel Box, then **RMB-click** and select **Lock and Hide Selected**.

5 Save your work

The final scene is called *17-meeperLegSetup_03.ma*.

Test the setup

You can now test your setup using five main controls:

leftFootManip

Controls the left leg and foot's heel-to-toe motion.

rightFootManip

Controls the right leg and foot's heel-to-toe motion.

leftPoleVector

Controls the rotate plane for the left leg IK.

rightPoleVector

Controls the rotate plane for the right leg IK.

hips

controls the root joint of the entire skeleton.

Explore how these objects work together. Move Meeper forward and begin experimenting with the leg manipulators. You may even set keys to preview how the Meeper skeleton will animate.

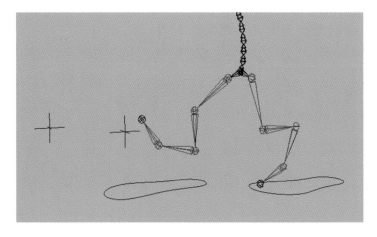

Lower body setup

Conclusion

In this lesson you created a reverse foot setup that uses different IK types and NURBS curves as control objects. You also added several custom attributes and pole vector objects to gain maximum control over Meeper's legs.

The foot setup created in this lesson is one among several other popular foot setups. You should keep your eyes open to all types of solutions as no clear standard for the *best* foot setup exists today. It usually depends on the situation the character is placed in.

In the next lesson, you will setup Meeper's arms and hands for animation.

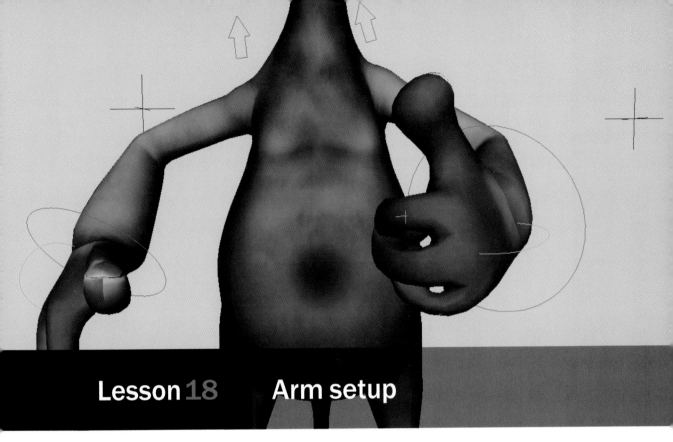

Lesson 18   Arm setup

In this lesson, you will create
Meeper's arm and hand
setup. To do so, you will define
manipulators, add rotate plane
IKs and create pole vector
objects, similar to what you
have done in the last lesson.

In this lesson you will learn the following:

- How to set up IK on Meeper's arms;

- How to work with the solver's end effectors;

- How to drive objects with manipulators;

- How to add constraints;

- An optional roll bone automation technique;

- How to add utility nodes;

- How to use Set Driven Keys.

Arm IK

You will use rotate plane IKs for the arm. One special thing to mention is that rather than placing the IK handle on the wrist joint, you will place it at the forearm roll joint. You will then move the chain's end effector to the wrist. This will allow the IK to control the arm as usual, but it will also allow the forearm roll bone to be free for setup.

1 Scene file

- Continue with your own scene.

Or

- Open the last lesson scene file *17-meeperLegSetup_03.ma*.

2 Rotate plane IK

- Select the **Skeleton → IK Handle Tool → □**.

- Set the following:

     Current Solver to **ikRPsolver**;

     Sticky to **Off**.

- Create an IK handle from the *LeftArm* joint to the *LeftForeArmRoll* joint.

- Rename the IK handle *leftArmIK*.

3 Rename the effector

- Select the *LeftForeArmRoll*.

- In the Outliner, press **f** to frame the selection.

You will see the end effector, which is parented under the LeftForeArm joint.

- Rename the end effector *leftArmEffector*.

End effector

When you create an IK handle, you also create another node called an *end effector*. The end effector defines the end of an IK solver chain. By default, the end effector is hidden and connected to a child joint of the last joint controlled in the IK chain, as if it were a sibling of that child joint of the last joint in the IK chain. So, when you move the end effector, the IK handle will go along for the ride. IK is not invoked when an end effector is moved. This gives you the ability to reposition the IK chain/IK handle without invoking IK.

As you will see, this is what you want to happen for Meeper's forearm. Because you want to control Meeper's arms from his wrist, you will need to translate the end of the IK chain from the forearm to the wrist. By changing the position of the effector, you are changing the end position of the IK handle down to the wrist without running IK through to the wrist.

Tip: *If you move the end effector, it is advisable to save a new preferred angle.*

1   Move the end effector

- In the Hypergraph or Outliner, select the *leftArmEffector*.

- Select the **Move Tool**, then press the **Insert** key to invoke the **Move Pivot Tool**.

- Hold down **v** to **Snap to Point**, then move the end effector pivot to snap it on the *LeftHand* joint.

Note: *If the arm joints move when you move the effector, the IK's stickiness was enabled and should not be. To fix the problem, simply undo the move, then open the Attribute Editor for the IK handle and set **Stickiness** to **Off**.*

- Press the **Insert** key to return to standard manipulator mode.

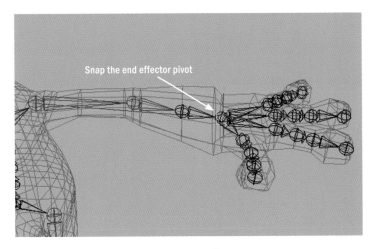

Move the end effector

2   Set the stickiness

- Select the *leftArmIK*.

- In the Attribute Editor, under the **IK Handle Attributes**, set **Stickiness** to **Sticky**.

3   Move the IK handle

- Select the *leftArmIK*.

- Move the IK handle along the **X-axis** to confirm that the forearm roll joint does not bend.

The IK handle can now be translated, bending the arm without bending the forearm roll bone. This is a necessary technique that enables you to rotate the hand while creating realistic movement and deformation on the forearm joints and skin. You will eventually drive the rotation of the roll bone joint based on the wrist rotation.

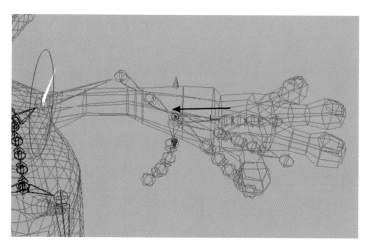

The forearm roll bone doesn't bend

- Undo the previous move.

4   Save your work

Constraints

Constraints are objects that you assign to control specific aspects of other objects' transformations. Following are descriptions of the constraints that will be used for the arm setup:

Point constraint

A point constraint is used to make one object move according to another object.

Orient constraint

An orient constraint is used to make one object rotate according to another object. An orient constraint will be set on a wrist manipulator to control rotation of the hand.

Parent constraint

A parent constraint is used to make one object behave as if it was parented to another object. A parent constraint will be used to constrain the clavicle to a manipulator.

Pole vector constraint

A pole vector constraint always points an IK's pole vector to the specified object. A pole vector constraint will be used to control the rotation of the arm and will provide a nice visual aid for positioning the elbows.

Hands and elbows

Now that you have set up an effective control system for Meeper's arms, you will create a control to easily manipulate the clavicles.

1 Scene file

- Continue with your own scene.

Or

- Open the scene file *18-meeperArmSetup_01.ma*.

2 Wrist manipulator

- Select **Create** → **NURBS Primitives** → **Circle**.

- Rename circle to *leftHandManip*.

- Press **v** to **Snap to Point**, then place the *leftHandManip* vertically over Meeper's left wrist.

- Scale the circle appropriately.

- Select **Modify → Freeze Transformations**.

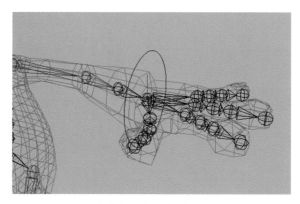

Left hand manipulator

3 Parent the IK handle

- Select *leftArmIK,* then **Shift-select** the *leftArmManip*.

- Press **p** to parent the IK to the manipulator.

4 Orient constrain

- Select the *leftArmManip*, then **Shift-select** *LeftHand* joint.

Tip: *Always select the object that you want to constrain last.*

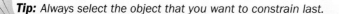

- Select **Constrain → Orient → ▢**.

- In the option window, make sure the **Maintain Offset** checkbox is set to **On**.

*The **Maintain Offset** option will make sure the wrist stays with its current rotation instead of snapping to the circle's rotation.*

- Click the **Add** button.

Constraining the LeftHand joint to the leftArmManip will keep the joint aligned with the control object. This will allow you to easily plant the hand.

5 Lock and hide attributes

Since *leftArmManip* is one of Meeper's control objects, you should lock and make non-keyable any channels that should not be changed. This will prevent users from manipulating the arm setup in ways it was not meant to be.

- Lock and hide the *leftArmManip*'s scale and visibility attributes.

6 Pole vector object

- Select **Create** → **Locator**.

- Using **v** to **Snap to Point**, move the locator to the left elbow.

- Translate the *locator* behind the elbow on its **negative Z-axis**.

- Select **Modify** → **Freeze Transformations**.

- Rename the *locator* to *leftArmPV*.

7 Pole vector constraint

- Select *leftArmPV*, then **Shift-select** the *leftArmIK*.

- Select **Constrain** → **Pole Vector**.

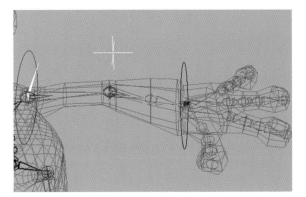

Pole vector object

8 Lock and hide attributes

- Lock and hide the *leftArmPV*'s rotation, scale and visibility attributes.

9 Repeat for the right side

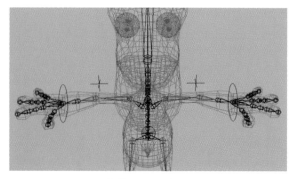

Both arms set up

10 Save your work

Clavicles

Now that you have set up an effective control system for Meeper's arms, you will create a control to easily manipulate the clavicles.

1 Scene file

- Continue with your own scene.

Or

- Open the scene file *18-meeperArmSetup_02.ma*.

2 Draw a manipulator

- Select **Create → EP Curves → ❑**.

- In the option window, set the **Curve Degree** to **Linear**.

- From the *front* view, draw an arrow pointing up as follows:

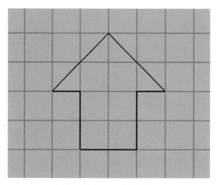

Clavicle manipulator

- Press **Enter** to exit the Curve Tool.

- Rename it *leftClavicleManip*.

- Move and scale the arrow so it is above the left shoulder.

- Parent the *leftClavicleManip* to the *Spine5* joint.

Tip: *Use* **x** *to Snap to Grid.*

3 Adjust the manipulator's pivot

- Select the *leftClavicleManip*.

- Press **Insert** to switch to the **Move Pivot Tool**.

- Press **v** to Snap the Pivot to the *LeftShoulder* joint.

- Press **Insert** again to toggle off the **Move Pivot Tool**.

- With the *leftClavicleManip* selected, select **Modify** → **Freeze Transformation**.

4 Parent Constrain

- Select *leftClavicleManip*, then **Shift-select** the *LeftShoulder* joint.

- Select **Constrain** → **Parent** → □.

- In the option window, make sure the **Maintain Offset** is set to **On**.

5 Lock and hide attributes

- Lock and hide the *leftClavicleManip*'s translate, scale and visibility attributes.

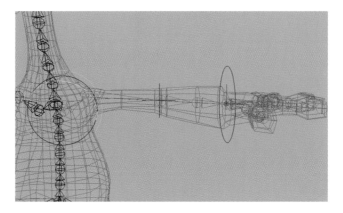

Left clavicle manipulator

6 Repeat for the right arm

IK handles

Now that Meeper's arms are set up, some final touches must be added to the manipulators. First, you will add the IK/FK blending functionality, then you will lock and hide the IK handles to prevent them from accidentally being manipulated.

1 Add an IK FK Blend attribute

- Select both the left and right arm manipulators.

- Select **Modify** → **Add Attributes**.

- Set the following:

  Attribute Name to ikFkBlend;

  Data Type to **Float**;

  Minimum to **0**;

  Maximum to **1**;

  Default to **1**.

- Click **OK**.

- Through the Connection Editor, connect this new attribute to the *Ik Blend* attribute of its respective IK handles.

- In the Attribute Editor, turn **On** the **Ik Fk Control** checkbox for both IK handles under the section **IK Solver Attributes**.

2 Connect the orient constraint

Since the IK blending will allow you to animate the arms with rotations, it is necessary to turn off the orient constraints on the wrists at the same time. Doing so will allow you to also manually rotate the wrist instead of using the manipulator.

- Through the Connection Editor, connect the *Ik Fk Blend* attribute to the *W0* attribute found on the *LeftHand_orientConstraint1* and *RightHand_orientConstraint1* nodes.

The W0 attributes stands for weight at index 0 and is usually prefixed with the name of the object it is constrained to. This attribute defines the weighting of the constraint; 1 for enabled and 0 for disabled.

Tip: *The constraints are always parented to the constrained nodes. You can find them easily through the Outliner.*

- Set the **Ik Fk Blend** attribute to **0** to see if you can rotate the bones appropriately.

- When you are done, undo any rotations and reset the **Ik Fk Blend** attribute to **1**.

3 Hide the IKs

- Select both the left and right arm IK handles.

- Set their **Visibility** attribute to **Off**.

- Highlight all the attributes listed in the Channel Box, then **RMB-click** and select **Lock and Hide Selected**.

4 Save your work

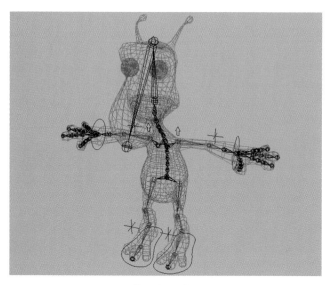

The rig so far

Roll bone automation

If you like automation, you can make connections in order to automate the roll bone. This is done by adding a utility node, which will give some wrist rotation to the roll bone.

> **Note:** *The technique shown in this exercise works well only when using the hand manipulators in IK and will not automate the roll bone when animating the arm in FK. To have this setup work for both IK and FK, you would need to write a MEL expression and control a separate roll bone.*

1   Create the utility node

- Select **Window** → **Rendering Editor** → **Hypershade**.

The Hypershade is a good place to create and connect utility nodes.

- Scroll down to the **General Utilities** section in the **Create** bar and locate the **Multiply Divide** node.

- **MMB-drag** a **Multiply Divide** node in the Work Area.

This will create the utility node in the scene.

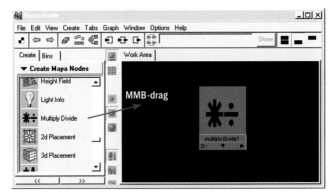

Multiply Divide utility node

2 Connect the utility node

- Select **Window** → **General Editor** → **Connection Editor**.

- Select the *leftArmManip* and load it on the left side of the Connection Editor, then select the *multipliDivide1* and load it on the right side.

- Connect the *Rotate X* attribute of the manipulator to the *Input1 X* attribute of the utility node.

- **Double-click** on the *multiplyDivide1* node in the Hypershade to open its Attribute Editor.

- In the **Multiply-Divide Attributes** section, set the *Input2 X* to **0.5**.

This specifies that half of the rotation from the wrist will go on the roll bone.

- In the Connection Editor, load the *multiplyDivide1* node on the left side, then load the *LeftForeArmRoll* joint on the right side.

- Connect the *Output X* attribute of the utility node to the *Rotate X* attribute of the roll bone.

You have now connected half of the wrist rotation to the LeftForeArmRoll rotation.

3 Repeat for the right arm

Tip: *Since you used only the X attribute on the utility node, you don't need to create another one. Just use the Y or Z attribute for the right arm.*

4 Save your work

Set Driven Keys

When you want to control attributes based on the animation of another attribute, you can use *Set Driven Keys*. Set Driven Key is a curve relationship between two attributes. In the Graph Editor, the horizontal axis represents the driver attribute values and the vertical axis represents the driven attribute values.

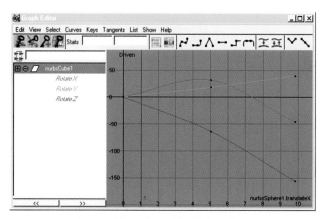

Graph Editor view of Set Driven Key

Because Set Driven Key is a curve relationship, it is possible to adjust the tangents of this curve and add additional keys. This can help you achieve some interesting behavior. For example, if the rotate attribute of an elbow is driving the size of a bicep muscle, the curve could be edited so that when the elbow is about to reach its maximum bend, the bicep shakes a little as it is flexed.

Finger manipulator

You will add another NURBS circle to the hand to use as a manipulator for articulating the fingers. It is a good idea to create another manipulator for the fingers in addition to the existing one for the arm because the arm's manipulator will be left behind when the arm is controlled in FK.

Note: *This exercise should be applied to your character only if you like complete hand automation. Since the driven keys on the fingers will connect their attributes, it will not be possible to manually animate the fingers. One way to use both the driven keys and manually animate the fingers would be to create overrides for joints in each finger. Creating an override means that every articulation needs two bones overlapping: one for the driven keys and another one for manual rotation.*

1   Scene file

- Continue with your own scene.

Or

- Open the scene file *18-meeperArmSetup_03.ma*.

2   Create the manipulator

- Select **Create** → **NURBS Primitives** → **Circle** and name the circle *leftFingersManip*.

- Press **v** to **Snap to Point** and move the manipulator to the *LeftHand* joint.

- Adjust the CVs so the manipulator looks like the following:

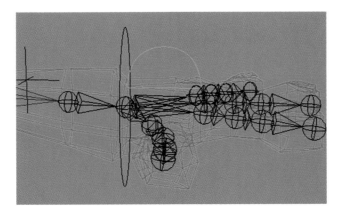

Finger manipulator

3   Parent and freeze transformations

- Parent the *leftFingersManip* to the *LeftHand* joint.

- Freeze the *leftFingersManip* transformations.

4   Lock and hide the attributes

- Highlight all the translate, rotate, scale, and visibility attributes in the Channel Box for the *leftFingersManip*, then **RMB-click** and select **Lock and Hide Selected**.

5   Add custom attributes

You will now add attributes to *leftFingersManip* to control the fingers.

- Select *leftFingersManip*.

- Select **Modify** → **Add Attribute**. Set the following:

    Attribute Name to **indexCurl**;

    Make Attribute Keyable to **On**;

    Data Type to **Float**;

    Minimum Value to **0**;

    Maximum Value to **10**;

    Default Value to **0**.

- Click the **Add** button.

- Repeat the steps outlined above to add the following attributes:

    middleCurl;

    ringCurl;

    thumbCurl.

Tip: You can also use the Script Editor to execute the `addAttr` *MEL command like this:* `addAttr -k 1 -ln middleCurl -at double -min 0 -max 10 -dv 0 leftFingersManip;`

- Add the following attributes to the *leftFingersManip* with their **Min**, **Max**, and **Default** values set to **-10**, **10**, and **0**, respectively:

    thumbRotX;

    thumbRotZ;

    fingerSpread.

All these custom attributes will be controlled with Set Driven Keys.

Tip: You can always edit the custom attribute's name, its keyable state, and its min/max values after they are created by selecting **Modify** → **Edit Attribute**.

Alias

Tip: *My favorite tool in Maya is Set Driven Key because it gives you the power to build action/reaction. You can build the causal relations between anything. It is very simple and efficient to use.*

Patrice Paradis | Application Engineer

Finger Set Driven Keys

Now that you have all the attributes to control the fingers' rotations, you need to connect the two together. In the case of bending the index finger, you can have its joints rotate when you change the value for the *indexCurl* attribute. When *indexCurl* is set to **0**, none of the index finger joints will be rotated, but when you change *indexCurl* to **10**, the finger will rotate to its maximum. For motions like spreading the fingers, the **Min** and **Max** should range from **-10** to **10**, where **-10** moves the fingers closer together and **10** moves them further apart.

The following exercise will set up the *indexCurl* attribute to rotate the index finger. You will have to repeat these steps for the remaining fingers on Meeper.

Note: *The technique used for setting up driven keys is the same for any other driven keys you want to create.*

1 Open the Set Driven Key window

- Select the **Animate** → **Set Driven Key** → **Set** → ❑.

The Set Driven Key window is displayed. It is divided into two parts, Driver and Driven. The attributes you just created will be the drivers and the joint rotations on the fingers will be the driven attributes.

2 Select the Driver node and attribute

- Select *leftFingersManip*.

- Click **Load Driver**.

Notice that leftFingersManip appears in the list of drivers, along with all of its keyable attributes.

- Select *indexCurl* from the list of keyable attributes.

3 Select the Driven nodes and attributes

The *rotateZ* attribute of the index joints will be the driven attributes.

- Select the three index joints (*LeftHandIndex1*, *LeftHandIndex2*, *LeftHandIndex3*).

- Click **Load Driven**.

Notice that the selected objects appear in the driven list.

- Highlight the driven objects, then select *rotateZ* from the list of attributes.

Note: *The local rotation axis must be set up so that the fingers only need to rotate around one axis to curl.*

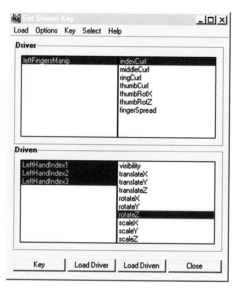

Set Driven Key window

4   Set an initial key position

- Click on the *leftFingersManip* in the Set Driven Key window to make it active and make sure that *indexCurl* is set to **0** in the Channel Box.

- Click **Key** in the **Set Driven Key** window.

Doing so sets keys on all three index joints.

5   Set a second key position

- Click on the *leftFingersManip* in the **Set Driven Key** window, then set *indexCurl* to **10** in the Channel Box.

- Rotate all the index joints on their **Z-axis** by about **-65 degrees**.

Note: *The* **Rotate Tool** *should be set to* **Local**.

The tip joint of the index should touch the palm of Meeper's geometry.

- Press **Key**.

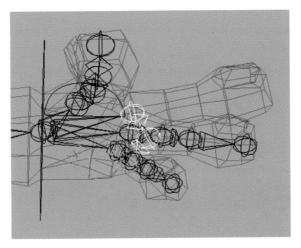

The index joints rotated

> **Tip:** Since the geometry does not deform at this time, you will need to visualize when the finger tip will touch the palm. It is better to over-rotate the joints than under-rotate them. If you don't rotate the joints enough, you may have to edit them later. If required, you will be able to change the driven key values through the Graph Editor.

6 Test the values

- Select *leftFingersManip*.

- In the Channel Box, highlight the *indexCurl* attribute.

- In the viewport, **MMB-drag** to invoke the virtual slider and change the selected attribute's value.

7 Use Set Driven Key for the other fingers

- Repeat this exercise to set up the curl for the *middle finger*, *ring finger* and *thumb*.

> **Note:** On their Y-axes, the fingers have three joints to curl while the thumb has only two.

Finger spread Set Driven Keys

You also want the hand to be able to spread its fingers. Use Set Driven Key again to control the action. This time, you'll use attributes that have a range between -10 and 10, with 0 being the rest position, or preferred angle.

1   Finger spread

- Load the *leftFingersManip* with its *fingerSpread* attribute as the **Driver**.

- Select *LeftHandIndex1, LeftHandMiddle1* and *LeftHandRing1* joints.

- Click **Load Driven**.

- Highlight the joints and their **rotateY** attribute.

- Set a key with **fingerSpread** at **0** with the finger joints at their default position.

- Set the *fingerSpread* attribute to **10**.

- Select the finger joints and spread them apart, then set a key for them.

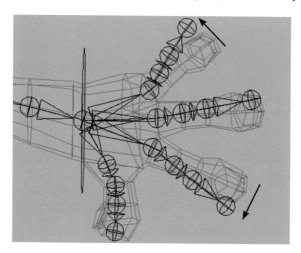

Fingers spread out

- Rotate the finger joints in a closed position, then set a key with *fingerSpread* at **-10**.

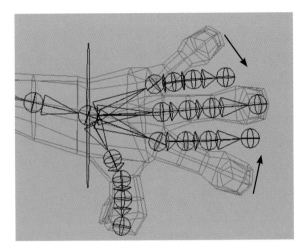

Closed finger spread

2   Test the results

- Test the range of motion between **-10** and **10** by changing the *fingerSpread* attribute.

Thumb rotation Set Driven Keys

The thumb is different from the other fingers in that its base pivots on a saddle joint and has much more freedom of movement than the finger joints. When you set up the thumb motion, you need to allow for flexible articulation that mimics the orbiting provided by a saddle type joint. This is broken down between the *thumbRotX* and *thumbRotZ* attributes.

1   Drive the rotation Y of the thumb

- Select *leftFingersManip* and click **Load Driver**.

- Select *LeftHandThumb1* and click **Load Driven**.

- Select *thumbRotX* as the **Driver** attribute and *rotateX* as the **Driven** attribute.

- Set a key with *thumbRotX* at **0** and the *LeftHandThumb1* joint at its default position.

- Set *thumbRotX* to **10**.

- Rotate the *LeftHandThumb1* on the **X-axis** in one direction.

- Click **Key**.

2   Set the second key position

- Set *thumbRotX* to **-10**.

- Rotate the *LeftHandThumb1* in the **X-axis** in the opposite direction.

- Click **Key**.

3   Drive the rotation Z of the thumb

- Select *thumbRotZ* as the **Driver** attribute and **rotateZ** as the **Driven** attribute.

4   Set keys on the Z-axis

- Set a key with *thumbRotZ* at **0** and the *LeftHandThumb1* joint at its default position.

- Set a key with *thumbRotZ* at **10** and rotate the *LeftHandThumb1* joint down on the **Z-axis**.

- Set a key with *thumbRotZ* to **-10** and rotate the *LeftHandThumb1* on the **Z-axis** in the opposite direction.

5   Test the operation of the thumb in this direction

Right finger manipulator

You must now recreate the finger manipulator and all its driven keys for the right hand.

Clean the scene

Since the rig is almost done, it is now time to do a small cleanup in your scene.

1   Delete history

- Select **Edit** → **Delete All by Type** → **History**.

2   Optimize scene size

- Select **File** → **Optimize Scene Size**.

3   Save you work

- The final scene file is called *18-meeperArmSetup_04.ma*.

Test the character rig

Meeper's rig is starting to take shape. You now have the basic control points for blocking out motion. Test the character's behavior by using the manipulators you created.

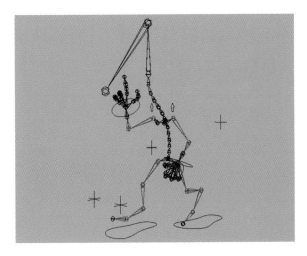

A pose for Meeper

You can also experiment with other setups. For instance, you could attempt to parent the pole vectors to the *root* joint. Maybe you would rather use the Twist attribute on the IK handles and create a custom attribute on the manipulators for it.

Conclusion

This lesson explored the use of rigging techniques associated with setting up arms. You learned how to add constraints in order to simplify your rig. You also learned about the multiply and divide utility nodes, which can be used instead of writing a MEL expression. Lastly, you implemented finger automation using driven keys.

In the next lesson, you will implement spline IKs onto Meeper's spine and you will finalize the setup hierarchy.

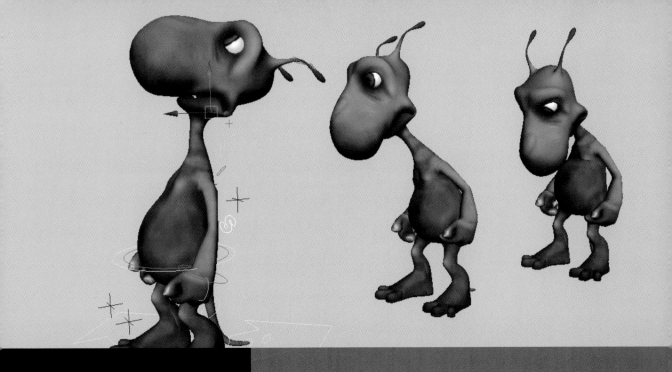

Lesson 19　Spine setup

In this lesson, you will add an IK spline solver to Meeper's spine. This will control how his back and neck sway and bend when he moves. It will also provide you with a realistic relationship between the pelvis and spine. Once the IK is in place, you will cluster points on the spline to help create manipulators.

Once that is done, you will finalize the rig in order to proceed to the next project where you will set up geometry deformations.

In this lesson you will learn the following:

- How to set up a basic IK spline solver;

- How to use clusters to gain control over the spline curve;

- How to parent the clusters to manipulators;

- How to associate Meeper's spine and pelvis motion;

- How to create global and local control mechanisms;

- How to create an eye aiming setup.

IK spline

When you use an IK spline, there are several things to keep in mind:

- Keep the spline curve as simple as possible for the IK spline. For the most part, the default of four CVs works well. Note that the curve created when setting up the IK spline solver will attempt to stay as simple as possible by default.

- Create clusters for the CVs to make selecting and animating easier. Clusters have translate, rotate and scale attributes while CVs only have position attributes. This means that CVs can't be keyframed as accurately as clusters, which will help for the animation.

- The IK spline should not be starting from a *root* joint. Also, as a rule, it should not cross any branching joints. In Meeper's case, you do not want the IK spline to start at the *Hips* joint, but rather at the first *Spine* joint. It should not start at the *root* joint because it would not only rotate the back but the hips as well. While the hips and back do rotate together in real life, this motion can be difficult to animate and control. You could also create a single IK spline on Meeper starting from the spine, going up to the head, but this will create problems when you need to rotate the neck separately from the back. The best solution for Meeper would be the following:

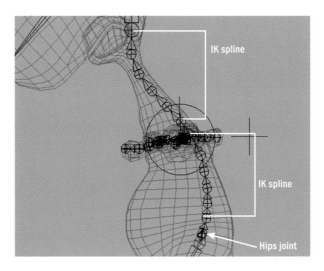

IK splines for Meeper

Adding the IK splines

The IK spline solver allows you to control a chain of joints, like Meeper's spine, with only a few control points. Animating a flexible back with forward kinematics requires you to keyframe the rotation of each joint individually. With a spline IK, you will control all of the back joints with three control points.

1   Scene file

- Continue with your own scene.

  Or

- Open the last lesson scene file *18-meeperArmSetup_04.ma*.

2   Add the first IK spline

- Select **Skeleton** → **IK Spline Handle Tool** → ☐.

- Click the **Reset Tool** button.

- Turn **Off** the **Auto Parent Curve** option.

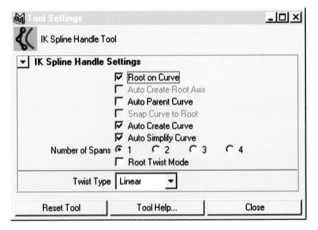

IK spline options

- Select the *spine* joint above the *Hips* joint to define the start joint of the chain.

- Select the last spine joint, *Spine5*, to place the IK handle.

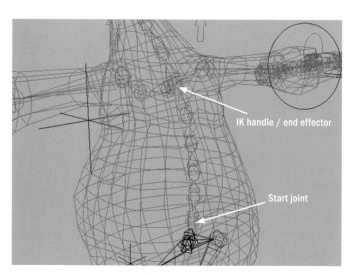

First IK spline

An IK system is created with a curve running through the selected joints. You can control the joints by selecting the CVs of this curve and translating them.

3   Add the first IK spline

- Press **y** to make the **IK Spline Handle Tool** active.

- Select the *Neck* joint to define the start joint of the chain.

- Select the *Head* joint to place the IK handle.

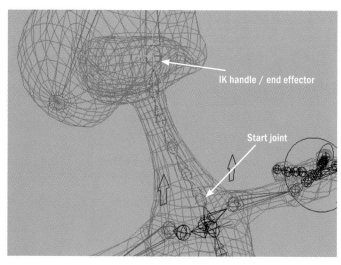

Second IK spline

4   Rename the new nodes

- Rename the new IK handles *backSplineIK* and *neckSplineIK*.

- Rename the new spline curves *backSpline* and *neckSpline*.

Test the IK splines

There are two ways to operate IK splines. The *Twist* attribute will rotate each of the joints in the solution around the X-axis, causing a twisting action up Meeper's spine or neck. Moving CVs in the *backSpline* or the *neckSpline* will allow you to pose Meeper's back or neck in a serpentine manner. Try both methods in order to understand how the IK spline operates.

1   The Twist attribute

- Select the *backSplineIK* handle.

Note: *The feedback window will tell you that some items cannot be moved in the 3D view. This warning simply means that spline IK handles cannot be translated the way that other IK handles are.*

- In the Channel Box, highlight the Twist attribute.
- **MMB+drag** in the viewport to change the value with the virtual slider.
- Reset the **Twist** value back to **0** when you are done.
- With the *backSplineIK* handle still selected, press **t** to show the manipulator for the back.
- **Click+drag** the top manipulator ring to twist the back.

This manipulator is another way to access the twist.

Note: *Experiment with the **Twist Type** attribute accessible through the Attribute Editor.*

2   Moving CVs

- Select the *backSpline*.

Tip: You can use the selection mask buttons to select the curve in the viewport. In Object mode, select **All Objects Off**, then toggle **On** the **Curve** icon.

- Switch to Component mode.

- Select any CVs on the curve and translate them.

- Undo until the *backSpline* is back to its original shape.

Note: You may notice that the lower CV in the curve should not translate since it causes the first joint to be translated. You may also notice that translating the top CV in the back curve does not move the neck. Both these issues will be resolved in the next exercise.

Clusters

Both curves used by the IK spline solver have four CVs. Currently, the only way to select these CVs is in Component mode. To make selection easier and consistent with the rest of Meeper's rig, you will add clusters to the CVs of the curves. The clusters will then be parented to NURBS manipulators.

1 Select the top CV

- Select the *backSpline*.

- Switch to Component mode and set the selection mask to **CVs** and **Hulls**.

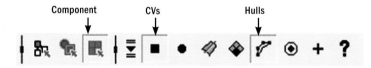

Selection mask buttons

- Select the top **two** CVs.

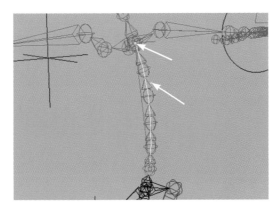

Top CVs selected

2 Create a cluster

- With the CVs still selected, select **Deform** → **Create Cluster** → □.

- Make sure to reset the option window.

- Press **Create**.

A small **c** *will appear in the viewport.*

- Rename this cluster *backTopCluster*.

You have created the top cluster using the first two CVs, allowing you to use the deformer to its maximum capability. As well, you can rotate it to get the wanted orientation of the upper back.

3 Create another cluster

- Now select the bottom **two** CVs and create a cluster with them.

- Rename the cluster *backBottomCluster*.

4 Parent the bottom cluster

- Select *backBottomCluster* and parent it to the *Hips* joint.

5 Lock and hide the bottom cluster

Since the bottom cluster will be used only to keep the tangency of the spine with the pelvis, you should not move this cluster. As a result, it will be hidden and locked.

- Select *backBottomCluster* and set its **Visibility** to **Off**.

- Highlight all of its attributes in the Channel Box, then **RMB-click** and select **Lock and Hide Selected**.

6   Create two other clusters for the neck

You will now repeat the previous steps, but this time to cluster the *neckSpline*'s CVs.

- Select *neckSpline* and display its CVs.

- Select the top **two** CVs and create a cluster with them.

- Rename the cluster *neckTopCluster*.

- Select the bottom **two** CVs and create a cluster with them.

- Rename the cluster *neckBottomCluster*.

- Parent the *neckBottomCluster* to the *Spine5* joint.

- Hide the *neckBottomCluster* and lock and hide all of its attributes.

7   Test the skeleton

- Translate and rotate the top neck cluster to test movement of the head.

- Rotate the *Spine5* joint to see the effect of the cluster on the lower neck.

- Translate and rotate the top back cluster to test movement of the upper back.

- Rotate the *Hips* joint to see the effect of the cluster on the lower back.

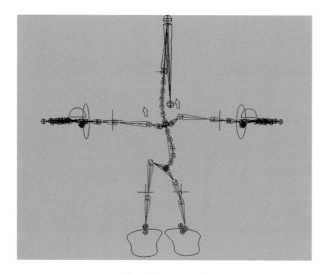

Hips joint rotated

8   Save your work

Manipulators for the clusters

To continue with the manipulators' scheme for Meeper, you will now create NURBS curves to be used as manipulators for the clusters.

1   Scene file

- Continue with your own scene.

Or

- Open the scene file *19-meeperSpineSetup_01.ma*.

2   Create NURBS manipulators

You will create two curves using the Text Tool. One for the *Spine* and one for the *Neck*.

- Select **Create** → **Text** → ❑.
- In the options window, type **"S N"** in the text field.
- Make sure that **Curves** is selected in the **Type** section.
- Click on the **Create** button.

3   Rotate the text object

- Rotate the text object **90 degrees** on the **Y-axis**.

4   Unparent and rename the curves

- Select the **S**.
- Select **Edit** → **Unparent** or press **Shift+p**.
- Rename the **S** to *spineManip*.
- Select, unparent and rename the *N* to *neckManip*.
- Delete the original group node from the Outliner.

5   Position the text curves

- In the *side* view, move and scale the two new manipulators next to their respective body parts.

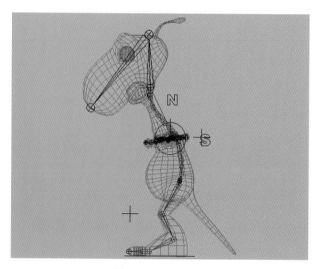

New manipulators

6 Move the manipulators' pivots

- Snap the *spineManip*'s pivot to the *Spine5* joint.
- Snap the *NeckManip*'s pivot to the *Head* joint.

7 Freeze Transformations

- Select **Edit → Freeze Transformations** for both manipulators.

8 Parent the clusters

- Parent the clusters to their respective manipulators.

Note: *Maya will automatically group the cluster before parenting to the manipulator. This is normal behavior since the cluster needs to preserve its relative position in space.*

9 Lock and hide attributes

- From the Outliner, select all children of the *spineManip*, then **Ctrl-select** all children of the *neckManip*.
- Set their **Visibility** to **Off**, then lock and hide all of their attributes.
- Lock and hide the scale and visibility attributes for the *spineManip* and *neckManip*.

10 Add custom attributes

- Select both the *spineManip* and *neckManip*.

- Select **Modify** → **Add Attribute**...

- Set the new attribute as follows:

  Attribute Name to *twist*;

  Data Type to **Float**.

- Click the **Add** button.

- Add another custom attribute as follows:

  Attribute Name to *ikFkBlend*;

  Data Type to **Float**;

  Minimum to **0**;

  Maximum to **1**;

  Default to **1**.

- Click the **OK** button.

11 Connect the custom attributes

- Connect both the *twist* and *ikFkBlend* attributes to their respective IK handles.

- Through the Attribute Editor, turn **On** the **Ik Fk Control** attribute for both IK spline handles.

12 Lock and hide the IK handles and splines

- Set the *backSplineIK*, *neckSplineIK, backSpline* and *neckSpline* visibility to off, then lock and hide all of their attributes.

13 Test the motion

- Move and rotate the new manipulators to see their effect on the characters.

- Set the manipulators back to their default attributes when you are done experimenting.

14 Save your work

Hips' manipulators

In order to complete Meeper's back setup, you will need manipulators for the hips. You will need one manipulator for the *Hips* root joint, and another one for the *HipsOverride* joint.

1   Scene file

- Continue with your own scene.

Or

- Open the scene file *19-meeperSpineSetup_02.ma*.

2   Create a NURBS circle

- Select **Create → NURBS Primitives → Circle**.

- Rename the circle *hipsManip*.

3   Position the manipulator

- Move and scale the *hipsManip* to fit Meeper's belly.

- Snap the pivot of the manipulator onto the *Hips* joint.

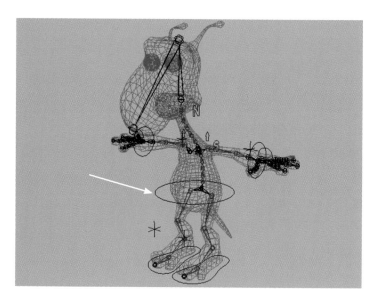

Hips manipulator

4   Duplicate the manipulator

- Select *hipsManip* and duplicate it.

- Rename the new manipulator to *hipsOverrideManip*.

- Parent the *hipsOverrideManip* to the *hipsManip* and **scale** it down.

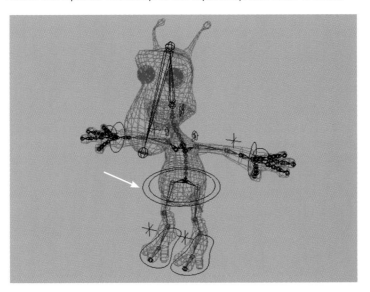

Hips override manipulator

5   Freeze and delete history

- Freeze the *hipsManip* and *hipsOverrideManip* transformations.

- Still with *hipsManip* and *hipsOverrideManip* selected, select
  Edit → Delete by Type → History.

Note: *It is important at this stage to not delete all the history in the scene
because that would delete important history, such as the clusters.*

6   Parent constraint the hips

- Select the *hipsManip* and the *Hips* joint, then select **Constrain → Parent**.

Note: *Make sure **Maintain Offset** is set to **On**.*

7 Orient constraint the HipsOverride

- Select the *hipsOverrideManip* and the *HipsOverride* joint, then select **Constrain** → **Orient**.

Note: *Make sure* **Maintain Offset** *is set to* **On**.

8 Lock and hide unnecessary attributes

Master node

You will now add an additional level of control to Meeper's rig by creating a master manipulator. When moving the master node, the entire rig should be moving forward.

1 Create the master manipulator

- Select **Create** → **EP Curve** → ❏.

- In the option window, make sure **Curve Degree** is set to **Linear**.

- From the *top* view, draw a four-point arrow as follows:

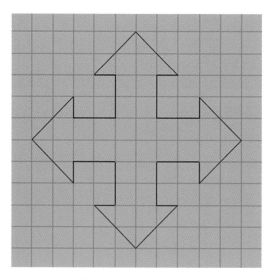

The master manipulator

- Rename the curve to *master*.

2   Position master at the center of the world

- With the *master* selected, select **Modify** → **Center Pivot**.

- Snap the *master* to the world origin.

- Scale it appropriately under Meeper.

- Freeze its transformations.

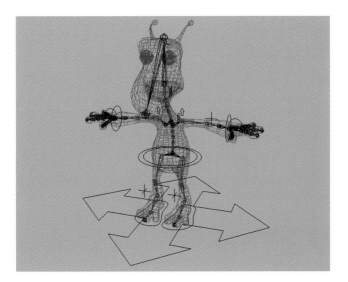

The well placed master node

3   Lock and hide attributes

- Lock and hide the *master*'s scale and visibility attributes.

4   Parent the rig to the master

Everything in the world used to move the rig must now be parented to the *master* node.

- Parent all manipulators and pole vectors to the master node.

Note: *Do not parent the Hips root joint since it is driven by the hipsManipulator.*

- Move the *master* to ensure everything follows.

Finishing touches

You will now parent everything that is part of Meeper's rig to a rig group and place that group on a rig layer. You will also see how to color code the various manipulators so they are easy to see and differentiate.

1   Group all top nodes together

In order to have a clean rig scene, you will group all the top nodes together under a single *rig* node.

- From the Outliner, select the *Hips* joint, all the *splines* and *spline IKs* and the *master,* then press **Ctrl+g** to group them together.

Note: *Do not group the geometry group, as it should be in a separate hierarchy.*

- Rename the new group *rig*.

- Lock and hide all the attributes of the *rig* group since the rig must never move.

2   Create a rig layer

- Create a new layer in the Layer Editor and name it *rigLayer*.

- Add the *rig* group to the new *rigLayer*.

You can now easily toggle the visibility of either the geometry layer or the rig layer.

3   Color code manipulators

- Select the *master* node.

- In the Attribute Editor, open the **Object Display** section, then the **Drawing Overrides** section.

- **RMB-click** on the **Enable Overrides** checkbox and select **Break Connection,** then turn it **On**.

Doing so will prevent the object from getting its color from the layer it is currently in.

- Change the **Color** slider to yellow.

By changing the color override, the object wireframe will have that color in the viewport.

> **Note:** *The object must be deselected in order to see the effect of the color override.*

- Repeat the steps outlined here for any other objects.

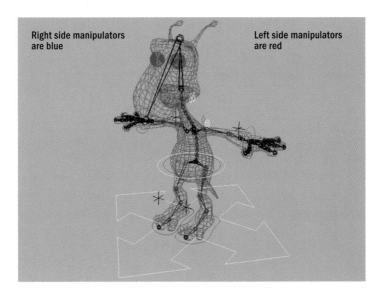

The color coded manipulators

Foolproof the rig

You have been conscientious about restricting access to Meeper's attributes, but it is a good idea to double-check every single node in the scene to ensure that any attribute that can potentially break the rig is hidden and locked. You can also display the selection handles of objects that are intended for animation but are not controlled by a manipulator.

1 Lock and hide potentially harmful objects and attributes

- Open the Hypergraph.
- Select **Options** → **Display** → **Hidden Nodes**.
- Go over each rig node one by one.

Tip: *You can lock and hide multiple attributes on nodes of the same type.*

2 Display selection handles

- Select the object for which you require a selection handle.

- Select **Display** → **Component Display** → **Selection Handles**.

Tip: *You can move a selection handle in Component mode.*

3 Save your work

Other Meeper setup

All the basics of the Meeper rig are final, but a few things are missing, such as the tail, the antennae and the eyes' setups. For characters more complex than Meeper, you might want to add control for the jaw and tongue, but this is not required here.

The following will finalize the rig:

1 Scene file

- Continue with your own scene.

Or

- Open the scene file *19-meeperSpineSetup_03.ma*.

2 Setup the tail

- Draw joints starting from the *Hips* going to the tip of the tail.

Note: *If you get a warning message saying Skipping Hips, it has non-zero rotations, check if the Hips joint is at its preferred angle.*

- Create an IK spline running through all tail joints.

Tip: *Increase the* **Number of Spans** *to* **3** *in the* **IK Spline Handle Tool** *options to give more definition to the tail curve.*

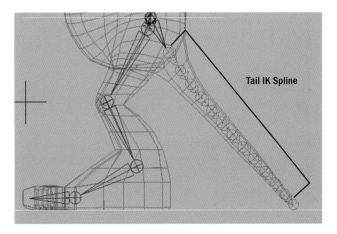

Tail IK Spline

The tail joints and the new IK spline

- Create clusters with the tail curve CVs.

- Create manipulators for the clusters.

- Rename all the new nodes accordingly.

- Lock and hide the appropriate objects and attributes.

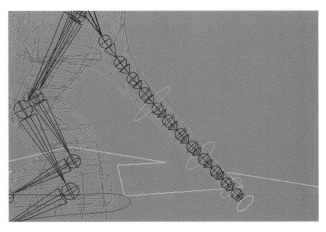

The tail setup

3   Antennae setup

- Draw joints starting from the *Skull* going to the tip of the antenna.

- Place the joints within Meeper's geometry.

- Orient the joints correctly.

- Rename the joints.

- Mirror the joints for the other antenna.

- Lock and hide the joints and their attributes.

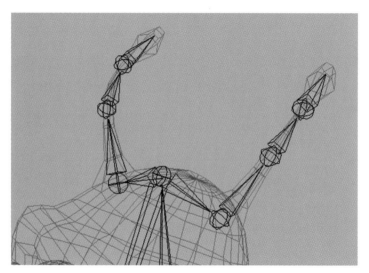

The antennae to be animated in FK

4   Eye joints

- Draw a single joint next to the eye geometry in the *side* view.

- Parent the new joint to the *Head* joint.

- Rename the new joint to *LeftEye*.

- Select Meeper's left eye geometry, then **Shift-select** the *LeftEye* joint.

- Select **Constrain** → **Point Constraint**, making sure the **Maintain Offset** is set to **Off**.

Doing so will snap the new eye joint exactly in the middle of Meeper's eye.

- Delete the constraint object that was just created.

> **Note:** *The goal of the point constraint was not to constrain the joint, but only to place the joint in the middle of the eye geometry for you.*

- Mirror the joint for the right eye.

You now have two well placed eye joints that will be used for the eye setup.

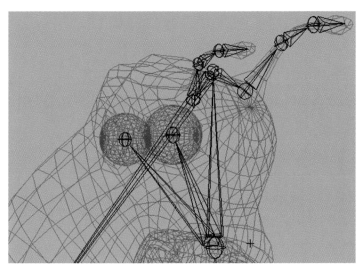

The eye joints

- Rename the new joint to *RightEye*.

> **Note:** *The eye joints will also be useful to see the eye location when animating without geometry.*

5   Eye setup

- Create a NURBS circle and rename it *eyeLookAt*.

- Place and edit the *eyeLookAt* so it looks as follows:

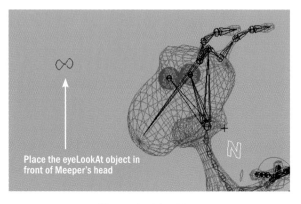

Place the eyeLookAt object in front of Meeper's head

The eyeLookAt object

- Create two locators and snap each one on its respective eye joint.

- Move both locators on their **Z-axes**, next to the *eyeLookAt* node.

- Parent both locators to the *eyeLookAt* node.

- Rename the locators to *leftEyeLookAt* and *rightEyeLookAt*.

- Freeze the transformations of the *eyeLookAt* and the two locators.

- Select the *leftEyeLookAt*, then **Shift-select** the *LeftEye* joint.

- Select **Constraint → Aim → ❏**.

- Make sure the **Maintain Offset** option is set to **On**, then add the constraint.

- Create an aim constraint for the other eye joint and locator.

- Lock and hide the appropriate objects and attributes.

Tip: *Don't lock the rotation and Scale X attribute of the eyeLookAt node, as they can be used to simulate crossed eyes.*

6   Save your work

- The final scene file is called *19-meeperSpineSetup_04.ma*.

433

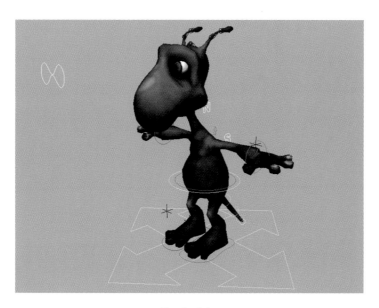

The final rig

Conclusion

The spline IK solver is ideal for controlling a long chain of joints such as those found in a snake, an animal's back or a tail. It is based on the use of a NURBS curve and therefore, is a powerful link to other parts of Maya. A NURBS curve, for example, can be deformed using non-linear deformers or animated as a soft body which utilizes dynamics to generate its animation. For Meeper, you used the cluster deformer, which allows you to move the individual NURBS CVs and keyframe his animation.

In the next project, you will set up all the deformation required for Meeper to be animated with his rig.

THE CHUBB CHUBBS GALLERY

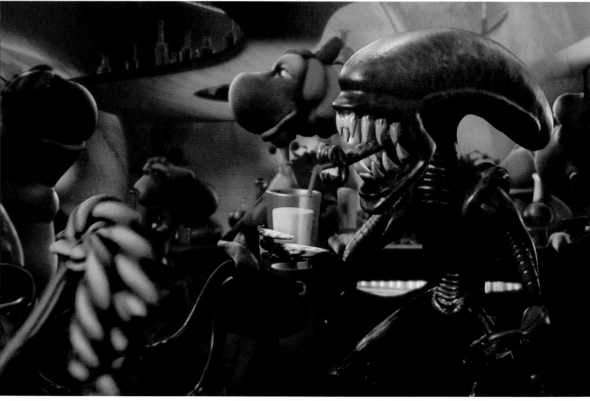

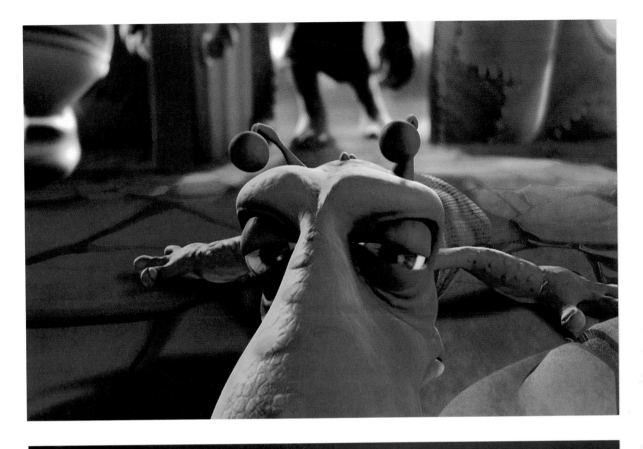

THE CHUBB CHUBBS **GALLERY**

Lessons

In Project Five, you will finalize and attach Meeper's geometry to the character rig from Project Four. First, you will generate all the blend shapes required for Meeper's facial expressions, and then you will bind his skin to the rig using smooth binding. You will also create influence objects and assign deformers to Meeper. Finally, you will create a low resolution model for animating in real time.

Lesson 20   Blend shapes

*In this lesson, you will bring
Meeper to life by creating
facial expressions. This will
be done by creating a blend
shape node to morph the
head. Once that is done, you
will set up a facial manipulator
that will give the animator
control over Meeper's
facial expressions.*

In this lesson you will learn the following:

- The basic phonemes;

- How to create blend shape targets;

- How to sculpt facial expressions;

- How to set up blend shape nodes;

- How to use in-between targets;

- How to edit a deformer set;

- How to connect the blend shape attributes to
  a manipulator.

Blend shape deformer

A *blend shape* is a powerful deformer that allows you to blend several target shapes onto a base shape. When computing the resulting blended shape, the deformer calculates the differences between the base and target shapes. The blend shape attributes, which range from 0 to 1, define the percentage of the target shapes to assign to the base shape.

The node has one attribute for each of the target shapes, which can be animated to get smooth transitions between shapes.

Blend shape deformers are usually used for facial expressions, but they can also be used in lots of other cases. For instance, you might want to use blend shapes to bulge muscles. You could also use blend shapes along with driven keys to correct geometry as it is being deformed. For Meeper, you will concentrate mostly on facial animation.

Facial animation

Facial animation can be broken down into several categories:

Mouth, cheeks and jaw

For lip-synching, phonemes are very important and must be created carefully so they can blend together without breaking the geometry. Generic phonemes such as *A, E, O, U,* can be used to establish mouth shapes that are formed recursively while talking. Along with the lips, the cheeks must also deform. The jaw must move down for phonemes that require an open mouth. The tongue must also be deformed to follow the different phonemes.

Eyes and eyebrows

Eye animation is critical when animating a character, since this is the site a viewer will be looking at the most. Shapes for blinking, squinting or to widen the eyes are very important. The eyebrows must also be taken care of, since they will describe all the emotions of the character. Most shapes in this category should be split to deform either the left or right side of the face.

Nose

Even though some nose movement comes as a result of other facial motion, the nose blend shapes are often forgotten. Having shapes for breathing in and out or flaring the nostrils will add realism to the facial animation.

Expressions

Sometimes, when facial expressions are recursive for a character, it is worthy to create entire facial expressions rather than using a blend of multiple shapes. Doing so will allow the expressions to be perfect and blend without breaking the geometry. It is especially good when the expressions are extreme.

Collisions

It is a good idea to add blend shapes for when the character's face is touched by something. Even if it is not possible to plan for every geometry collision, you should take some time to determine if the character will be pulling its ear or receiving a punch on the nose, and create those shapes. This will also add realism to the animation.

Additional shapes

You must not forget about additional shapes that could be useful for facial animation, such as the neck muscles contracting, swallowing, or a bulging thorax as a character breathes in.

Phonemes

Below and on the following page is a simple chart of the basic phonemes used in the English language. You can use this list to create the different target shapes for your character, and also as a guide to breakdown the phonetics of a speech.

Note: *Since Meeper does not have a tongue or teeth, the phonemes shown here are based only on the lips' position.*

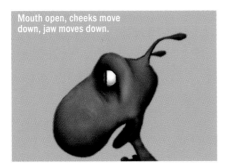

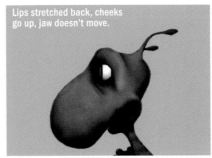

A phoneme as found in words like *alright*, *autumn* and *car*.

E phoneme as found in words like *he*, *tree* and *believe*.

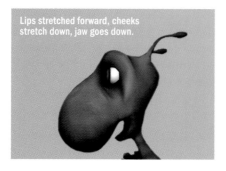

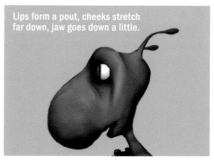

O phoneme as found in words like *flow*, *go* and *toy*.

U phoneme as found in words like *you*, *stew* and *noodle*.

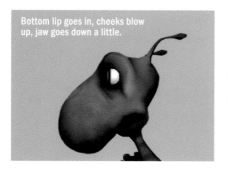

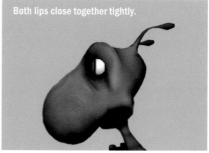

V and **F** phonemes as found in words like very and fabulous.

B, **M** and **P** phonemes as found in words like *big*, *mat* and *put*.

Tip: *For characters with a full inner mouth, other phonemes such as* **Th** *and* **Sh** *can be added.*

From these basic shapes, you can achieve most mouth shapes in the English language. The tricky part is getting all these shapes to transition properly from one shape to the next. In order to achieve an appropriate blending, you will need to study how each phoneme is formed.

Alias

Tip: *Chris Landreth sat near me while the Maya 1.0 development was going on, and was working on the short film Bingo as a production test. It was meant to test the system and make sure it held up to a real-world environment (and Bingo not only did the testing in spades, it garnered acclaim in its own right). One day I was wandering around looking over his shoulder when I saw the most hideously complex graph display I had ever seen (to that point). It was his implementation of a facial muscle set designed to emulate phonemes for lip sync. There are about 90 muscles in the face and I bet he had a half dozen nodes for each one. He would be sitting there with anatomy books, matching graph nodes to individual muscles or muscle groups, and tweaking deformation parameters to get the graph node to behave in a close approximation of how the muscle itself worked. It was an awesome example of art imitating life -literally. It was a very visceral lesson for me in the talent our software users brought to bear in their work*

Kevin Picott | Principal Engineer, Product Development

Meeper's first blend shape

You will now create Meeper's first blend shape target. By doing this, you will learn the workflow for the rest of the shapes to be created.

1 Scene file

- Continue with your own scene.

Or

- Open the last project scene file called *19-meeperSpineSetup_04.ma*.

2 Set the layers

- Set the *rigLayer*'s **Visibility** to **On**.

- Set the *geometryLayer* to be displayed normally.

3 Duplicate Meeper's geometry

You will now duplicate Meeper's geometry in order to sculpt the shape in a different geometry, thus keeping the base shape untouched.

- Select the *geoGroup* from the Outliner.

- Press **Ctrl+d** to duplicate it.

- Translate the new group on the **X-axis** by **10** units in order to have two heads side by side.

Note: *The geometry group is duplicated in order to keep the eyes with the duplicate. This will make it easier to shape the area around the eye once you get there.*

4 Rename the duplicate geometry

When you create the blend shape node, it uses the name of each target shape to name the corresponding blend attribute. Because of this, you should always give your blend shape targets concise and informative names.

- Rename the duplicated geometry to *E*.

Note: *Rename the geometry and not the geometry group.*

5 Sculpt Polygons Tool

There are several ways to sculpt the target shape. For instance, you might want to use a wire deformer, a cluster or a sculpt deformer. For Meeper's blend shapes, you will be sculpting the geometry using the Sculpt Polygons Tool.

- Select **Edit Polygons** → **Sculpt Polygons Tool** → ❑.

- In the **Stroke** section, set the **Reflection** checkbox to **On** and specify the **Reflection Axis** to **X**.

By enabling this option, any sculpting will be reflected on the other side of the geometry.

Tip: *Press **5** or **6** to be in shaded mode while sculpting.*

6 Sculpt the E target

Using the various sculpt operations, sculpt the E target shape as best you can. First, stretch the lips back and open them slightly. Make sure to also move the cheeks and cheekbones up.

Tip: *Always keep a mirror close to you when sculpting facial shapes.*

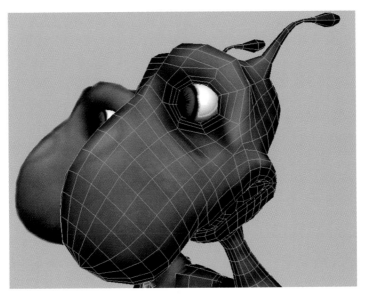

E target shape

Note: *When sculpting a shape, try to keep your edits localized. For instance, don't sculpt the eye area. Also, try not to sculpt other parts of the body by mistake.*

Test the shape

You will now test the effect of the E target on Meeper's original head by creating a temporary blend shape deformer. This will allow you to see how the shape is blending in. Since construction history will be kept, you will be able to bring modifications onto the target shape, which will automatically update the blend shape deformer.

1 Create the blend shape deformer

- Select the E target geometry, then **Shift-select** *Meeper*'s original geometry.

Note: *The base shape must always be selected last.*

- Under the **Animation** menu set, select **Deform** → **Create Blend Shape** → ❑, and make sure the options are reset to their default values.

- Create the blend shape deformer.

2   Test the blend shape

- Select **Window** → **Animation Editor** → **Blend Shape**.

The **Blend Shape** *window will appear, listing a single slider for the target E.*

Note: *You can also access blendShape1's attributes through the* **Input** *section of the Channel Box.*

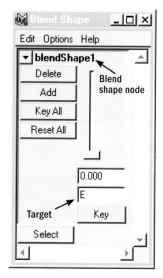

- Use the slider to see the effect of the blend shape on the original Meeper geometry.

Tip: *It is better to see the wireframe over the geometry in order to see the subtle movement of Meeper's skin.*

The Blend Shape window

3   Make corrections

- If needed, make corrections on Meeper's E target shape.

Doing so will automatically update the blend shape node because of construction history.

4   Delete the blend shape deformer

Since the blend shape deformer created above was only temporary, you will now delete it.

- In the **Quick Selection** field located at the top-right corner of the main Maya interface, type *blendShape1*, then hit **Enter**.

The blend shape node gets selected.

- Press **Delete** on your keyboard to delete the blend shape deformer.

5   Add a targets layer

- Create a new layer called *targetsLayer* and add the shapes to it.

- Set layer's **Visibility** to **Off**.

Doing so will keep your scene refresh fast as you create more and more geometry.

6   Save your work

All Meeper's blend shapes

You are now ready to create all the remaining blend shapes required for Meeper's animation.

1   Scene file

- Continue with your own scene.

Or

- Open the scene file *20-meeperBlendShapes_01.ma*.

2   Create a target shape

- Duplicate the original Meeper's *geoGroup*, and move it aside.

- Rename Meeper's target geometry to the desired shape name.

- Sculpt the target shape.

Tip: Turn **Off** the **Sculpt Polygons Tool's Reflection** *option for shapes that are separate for each side of the face.*

- Test the blending if required, then delete the blend shape node.

- Hide the target shape.

- Save your work.

3 Repeat step 2 for all the shapes

Next is a list of the different shapes you can create:

Phonemes: *A, E, O, U, V, M*

Mouth shapes: *jawDown*, *smile*, *blowCheeks*

Eyebrows: *leftBrowUp, leftBrowSad, leftBrowMad, rightBrowUp, rightBrowSad, rightBrowMad*

Eyes: *leftWideOpen, leftLowerLidUp, leftBlinkMid, leftBlink Max,rightWideOpen,rightLowerLidUp, rightBlinkMid, rightBlinkMax*

Others: *breath*

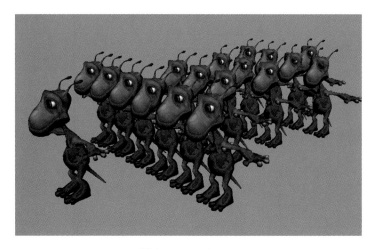

All the target shapes

Tip: *Your shapes will look more natural if they are not all perfect. For instance, moving one eyebrow up can move the cheeks and stretch the other eyebrow.*

In-between targets

The blend shape deformer has the ability to have *in-between* targets. This means that you can have multiple target shapes placed one after the other in the same blend shape attribute. This kind of blending is said to be in *series*, and the in-between shape transition will occur in the order in which you added the target shapes. The effect will be that the blend shape will be able to change from the first target object shape to the second, and so on.

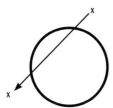
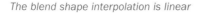
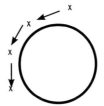

The blend shape interpolation is linear   *The blend shape interpolation with in-between targets*

In the last exercise, you created two different blend shapes for the blinking eyes: a blink *mid* shape and a blink *max* shape. The reason you had to do this is because if you blend from the eye open straight to the eye closed, the vertices of the eyelid could go straight through the eye rather than following the eye curvature.

1   Scene file

- Continue with your own scene.

Or

- Open the scene file *20-meeperBlendShapes_02.ma*.

Note: *This scene file contains all of Meeper's shapes. For simplicity reasons, the rest of the exercise will explain a workflow starting from this file.*

2   In-between targets

- Show only the *targetsEyesLayer* and the original *geometryLayer*.

Doing so displays the original Meeper geometry along with all the eye related blend shape targets.

- From the Outliner, select the *leftBlinkMid* target shape, which is child of the *blinkMidGroup*, under the *eyeGroup*.

- **Ctrl-select** the *leftBlinkMax* target shape, which is child of the *blinkMaxGroup*, under the *eyeGroup*.

- **Ctrl-select** the original *Meeper* geometry.

You should now have three objects selected in the following order: leftBlinkMid, leftBlinkMax and Meeper.

- Select **Deform** → **Create Blend Shape** → ❑.

- In the option window, make sure the **In-Between** checkbox is turned **On**.

- Click the **Apply** button.

3 Test the blink blending

- Select the original *Meeper* geometry.

- In the Channel Box, highlight the *blendShape1* node in the **Inputs** section.

- Highlight the *leftBlinkMax* attribute, then **MMB-drag** in the viewport to invoke the virtual slider.

*You will notice Meeper is shaped like leftBlinkMid at **0.5** and shaped like leftBlinkMax at **1**.*

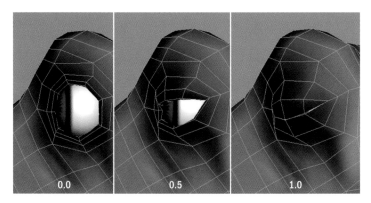

The in-between blending

4 Rename the attribute

Since the blink attribute is named *leftBlinkMax*, rename it to *leftBlink* by typing the following MEL command:

```
aliasAttr leftBlink blendShape1.leftBlinkMax;
```

Note: *You could also give the last target selected a proper name before creating the blend shape node.*

5 Add to a blend shape node that already exists

You will now add the right blink target to the blend shape node.

- Select the following objects in order: *rightBlinkMax* and *Meeper*.

- Select **Deform** → **Edit Blend Shape** → **Add**.

A new blend shape attribute is now added to the original blendShape1 node.

- Rename the attribute by typing the following MEL command:

```
aliasAttr rightBlink blendShape1.rightBlinkMax;
```

6 Add in-between to a blend shape node that already exists

- Select the following objects in order: *rightBlinkMid* and *Meeper*.

- Select **Deform** → **Edit Blend Shape** → **Add** → ❑.

- In the option window, set the following:

> **Specify Node** to **On**;
>
> **Add In-Between Targets** to **On**;
>
> **Target Index** to **2**;
>
> **In-Between Weight** to **0.5**.

Note: *The **Target Index** denotes which blend shape attribute the in-between should be added to, and the **In-Between Weight** is the position in the attribute in which it should reach that shape.*

- Click the **Apply** button.

The right eye now blinks properly with in-betweens.

Finalize the blend shape

You will now finalize Meeper's blend shapes by adding all the remaining shapes to its current blend shape node. In order to have coherence in the list of attributes of the blend shape node, you will have to select all the new targets in the order you want them to appear.

Once the blend shape node is final, you will optimize it by removing unused vertices from the blend shape deformer set. Once that is done, you will delete all the target shapes.

1   Add the targets

- Select the following objects in order:

    leftWideOpen, *rightWideOpen*, *leftLowerLidUp*, *rightLowerLidUp*, *A*, *E*, *O*, *U*, *F*, *M*, *jawDown*, *smile*, *blowCheeks*, *leftBrowUp*, *rightBrowUp*, *leftBrowSad*, *rightBrowSad*, *leftBrowMad*, *rightBrowMad*, *breath* and *Meeper*.

- Select **Deform → Edit Blend Shape → Add → ❑**.

- In the option window, reset all of the options to their default values.

- Click the **Apply** button.

2   Remove unwanted vertices from the deformer set

When you created the blend shape node, it listed all the vertices of Meeper's geometry in order to blend them, even if the vertices would never be affected by the deformer. For this reason, you will edit the deformer set in order to remove any vertices that will not be moved by any of the targets.

- Select the *Meeper* geometry.

- Select **Window → Relationship Editors → Deformer Sets**.

A window will be displayed with the deformer sets on the left panel and the scene objects in the right panel.

- Highlight the *blendShape1Set* on the left panel.

geometryLayer	
blendShape1	
tweak4	
Envelope	1
leftBlink	0
rightBlink	0
leftWideOpen	0
rightWideOpen	0
leftLowerLidUp	0
rightLowerLidUp	0
A	0
E	0
O	0
U	0
F	0
M	0
jawDown	0
smile	0
blowCheeks	0
leftBrowUp	0
rightBrowUp	0
leftBrowSad	0
rightBrowSad	0
leftBrowMad	0
rightBrowMad	0
breath	0

The blend shape node finalized

- **RMB-click** on the *blendShape1Set* to display its context menu, then select **Select Set Members**.

Doing so will select all the vertices of Meeper that are currently being affected by the blend shape deformer.

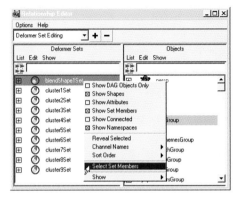

Select Set Members

- From the *front* view, while in Component mode, select all the vertices that are not moved by any of the blend shapes.

Note: *Don't select the vertices of the chest and back since the breath shape affects these vertices.*

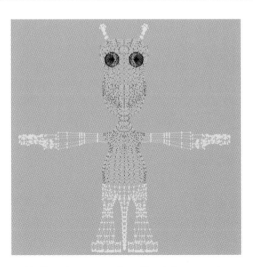

Vertices to remove from the deformer set

- In the Relationship Editor, still with the *blendShape1Set* highlighted, select **Edit** → **Remove Selected Items** from the left side panel.

3 Make sure the deformer set is good

- Deselect all the vertices.

- **RMB-click** on the *blendShape1Set* to display its context menu, then select **Select Set Members**.

Only the vertices deformed by the blendShape1Set get selected.

4 Test the blend shapes

- Test Meeper's blend shapes and make sure all of them still work correctly.

5 Delete the targets

- Select all target groups from the Outliner and delete them.

Note: *You might want to keep a version of the scene with all the target shapes in case you need them later on. Otherwise, the targets shapes can be extracted from the blend shape deformer.*

- Select **File** → **Optimize Scene Size** to remove any obsolete nodes.

6 Save your work

Blend shape manipulator

To continue with the manipulator theme and to make it easy for the animator to access Meeper's blend shapes, you will create a manipulator that will list all of Meeper's blend shapes.

1 Scene file

- Continue with your own scene.

Or

- Open the scene file *20-meeperBlendShapes_03.ma*.

2   Create a manipulator

- Select **Create** → **NURBS Primitives** → **Circle** → ❑.

- Set **Degree** to **Linear** and change the **Number of Sections** to **16**.

- Click the **Create** button.

- Rename the circle to *blendShapesManip*.

- Edit the manipulator so it looks like the following and place it above Meeper's head:

The blend shape manipulator

3   Place the manipulator in the rig

- Enable the visibility of the *rigLayer*.

- Parent the manipulator to the *Head* joint.

- Freeze the manipulator's transformations.

- Select **Edit** → **Delete by Type** → **History**.

- Lock and hide all of its attributes.

4   Add custom attributes

- Add a custom attribute for each shape in the blend shape deformer with the following values:

  Data Type to **Float**;

  Minimum to **0**;

  Maximum to **1**;

  Default to **0**.

Tip: *Add the attributes in the appropriate order. Use MEL to speed things up.*

- Through the Connection Editor, connect all the blend shape attributes to the manipulator's attributes.

Tip: *You can either select the blend shape node or highlight its name in the Channel Box to be able to load it in the Connection Editor. The Blend attributes are listed under the weight attribute.*

5   Save your work

- The final scene file is called *20-meeperBlendShapes_04.ma*.

Conclusion

In this lesson, you learned how to channel the power of the blend shape deformer. You recognized that you could create as many target shapes as needed to control a base shape. You also learned about in-between targets, which can refine the deformation for complex blends. Then you learned how to edit a deformer set, which is an essential concept to understand when dealing with deformers.

This lesson also covered specific facial behavior intended for lip-synching. Generating the appropriate facial expressions will breathe life into your character as it expresses itself.

In the next lesson, you will bind Meeper's skin to its skeleton.

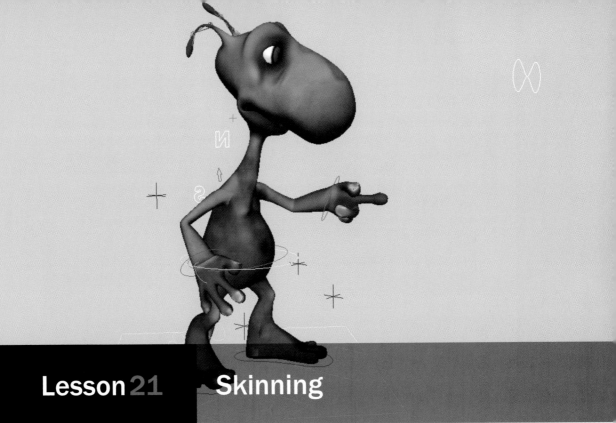

Lesson 21   Skinning

In this lesson, you will explore
the smooth bind deformer.
Smooth binding provides
smooth deformations around
joints by allowing multiple
joints to have influence on
the same vertex.

In this lesson you will learn the following:

- How to smooth bind surfaces to bones;

- How to edit weights with the Paint Skin
  Weights Tool;

- A recommended painting workflow;

- Tips and tricks for weighting smooth
  skinned surfaces.

Binding

Bound geometry points (CVs, vertices, lattice points) can be thought of as *skin points*. Smooth binding is the most common technique used to attach geometry to skeletal joints. Unlike rigid binding where a skin point is fully assigned to a particular joint, smooth binding allows the skin points to be weighted across many different joints. You can then refine a point's binding by changing the weights coming from each of the influences. These points all have a total weight of 1.0, but the weights can be shared between many different joints and influences.

The weight or participation of a skin point's influences can be locked or held to a specific value. This will inhibit the weight from changing as adjacent skin weights are adjusted and a total value of 1.0 is maintained.

1   Scene file

- Continue with your own scene from the last lesson.

Or

- Open the last lesson scene file called *20-meeperBlendShapes_04.ma*.

2   Hide what doesn't need to be bound

- In the *Perspective* view, select **Show** → **None**, then select **Show** → **Polygons** and **Show** → **Joints**.

3   Select the appropriate skeleton joints

In order to keep the skinning as simple as possible and to reduce the amount of influences to be calculated in Meeper's skinning, you will manually pick the joints that will influence the geometry.

- Select all the joints that you judge important to be part of the influences of the binding.

Tip: *Do your selection from the Outliner to ensure you don't forget any important joints.*

Note: *For instance, don't select the Hips joint, but rather the HipsOverride joint. Also, any joints at the tip of a joint chain don't need to be selected.*

4   Select the surface

- **Shift-select** *Meeper*'s skin.

5   Smooth Bind Meeper

- Select **Skin** → **Bind Skin** → **Smooth Bind** → ❐, and set the **Bind to** option to **Selected Joints**.

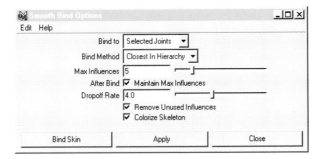

Smooth Bind Options window

Following are some explanations of the Smooth Bind options:

Closest In Hierarchy *specifies that joint influence is based on the skeleton's hierarchy. In character setup, you will usually want to use this binding method because it can prevent inappropriate joint influences. For example, this method can prevent a right leg joint from influencing nearby skin points on the left leg.*

Max Influences *are the number of joints that will have influence on an individual skin point. Setting the* **Max Influences** *to* **5** *means that each skin point will not have more than* **5** *joints affecting it.*

Setting the **Dropoff Rate** *is another way to determine how each skin point will be influenced by different joints. The Dropoff Rate controls how rapidly the influence of each joint on individual skin points are going to decrease with the distance between the two. The greater the dropoff, the more rapid the decrease in influence with distance. Max Influences and Dropoff Rate are described in greater detail later in this lesson, under the heading Paint Weight Tips.*

Tip: *The Dropoff Rate can be adjusted on individual joints after the character is skinned. The Max Influences can also be adjusted after the character has been skinned, except the new setting takes effect only on selected surfaces instead of the entire character with multiple surfaces.*

- Press the **Bind Skin** button to attach the skin to the skeleton and establish weighting.

6   Set IKs to FK

In order to test the skinning, you should first disable the IK handles. You want to rotate each bone individually in FK and watch the effect on the geometry.

- Set the **Ik Fk Blend** attribute to **0** for the arms, legs, back, neck and tail manipulators.

You can now rotate each bone using FK.

Tip: *You could also select* **Modify** → **Evaluate Nodes** → ❒ *and turn* **Off** *the* IK **Solvers** *and* **Constraints** *evaluation.*

7   Test the results

- Test the results of the smooth binding by rotating Meeper's arms and legs. Pay particular attention to Meeper's articulations.

- Return Meeper to his original pose by selecting **Assume Preferred Angle**.

8   Save your work

Editing weights

Weighting a character has traditionally been a long and tedious task. Fortunately, the Paint Skin Weights Tool eases the burden of this process by allowing you to paint weights directly on the geometry using a visual feedback.

When a character is bound, a skin cluster node is created for each of the surfaces that is bound to the skeleton. A skin cluster holds all the skin points' weights and influences, and you can edit the assignment of each point to different joints to achieve better deformations.

After moving Meeper around in the last exercise, you may notice that the settings you used for the smooth binding provide good quality deformations, but there are some problem areas such as the pelvis and shoulder. These areas will be improved by editing the weights of the skin points for the different influence joints.

Paint Skin Weights Tool

You will now use the Paint Skin Weights Tool to refine the arms' binding. To ensure that you are improving the skinning as you are painting, you will put Meeper into various poses that will bring out problematic areas.

1 Scene file

- Continue with your own scene.

Or

- Open the scene file *21-meeperSkin_01.ma*.

2 Pose Meeper to show problem areas

A good technique for simplifying the painting process is to keyframe Meeper while in extreme poses. This allows you to scroll in the time slider to see the deformations.

- Select the *LeftArm* joint.

- Go at frame **1** and set a keyframe.

- Establish several arm poses every **10** frames:

> *Arm up* at frame **10**;
>
> *Arm down* at frame **20**;
>
> *Arm forward* at frame **30**;
>
> *Arm backward* at frame **40**.

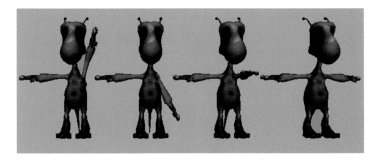

Arm poses

Tip: *You can create poses that are extreme, but try to keep them humanly possible.*

3 Paint Tool

- Select the *Meeper* geometry.

- Select **Skin** → **Edit Smooth Skin** → **Paint Skin Weights Tool** → ❑.

The Paint Skin Weights window

- Within the **Influence** list, find and highlight *LeftArm*.

- Within the **Stroke** section, turn **Screen Projection** to **On**.

- Within the **Display** section, set **Color Feedback** to **On**.

*This allows you to see a grayscale representation of the weighting values associated with the surface being painted. White corresponds to a value of **1**, black a value of **0**. The shades of gray represent a value between **0** and **1**.*

Visual feedback

Note: *In the above image, the* **Show Wireframe** *option was set to* **Off**.

4   Painting weights

If you look closer at the shoulder area, you will notice a gray color on the side of the chest. This kind of influence will deform the chest as you rotate the arm in an up position, such as the one at frame 10.

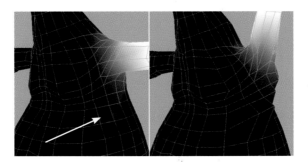

Chest influence at frame 0 and 10

- Select the second **Profile** brush.

- Set the **Paint Weights** operation to **Replace**.

- In the **Paint Weights** section, set **Value** to **0.0**.

By setting the painting value to 0, you are telling Maya to remove any weight coming from this bone and to reassign the removed weights to other bones already influencing this area, such as the spine bones.

- Paint the chest and armpit until the chest is no longer deformed by the *LeftArm*.

Tip: *Hold down the **b** key and **click+drag** to increase or decrease the brush size.*

- Scroll in the time slider between frame **1** and **10**.

You will notice that despite the fact you have painted the entire chest area black, some of the chest vertices are still moving. This is because there are weights assigned on other bones of the arm.

Those vertices are still moving

Corrected chest influence

- Select the *LeftForeArm* in the **Influence** section.

- Select the third **Profile** brush.

- Attempt to paint some black on the problematic vertices to see if that fixes the problem.

Note: *With the values so close to 0, you might not see the color difference with the color feedback.*

- If the previous step did not entirely fix the problem, try to paint the other arm joints black as well.

Note: *Painting weights on a character is an iterative process, so there will generally be some going back and forth between the influences.*

5 MMB-dragging

Another quick and easy technique to test the influence of the different bones, is to use the middle mouse button (MMB) and drag in the viewport.

- Go to frame **1**.
- Select the *LeftArm* joint.
- Select **Edit** → **Delete by Type** → **Channels**.

Doing so will remove the animation on the arm.

- With the *LeftArm* influence selected, **MMB+drag** in the viewport.

By dragging the mouse, the influence is rotated according to the current camera angle.

- Tumble around the arm to watch it bend under different angles.
- When you are done testing the rotations, you can either Undo or **RMB-click** and select **Assume Preferred Angle** to reset the joint's rotation.
- Click on the *Meeper* geometry to continue painting weights.

6 Smoothing weights

- Switch the **Paint Weight** operation to **Smooth**.
- Paint the shoulder and armpit area to smooth the *LeftArm* influences.

Smoothing will help to even out the deformation.

7 The clavicle

You are now ready to refine the influence on another part of the body.

- Select the *LeftShoulder* influence.

There is probably too much influence coming from this joint on the entire chest area.

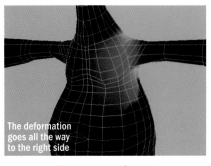

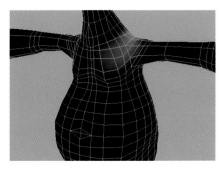

The deformation goes all the way to the right side

Bad clavicle influence   Corrected clavicle influence

- Set the **Paint Operation** to **Replace** and paint black on the chest. This will contain the influence on the pectoral muscle and the top of the shoulder.

Note: *Since the clavicle's rotation is used by the leftClavicleManip, you will not be able to use the **MMB-drag** technique. Use the manipulator to test the influence.*

8   Adding weights

So far, you have been painting the influences by painting zero weights (black). Doing so establishes the general influence of a joint, but you might not always be sure of where the removed influence will go. For instance, now that you removed weights from the clavicle influence, it is not clear where the influence went.

Tip: *As a general workflow, you should remove weights only when roughing out the weights on the entire character. Once that is done, you can start refining the influences by adding weights. If you stick to this, you will be certain to get the best possible results from the Paint Skin Weights Tool.*

- With the *LeftShoulder* influence still selected, set the **Paint Operation** to **Add**.

- Set the **Value** to **0.1** and select the second **Profile** brush.

- **Add** and **Smooth** the influence to the clavicle by painting the shoulder blade.

Doing so will greatly improve the clavicle influence by simulating the shoulder blade moving under the skin.

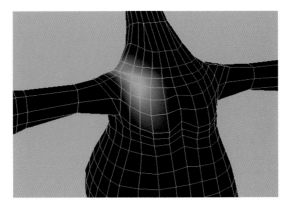

Shoulder blade influence

Tip: *Make sure you don't paint too much, as it will result in a harsh deformation.*

9 Flooding weights

The Paint Skin Weights Tool has the ability to flood the entire geometry with the specified operation. For instance, if a joint has no influence at all on the geometry, you can set the **Paint Operation** to **Replace** with a value of **0**, then click the **Flood** button. Another great way of using the Flood button is to smooth the entire influence of a joint in one click.

- Select the *Spine* influence.

- Set the **Paint Operation** to **Smooth**.

- Click on the **Flood** button.

The entire Spine influence was smoothed.

- Click the **Flood** button multiple times in order to really smooth an influence.

Tip: *You should especially flood smooth values after roughing out the entire character's influences, to avoid reassigning some weights onto other unknown influences.*

10 Save your work

Painting weights workflow

Now that you have learned the basics about painting weights, you can proceed to rough out the entire character. Once that is done, you can start smoothing the weights using the flood technique. Finally, when you have managed to assign adequate influences everywhere, you can add and smooth the localized area.

Following are the primary steps to take in order to weight the entire character perfectly:

1 Scene file

- Continue with your own scene.

Or

- Open the scene file *21-meeperSkin_02.ma*.

2 Roughing out the entire character

The following images show the roughing stage for all the influences. This was achieved by going through them one by one, and painting with the **Paint Operation** set to **Replace** with a value of **1**. You can then precisely define the regions you want certain influences to act upon.

Tip: Since Meeper is symmetrical, don't bother painting the joints with a name containing right since you will be using the **Mirror Skin Weights** to copy the weights from the left side to the other.

Complete character rough influences

Note: *In the above images, Meeper is displayed using the* **Multi-color Feedback** *available under the* **Display** *section of the Paint Skin Weights Tool, with the* **Wireframe** *turned* **Off.**

3 Mirror the influences

- With the *Meeper* geometry selected, select **Skin → Edit Smooth Skin → Mirror Skin Weights → ❐**.

- In the option window, set the **Mirror Across** option to **YZ** and turn **On** the **Positive to Negative** checkbox.

- Press the **Mirror** button.

4 Save your work

- Name the scene file *21-meeperSkinning_03.ma*.

5 Flood smoothing

Now that the entire character is weighted correctly, but with skin points influenced by only one joint, it is time to smooth out the weighting. If you bend Meeper at this time, the binding would look like rigid binding, causing the geometry to crack as it is being folded.

In order to smooth out the binding, you will use the flood smooth technique starting from the extremities of Meeper's limbs, working your way toward the pelvis.

- In the **Paint Skin Weights Tool** window, select the **Smooth** operation.

- Starting from the tip of the left fingers, press the **Flood** button for each finger influence.

Tip: *Rather than pressing the* **Flood** *button multiple times, go back and forth among the finger influences to smooth the binding. Doing so will even out the binding better than weighting.*

- Press the **Flood** button again, going from the left palm to the left clavicle.

- Press the **Flood** button again, going from the tip of the left antenna down to the base of the neck.

- Keep going down to the first spine bone.

Tip: *Since many bones are meeting in the hip area, you might have to repeat the smooth process, going back and forth between the influences.*

- Do the same, going from the tip of the tail up to the buttocks.

- Do the same, going from the left toes up to the hips.

- Lastly, do the reverse process, going from the hips to the extremities.

You should now have fairly smooth influences throughout the body.

Tip: *Once again, do not bother with influences with right in their name, since you will be mirroring the weights.*

6 Prune small weights

Pruning small weights will reassign weight from all the influences that are below a specified threshold.

- Select the *Meeper* geometry.

- Select **Skin** → **Edit** → **Smooth Skin** → **Prune Small Weights** → ❑.

- In the option window, set the **Prune Below** option to **0.1**.

The idea here is to prune fairly big weights in order to keep the skinning somewhat rough, and to be able to manually refine the influences later on. Toward the end of the painting process, you will be using a much smaller value for pruning.

- Click the **Prune** button.

Note: *Without weights lower than 0.1 on your character, it is more likely you will notice zones of skin points that are not well assigned and gray.*

7 Mirror the influences

- With the *Meeper* geometry selected, select **Skin** → **Edit Smooth Skin** → **Mirror Skin Weights**.

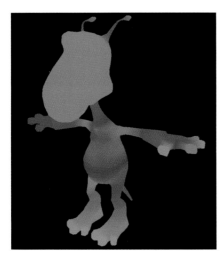 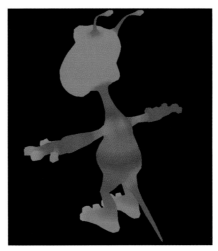

Complete character rough influences

8 Test the influences

- Rotate the various joints to see their individual effects, and note the places creating problems.

Tip: *Using the IK splines to test the deformation of the spine, neck and tail might yield better results.*

- If necessary, do another pass of smoothing on the entire character or only on specific body parts where you find the influence to be too rough.

9 Save your work

- Name the scene file *21-meeperSkinning_04.ma*.

10 Refining

It is now time to refine all the influences by hand. Use the **Add** and **Smooth** operations as much as possible along with the **MMB-drag** technique to test the deformation. Try to bend your character in all possible ways as you refine folds, but keep in mind that your character can have limitations. It is almost impossible to generate geometry, skin and rig that look good in all possible extreme positions.

Tip: You can use the **Alt+b** hotkey to cycle the background color between the default gray and black. A black background color along with the color feedback of the Paint Tool will make the influence area more apparent.

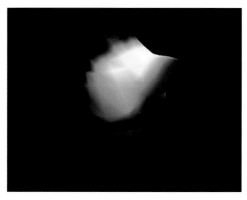

Shoulder influence with color feedback and black background

Tip: When you are happy with the weighting of an influence, you can press the **Toggle Hold Weights on Selected** button to lock the weights for that influence. Be careful using this feature, because when Maya cannot find an unlocked influence to put weight on, it might end up adding it to unwanted places.

11 Prune small weights

- Select the *Meeper* geometry.

- Select **Skin** → **Edit** → **Smooth Skin** → **Prune Small Weights** → ❑.

- In the option window, set the **Prune Below** option to **0.02**.

- Click the **Prune** button.

You are now sure that very small weight values won't influence the geometry in unintentional ways.

12 Mirror the influences

- With the *Meeper* geometry selected, select **Skin** → **Edit Smooth Skin** → **Mirror Skin Weights**.

13 Save your work

- Name the scene file *21-meeperSkinning_05.ma*.

Final touches

There is only one more thing to add to Meeper for him to be fully animatable.
You must skin the eyes to the eye joints. Once that is done, you will be able to
move the lookat target and see Meeper come to life.

1 Scene file

- Continue with your own scene.

Or

- Open the scene file *21-meeperSkin_05.ma*.

2 Bind the eyes

- Select the *left* eye geometry, then **Shift-select** the *LeftEye* joint.

Tip: *Make sure that* **Show** → **NURBS Surfaces** *as well as* **Show** → **NURBS**
Curves *are turned* **On** *in the viewport.*

- Select **Skin** → **Bind Skin** → **Smooth Bind**.
- Repeat for the other eye.

3 Test the eye motion

- Press **6** to see Meeper's textures.
- Select and move the *eyeLookAt* manipulator.
- Try to scale and rotate the *eyeLookAt* manipulator to see the effect
on Meeper.

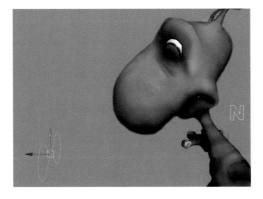

Meeper can now look where he wants

4   Test the skinning

- Set all the manipulators with the *ikFkBlend* attribute back to **1**.

- Attempt to pose Meeper to see if everything follows and deforms properly.

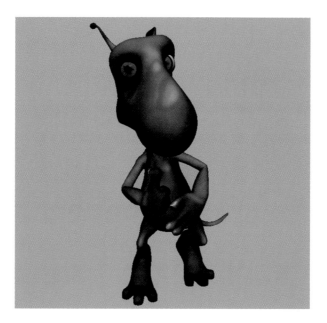

Final skinned Meeper

5   Save your work

- The final scene file is called *21-meeperSkinning_06.ma*.

Paint weight tips

Although smooth binding and the Paint Skin Weights Tool simplify the process of deforming a character, you may still encounter some pitfalls, depending on the character you are working with. The following section provides some general tips and guidelines for making the smooth skinning process more efficient, and also summarizes some of the key points of the workflow you just completed.

Paint Scale Operation

The **Scale Operation** in the **Paint Skin Weights Tool** was not mentioned in this lesson, but you might find it very handy. Scaling weights at a value of 0.9 for instance, will remove 10% of the weight of the selected influence and redistribute it proportionally among the other influences in the painting area. This is a good feature to use since the tool will not attempt to add all the removed weights to other influences, but it will rather scale the values you have already defined.

Numeric weighting

Each skin point has a total weight value of **1.0**, but that weight can be spread across many influences. If a group of skin points isn't behaving the way you want it to, it is possible they are getting weights from different (and perhaps unwanted) influences.

To check or modify the assignments of weights of each skin point, do the following:

- Select some bound vertices or CVs.

- Select **Window** → **General Editors** → **Component Editor**.

- Select the **Smooth Skins** tab.

- Enable **Option** → **Hide Zero Columns** to hide any influences that don't affect the selected skin points.

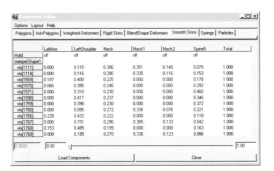

The Component Editor

Tip: Highlight entire columns by clicking on their influence label, then set the focus on any weight field and type **0**. Then hit **Enter** to remove any weight coming from the selected influences. This is very useful when you want to select a bunch of points and ensure they are not affected by unwanted influences.

Adjust the Dropoff Rate

When you initially smooth bind the skin, you can set the **Dropoff Rate** for each of the influences manually. The Dropoff Rate determines how much the weighting decreases as the distance between the influence and the skin point increases. Increasing the Dropoff Rate helps localize the weighting for the selected joint.

To adjust the Dropoff Rate after skinning, do the following:

- Select the desired joint.

- Adjust the **Dropoff** in the **Smooth Skin Parameters** section of the Attribute Editor.

- Click the **Update Weights** button.

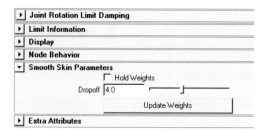

Adjusting the selected joint's Dropoff Rate

Adjust the Max Influences

You have an option to set the number of **Max Influences** on each bound surface. For Meeper, you set the **Max Influences** to **5**, which means that a total of five influences can participate in the weighting on a given skin point. This adds up to a lot of weighting and re-weighting since changing the weighting of one skin point has a *rippling* effect on the weights of the other skin points. As the number of max influences increases, so does this complexity of interdependent weighting.

In many cases, it is easier to lower the **Max Influences** of each surface than trying to track down which influence controls which skin point. Lower Max Influence settings will help to localize the control of the weighting.

To change the Max Influence setting, do the following:

- Select a smooth bound surface.

- Select **Skin → Edit Smooth Skin → Set Max Influences...**

- Set the new amount of maximum influences allowed.

- Click the **Apply and Close** button.

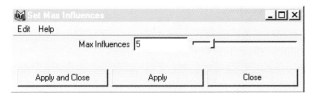

Adjusting Max Influences

Note: *A* **Max Influence** *setting of* **1** *causes the surface skinning to behave like rigid binding.*

Equalize weights on multiple surfaces

If the tangency between two NURBS patches is giving you problems, it is often easiest to set the same weighting value on the two surfaces to get a uniform weight across the seam. You can then smooth out the weighting between the two surfaces. This technique is helpful because all of the values are set to a uniform state before the smoothing process begins.

Using wrap deformer

Another technique used to bind a NURBS patch model is to convert the NURBS patches to a single combined polygonal object and then use a wrap deformer to deform the patches. Doing so greatly simplifies the weighting process of a model since there is only a single poly object to bind and weight.

Toggle hold weights

There are times you can feel like you are chasing your tail when weighting complex surfaces and influence objects. You can toggle **On** and **Off** a **Hold** flag for each influence object. This will lock the value and prevent it from changing.

When you add an influence object to a skinned object, it is a good idea to lock this influence object to a value of 0 when it is created. This will help prevent the new influence object from disrupting your existing weighting. This will be explored more in-depth in the next lesson.

Flood values

As you have seen, depending on the number of **Max Influences** set when the
original **Smooth Bind** function is applied, there can be many joints affecting
the same skin point. At times, it is easiest to select the surfaces and an
influence and **Replace** all weighting values with a common value using the
Flood button.

This is particularly useful for removing unwanted weighting applied to the
root joint, or other joints that should not have any influence on the surface.

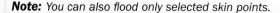

Note: *You can also flood only selected skin points.*

Prune small weights

After spending time weighting a character, you might notice that a small
amount of weight might be added to many different influences. Generally,
the amount of weight is very small and hard to detect, but it does affect
where weights are distributed when they are adjusted on a particular
influence. When you take weight away from a surface, the weight gets
distributed to every surface that has an influence on it, even if it is only
a small weight. This also might have a significant influence on speed,
performance and the size of the file.

Pruning small weights will remove weight from all influences below a
specified threshold. To prune weights, do the following:

▪ Select all of the surfaces that you would like to prune.

▪ Select **Skin → Edit → Smooth Skin → Prune Small Weights → ❐**.

▪ Specify the value of small weight to prune as needed.

▪ Click the **Prune** button.

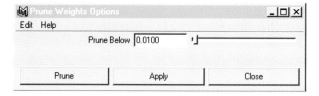

Prune Weights Options

Copy Skin Weights

The **Copy Skin Weights** command can greatly speed up a weighting task. For instance, you could weight a lower resolution model and copy the skin weights to a higher resolution model. As a result, you could have a good starting point to refine the higher resolution model.

Import and export skin weights

There is a possibility to export and import skin weights if needed. Doing so will generate one grayscale image per influence object and write it to disk. The images exported are relative to the model's UVs, so if your model doesn't have proper UVs or overlapping UVs, importing the weight maps might give undesirable results.

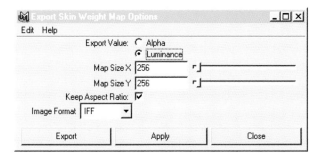

Export Skin Weight Map Options

Tip: *If you want to transfer skin weights based on spatial location rather than UVs, use **Copy Skin Weights**. With Copy Skin Weights, your source and target skinned geometry do not need to have the same UVs.*

Conclusion

Smooth and rigid skinning are the two basic types of skinning available in Maya. Smooth skinning allows for more control over the skinned surface using influence objects, while rigid skinning relies on clusters of points to be deformed by the influence objects.

In this lesson, you learned how to bind a character and how to use the Paint Skin Weights Tool. You also experienced a typical weighting workflow and learned several tips and tricks for speeding up the weighting process.

In the next lesson, you will learn about influence objects.

Lesson 22

Influence objects

In this lesson, you will examine how influence objects aid the deformations of smooth bound geometry. Their transforms can be used to manipulate the position of skin points to either smooth out deformations or add effects to the skin. For Meeper, you are going to add influence objects to refine the belly, shoulder and bicep areas.

In this lesson you will learn the following:

- How to create influence objects;

- How to weight influence objects and the surrounding skin to provide realistic deformations;

- How to use curves to create a nice bone effect;

- How to automate deformations using Set Driven Keys;

- How to mirror influence weights.

Influence objects

Influence objects are external sources used to deform smooth bound skin. These objects can be any type, such as geometry or locators, and they can behave in a similar way to joint influence. You will see in this lesson that using geometry as an influence object can really improve your skin deformation. An influence object's default setting uses the transform of an object to affect the skin surface, but it can be set to use components, such as vertices or CVs, to determine the offset of skin points.

For instance, you can add an influence object to simulate a bicep bulging while the arm bends, and the skin vertices would bulge along. You could also use an influence object that is affected by any type of dynamics or deformers. The potential of influence objects is endless.

Belly influence

The smooth binding done in the previous lesson has very good deformations, but parts of the character could be improved even more. For this exercise, you are going to add an influence object to smooth out the roundness of the belly using NURBS.

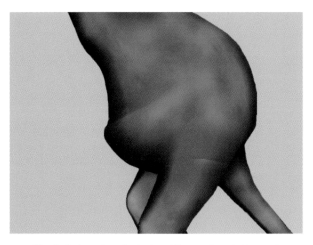

The belly is not perfect when Meeper bends forward

1   Scene file

- Continue with your own scene from the last lesson.

Or

- Open the last lesson scene file called *21-meeperSkin_06.ma*.

2   Return to bind pose

It is recommended to return Meeper to his bind pose before inserting influence objects.

- Select **Modify** → **Evaluate Nodes** → **Ignore All**.
- Select Meeper's *Hips* joint.
- Select **Skin** → **Go to Bind Pose**.

Tip: *Resetting all manipulators to their default positions should also do the trick.*

3   Create a NURBS plane

You will now create a NURBS plane to be used as the influence object onto Meeper's belly.

- Select **Create** → **NURBS Primitives** → **Plane**.
- Set the plane's **Patches U** and **Patches V** to **2** in the **Inputs** section of the Channel Box.
- Rename the plane to *bellyInfluence*.

4   Place the plane appropriately

- Rotate the *bellyInfluence* on the **X-axis** by **90 degrees**, then translate and scale it in front of Meeper's belly.

- Switch to Component mode and edit the *bellyInfluence* to look like this:

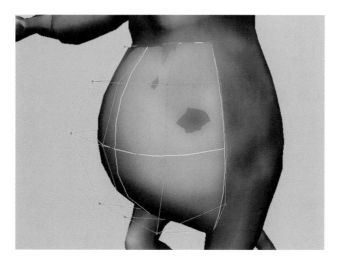

bellyInfluence positioned correctly

- Go back to Object mode and delete the *bellyInfluence*'s history.

5 Add the influence object

- Select the *Meeper* geometry, then **Shift-select** the *bellyInfluence*.

- Select **Skin → Edit Smooth Skin → Add Influence → ❑**.

- In the option window, reset the settings, then set the following:

   Use Geometry to **On**;

   Lock Weights to **On**;

   Default Weight to **0.0**.

- Click the **Add** button.

When the influence object is created, the object is duplicated and hidden. That object is a base object, which stores the component information of the influence object at its default position. Without the base object, you would not be able to manipulate the components of the influence object.

> **Note:** The **Lock Weights** option specifies that the influence object should not get any weights at this time for the surface. You will be painting the weights manually later in the lesson.

6 Bind the influence object

You are going to smooth bind the influence object to the skeleton so it moves with the rest of the skeleton.

- Select the joints to bind the influence object to, such as the *HipsOverride*, *LeftUpLeg*, *RightUpLeg*, *Spine*, *Spine1*, *Spine2*, *Spine3* and *Spine4*.

- **Shift-select** the *bellyInfluence*.

- Select **Skin** → **Bind Skin** → **Smooth Skin** → ⊓.

- Make sure **Bind to** is set to **Selected Joints** in the option window, then click the **Bind Skin** button.

7 Adjust weighting

- Select the *bellyInfluence*, then select **Skin** → **Edit Smooth Skin** → **Paint Skin Weights Tool** → ⊓.

- Paint the weights on the *bellyInfluence*.

Tip: *You should definitely assign some weight to the HipsOverride joint, as it is where the belly should hook itself.*

8 Test the binding

At this point, you want to test the *bellyInfluence* binding to see if it bends correctly with the skeleton.

Belly influence deforms much smoother

9 Save your work

Paint influence on Meeper

Now that the influence object is inserted into Meeper's skinning and it is well bound to the skeleton, you can paint some influence coming from the influence object onto Meeper's belly.

1   Scene file

- Continue with your own scene.

Or

- Open the scene file called *22-meeperInfluence_01.ma*.

2   Hide the influence object

- Select the *bellyInfluence* and press **Ctrl+h** to hide it.

3   Unlock the influence object weight

- Select the *Meeper* geometry.

- Select **Skin → Edit Smooth Skin → Paint Skin Weights Tool → □**.

- In the tool window, scroll down to the bottom of the list of influences and highlight *bellyInfluence (Hold)*.

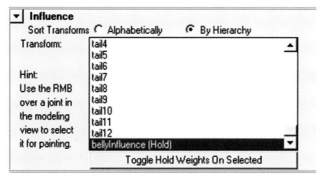

The bellyInfluence is listed

Alias

Tip: *Maya Artisan is the best feature - the brush paradigm is so natural for users. Having the ability to select, paint, edit and animate attributes as well as add, remove and sculpt geometry with a brush is a powerful high-level interface to what would otherwise require tedious and error prone manipulation of many individual elements..*

Shai Hinitz | Sr. Product Manager, Rendering and Animation

Note: *The influence was locked when you created it earlier in this lesson.*

- Since you are about to paint the weights for the influence, click the **Toggle Hold Weights On Selected** button to disable the locking of its weight.

By doing so, the influence's name in the list will change from bellyInfluence (Hold) to bellyInfluence. This confirms that you will be able to paint for the selected influence.

4   Paint the weight coming from the influence

- Select the **Add** operation with a value of **0.2**.
- Select the first **Profile** brush.
- Paint some influence to cover most of Meeper's belly.

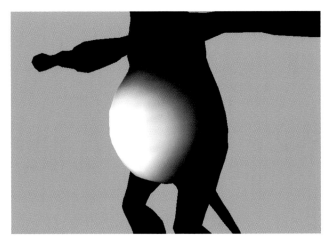

The bellyInfluence's weight

5   Use components

If you attempt to move the rig at this time, you will notice that the skin points influenced by the *bellyInfluence* do not move. This is because the smooth skin node doesn't know you want to use the components of the influence object to drive the points and it is using the transform information instead. Since the transform of the *bellyInfluence* stays still (only the points move because of the skinning), the skin points end up not moving.

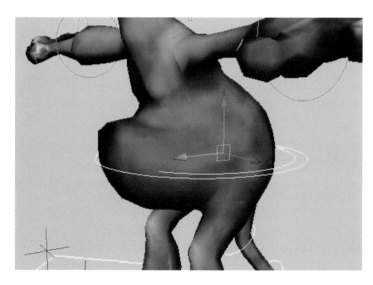

The skin points do not move

There is an attribute in the smooth skin node that allows you to select between using the object's transform node or its components as the driving force to create the deformations. In this case, you will use its component information to get the desired deformations.

- Select the *Meeper* geometry.

- In the Channel Box, highlight the *skinCluster1* node.

- Change the **Use Components** attribute to **On**.

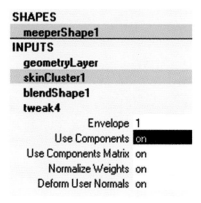

Enable the Use Components attribute

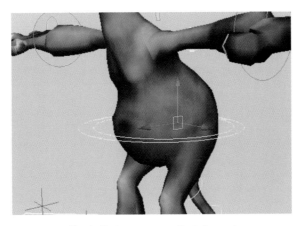

The belly is now correctly deformed

6 Tweak the bellyInfluence binding

Now that you can see the influence of the NURBS plane on the belly, it might be a good idea to ensure the binding of the plane is refined to allow maximum bending. At the same time, you must make sure the weight coming from the influence object is adequate to allow Meeper to have a proper deformation.

Tip: Select **Display → Show → Show Last Hidden** or press **Ctrl+Shift+h** *in order to display the bellyInfluence that was hidden earlier in the lesson.*

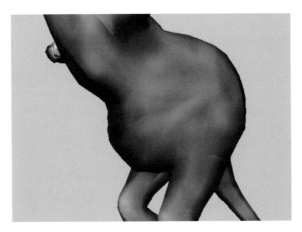

Meeper can now bend forward much further

7 Save your work

Clavicles

You will now use another influence object to increase the display of the clavicle bones when Meeper is moving his clavicles forward. The following exercise can also be done in similar ways to achieve a nice bump caused by a ligament, a bone, or other cases requiring the skin to stretch.

1 Scene file

- Continue with your own scene.

Or

- Open the scene file called *22-meeperInfluence_02.ma*.

2 Make Live

Making a piece of geometry live allows you to draw or snap points directly onto a surface.

- Select the *Meeper* surface.

- Click on the **Make Live** button located at the top right of the main interface.

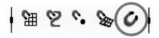

The Make Live button

The Meeper geometry will change to be displayed in green wireframe.

3 Draw a curve

- Select **Create** → **EP Curve** → □, and make sure the **Curve Degree** is set to **Linear**.

- Draw **three** curve points directly on Meeper, starting from the shoulder, going to the center of the neck, then on to the other side to represent the clavicle bones.

Note: *For simplicity reasons, the clavicle curve will be basic, but increasing its resolution could achieve smoother results.*

- Press **Enter** to confirm the curve creation and exit the tool.

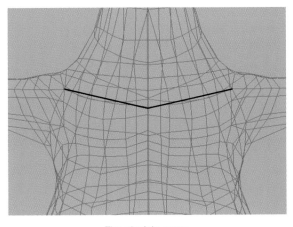

The clavicle curve

Tip: *Try to follow one of Meeper's geometry edge loops.*

- Click the **Make Live** button to return *Meeper* to his original state.
- Select the newly created curve and rename it to *clavicleInfluence*.
- Select **Modify** → **Center Pivot**.

4 Insert the curve as an influence object

- Select the *Meeper* geometry, then **Shift-select** the *clavicleInfluence*.
- Select **Skin** → **Edit Smooth Skin** → **Add Influence**.

The curve is now part of Meeper's influences with zero weight.

5 Rigid bind the curve

- Select the following joints: *Spine5*, *LeftShoulder*, *RightShoulder*.
- **Shift-select** the *clavicleInfluence*.
- Select **Skin** → **Bind Skin** → **Rigid Bind** → ❐.
- In the option window, make sure **Bind to** is set to **Selected Joints**, then click the **Bind Skin** button.

The default binding should assign the points to the good bones right away.
The CVs on the extremities of the curves should go to their respective clavicle
bones, and the center CV should be assigned to the spine bone.

Tip: *You can select the* **Deform → Edit Membership Tool** *to double-check if the vertices are well bound to the bones.*

6 Paint the weight of the influence object

If you rotate the clavicle forward, you will see that the curve defines a straight line between the chest and the shoulder. Your goal is to paint the influence of the curve on Meeper's geometry to get the clavicle to stand out.

- Select **Skin → Edit Smooth Skin → Paint Skin Weights Tool → ❐**.

- Scroll to the bottom of the influence list and highlight the *clavicleInfluence*.

- Click the **Toggle Hold Weights On Selected** button to disable the locking of its weight.

- Zoom in on the clavicle region and paint weights as follows:

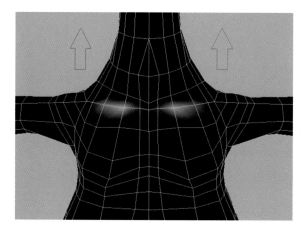

The clavicleInfluence weights

7 Rotate the clavicles to test the deformation

- Hide the *clavicleInfluence* curve.

- Rotate the clavicle manipulators and make any adjustments necessary to refine the deformation.

Tip: *Clavicle bones don't usually move that much, so keep the rotations humanly possible.*

8   Save your work

Biceps

Despite the fact that Meeper is a pretty skinny character, it might be a good idea to add a bulging bicep as he bends his arm. To do so, you will use a locator as an influence object.

1   Scene file

- Continue with your own scene.

Or

- Open the scene file called *22-meeperInfluence_03.ma*.

2   Create a locator

- Select **Create** → **Locator** and rename it to *leftBicepInfluence*.

Tip: *Make sure that* **Locators** *is turned* **On** *in the* **Show** *menu.*

- Parent the *leftBicepInfluence* to Meeper's *LeftArm* joint.

3   Place the locator

- Move the *leftBicepInfluence* to the bicep area of the arm.

4   Add the influence

- Select the *Meeper* geometry, then **Shift-select** the *leftBicepInfluence*.
- Select **Skin** → **Edit Smooth Skin** → **Add Influence**.

The locator is now part of Meeper's influences with zero weight.

5   Paint the influence

- Select **Skin** → **Edit Smooth Skin** → **Paint Skin Weights Tool** → ❒.
- Scroll to the bottom of the **Influence** list and highlight the *leftBicepInfluence*.
- Click the **Toggle Hold Weights On Selected** button to disable the locking of its weight.

- Zoom in on the bicep region and paint weights as follows:

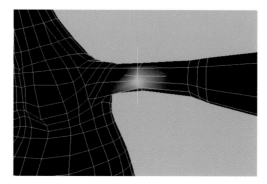

The leftBicepInfluence weights

6   Set Driven Keys

You now want the locator to bulge the bicep as the forearm bends.
The best way to do this is by setting driven keys that will automate the
bulging animation.

- Select **Animate** → **Set Driven Key** → **Set** → □.

- Load the *LeftForeArm rotateY* as the **Driver**.

- Load the *leftBicepInfluence* as the **Driven** and highlight all of its translation
  attributes.

- Click the **Key** button to set the default position of the influence object.

- Rotate the *LeftForeArm*.

- Move the *leftBicepInfluence* to bulge the bicep.

- Click the **Key** button to set the bulge position of the influence object.

The bulged position of the leftBicepInfluence

Tip: *The arm must be in FK to rotate the joint manually.*

7 Test the influence

- Rotate *LeftForeArm* back and forth to see the effect of the influence object on the bicep.

8 Set Driven Keys

The bulging of the bicep should look pretty good, but you might notice snaps when it starts and stops moving. This is because the Set Driven Keys are linear. You will now change the influence's animation curve to ease in and out.

- Select the *leftBicepInfluence*.

- Select **Window** → **Animation Editors** → **Graph Editor...**

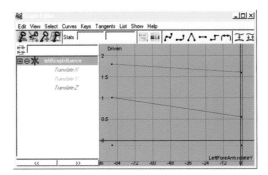

The leftBicepInfluence animation curves

- Select all the animation curves, then select **Tangents** → **Flat**.

The animation curves now have flat tangents, which will help for progressive animation of the influence object.

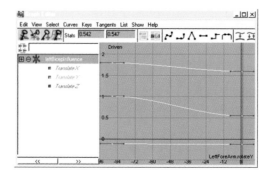

The corrected animation curves

9   Save your work

Mirror influences

You could repeat the last exercise for the other arm of Meeper's body, but fortunately, you don't have to redo everything. The influence objects can be duplicated and the weighting of the influence can be mirrored, just like bone influences.

1   Scene file

- Continue with your own scene.

Or

- Open the scene file called *22-meeperInfluence_04.ma*.

2 Mirror the influence objects

The following steps will duplicate and mirror the locator to the other arm.

- Select the *leftBicepInfluence*.
- Press **Ctrl+d** to duplicate it.
- Press **Shift+p** to unparent it.
- Press **Ctrl+g** to group it.
- Set the **Scale X** value for the new group to **-1**.
- Select the new *leftBicepInfluence1* object on Meeper's right arm, and rename it to *rightBicepInfluence*.
- Select the *rightBicepInfluence,* then **Shift-select** the *RightArm* joint.

- Press **p** to parent the locator to the joint.

- In the Outliner, delete the temporary group used to mirror the locator.

3 Add the influence object

- Select the *rightBicepInfluence*, then **Shift-select** the *Meeper* geometry.

- Select **Skin → Edit Smooth Skin → Add Influence**.

4 Unlock the weighting for the influence objects

You are about to mirror the weighting from the left side of Meeper's body to the right side. Before you can do that, the new influence object must have its weight unlocked so that it can receive the new weighting values.

- Select the *Meeper* surface.

- Open the **Paint Skin Weights Tool** window.

- Press the **Toggle Hold Weights On Selected** button with the *rightBicepInfluence* highlighted to unlock its weighting.

5 Mirror the shirt's weighting

Now that the duplicate locator has been made as an influence object and its influence weight is unlocked, you can mirror the weighting from the left side of Meeper's body to the right side.

- Select the *Meeper* surface.

- Select **Skin → Edit Smooth Skin → Mirror Skin Weights**.

Tip: *Make sure that* **Mirror Across** *is set to* **YZ***, and that* **Direction Positive to Negative** *is toggled* **On**.

- Double-check that the influences of the biceps were mirrored.

Note: *By mirroring at this time, you also made the belly and clavicle influences symmetrical.*

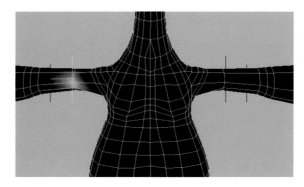

Bicep weight mirrored correctly

6   Recreate the Set Driven Keys

As in the last exercise, use Set Driven Keys and the rotation of the *RightForeArm* to control the bulging of the bicep. Also, change the animation curves to have flat tangents.

7   Lock and hide objects and attributes

- Select the *leftBicepInfluence* and *rightBicepInfluence*.

- Set their visibility attribute to **Off**.

- Lock and hide all of their attributes from the Channel Box.

8   Test the weighting

Pose Meeper to check if the weighting is correct over all of his body. When you're done, return Meeper to his original position.

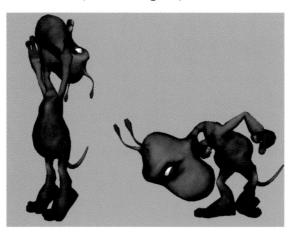

Influence objects provide good results

Final touches

In order to keep the scene clean, you will group all the influences together and parent them in the rig hierarchy. You will also lock all their attributes to prevent erroneous manipulations.

1 Group the influence objects

- From the Outliner, select the unparented influence objects along with their base objects created earlier in this lesson.

- Press **Ctrl+g** to group them together.

- Rename the group to *influenceGroup*.

- Parent the *influenceGroup* to the *rig* group.

2 Lock and hide attributes

- Select the *influenceGroup* and all its children.

- Highlight all the attributes in the Channel Box, then **RMB-click** and select **Lock and Hide Selected**.

3 Save your work

- The final scene file is called *22-meeperInfluence_05.ma*.

Conclusion

In this lesson, you learned about influence objects and their workflows. Influence objects can be any transforms, such as locators, curves, or geometry. They get carried along with the joint hierarchy to influence the skin points. Very powerful rigs can be established using influence objects. Influence objects can even be driven by dynamics as soft bodies or by using the jiggle deformer to establish secondary or reactive movements under the skin. Influence objects can also be used to improve problematic areas.

In the next lesson, you will finalize Meeper by adding deformers that will add automated secondary animation. You will also build a low resolution model that will react in real-time as the animator plays with it. Finally, you will apply a poly smooth to generate a higher resolution model that you will be able to turn on or off before rendering.

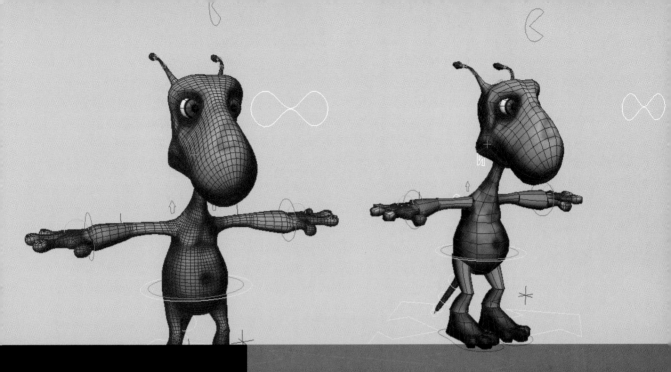

Lesson 23 Final touches

In this lesson, you will finalize the Meeper character by adding a few deformers that will help generate secondary animation. You will also create both a low resolution and high resolution file to use as references in Project 7.

In this lesson you will learn the following:

- How to set up a jiggle deformer;

- How to use the jiggle deformer on an influence object;

- How to use a sculpt deformer;

- How to use a motion path with a custom attribute;

- How to change the deformation order;

- How to create a low resolution version of the model;

- How to copy skin weights;

- How to detach a skin;

- How to create a high resolution version of the model.

Jiggle deformer

Jiggle deformers cause points on a surface or curve to shake as they move, speed up, or slow down. You can apply jiggle to specific points or to the entire object. In the context of jiggle deformers, the term points means CVs, lattice points, or the vertices of polygonal or subdivision surfaces.

In this exercise, you will be using the jiggle deformer on Meeper's nose.

1 Scene file

- Continue with your own scene from the last lesson.

Or

- Open the last lesson scene file called *22-meeperInfluence_05.ma*.

2 Assign jiggle

- While in Component mode, with the *Meeper* vertices displayed, select the nose vertices as follows:

 Tip: *You can use the Lasso Tool to select the vertices.*

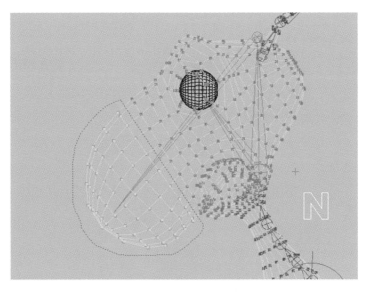

The nose vertices selected using the Lasso Tool

- Select **Deform** → **Create Jiggle Deformer**.

The jiggle deformer is now added and will affect only the selected vertices.

3   Paint jiggle weights

Just like skin weights, you can paint jiggle weights by using the Paint Tool. You will now smooth the jiggle's influence to deform the nose more evenly.

- Select **Deform** → **Paint Jiggle Weights Tool** → ❑.

You should see the the influence of the jiggle on the nose with the color feedback of the Paint Tool.

- Set the **Paint Operation** to **Smooth** and press the **Flood** button several times to get the following result:

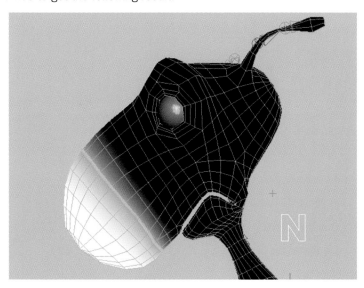

The nose's jiggle weights

4   Test the motion

In order to test the motion of the jiggle on the nose, you need to move the head so that the jiggle affects the geometry.

- Select the *Head* joint.

- Set keyframes at frame **1**, **5**, **10** and **15** with different head rotations going up and down.

- Playback the results.

You should notice the jiggle affecting Meeper too much.

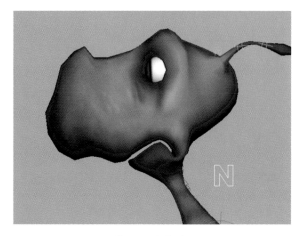

Too much jiggle

5   Adjust jiggle settings

You will now change jiggle's attributes to adjust the different dynamic settings and even out the jiggling of the nose.

- Select the *Meeper* geometry and highlight the *jiggle1* node in the **Inputs** section of the Channel Box.

The different attributes of the deformer are displayed.

- Set the following on the *jiggle1* node:

> **Stiffness** to **0.4**;
>
> **Damping** to **0.3**;
>
> **Jiggle Weight** to **0.4**.

- Playback the results.

The jiggle should be much more subtle and realistic.

Note: *You can get more jiggling by increasing the* **Jiggle Weight***.*

6   Remove the head animation

- Select the *head* joint.

- In the Channel Box, highlight the **Rotation** attributes.

- **RMB-click** and select **Break Connections**.

- Set the **Rotation** attributes back to **0**.

7   Save your work

More jiggling

You will now add jiggling to Meeper's belly, using the *bellyInfluence* object.

1   Scene file

- Continue with your own scene.

Or

- Open the scene file called *23-meeperFinal_01.ma*.

2   Display the bellyInfluence object

- Through the Outliner, select the *bellyInfluence* object.

- Unlock the visibility attribute using **Window** → **General Editors** → **Channel Control…**

- Select **Display** → **Show** → **Show Selection** or press **Shift+h** to display the *bellyInfluence* object.

3   Assign jiggle

- While in Component mode, select the following *bellyInfluence* CVs:

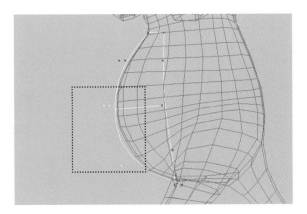

Assign jiggle to the bellyInfluence CVs

- Select **Deform** → **Create Jiggle Deformer**.

- Select **Deform** → **Paint Jiggle Weights Tool** → ❑.

- Set the **Paint Operation** to **Smooth** and press the **Flood** button to get the following result:

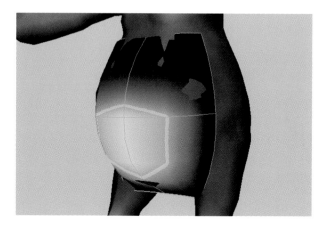

Belly's jiggle influence

4   Adjust the jiggle settings

- Highlight the *jiggle2* node in the **Inputs** section of the Channel Box.

- Set the following:

> **Stiffness** to **0.2**;
>
> **Damping** to **0.2**;
>
> **Jiggle Weight** to **1**.

5   Hide the bellyInfluence object

- Lock and hide the *bellyInfluence* object.

6   Test the motion

Again, in order to test the motion of the jiggle on the belly, you need to animate the hips.

- Select the *hipsManip*.

- Set keyframes at frame **1**, **5**, **10** and **15** in different positions going up and down.

- Playback the results.

7   Remove the animation

- Select the *hipsManip*.

- In the Channel Box, highlight the animated attributes.

- **RMB-click** and select **Break Connections**.

- Set the attributes back to their default values.

8   Save your work

Sculpt deformer

In this exercise, you will add swallowing capability to Meeper. To do so, you will create a sculpt deformer and animate it along a path following the throat. You will then edit the order of deformation so the sculpt deformer is evaluated before any other deformers. Doing so will allow the swallowing motion to be accurate even when Meeper is animated.

1   Scene file

- Continue with your own scene.

    Or

- Open the scene file called *23-meeperFinal_02.ma*.

2   Sculpt deformer

- With the *Meeper* geometry selected, choose **Deform → Create Sculpt Deformer**.

    A sculpt deformer will be created.

- In the Outliner, parent the *sculpt1StretchOrigin* node to the *sculptor1* node.

    Doing so will allow you to slide the deformer under Meeper's skin.

3   Place the sculpt deformer

- Select the *sculptor1* node.

- Place the deformer in Meeper's throat as follows:

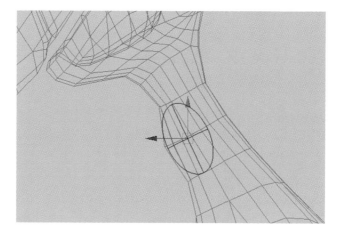

The deformer in Meeper's throat

4   Path curve

Now that the sculpt deformer is in place, you need a way to animate it along Meeper's throat, even when he is moving around and bending his neck.

- Select **Create** → **EP Curve** → ☐, and make sure the **Curve Degree** is set to **Cubic**.

- Draw the curve in Meeper's throat, following where the sculpt deformer should pass.

The throat curve

Tip: *Meeper must be in his default position.*

- Rename the curve to *throatPath*.

5   Motion path

You must now attach the sculpt deformer to the curve as a motion path.

- Select *sculptor1* and **Shift-select** the *throatPath*.
- Select **Animate** → **Motion Paths** → **Attach to Motion Path** → ❑.
- In the option window, set the **Front Axis** to **Y**.
- Click the **Attach** button.

6   Custom attribute

The rig needs a custom attribute so you can control the position of the sculptor in the throat. The best place to add such an attribute is on the *blendShapesManip*.

- Select the *blendShapesManip*.
- Select **Modify** → **Add Attribute**.
- Set the following:

> **Attribute Name** to *swallow*;
>
> **Data Type** to **Float**;
>
> **Minimum** to **0**;
>
> **Maximum** to **1**;
>
> **Default** to **0**.

- Click the **OK** button.

7   Connect the attribute

Right now, the sculpt deformer is animated along its path using the current time. Since you want to control the sculpt deformer using the attribute you just added, you will need to break the time connection.

- Select **Window** → **General Editors** → **Connection Editor...**
- Load the *blendShapesManip* on the left side.
- Load the *motionPath1* on the right side.

Tip: *You can use the quick selection box at the top right of the main interface.*

- Connect the swallow attribute to the U Value attribute of the motion path.

  Doing so will break the time connection of the motion path automatically.

8 Test the swallowing motion

- Select the *blendShapesManip* and change the swallow attribute to see if the sculpt deformer works appropriately.

Note: *The swallowing motion works well at this time, but it will stop working as soon as you animate Meeper. To fix this, you must change the order of deformation, which is covered in the next exercise.*

9 Throat setup

- From the Outliner, select the *sculptor1* and the *throatPath*.

- Press **Ctrl+g** to group them together.

- Rename the new group *throatSetup*.

- Parent the *throatSetup* to the *rig* group.

- Lock and hide all objects and attributes.

Deformation order

It is important to understand that deformers are executed sequentially, before achieving the final deformation of a piece of geometry. In the previous exercise, the sculpt deformer was inserted after all other deformers, which will cause unwanted results as soon as the character moves away.

Currently, Meeper is first affected by his blend shapes, then the skinning is evaluated, then the jiggle kicks in and lastly, the sculptor deforms the surface. In order for the sculpt deformer to work properly, you need the character to be in its original position. It would be logical to change the order of deformation so the sculpt deformer is evaluated first.

Fortunately, it is possible to switch the deformation order around quite easily. The following shows how to view and change a model's deformation order:

1   View the deformation order

- **RMB-click** on the Meeper geometry and select **Inputs** → **All Inputs** from the context menu.

This opens up a window that shows the list of deformers currently affecting the geometry.

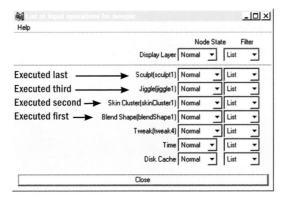

Order of deformation

Note: *The Tweak, Time and Dwwisk Cache are Maya related nodes that should not be reordered.*

2   Reorder the deformers

- **MMB-drag** the *Sculpt* deformer over the *Blend Shape* deformer item in the list.

Doing so will swap and reorder the deformers.

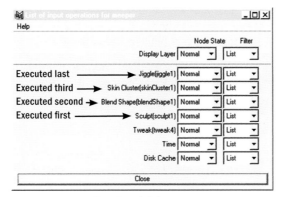

Reordered deformers

3   Pose the rig and test the swallowing

4   Save your work

Low resolution body

Congratulations! Meeper's rig is done, but you should now think about creating a low resolution version of Meeper to speed up loading and playback time. This file will not need things like jiggle deformers or influence objects, but it will require all animated items to stay in the scene. Doing so will allow you to switch a reference from the low resolution model to the high resolution model without any problems.

1   Scene file

- Continue with your own scene.

Or

- Open the scene file called *23-meeperFinal_03.ma*.

2   Rename and save scene

- Save the scene as *23-meeperFinal_lores_04.ma*.

3   Low resolution layer

- Create a new layer.

- Rename the layer *loresLayer*.

- Make the *geometryLayer* templated.

4   Generate the low resolution model

There are several ways to create a low resolution model. One simple technique is to *primitive up* a model. To do this, you must take primitive objects, such as cylinders, and simplify the different limbs of the character to their minimum.

- Create a new NURBS cylinder.

- Move and edit the cylinder to fit Meeper's upper arm.

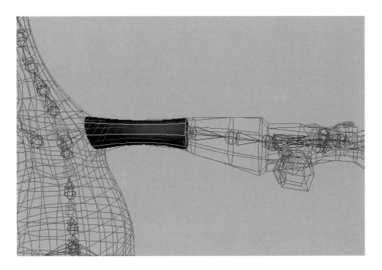

NURBS cylinder upper arm

- Rename the cylinder to *loLeftUpperArm*.

- Add the model to the *loresLayer*.

- Repeat the previous steps to create low resolution models for the following body parts:

    loLeftForeArm;

    loLeftUpperLeg;

    loLeftShinLeg;

    loTail.

Tip: *The default cylinder resolution is enough to give proper results for most of the limbs, but for the tail, make sure to add enough resolution to be able to bind it appropriately.*

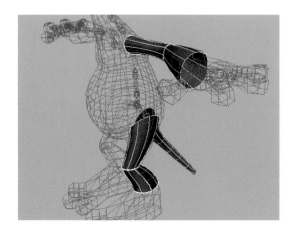

NURBS cylinder limbs

5   Low resolution hand

Since it is important to keep the hands accurate on the low resolution model, you will duplicate the geometry and keep only one hand, which you will rebind later in this exercise.

- Select the *Meeper* geometry and duplicate it.

- Press **Shift+p** to unparent the new model.

- Rename the new model *loLeftHand*.

- Add the new model to the *loresLayer*.

- In Component mode, delete the faces on the *loLeftHand* model, keeping only the hand.

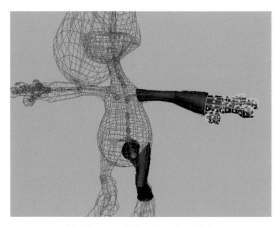

The low resolution hand model

Tip: *Delete details at will, but try to keep the shape and proportions of the hand.*

6 Low resolution foot

- Repeat the previous step, but this time to generate the *loLeftFoot* model.

The low resolution foot model

7 Low resolution torso

- Repeat the previous step, but this time to generate the *loTorso* model.

- Simplify the torso by selecting loops of edges using **Edit Polygons →
Selection → Select Contiguous Edges** and deleting edges using **Edit
Polygons → Delete Edge**.

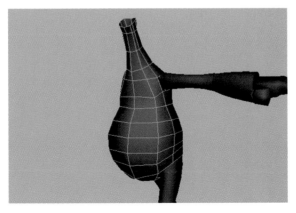

Low resolution torso

8   Mirror on the other side

- Select all the left low resolution models.

- Press **Ctrl+d** to duplicate them.

- Press **Ctrl+g** to group the new models.

- Set the **Scale X-axis** of the new group to **-1** to mirror the geometry on the right side of Meeper.

- Rename the models to *loRight*.

9   Clean up

- Select all the low resolution models.

- Through the **Window → General Editors → Channel Control...** unlock the transform attributes of the geometry.

- Select all the right low resolution models, then press **Shift+p** to unparent them.

- Select all the low resolution models, then select **Modify → Freeze Transformations**.

- Select **Edit → Delete by Type → History**.

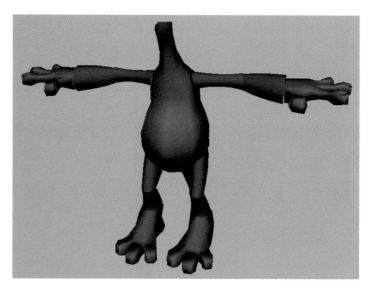

The low resolution body

10 Copy skinning

Now that the low resolution body is created, you can bind it to the skeleton and copy the weighting of the high resolution model to the low resolution model.

- Delete the *influenceGroup* and the *bicepInfluences*.

By deleting the influences, Maya will remove their weights from Meeper's skinning and reassign them to their respective bones.

- Enter the following MEL command in the Command Line:

```
select `skinCluster -q -inf meeper`;
```

This command tells Maya to select all the joints that influence the Meeper geometry.

- **Shift-select** the *loTorso*.

- Select **Skin** → **Bind Skin** → **Smooth Bind**.

Doing so will bind the selected geometry to the selected joints.

- Select the original *Meeper* geometry, then **Shift-select** the *loTorso*.

- Select **Skin** → **Smooth Skin** → **Copy Skin Weights**.

Since the low resolution geometry was bound to the same skeleton as the high resolution geometry, copying the weights will give adequate skinning on the low resolution model.

- Repeat the previous steps to copy the original skinning to the hands, feet and tail.

11 Rigid bind

- Select the remaining unbound geometry one by one and select **Skin** → **Bind Skin** → **Rigid Bind** to rigid bind them to their respective joints.

12 Save your work

Low resolution head

You have now bound the low resolution model, which is missing a head. Since the head needs as much detail as possible for accurate facial animation, you will need to keep all of its details along with all of its blend shapes.

1   Scene file

- Continue with your own scene.

Or

- Open the scene file called *23-meeperFinal_lores_04.ma*.

2   Delete faces

- Make the *geometryLayer* untemplated.

- Hide the *rigLayer* and *loresLayer*.

- Select and delete all the lower body faces.

- Rename the *Meeper* geometry to *loHead*.

3   Delete deformers

- With the *loHead* selected, select **Skin → Detach Skin**.

- Select the *jiggle1* node through the **Quick Selection** field and delete it.

The loHead now only has the blendShape1 deformer and the deleteComponent1 inputs.

4   Skin the head

- Select the *head* joint along with all the *antennae* joints.

- **Shift-select** the *loHead* geometry.

- Select **Skin → Bind Skin → Smooth Bind**.

- Review the *loHead* weights using the **Paint Skin Weights Tool**.

5   Final touches

- Parent all the low resolution models to the *geoGroup*.

- Delete the *loresLayer*.

- Select **File → Optimize Scene Size**.

The low resolution Meeper

6 Save your work

- The final low resolution scene file is called *23-meeperFinal_lores_05.ma*.

High resolution Meeper

In order to create the high resolution Meeper, all you have to do is add a polygonal smooth to the setup.

1 Scene file

- Continue with your own scene.

Or

- Open the scene file called *23-meeperFinal_03.ma*.

2 Save the scene under another name

- Save the scene as *23-meeperFinal_hires_04.ma*.

3 Poly Smooth

- Select the *Meeper* geometry.

- Select **Polygon** → **Smooth**.

The smooth applied to Meeper

4 Create a custom attribute

- Select the *master*.

- Select **Modify** → **Add Attribute**.

- Set the following:

    Attribute Name to *smooth*;

    Data Type to **Integer**;

    Minimum to **0**;

    Maximum to **3**;

    Default to **1**.

- Click the **OK** button.

Tip: *If you will be switching often between the low resolution model to the high resolution model, you might want to also add this same attribute to the low resolution file. Doing so will maintain any value that you set or animate.*

5   Connect the custom attribute

- Select **Window** → **General Editor** → **Connection Editor**.

- Load the *master* on the left side.

- Load the *polySmooth* node that is on the *Meeper* geometry on the right side.

- Connect the smooth attribute to the divisions attribute.

The rig now has a special attribute just for smoothing the geometry before rendering.

6   Eye tessellation

- Select the *lEye* and open its Attribute Editor.

- Under the **Tessellation** section, set the following:

    Curvature Tolerance to **High Quality**;

    U and V Division Factor to **5.0**.

- Repeat for the *rEye*.

7   Save your work

- Save the final low resolution scene file *23-meeperFinal_hires_04.ma*.

Conclusion

In this lesson, you learned about the jiggle and sculpt deformers. You also learned about the order of deformation, an essential concept all animators should understand. Lastly, you generated low and high resolution versions of Meeper, which you will be able to interchange when they are used as references.

In the next project, you will reuse Meeper's rig for the Diva model.

Project Six

In Project Six, you are going to set up Diva. You will start by reusing and modifying Meeper's rig. Once that is done, you will convert her to polygons and skin her, so that everything follows as you animate the rig. Along the way, you will also create basic blend shapes so that she can have facial expressions and lip-synching capabilities.

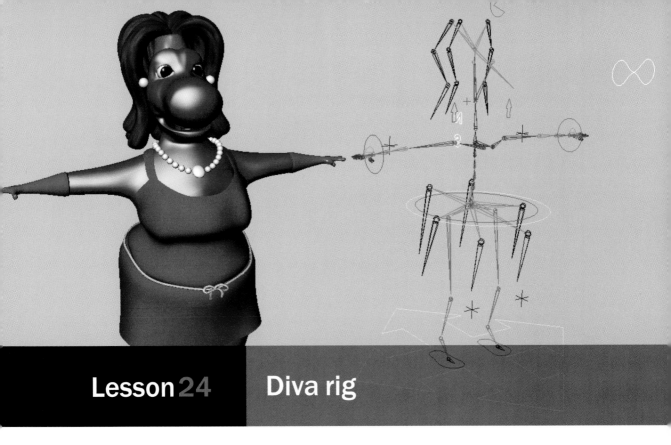

Lesson 24   Diva rig

In this lesson you will learn the following:

- How to reuse an existing setup;

- How to scale bones in an IK chain;

- How to connect joints;

- How to freeze transformations;

- How to use MEL scripting to lock attributes.

In this lesson, you will take Meeper's rig and modify it for Diva. Doing so will save you some valuable time in the rigging operation.

Import Meeper's rig

You will now import Meeper into the Diva scene and make the two characters to scale. You will also need to remove and modify certain joints on the rig, but the overall process will be much faster than rebuilding an entire rig from scratch.

1 Open an existing scene file

- Open the last scene from Project Two called *09-divaTextures_02.ma*.

2 Import Meeper

- From Project Five, import the Meeper scene file called *23-meeperFinal_lores_05.ma.*

3 Scale Diva

- Select the Diva's main group.

- Scale her up and move her so her feet stand at the center of the world grid.

Meeper imported with Diva

Note: *In the above image, Meeper was moved beside Diva. If you do the same, make sure to place Meeper back at the origin before continuing.*

4   Delete Meeper's geometry

- Delete Meeper's *geoGroup*.

- Select **File** → **Optimize Scene Size** in order to also remove any nodes and material related to Meeper.

5   Freeze Diva's transformations

- Select Diva's main group.

- Select **Modify** → **Freeze Transformations**.

- Change the **Shading** of the view to **X-Ray**.

- Set Diva's geometry layer to reference.

6   Delete obsolete rig parts

- Delete nodes such as the *tail*, *tail manipulators*, *tail IK spline* and *antennae*.

7   Make the rig to scale

- Select the *hipsManip*, both *armManips,* the *poleVector*, the *spineManip* and the *neckManip*.

- Move all the nodes simultaneously until the *Hips* joint is located appropriately in the Diva geometry.

- Deselect the *hipsManip*.

- Move the remaining selected nodes until the *armManips* and *poleVector* are in line with Diva's arms.

- Move the *armManips* to fit Diva's wrists.

- Move the *neckManip* on its own until the *Head* joint fits the Diva's head.

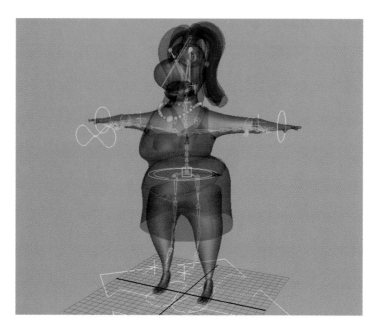

The manipulators moved to fit Diva's geometry

8 Scale joints

Now that most manipulators have been moved to better locations, you will now scale the bones up to suit Diva's geometry. Before you can do so, you must first unlock the joints' Scale attributes.

- Select **Edit** → **Select All By Type** → **Joints**.

- Select **Window** → **General Editors** → **Channel Control**.

- Make sure the checkbox **Change all selected objects of same type** is set to **On**.

- Select the **Locked** tab.

- Move all the *Scale* attributes from the **Locked** side to the **Non Locked** side.

- Select the **Keyable** tab.

- Move all the Scale attributes from the **Nonkeyable Hidden** side to the **Keyable** side.

Note: *Since the rig was carefully locked in order to prevent bad manipulations, several steps outlined next will require you to unlock attributes. A nice workflow is to create macro buttons to lock and unlock the attributes of the selected nodes.*

9   Scale the hips

- Select the *HipsOverride* and scale it uniformly to enlarge the pelvis.

Tip: *Since the scale pivot is off center, it is important to scale the joint uniformly by **clicking+dragging** the middle manipulator of the **Scale Tool**.*

10 Reverse feet

- Select both *RevHeel* joints and make them visible.

- Select both *footManips*, then scale and move them to fit Diva's feet.

- Select the reverse foot joints, then **scale** and move them to fit Diva's feet.

The reverse feet should now fit Diva's feet perfectly. Now you must scale the legs and foot joints to reach them.

Note: *The reverse heel joint should be aligned with the bottom of the high heel on the floor and not Diva's actual heel.*

11 Scale leg joints

- Select both *UpLeg* and *Leg* joints.

- Scale them on the **X-axis** until the ankles reach their reverse foot joint and the knees start bending.

Note: *If you find the knee joints to be too high or too low compared to Diva's knees, try scaling the UpLeg and Leg joints individually until they align with the geometry.*

- Move the leg *poleVectors* to align the knees toward the front.

12 Scale foot joints

- Select both *Foot* joints.

- Scale them on the **X-axis** until they reach their respective reverse foot joint.

- Select both *ToeBase* joints.

- Scale them on the **X-axis** until they reach their respective reverse foot joint.

13 Feet manipulator shape

- Hide the reverse foot chains.

- Select both *footManips*.

- While in Component mode, scale the manipulator curve CVs to be visible around the feet.

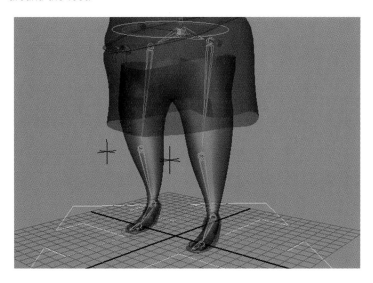

The legs and feet are now well suited for Diva

14 Spine joints

- Select the *backSpline* curve and make it visible.

- Change the shape of the curve by moving CVs to straighten it up Diva's back.

- Select all the *Spine* joints, then **scale** them to place the shoulders appropriately in Diva's geometry. Align the geometry at the end of the *backSpline*.

15 Arm joints

You will now place the clavicle, arms and fingers in Diva's geometry. Since the clavicles are driven by constraints, you will delete these constraints and recreate them later.

- Select the clavicles' parent constraints and delete them.

- Move and scale the *Shoulder* joints.

Note: *IK handles must be set to* **Sticky** *if you want them to correctly update while scaling joints.*

- Scale the *Arm*, *ForeArm* and *ForeArmRoll* joints.

- Scale the *ForeArmRoll* joints to match the *Hand* joints with the IK handles.

- Place the *clavicleManips* correctly and snap their pivots to their respective bones.

- Parent constraints to their manipulators.

16 Hand joints

- Scale and move the *Hand* and *Finger* joints appropriately.

Note: *Translating Finger joints will offset their local rotation axes, but it will allow you to conserve their driven keys animation.*

17 Neck joints

Because Meeper has a pretty long neck, you do not require as many joints for Diva's neck. In order to remove joints, you will need to first delete and recreate the IK spline.

- Delete the *neckSpline* and *neckSplineIK*.

- Select the *Head* joint and unparent it temporarily.

- Delete all the *Neck* joints except the first one: *Neck*.

Doing so will leave you with only a single neck joint, which should be enough for this character.

- Select the *Head* joint, then **Shift-select** the *Neck* joint.

- Select **Skeleton** → **Connect Joint** → ❑.

- In the option window, select **Parent joint**, then click the **Connect** button.

Doing so is different than simply parenting a joint since it recreates a special connection that compensates for the parent's scaling. Without this connection, if you were to scale the Neck joint, the entire head would deform.

- Scale and move the *Neck* and *Head* joints appropriately.

- Reuse the *neckManip* for the remaining *Neck* joint by snapping its pivot to the joint and creating a **Parent** constraint between the joint and the manipulator.

- Parent the *neckManip* to the *Spine5* joint.

Tip: *Make sure to unlock all the attributes of the manipulator before parenting it.*

18 Head joints

- Move the *Skull* and *Nose* joints that are used for reference.

- Use a **Point** constraint on the *Eye* joints to center them in the eye geometry.

Just like what was done with Meeper, this is only a trick to center the joints within the eye. The constraint must be removed.

- Delete the point constraints.

19 eyeLookAt manipulator

- Move the eye*LookAt* up to align it with Diva's eyes.

20 Hips' manipulators

- In Component mode, tweak the shape of the *hipsManip* and *hipsOverrideManip* to better surround Diva's waist.

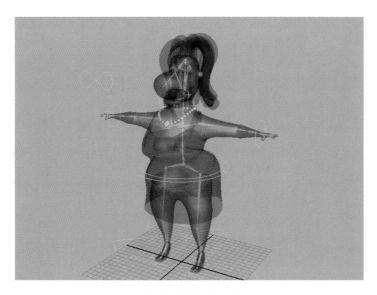

The updated Diva rig

21 Save your work

- Save the scene as *24-divaRig_01.ma*.

Add Diva controls

Now that you have changed Meeper's rig for Diva, you must add extra controls specific to her. In this exercise, you will add joints for her dress and hair.

1 Scene file

- Continue with your own scene.

    Or

- Open the scene called *24-divaRig_01.ma*.

2 Dress joints

In order to manually animate the dress, you must add a series of joints all around her pelvis, which you will be able to rotate and scale to lift the dress as needed.

- Select **Skeleton → Joint Tool**.

- From the *side* view, draw three chains of bones pointing down as follows:

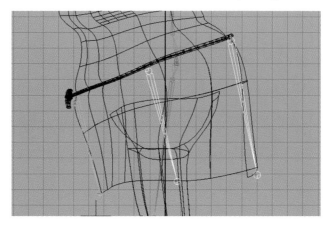

Dress bones

- Move the joints to fit the dress over Diva's left leg.
- Select each joint and select **Skeleton → Mirror Joint** to go over the right leg.

You should now have six joints going all around the dress.

- Rename all the joints *dressJoint*.
- Group all the joints together and rename it *dressJoints*.
- Parent the joints to the *HipsOverride*.

Note: *If you do not group all the joints together before parenting them, extra transform group nodes are created in the hierarchy for the joints to maintain their positions, since the HipsOverride joint was scaled.*

- Snap the pivot of the *dressJoints* group on the *HipsOverride* joint.
- Select **Modify → Freeze Transformations**.
- With all the dress joints selected individually, select **Skeleton → Orient Joint**.

Doing so will ensure that the joints' local rotation axes point toward their first child correctly.

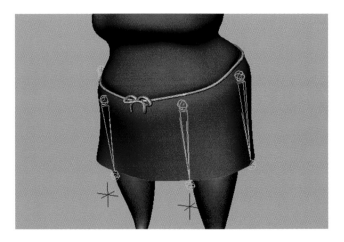

All the dress bones in position

3   Hair joints

Following the same idea as for the dress, you will use joints to manually animate the hair. You could create a series of joints for each unique dread, but in order to simplify things, you will regroup the dreads to be animated with three joint chains.

- Select **Skeleton** → **Joint Tool**.

- From the *side* view, create a series of **four** joints as follows:

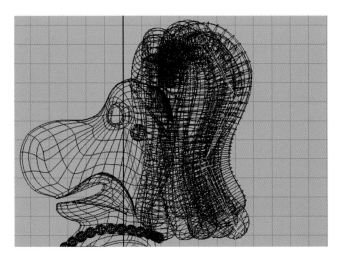

The hair joints

- Duplicate the joint chain **two** times and place the new chains on both sides of the head.

- Group them together, then snap the group's pivot to the *Skull* joint.

- Rename everything properly.

- Parent the group to the *Skull* joint.

- Select **Modify** → **Freeze Transformations**.

- With all the hair joints selected, select **Skeleton** → **Orient Joint**.

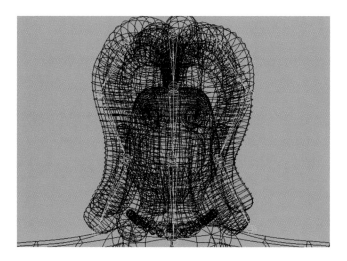

All the hair joints in position

Final touches

Throughout the process of modifying the rig, you have unlocked, shown and moved quite a lot of nodes and attributes. You should now look at each node and make sure they are properly frozen and locked to prevent erroneous manipulation by the animator.

1   Freeze transformations

Since you moved most of the manipulators while placing the rig, it is a good idea to freeze their transformations so they are at their default positions with default attributes. In order to be able to freeze transformations, you must unlock the attributes to be frozen of the node and its children.

Following is the workflow to use while freezing transformations:

- Select the object to be frozen.

- Unlock the attributes to be frozen, which are usually **rotation**, **translation** and **scale**.

- Unlock the same attributes on all children of the object.

- Freeze the transformations of the object.

All the children will also be frozen.

Tip: *If you don't need to freeze the transformations of the children, unparent them temporarily while you freeze the transformations. If the objects move as you unparent them, make sure to unlock their attributes first.*

- Repeat this for all the objects that are to be frozen, such as manipulators and locators.

Tip: *If an object's attributes are to be locked to prevent the animator from using the object, you might not need to freeze its transformations.*

2   Set preferred angle

- Select the *Hips*, then select **Skeleton** → **Set Preferred Angle**.

Doing so will ensure that all the joints have a proper, saved preferred angle.

Note: *The only drawback of reusing a rig is that joints driven by IKs might get values in their rotation attributes. The best solution is still to create an entire new skeleton.*

3   Lock and hide attributes and nodes

- In the Hypergraph or the Outliner, go over each node and make sure you lock and hide them correctly.

> **Tip:** Using a MEL script to do this could really speed up the task. For instance, the following script would lock and hide the translation attributes for all selected nodes:
>
> ```
> for($each in `ls -sl`)
>
> {
>
>         setAttr -k 0 ($each + ".tx");
>
>         setAttr -k 0 ($each + ".ty");
>
>         setAttr -k 0 ($each + ".tz");
>
>         setAttr -l 1 ($each + ".tx");
>
>         setAttr -l 1 ($each + ".ty");
>
>         setAttr -l 1 ($each + ".tz");
>
> }
> ```

The finished rig

4   Save your work

- Save the scene as *24-divaRig_02.ma*.

Conclusion

In this lesson, you saved some valuable time by reusing Meeper's rig for Diva. The goal of this lesson was not to create an entire rig, but to show that there are ways to reuse work. If the rig created here is not good enough for your needs, you can at least reuse bone placements to create a new skeleton, and also reuse most of the manipulators.

In the next lesson, you will bind Diva to the skeleton.

Conversion and skinning

*In this lesson, you will bind
Diva to her skeleton. In order
to keep the lesson fast and
simple, you will convert
the NURBS patch model to
polygons. You will then bind
that new geometry to the
skeleton. You will also see
how to use a wire deformer to
deform the necklace.*

In this lesson you will learn the following:

- How and why to convert the NURBS model
  to polygons;

- How to bind the polygons and accessories;

- How to use a wire deformer to bind
  the necklace;

- How to edit weights of a curve.

NURBS or polygons?

At this point, you have two choices concerning the binding of Diva. The first choice is to continue with the model entirely in NURBS, and bind using heavy tools that will maintain the stitching and tangency of the character together while being deformed. The second solution is to convert the model to polygons and bind it using the same tool that you used to bind Meeper.

For this lesson, the choice is to convert the NURBS patch model to polygons and bind that new geometry to the skeleton. That way, the process of skinning the character will be much easier, since you will only need to weight a simple polygonal mesh rather than numerous individual NURBS patches.

Note: *You will have to create a new texture reference object when converting to polygons at this stage.*

Convert to polygons

1   Open an existing scene file

- Open the last scene from the previous lesson called *24-divaRig_02.ma*.

2   Hide the rig

- Set the *rigLayer*'s visibility to **Off**.

- Turn **Off** the referencing of the *divaLayer*.

3   Convert to polygons

To create the polygonal mesh, you will only need to convert the NURBS patches that define Diva's body. For instance, you will not convert any of her accessories such as jewelry, eyes, hair, belt or high heels.

- Select all of Diva's skin and dress surfaces.

The geometry to convert

- Select **Modify** → **Convert** → **NURBS to Polygons** → ❐.

- In the option window, set the following:

  Type to **Quads**;

  Tessellation Method to **General**;

  U Type to **Per Span # of Iso Params**;

  Number U to **3**;

  V Type to **Per Span # of Iso Params**;

  Number V to **3**;

- Click the **Tessellate** button.

The new polygonal surfaces are created and the original NURBS surfaces will be hidden.

- Hide the *divaLayer*.

You should now see only the polygonal surfaces.

The converted geometry

Note: *If you intend to smooth the meshes later in the process, you could convert sections of the Diva geometry, such as the head, hands and feet, with less density if needed.*

4   Combine the polygons

You now need to combine the polygonal meshes into a single mesh.

- Select all polygonal meshes.

- Select **Polygons** → **Combine**.

- Select **Edit Polygons** → **Merge Vertices** with a **Distance** of **0.01**.

- Select **Display** → **Custom Polygon Display** → ❑.

- In the option window, make sure to set **Border Edges** to **On**, then click the **Apply and Close** button.

5   Close borders

The gaps between the dress and skin are unimportant, but any other border edges on the geometry should be properly closed. To do so, you need to split polygonal faces and snap vertices together to close the border edges.

- Select **Edit Polygons** → **Merge Edge Tool** to close borders that were not closed in the previous step.

Or

- Split polygonal faces where there are vertices missing in the neck and hands area.

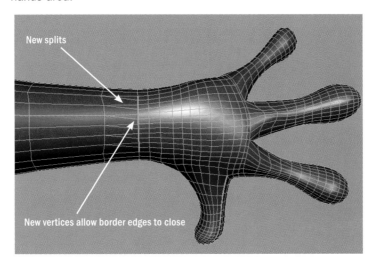

New splits

New vertices allow border edges to close

Splits to close the border edges

- Using snap to point, snap border edge vertices together.

- Select **Edit Polygons** → **Merge Vertices**.

- Repeat until all border edges, other than the dress and eye openings, are closed.

Tip: *You can delete half the model and mirror it if you don't want to repeat the previous steps for the other side.*

6   Finish the polygonal model

- Select the polygonal mesh and rename it *diva*.

- Select **Edit Polygons** → **Normals** → **Soften/Harden** to make the geometry look smooth.

Note: You will also be using this geometry as your low resolution model later in the project.

- Select the *divaLow*, then select **Edit** → **Delete By Type** → **History**.

Note: Do not use **Delete** → **All by Type** → **History** because the rig is using some history.

7   Save your work

- Save the scene as *25-divaBound_01.ma*.

Skinning

Now that you have proper polygonal geometry, you can bind it to the skeleton and paint its weights.

1   Scene file

- Continue with your own scene.

Or

- Open the scene called *25-divaBound_01.ma*.

2   Bind to skeleton

- Display the *rigLayer*.

- Select all joints that you deem important for the binding of Diva, then **Shift-select** the *divaLow* geometry.

- Select **Skin** → **Bind Skin** → **Smooth Bind** → ❑.

- In the option window, make sure **Bind to** is set to **Selected Joints**.

- Click the **Bind Skin** button.

3   Paint weights

Using the same technique used to bind Meeper, paint the weights of the *divaLow* geometry. The following outlines the steps to follow:

- Select *divaLow*.

- Select **Skin** → **Edit Smooth Skin** → **Paint Skin Weights Tool** → ❒.

- Paint the weights to a value of **1** to clearly define which influence goes where.

Tip: *Only bother painting the left side of the body since you will mirror the joint influences.*

- Select **Skin** → **Edit Smooth Skin** → **Mirror Skin Weights**.

- Refine the binding by smoothing out the influences.

- Select **Skin** → **Edit Smooth Skin** → **Prune Small Weights**.

- Select **Skin** → **Edit Smooth Skin** → **Mirror Skin Weights**.

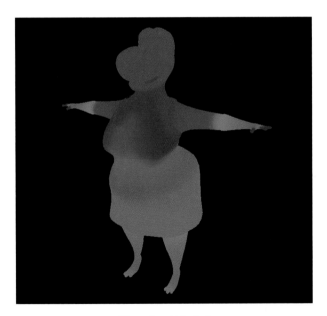

The refined binding

4   Save your work

- Save the scene as *25-divaBound_02.ma*.

Other skinning

Now that the body and dress are bound, you can bind the remaining
Diva objects.

1 Scene file

- Continue with your own scene.

Or

- Open the scene called *25-divaBound_02.ma.*

2 Delete unused surfaces

- Delete all skin and dress NURBS patches that were converted earlier.

3 Bind the eyes

- Smooth bind the eyes to the *Eye* joints.

4 Bind the hair

- Rigid bind the hair band to the *Head* joint.

- Smooth bind the dreads (by group) to the *Hair* joints.

5 Bind the high heels

- Smooth bind the high heels to the *Foot* and *ToeBase* joints.

6 Bind the earrings

- Rigid bind the earrings to the *Head* joint.

7 Bind the belt

- Smooth bind the belt to the *HipsOverride* and *Dress* joints.

- Paint the weights as needed.

Necklace deformer

The necklace is somewhat problematic to deform since it needs to keep its
shape and follow the skin's deformation. Rather than keyframing it or using
dynamics to have the pearls follow the chest, you will simply use a wire deformer
which will in turn be bound to the rig.

1 Necklace curve

- If you no longer have the necklace curve in your scene, create a primitive circle and tweak to fit the shape of the necklace.

- Delete the construction history of the circle.

- Rename the curve *necklaceCurve*.

2 Necklace curve

- Select **Deform** → **Wire Tool**.

The tool will prompt you to select the geometry to deform.

- Select all of the necklace pearls, then hit **Enter**.

- Select the *necklaceCurve*, then hit **Enter**.

Doing so will create the wire deformer as intended.

3 Test the necklace deformation

- Switch to Component mode and move the *necklaceCurve*'s CVs to see if it deforms the necklace correctly.

At this time, the pearls tend to stretch back to their original positions because the wire influence is not strong enough.

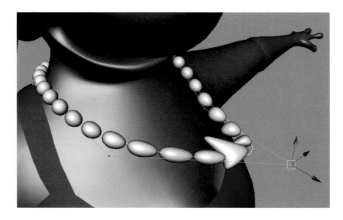

The wire default deformation

- In the Channel Box, under the **Outputs** section, highlight *wire1*.

- Set the **Dropoff Distance** to a high value, such as **100.0**.

Now the necklace will deform better.

4   Bind the necklace curve

- Smooth bind the *necklaceCurve* to all joints that are at risk of affecting the necklace area.

At this time, the curve has default binding to the skeleton, but it would be nice if it could precisely follow the binding of the geometry.

- Select the *Diva* body, then **Shift-select** the *necklaceCurve*.

- Select **Skin** → **Edit Smooth Skin** → **Copy Skin Weights**.

The weighting of the curve is now similar to the weighting of the body, which will help the necklace to follow the body deformation.

5   Tweak the binding of the curve

Weighting a curve is different than weighting a surface since there is no color feedback along the curve to represent the influence values. In order to refine the binding of a curve, you must select its CVs and manually enter weighting values through the Component Editor.

- Switch to Component mode and select the *necklaceCurve*'s CVs to be edited.

- Select **Window** → **General Editor** → **Component Editor**, then select the **Smooth Skins** tab.

Here you can edit weighting values by directly entering weighting values for the curve.

- Change the weighting values of the curve, if needed.

You should now have a properly deforming necklace.

Final touches

1   Delete the old texture reference objects

Since you converted the model to polygons, some of the texture reference objects created in Project Two are no longer used. You will now delete the old texture reference object and create another one for the polygonal body.

- Under the *txtRefGroup*, delete the texture reference objects for the *skinGroup* and *dressGroup*.

- Select the *Diva* polygonal body.

- In the **Rendering** menu set, select **Texturing** → **Create Texture Reference Object**.

- Parent the new texture reference object to the *txtRefGroup*.

2   Make sure everything is parented and well named

3   Optimize the scene size

4   Test Diva's binding

- Try to pose Diva to see if everything deforms well.

- Make any required changes.

The bound Diva

5   Save your work

- Save the scene as *25-divaBound_03.ma*.

Conclusion

In this lesson, you converted a NURBS model to polygons for simplicity reasons, but feel free to experiment and try another workflow. You also gained added experience in skinning a more complex character.

In the next lesson, you will model blend shapes for Diva.

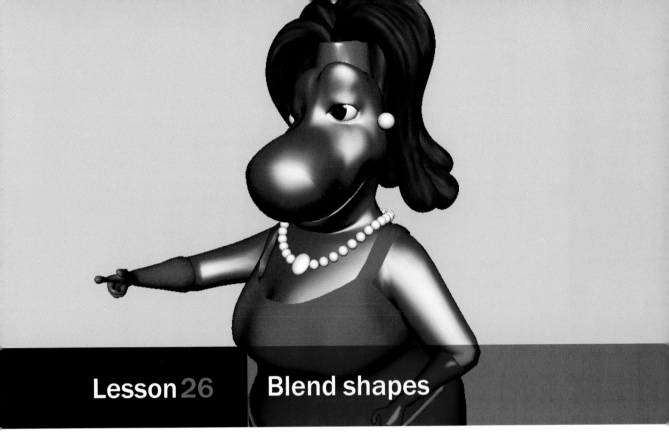

Lesson 26 | Blend shapes

In this lesson, you will create blend shapes for Diva by using the original NURBS patch model. You will then use the wrap deformer to transfer blend shapes from the NURBS model to the polygonal model.

In this lesson you will learn the following:

- How to sculpt NURBS patches;

- How to create blend shapes with multiple surfaces;

- How to use a wrap deformer;

- How to use a wrap deformer with mirrored geometry;

- How to create blend shapes extracted from a wrap deformer.

NURBS or polygons?

Since you used the sculpt deformer on polygons to create Meeper's blend shapes, in this lesson you will sculpt NURBS and use a wrap deformer to create Diva's blend shapes.

If you don't feel comfortable creating the blend shape on NURBS patches, you can simply redo Lesson 20 using Diva's polygon skin. This lesson explores another workflow, which could be useful in other situations.

Sculpt target shapes

In this exercise, you will sculpt the Diva NURBS model to create her blend shapes.

1   Open an existing scene file

- Open the scene called *24-divaRig_01.ma*.

You will use this scene because it Diva has proper scaling and is made of NURBS patches.

- Delete the *rig* group.

- Delete all surfaces that are not intended to be part of the blend shapes.

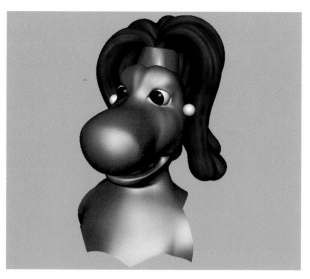

Diva's head is used for blend shapes

Tip: *Keep any surfaces that are likely to help with the deformations, such as the eyes, earrings and hair.*

2 Duplicate

You can now duplicate the head to sculpt Diva's facial expressions.

- Rename the *divaGroup* to *original*.

- Duplicate the *original* group.

- Rename the new group to *leftBlink*.

3 Sculpt

- Sculpt the skin surfaces by manipulating CVs, using wire deformers or by using the **Edit NURBS → Sculpt Geometry Tool**.

Tip: *One of the easiest ways to create blend shapes on NURBS surfaces is by duplicating surface curves and using that curve as a wire deformer.*

- Sculpt the following target shapes:

  leftBlink, leftBlinkMid, leftWideOpen, leftLowerLidUp;

  A, E, O, U, F, M;

  jawDown, smile, blowCheeks;

  leftBrowUp, leftBrowSad, leftBrowMad.

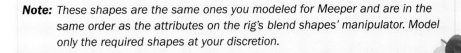

Note: *Since you will be using a wrap deformer to transfer the blend shapes to the polygonal mesh, you only need to carefully sculpt one side of the face. You will then mirror half the head to create the other side of the blend shapes.*

Note: *These shapes are the same ones you modeled for Meeper and are in the same order as the attributes on the rig's blend shapes' manipulator. Model only the required shapes at your discretion.*

Diva's blend shapes

4 Save your work

- Save the scene as *26-divaBlendShapes_01.ma*.

Blend shape deformer

Now that all the blend shapes have been modeled, you can create the blend shape deformer for all the face surfaces. Just like for Meeper, you will create an in-between shape first, and then add the rest of the targets.

1 Scene file

- Continue with your own scene.

Or

- Open the scene called *26-divaBlendShapes_01.ma*.

2 In-between shapes

- From the Outliner, select the *leftBlinkMid* group, then the *leftBlink* group.

- Add the *original* group to the selection.

- Select **Deform → Create Blend Shape → ❏**.

- In the option window, turn **On** the **In-Between** checkbox.

- Click the **Create** button.

You now have a proper blinking blend shape with an in-between shape to prevent the surface from interpenetrating the eye.

3   Rest of the shapes

- From the Outliner, select all the remaining target groups.

- Add the *original* group to the selection.

- Select **Deform** → **Edit Blend Shape** → **Add** → ❑.

- In the option window, turn **On** the **Specify Node** checkbox.

- Click the **Apply and Close** button.

All the target shapes are now part of the blend shape deformer on the base shape.

4   Test the shapes

- Test the blend shape deformer and bring any changes required on the target shapes.

5   Delete the targets

- It is now safe to delete all the target groups.

6   Delete the accessories

- Delete all the accessories and keep only Diva's *skinGroup*.

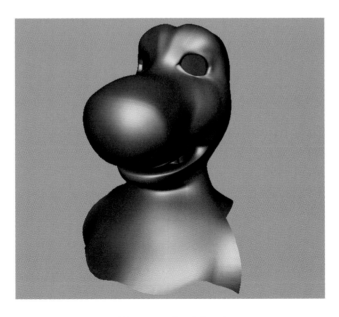

All accessories deleted

7   Split the head

Since the blend shapes will be mirrored, you only need to have half of the head. The head will then be duplicated and mirrored on the other side.

- **RMB-click** on the central surfaces and select **Isoparm**.

- Select all the central isoparms, then detach the surfaces.

You should now have the entire head split in half.

- Parent all the new surfaces to the *skinGroup*.

- Group the right surfaces and rename the group *notUsed*.

- Hide the *notUsed* group.

- Group the left surfaces and rename the group *goodSurfaces*.

Note: *You must hide the surfaces because if you delete them, the blend shape deformer would no longer work correctly.*

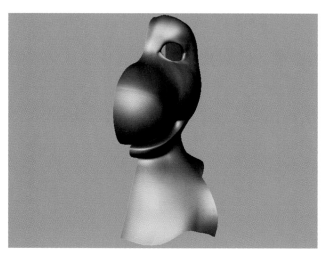

Half the head is hidden

8   Mirror the head

- Select the *skinGroup*, then select **Edit → Duplicate → ❑**.

- Turn **On** the **Duplicate Input Graph** checkbox.

- Click the **Duplicate** button.

Doing so will duplicate the entire head, along with its blend shape deformer.

- Set the **Scale X** attribute of the new *skinGroup* to **-1**.

You should now have the entire head again, but with a blend shape deformer to control each half.

- Group *skinGroup* and *skinGroup1* together.

9   Group the good surfaces together

It is important that all the good deforming surfaces used in the wrap deformer be grouped together.

- Group both *goodSurfaces* together and rename the new group *wrapObjects*.

10 Save your work

- Save the scene as *26-divaBlendShapes_02.ma*.

Wrap deformer

You will now open the bound Diva scene file, and import the scene created in the previous exercise. You will then create wrap deformers between the base shape and the polygonal Diva geometry.

1   Open an existing scene file

- Open the scene called *25-divaBound_03.ma*.

2   Import the blend shapes

- Select **File → Import** and select the scene called *26-divaBlendShapes_02.ma*.

You now have the bound Diva along with the blend shapes in your scene.

3 Prepare the model

- Hide the *rigLayer*.
- Select the *Diva* polygonal geometry.
- In the Channel Box, under the **Inputs** section, highlight the *skinCluster* node.
- Set the **Envelope** attribute to **0.0**.

Setting this attribute to zero disables a skinning deformer. By disabling this, you are temporarily turning off the skinning of Diva, which will ensure that she is in her default position. It is important for the skin to be in its default position for the blend shapes to work correctly.

4 Wrap deformer

- Select the *Diva* polygonal geometry, then **Shift-select** the *wrapObjects* group.
- Select **Deform → Create Wrap**.

After a few seconds, the wrap deformer will be created.

5 Test the wrap deformer

- Hide the *wrapObjects* group.
- Through the Outliner, select one of the surfaces in the *wrapObjects* group.
- In the Channel Box, under the **Inputs** section, highlight the *blendShape* node.
- Test the blend shapes and see how Diva's polygonal geometry deforms.

The wrap deformer affecting the polygonal geometry

Note: *In order to have the blend shapes affecting both sides of the head, you must edit the values of both blend shape deformers.*

6 Duplicate the polygonal geometry for each shape

- Turn **On** the *leftBlink* blend shape.
- Select the *Diva* geometry.
- Select **Edit → Duplicate → ❑**.
- Turn **Off** the **Duplicate Input Graph** checkbox.
- Click the **Duplicate** button.
- Move the duplicated geometry aside and rename it *leftBlink*.
- Hide the *leftBlink* geometry.
- Continue to extract each polygonal target shape:

  leftBlink, leftBlinkMid, leftWideOpen, leftLowerLidUp;

  rightBlink, rightBlinkMid, rightWideOpen, rightLowerLidUp;

  A, E, O, U, F, M;

  jawDown, smile, blowCheeks;

  leftBrowUp, leftBrowSad, leftBrowMad;

  rightBrowUp, rightBrowSad, rightBrowMad.

Tip: *The weight of the blink mid in-between target is* **0.5**.

7 Remove the wrap deformer

- Delete the *group1,* which contains the imported NURBS patches head.

  The wrap will automatically be deleted.

8 Group the targets

- Group all the target shapes that you created in the previous steps.

9 Create the blend shape deformer

▪ Create all the target shapes (beside *blinkMid*), for the *Diva* geometry.

Tip: *Make sure when you create the blend shape deformer that you set the* **Deformation Order** *option to* **Front Of Chain.** *That way, the deformer will go before the skinning, which is what you want.*

▪ Add the in-between shapes for the *leftBlinkMid* and *rightBlinkMid* to the Diva's blend shape node.

Note: *Set the* **In-Between Weight** *to* **0.5.**

10 Test the blend shapes

▪ Test the blend shapes and bring any changes to the target shapes, if needed.

11 Deformer set

Just like you did for Meeper, you will now remove unaffected vertices from the blend shape deformer set. Doing so will greatly speed up the blend shape deformer.

▪ Select the *Diva* geometry, and switch to Component mode.

▪ Select all the vertices that are not in danger of being deformed by the blend shapes.

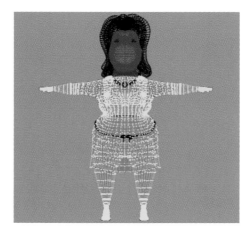

Vertices that can be removed from the blend shape deformer set

- Select **Window** → **Relationship Editors** → **Deformer Sets**.
- In the left column, highlight the *blendShape1Set*.
- In the left column menu, select **Edit** → **Remove Selected Items**.

The selected vertices will be removed from the blend shape deformer set.

12 Double-check the deformer set members

- Deselect all the vertices.
- In the Relationship Editor, **RMB-click** on the *blendShape1Set* and select **Select Set Members**.

Only the head vertices should be selected.

13 Delete the targets

- Delete the target shapes.

14 Enable the skin cluster

- Select the *Diva* geometry.
- In the Channel Box, under the **Inputs** section, highlight the *skinCluster* node.
- Set the **Envelope** attribute to **1.0**.

15 Optimize scene size

16 Connect blendShapesManip

- Show the *rigLayer*.
- Select **Window** → **General Editors** → **Connection Editor**.
- Load the *blendShapesManip* on the left side.
- Load the *blendShape1* node on the right side.
- Connect the attributes of the *blendShapesManip* to the *blendShape1* node.

> **Note:** *There are no breath and swallow shapes in the example files. Hide them from the Channel Box, if desired.*

17 Test the rig

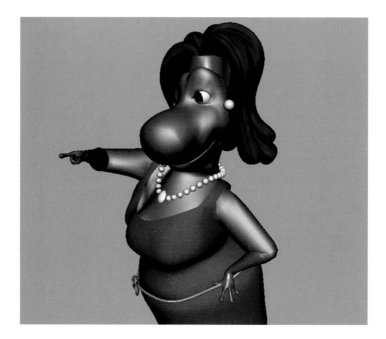

A Diva pose using blend shapes

18 Save your work

- Save the scene as *26-divaBlendShapes_03.ma*.

Conclusion

In this lesson, you saw how to model blend shape targets starting from a NURBS patch model. As well, using both the wire deformer and wrap deformer were good ways to learn different methods of deforming geometry. By utilizing mirroring, you only had to create half the blend shapes, thus saving you some valuable time.

In the next lesson, you will finalize Diva's setup by adding secondary animation and creating a low resolution model.

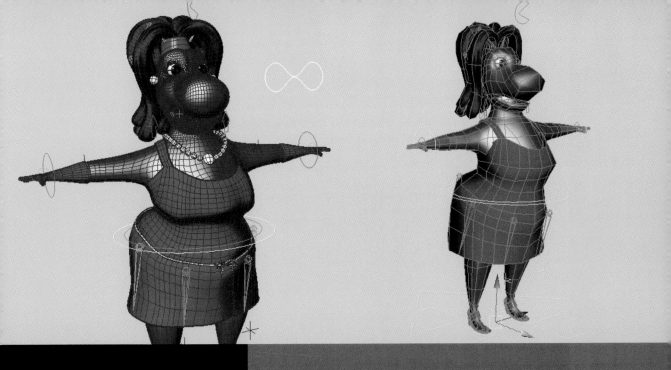

Lesson 27   Final touches

In order to finalize Diva's setup, you will add secondary animation to give life to your animations. You will use jiggle deformers on the breasts, dress and hair, and you will add a non-linear deformer on the dress to simulate a subtle wind movement. Lastly, you will generate a low resolution setup for animation.

In this lesson you will learn the following:

- How to grow a selection;

- How to use a non-linear deformer;

- How to create a low resolution model from the NURBS patch model.

Jiggle deformers

Since she will be moving a lot as she is dancing, jiggle deformers will add dynamic secondary animation to Diva.

1 Scene file

- Open the last scene from the previous lesson called *26-divaBlendShapes_03.ma*.

2 Hair selection

- Hide the *rigLayer*.

- Select all the hair dreads, then switch to Component mode.

- Select a single horizontal hull per dread near the bottom of the hair.

- Select **Edit NURBS** → **Selection** → **Grow CV Selection**.

- Repeat the **Grow CV Selection** command until the selection CVs reach the highest point of the dreads.

Tip: *Tear-off the **Selection** menu to access the command faster.*

3 Hair jiggle

You should now have CVs selected that start at the tip of the dreads and go up to the top of the head (not the entire group of dreads).

- With the CVs still selected, select **Deform** → **Create Jiggle Deformer** → ❒.

- In the option window, set the following:

> **Stiffness** to **0.2**;
>
> **Damping** to **0.2**.

- Click the **Create** button.

A jiggle deformer is created for each surface.

4 Hair jiggle weights

- Go back to Object mode.

- Select **Deform** → **Paint Jiggle Weights Tool** → ❒.

- In the tool window, set the **Paint Operation** to **Smooth**.

- Click the **Flood** button repeatedly until you get a result similar to the following:

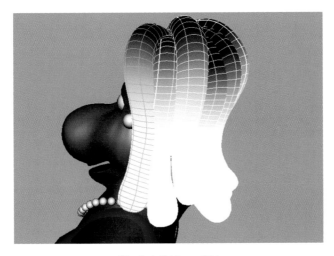

The hair jiggle weight

5   Preferences

- Select **Window** → **Settings/Preferences** → **Preferences**.

- In the **Timeline** category, make sure **Playback Speed** is set to **Play every frame**.

Tip: *Always make sure to play every frame before playing dynamic animation.*

- Click the **Save** button.

6   Test the hair jiggle

- Go at frame **1**.

- Select the *hipsManip*, and press **s** to set a keyframe.

- Move the *hipsManip*, and press **s** to set a keyframe at frames **10**, **20** and **30**.

- Playback the scene to see the behavior of the jiggle deformer.

Note: *Don't forget to delete the animation when you are done.*

7 Tweak the jiggle attributes

Since there are multiple jiggle deformers on the hair, you will now change them all at once.

- In the **Entry Field** located at the top right of the main interface, set its option to **Quick Selection**.

- Type *jiggle** to select all the jiggle nodes in the scene.

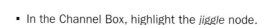

Note: *The * is a wildcard, meaning anything that starts with jiggle. You could also use* ? *as a wildcard for a single character.*

- In the Channel Box, highlight the *jiggle* node.

- Tweak the attributes of the deformer and playback the scene to see its effect.

8 Dress jiggle

- Repeat the previous steps to create a jiggle deformer on the dress as follows:

The dress jiggle weight

9   Breast jiggle

Since there is already a jiggle deformer on the Diva body, you will need to add the breast vertices in the jiggle deformer set. Then you will be able to paint some jiggle weights.

- Select the *Diva* geometry and switch to Component mode.

- Select the breast vertices of the dress and the skin.

- Select **Edit Polygons → Selection → Grow Selection Region**.

- Repeat the **Grow Selection Region** command as needed.

- Select **Window → Relationship Editors → Deformer Sets**.

- Note the name of the *jiggle* node in the Channel Box and highlight the same one in the left side of the Relationship Editor.

- Still in the Relationship Editor, select **Edit → Add Selected Items**.

Doing so will add the selected breast vertices to the jiggle deformer.

Note: *Keep the breast vertices selected for the next step.*

10 Paint breast jiggle

The following steps will prevent the flood smooth operation from affecting the dress jiggle, thus, only smoothing the weights on the breasts.

- With the breast vertices still selected, select **Deform → Paint Jiggle Weights Tool → ❑**.

- In the tool window, set the **Paint Operation** to **Replace**.

- Set the **Value** to **0.3**.

- Click the **Flood** button to change the weights of the selected vertices.

- Set the **Paint Operation** to **Smooth**.

- Click the **Flood** button repeatedly to smooth only the selected vertices.

The breasts' jiggle weight

Tip: *The breasts' jiggle should be kept very low compared to the dress and hair weights. A low jiggle will also prevent the skin from interpenetrating with the dress.*

11 Save your work

- Save the scene as *26-divaFinal_01.ma*.

Non-linear deformer

In this exercise, you will add a non-linear sine deformer, which will simulate subtle wind movement in the dress. A sine non-linear deformer will move the affected vertices in a sinusoidal way, according to the placement of the deformer handle. The deformer will be inserted in front of the deformation order, so it will affect the dress before it is deformed by the rig.

1 Scene file

- Continue with your own scene.

Or

- Open the scene called *26-divaFinal_01.ma*.

2   Sine deformer

- Select the dress vertices to be deformed by the sine deformer.

- Select **Deform → Create Nonlinear → Sine**.

The sine deformer is created and selected.

- Move the sine deformer in front of Diva.

3   Tweak the sine deformer

- In the **Inputs** section of the Channel Box, select the *sine1* node.

- Set the following:

  Amplitude to **0.1**;

  Wavelength to **1.0**;

  Dropoff to **-1.0**;

  Low Bound to **-2.0**;

  High Bound to **0.0**.

4   Test the sine deformer

- Highlight the **Offset** attribute in the Channel Box, then **MMB-drag** in the viewport to see the effect of the sine deformer on the dress.

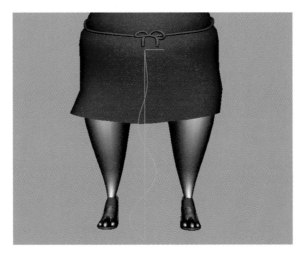

The dress sine deformer

- Tweak the sine deformer as needed.

Note: *The orientation and placement of the deformer handle will change the way the deformer affects the geometry.*

5   Deformation order

- **RMB-click** on the *Diva* geometry, then select **Inputs** → **All Inputs**.

- **MMB-drag** *Non Linear(sine1)* on *Blend Shape(blendShape1)*.

  Doing so will change the deformation order so the sine deformer will affect the geometry before any other deformers.

- Click the **Close** button.

6   Parent the sine deformer

- Parent the *sine1Handle* node to the *rig* group.

Note: *Since the deformer affects the geometry at its default position, it must remain at the center of the world in order to deform the dress correctly. Since you might want to move it to deform the dress in different ways, no lock will be required.*

Tip: *Remember to animate the* **Offset** *attribute of the sine1 node to activate the wind on the dress.*

7   Save your work

- Save the scene as *26-divaFinal_hires_01.ma*.

Low resolution model

Before calling the rig final, you will need to generate a low resolution model for realtime animation. The low resolution model will be created starting from the NURBS patch model.

1   Scene file

- Open the scene called *24-divaRig_02.ma*.

Note: *This scene contains the NURBS patch Diva model.*

2   Clean up

- Delete the *rig* group.

- Delete any accessories not needed for the low resolution model, such as the *belt*, the *jewelry* and the *hair band*.

Tip: *Keep the high heels since they are already low resolution enough for your needs.*

3   Rebuild

- Select the *bodyGroup* and *dressGroup*.

- Select **Edit NURBS → Rebuild Surfaces → □**.

- In the option window, set the **Number of Spans U** and **V** to **2**, then click the **Rebuild** button.

Doing so will rebuild all the NURBS patches to be low resolution.

4   Convert

- Select the *bodyGroup* and *dressGroup*.

- Select **Modify → Convert → NURBS to Polygons → □**.

- In the option window, set the following:

    Type to **Quads**;

    Tessellation Method to **General**;

    Number U and **V** to **1**.

- Click the **Tessellate** button.

There is now a low resolution polygonal Diva body.

5   Tweak the conversion

There might be some surfaces that need a higher resolution in order to be good enough for the low resolution model. For instance, the dress straps could use more resolution.

- Hide the *divaLayer*.

- Select the dress straps, then highlight the *nurbsTessellate* node in the Channel Box.

- Tweak the **U** and **V Number** to add some resolution to the model.

- Repeat the previous step for any other surfaces that requires more resolution.

6   Combine and merge

- Combine the low resolution surfaces and **Merge Vertices**.

- Tweak the low resolution surface to improve its quality.

Tip: *You can choose to tweak half the model, and then mirror and combine them together.*

- Set the normals of the geometry to be soft.

7   Other objects

- Show the *divaLayer*.

- Rebuild the hair to **4** spans in **U** and **V**.

8   Delete all history

9   Optimize scene size

The low resolution Diva

10 Save the low resolution model

- Save the scene as *27-divaFinal_lores_01.ma*.

11 Open the final Diva and merge the low resolution model

- Open the scene called *27-divaFinal_hires_01.ma*.

- Import the scene called *27-divaFinal_lores_01.ma*.

12 Skinning

- Select the original *Diva* geometry.

- Execute the following MEL script:

```
select `skinCluster -q -inf`;
```

*The above MEL command will select all the influences affecting
the Diva geometry.*

- **Shift-select** the low resolution *Diva* geometry.

- Select **Skin** → **Bind Skin** → **Smooth Bind**.

13 Copy skinning

- Select the original *Diva* geometry, then **Shift-select** the low
  resolution geometry.

- Select **Skin** → **Edit Skin** → **Copy Skin Weights**.

14 Bind the rest of the low resolution model

15 Blend shapes

Use what you have learned in this project to transfer the blend shapes from the high resolution model to the low resolution model.

The low resolution Diva rigged

16 Clean the scene

Clean up the scene by deleting the high resolution models. Then make sure everything is named appropriately and optimize the scene size.

17 Save your work

- Save the scene as *26-divaFinal_lores_02.ma*.

Conclusion

You have now managed to add secondary animation to Diva's setup using various deformers. You have also created a low resolution model which will come in handy when you will start animating.

In Project seven, you will animate Meeper and Diva together in a bar scene.

Lessons

In Project Seven, you will animate scenes with Meeper, Diva and her accessories. You will first experience keyframing by animating a simple walk with Meeper. Once that is done, you will learn about references and set up a simple scene.

While building the scene, you will set up some constraints on Diva for her to sing with a microphone. You will then block out an animation where Meeper interrupts Diva's singing and grabs the microphone.

By the end of this project, you should feel comfortable with most animation tasks.

Lesson 28   Simple walk

Now that you have finished creating the character rigs, it is time to animate them. You will start by animating Meeper walking forward. This is where you put the controls you worked on over the last few lessons to the test.

In this lesson you will learn the following:

- How to organize your keyable attributes into character sets;

- How to set keyframes;

- How to set breakdown keys;

- How to use Auto Key;

- How to edit animations in the Graph Editor with buffer curves;

- How to delete static channels.

Workflow

There are several approaches to animating a character. This lesson is by no means meant to be an exhaustive examination of character animation, but it will go through a basic animation workflow that can easily be adapted to your own personal workflow requirements.

Character sets

Before you start, you will create *character sets* to simplify the selection and keyframing process. A character set is a collection of attributes organized in a central place from the same or separate objects that are intended to be animated together. Character sets don't have to be actual physical characters like Meeper; specifically, they are a collection of attributes that you want to animate all together.

The benefit of working with character sets is that you don't have to keyframe each individual attribute in the set. Once the character set is active, simply pose your selections and when you set a key, each attribute in the character set gets keyframed.

You created the Meeper rig to be easily controlled by only a few control objects. Now you are going to organize those objects into a central collection, further simplifying the animation process.

> **Note:** *The attributes of a character set are aliased to the original attributes, which means they are intermediate attributes that are directly connected to the ones you are animating.*

You can select character sets from either the Outliner or Hypergraph, or you can use the menu **Character → Select Character Set Nodes**.

You can set the current character set from the menu **Character → Set Current Character Set**, or from the pull-down menu in the lower right corner of the timeline.

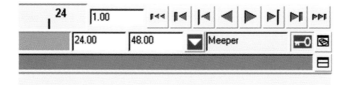

Character menu

Create a character set

1   Open an existing scene

- Open the scene file called *28-simple walk_01.ma*.

Note: *This scene contains the Meeper setup created in Project 5.*

2   Select the appropriate objects

The first step to creating a character set is selecting all of the objects that are going to be included in that set.

- Select all of the manipulators and locators.
- Select the *Head* and *antennae* joints.

Note: *Do not include non-animated objects because their attributes might end up with animation curves, which could increase the scene file size as well as slow down loading time and playback speed.*

3   Create the character set

- Select **Character** → **Create Character Set** → □.
- In the option window, select **Edit** → **Reset Settings**.
- Set the **Name** to *Meeper*.
- Press the **Create Character Set** button.

The attributes in the Channel Box should now appear yellow, which means they are connected and included in the character set.

4   Editing the character set

When you created Meeper's rig, you restricted unnecessary attributes by locking them and making them non-keyable. Because of this, Meeper's character set does not contain any superfluous attributes.

Although you have taken care to prevent unwanted attributes in the character set, it is a good idea to check the attributes of the character set in the Relationship Editor to make sure there is nothing missing or unessential.

- Select **Window** → **Relationship Editors** → **Character Sets...**

- Click on the **+** beside the *Meeper* character set in the left column.

All of the attributes in this character set will be listed.

- Check to make sure that the *Meeper* character set does not contain unwanted attributes.

Tip: *For instance, you might not want the master.Smooth attribute to be keyframed with the character set.*

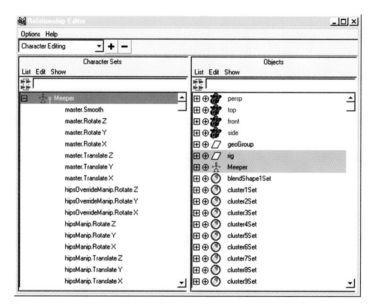

Relationship Editor

5 Edit attributes in the character set

- If you find attributes that don't belong to the character set, highlight them, then select **Edit** → **Remove Highlighted Attributes** from the left side of the Relationship Editor.

- If you find attributes missing from the character set, highlight them in the right column of the Relationship Editor.

Note: *You can also add and remove attributes from the selected character set by using* **Character** → **Add to Character Set** *and* **Character** → **Remove from Character Set.**

Keyframing preparation

Before you begin to set keys for the walk cycle, it is a good idea to change the **Move Tool** and **Rotate Tool** settings.

1 Transformation modes

- Select **Modify** → **Transformation Tools** → **Move Tool** → ☐.

- In the option window, set **Mode** to **Local**.

Using the **Move Tool** *in the* **Local** *option will allow you to move objects according to their local space, rather than world space, which is generally preferable when animating a character.*

- Select **Modify** → **Transformation Tools** → **Rotate Tool** → ☐.

- In the option window, set **Rotate Mode** to **Local**.

2 Key options

- Click on the **Animation Preferences** button at the right of the timeline.

- In the **Categories** column, select **Settings** → **Animation**.

- In the **Tangents** section of the **Animation Key Preferences**, set **Weighted Tangents** to **On**.

Weighted tangents provide more control over the shape of a curve between keys in the Graph Editor.

- Set the **Default In Tangent** and **Default Out Tangent** to **Clamped**.

Clamped keys are a good starting point for character animation because they prevent values from overshooting between keys of similar value, while providing spline smoothness between keys of different values.

- Click on the **Save** button.

3   Animation range

- Set the **Start Time** to **1** and the **End Time** to **120**.

- Set the **Playback Start Time** to **1**, and the **Playback End Time** to **30**.

*Setting the start/end times and playback start/end times differently will allow you to focus on the animated cycle, which will go from **1** to **30**. The rest of the animation will then be cycled from frames **30** to **120**.*

Time Slider

4   Save your work

- Save the scene as *28-simple walk_02.ma*.

Animating the walk

Artistically, a good walk cycle should not only get the character from point A to point B, but also express the character's personality. Technically, a good walk cycle should start with a generic walking pose that can easily be modified to reflect the character's mood.

Creating a walk cycle involves animating a character in several key positions. You want to start with both feet on the ground, then animate one leg lifting as it shifts forward. The first part of this process is the animation of the feet sliding on the ground. The lifting of the feet will be added later.

1   Go to frame 1

2   Set Meeper's arms to FK

While Meeper's arms could be animated with IK, FK is generally more appropriate for the type of action made here.

- Select the *leftArmManip* and *rightArmManip*.

- Set the **Ik Fk Blend** attributes to **0**.

3   Current character set

- Make sure that the name *Meeper* is displayed in the **Current Character Set** field at the right of the timeline.

- If *Meeper* is not the current character set, click on the **down arrow** button next to the character set field and select *Meeper*.

Now when you set a key, a keyframe will be set on all Meeper attributes.

4   Pose Meeper

The first step in animating Meeper's walk cycle is posing him.

- Select *leftFootManip* and **move** it to **-5** on the **Z-axis**.

Note: At this point, Meeper's feet will lift away from the manipulator. This will be corrected later by animating Meeper's foot attributes.

- Select *rightFootManip* and **move** it to **2** on the **Z-axis**.

Meeper posed at frame 1

For a cycled walk to behave properly, it is important to have a constant stride length for the feet and hips. If you calculate the distance between the feet (from the values set above), you will see that a stride will be equal to **7** units and a full step will be equal to **14** units.

5 Set a key

- Hit the **s** key to set a key.

Because the current character is set to Meeper, a keyframe is set on all of Meeper.

6 Advance to frame 15

7 Move the left leg forward

- Select the *leftFootManip* and move it forward by **14** units relative to the current value in the Channel Box, ending up at **9** units.

- Select the *leftPoleVector* and also move it forward by **14** units, ending up at **16** units.

8 Move the globalControl forward

- Select the *hipsManip* and move it forward by **7** units.

9 Set a key

10 Test the animation

- **Click+drag** between frames **1** and **15** in the Time Slider to test the animation.

11 Advance to frame 30

12 Move the right leg and hips forward

- Select the *rightFootManip* and move it forward by **14** units.

- Select the *rightPoleVector* and move it forward by **14** units.

- Select the *hipsManip* and move it forward by **7** units.

13 Set another key

14 Test the animation

- Playback the animation.

15 Save your work

- Save the scene as *28-simple walk_03.ma*.

Cycle the animation

Now that the first step has been animated, you will cycle the curves to keep Meeper walking beyond the current frame range.

1   Open the Graph Editor

- Select **Window** → **Animation Editors** → **Graph Editor**.

- Select the *Meeper* character set in the left column of the Graph Editor.

Note: *If you don't see it, make sure the Meeper character set is currently selected.*

- Select **View** → **Frame All** to display all *Meeper* character set animation curves.

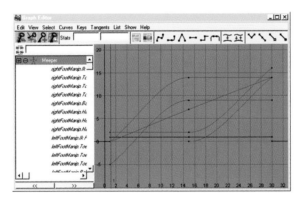

Animation curves in Graph Editor

2   Select the animation curves

- **Click+drag** a selection box over all of the curves.

- To display the values of the animation curves outside the recorded keyframe range, select **View** → **Infinity**.

3 Cycle the curves

- Select **Curves** → **Pre Infinity** → **Cycle**.

Cycling before the keys is not essential, but can be helpful once you start editing animation curves.

- Select **Curves** → **Post Infinity** → **Cycle**.

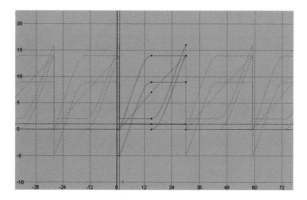

Cycled animation curves

4 Increase the playback range

- **Click+drag** on the box at the end of the current Range Slider and drag it until the playback range is from **1** to **120**.

5 Play the animation

Instead of moving forward, Meeper keeps covering the same ground every **30** frames. This is because the **Cycle** option was used. For Meeper to move forward in the cycle, the **Cycle With Offset** option must be selected.

6 Cycle the curves with offset

- With the curves still selected in the Graph Editor, select **Curves** → **Post Infinity** → **Cycle With Offset**.

- Select **Curves** → **Pre Infinity** → **Cycle With Offset**.

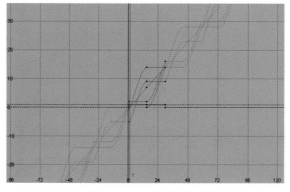

Animation curves cycled with offset

7 Play the animation

Meeper should now continue to move forward as he walks.

8 Turn off the character set

For the time being, the *Meeper* character set should be turned off so that individual attributes can be edited.

- Select **None** in the **Current Character Set** menu.

9 Curve tangencies

As you watch the animation, you will notice that Meeper seems to be limping. This is because the tangency of the animation curves are broken between the cycles.

- Select both foot manipulators.

Since there are no active character sets, you can see the animation curves in the Graph Editor.

- Select **Translate Z** in the left column for each manipulator.

Selecting attributes displays only those animation curves. You can see there is a clear break in tangency of those curves.

- Select both animation curves.

- Select **Tangents** → **Flat**.

- Playback the animation.

The motion of the legs is now correct.

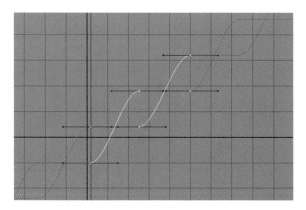

Translation Z animation curves with flat tangency

Note: *It is important when working with cycled animation that the curves interpolate appropriately from the last frame in the cycle to the first frame in the cycle.*

10 Save your work

- Save the scene as *28-simple walk_04.ma*.

Raising the feet

Currently, Meeper's feet drag on the ground as he walks. Now you will animate the raising of his feet using *breakdown keys*. Breakdown keys are different from standard keys in that they maintain their relative position between regular keyframes. This is useful for actions that, by their nature, tend to have relative timing. In the case of Meeper's walk, the timing of the foot raise is relative to the foot hitting the ground, so it is beneficial for the timing of the raise to adjust according to changes made in the timing of the fall.

1 Go back to frame 1

- Go back to frame **1** and set the playback range to go from **1** to **30**.

2 Lift the left foot

- Select the *leftFootManip*.

- Switch to the *side* view and **click+drag** in the Time Slider until the left foot lines up with the right foot.

- Translate the *leftFootManip* **2** unit on the **Y-axis**.

- Rotate it **15 degree** on the **X-axis**.

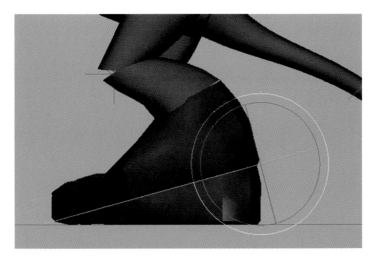

Left foot raised and rotated

3 Set a breakdown key

- Select **Animate** → **Set Breakdown**.

A blue tick will appear in the timeline denoting a breakdown key.

4 Repeat for the right foot

- Advance to the frame where the right foot lines up with the left foot.

Note: *You may find that the feet don't perfectly line up as they pass each other. Select the frame where they are the closest.*

- Move and rotate the *rightFootManip* like you did for the left foot.

5 Set another breakdown key

6 Set the playback range from 1 to 120

7 Playback the animation

8 Change the tangency of the curves

- In the Graph Editor, display the **Translate Y** animation curve for the *leftFootManip*.

- Select the key at frame **15**.

- Select **Tangent** → **In Tangent** → **Linear**.

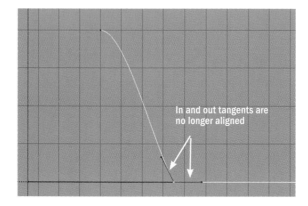

Frame 15 with In Tangent set to Linear

Before changing the In Tangent of this key, the curve decelerated as it interpolated into the key, causing the foot to decelerate as it approached the ground. Now, the curve interpolates into the key at more of a constant speed, causing the foot to hit the ground at a constant speed.

- Select the **Translate Y** animation curve for *rightFootManip*.

- Select the key at frame **15** and change its **Out Tangent** to **Linear**.

9 Play the animation

10 Save your work

- Save the scene as *28-simple walk_05.ma*.

Animate the rolling heel action

Now you will animate the motion of Meeper's heels as they hit and peel off the ground.

1 Right foot's heel rotation

- Go to frame **1**.

- Set *rightFootManip*'s **Heel Rot Z** attribute to **10**.

- Highlight the attribute, then **RMB-click** and select **Key Selected**.

- Go to frame **4**.

- Set **Heel Rot Z** to **0**.

- Set a key.

- Go to frame **30**.

- Set **Heel Rot Z** to **10**.

- Set a key.

2 Left foot's heel rotation

- Go to frame **15**.

- Set *leftFootManip*'s **Heel Rot Z** attribute to **10**.

- Set a key.

- Go to frame **18**.

- Set **Heel Rot Z** to **0**.

- Set a key.

3 Heel tangencies

The heel action is good, but the animation curves can be improved.

- Display the curves for the *left* and *rightFootManip* in the Graph Editor.

- Select both **Heel Rot Z** animation curves and change their tangency to **Flat**.

4 Break tangents

- Select the **Heel Rot Z** attribute for the *rightFootManip*.

- Select the key at frame **4**.

- Select **Keys** → **Break Tangents** in the Graph Editor.

With its tangency broken, the In and Out Tangent handles on the key can be independently edited.

- Select the tangent handle on the left side of the key and invoke the **Move Tool**.

- **MMB-drag** so that the tangent handle points toward the key at frame **1**.

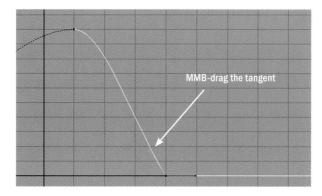

MMB-drag the tangent

Key at frame 4 with edited broken tangency

5 Weight tangents

- Select the key at frame **22**.

- Select **Keys** → **Free Tangent weights** in the Graph Editor.

> **Note:** *When animation curves are non-weighted and you wish to make them weighted, simply select* **Curves** → **Weighted Tangents**. *Doing so specifies that the tangents on the currently selected animation curves can be weighted.*

- Select the tangent handle on the right side of the key.

- Hold down the **Shift** key, then **MMB-drag** to adjust the shape of the curve.

Changing the tangent weight adjusts the timing of the curve. In this case, the timing out of the key is made slower.

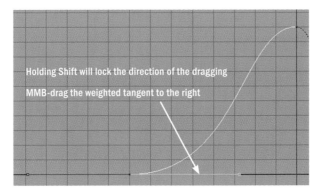

Key at frame 22 with tangent weight adjusted

6   Adjust the left foot

- Select the key at frame **18**, break its tangency, and point the left tangent handle at the key at frame **15**.

- Select the key at frame **8**, free its tangent weight, then adjust the shape.

Make sure the animation curves for both feet have basically the same shape. If necessary, adjust the curves so they match each other.

7   Save your work

- Save the scene as *28-simple walk_06.ma*.

Animating the foot peeling off the ground

Now that you have animated the heel action, you will animate the foot peeling off the ground.

1   Left foot's ball rotation

- Go to frame **1**.

- Set *leftFootManip*'s **Ball Rot** value to **-40**.

- Set a key.

- **MMB-drag** the current time in the Time Slider to frame **30**.

MMB-dragging *in the Time Slider will cause the time to change, but not the animation. You can then keyframe an attribute with the exact same value.*

- Set another key.

- Go to frame **25**.

- Set *leftFootManip*'s **Ball Rot** value to **0**.

- Set a key.

2 Right foot's ball rotation

- Go to frame **15**.

- Set *rightFootManip*'s **Ball Rot** value to **40**.

- Set a key.

- Go to frame **10**.

- Set *rightFootManip*'s **Ball Rot** value to **0**.

- Set a key.

3 Playback the animation

4 Flat animation curves

- Flatten the tangents of the **Ball Rot** animation curve for both feet.

5 Save your work

- Save the scene as *28-simple walk_07.ma*.

Hips motion

Now that Meeper's basic forward motion has been established, you will animate the up and down motion as he walks.

1 Enable the Auto Key

- Turn **On** the **Auto Key** button located on the right side of the Time Slider.

The Auto Key option will set a keyframe automatically as soon as you change the values of keyed attributes.

Note: *There must be at least one keyframe on the changing attribute in order for Auto Key to set a keyframe.*

2   Hips moving down keyframes

- Select the *hipsManip* and **key** its **Translate Y** attribute at **0** at frame **1**, **15** and **30**.

3   Animate the hips moving up

- Advance to the frame where the left foot passed the right foot, at frame **8**.

- Move the *hipsManip* up on the **Y-axis** by **0.5** units.

A key is automatically set on this attribute.

- **MMB-drag** to frame **22** in the Time Slider.

Note: *Since you didn't change the attribute's value in this step, Auto Key did not keyframe the attribute for you. Thus, you need to manually set a keyframe.*

- Set a key on the *hipsManip*'s **Y-axis** attribute in the Channel Box.

4   Weight shift

Now you will animate Meeper's side-to-side motion so that it looks like he's shifting his weight on the grounded foot.

- Go to frame **8**.

- Select *hipsManip* and set its **Translate X** to **-1.**

- Select *hipsOverrideManip* and set its **Rotate Z** to **-5.**

Weight shift at frame 8

5   Advance to the weight shift frame

- Go to frame **22**.

- Select *hipsManip* and set its **Translate X** to **1**.

- Select *hipsOverrideManip* and set its **Rotate Z** to **5**.

6   Play the animation

- Increase the **playback range** to **1** to **120** and playback the animation.

7   Save your work

- Save the scene as *28-simple walk_08.ma*.

Compensating for Meeper's center of gravity

Now that you have animated Meeper's side-to-side action, it's a good time to adjust the movement of his feet and body to compensate for his shifting center of gravity. First you will adjust his feet.

1   Lifted left foot

- Select *leftFootManip* and go to frame **8**.

- Set its **Translate X** value to **-1.5**.

- Set its **Y-Rotation** attribute so the foot points a little bit outward.

- Set a breakdown key for these attributes.

> **Note:** *You are using a breakdown key because the other keys you set for this object at frame **8** were breakdown keys.*

2   Lifted right foot

- Select *rightFootManip* and advance to frame **22**.

- Set its **Translate X** value to **1.5**.

- Set its **Rotation** attribute so the foot points a little bit outward.

- Set a breakdown key for this channel.

3 **Adjust the spine**

- Select *spineManip*.

- Go to frame **8**.

- Set *spineManip*'s **Translate X** to **0.2**.

- Advance to frame **22**.

- Set *spineManip*'s **Translate X** to **-0.2**.

4 **Adjust the head**

- Select *neckManip*.

- Go to frame **8**.

- Set *neckManip*'s **Rotate Y** to **-5**.

- Advance to frame **22**.

- Set *neckManip*'s **Rotate Y** to **5**.

5 **Play the animation**

6 **Adjust the curves as necessary**

7 **Save your work**

- Save the scene as *28-simple walk_09.ma*.

Put one foot in front of the other

As you watch Meeper's animation, you will notice that he walks strangely, not putting one foot in front of the other. You will now correct that.

1 **Left foot motion**

- Select the *leftFootManip*.

- In the Graph Editor, highlight its **Translate X** animation curve.

- Select the keys that have zero values at frame **1**, **15** and **30**.

- In the value field at the top of the Graph Editor, enter **-1.0**, then press **Enter**.

2 Right foot motion

- Select the *rightFootManip*.

- In the Graph Editor, highlight its **Translate X** animation curve.

- Select the keys that have zero values at frame **1**, **15** and **30**.

- In the **Selected Key's Value** field at the top of the Graph Editor, enter **1.0**, then press **Enter**.

3 Play the animation

4 Adjust the curves as necessary

Offset the hips timing

Meeper's basic body motion is complete. Now is a good time to refine it a little by offsetting the timing of some of his actions.

1 Offset animation curves

- Select *hipsManip*.

- In the Graph Editor, select all of the animation curves.

- In the **Selected Key's Time** field type `+=1`.

  +=# is a very useful tool for adjusting the values of a curve as a whole. In this case, typing +=1 will push each key in the selected curves forward one frame in time. This function also works with subtraction, multiplication and division.

2 Play the animation

3 Save your work

- Save the scene as *28-simple walk_10.ma*.

Animating Meeper's arms

Meeper's arms now need to swing at his side, and you will use FK rather than IK. Since Meeper's arm joints weren't included in the *Meeper* character set when it was created, they should be added before they are animated.

1 Go to frame 1

2   Select the elbow and shoulder joints for both arms

- Select the *Left* and *RightArm* and *ForeArm* joints.

3   Add the arm joints to the Meeper character set

- Select **Window** → **Relationship Editors** → **Character Sets...**

- Select the *Meeper* character set in the left column.

- Select **Edit** → **Add Objects To Character Set**.

The rotation attributes of the arm joints are now part of the Meeper character set.

4   Rotate the arms down

- Select the *LeftArm* and *RightArm* joints.

- Set their **Rotate Z** attributes to **-70 degrees**.

5   Balance the arms back and forth

- Set the **Rotate Y** attribute of the *LeftArm* to **40 degrees**.

- Set the **Rotate Y** attribute of the *RightArm* to **-20 degrees**.

- Key the rotation for both joints by pressing **Shift+e**.

- **MMB-drag** to frame **30**.

- Press **Shift+e** again.

- Go to frame **15**.

- Set the **Rotate Y** attribute of the *LeftArm* to **-20 degrees**.

- Set the **Rotate Y** attribute of the *RightArm* to **40 degrees**.

- Key the rotation of both joints.

6   Balance the elbows

- Go to frame **1**.

- Set the **Rotate Y** for *LeftForeArm* to **-20**.

- Set a key for that attribute.

- **MMB-drag** to frame **30**.

- Set a key for **Rotate Y** again.

- Go to frame **15**.

- Set a key for **Rotate Y** at **0 degrees**.

- Go to frame **1**.

- Set the **rotate Y** for *RightForeArm* to **0** and set a key.

- **MMB-drag** to frame **30**.

- Set a key for **Rotate Y** again.

- Go to frame **15**.

- Set a key for rotate Y at **-20 degrees**.

7   Cycle the animation

- Select the *Left* and *RightArm* and *ForeArm* joints.

- Cycle their animation curves in the Graph Editor and correct the tangency as is necessary.

8   Offset the animation

- Select both arm joints and offset their timing by using +=1.

- Select both *ForeArm* joints and offset their animation using +=3.

9   Playback the scene

Meeper's animated arms

10 Save your work

- Save the scene as *28-simple walk_11.ma*.

Buffer curves

When animating, you will often find it helpful to compare the results of a change made to an animation curve with the original curve. *Buffer curves* allow you to easily switch back and forth between two versions of the same channel.

1 Select both ForeArm joints

2 Open the Graph Editor

3 Select the animation curves

4 Create buffer curve snapshots

- Select **Curves** → **Buffer Curve Snapshot**.

Duplicates of the rotation curves have been saved into memory.

- Select **View** → **Show Buffer Curves**.

You will not see a change at the moment as the buffer curves are in exactly the same position as the original curves.

5 Scale the curves

- Select **Edit** → **Scale** → ❑.

- Reset the **Scale Keys** options.

- Set the **Value Scale**/**Pivot** values to **2.0** and **0.0**.

*This will scale the values of the keys by a factor of **2.0**, using **0.0** as the scale pivot.*

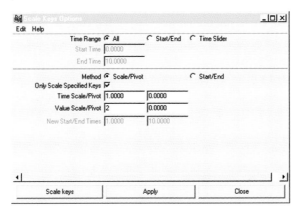

Scale Keys window

- Click the **Scale Keys** button.

The values of the curves have now been doubled and the buffer curves show the original values.

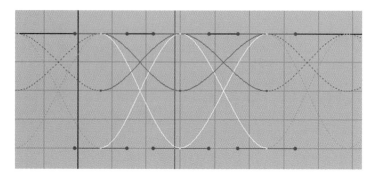

The animation curves and the buffer curves

6   Play the animation

7   Swap the buffer curves

The motion of the forearms is different, but it's hard to say whether or not it's better. You will now swap these curves with the buffer curves, which currently store the original rotation values.

- In the Graph Editor, select **Curves** → **Swap Buffer Curves**.

The Graph Editor now uses curves with the original rotation values.

8   Play the animation

Decide which curve you prefer and make it the current curve.

9   Save your work

- Save the scene as *28-simple walk_12.ma*.

Meeper's overall animation

The principle advantage of this approach to animating a walk cycle is that once it is set up, it is easy to edit and modify the walk. You will now make adjustments to the curves to change how Meeper walks.

1   Scale the hips and feet to create a faster and longer walk

- Select the *hipsManip*, both *footManips* and both legs' poleVectors.

- Select the **Translate Z** animation curves for all three nodes in the Graph Editor.

- Select **Edit** → **Scale**.

- Reset the **Scale Keys** options.

- Set the **Value Scale/Pivot** values to **1.5** and **1.0**.

*This will scale the values of the keys by a factor of **1.5**, using frame **1** as the scale pivot.*

- Click the **Scale Keys** button.

2   Play the animation

Meeper now covers fifty percent more ground in the same time.

3   Adjust Meeper's vertical motion

Since Meeper's knees now snap due to overextending, you will need to compensate with an up and down hip motion.

- Select *hipsManip*'s **Translate Y** curve in the Graph Editor.

- Select all the keys.

- Invoke the **Move Tool**.

- Hold down **Shift** and **click+drag** the keys down.

- Stop when Meeper's knees no longer snap throughout the animation.

4   Scale keys manipulator

- Select *hipsOverrideManip*'s **Rotate Z** curve in the Graph Editor.

- From the main interface, select **Modify** → **Transformation Tools** → **Scale Tool** → ❐.

- Click on the Graph Editor's title bar.

A new set of options will appear in the Scale Tool's options window.

- Select **Manipulator**.

- A box will appear around the selected curve.

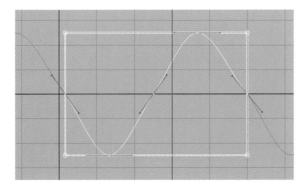

The scale keys manipulator

- Playback the animation and scale the curve by adjusting the manipulator.

Be careful to only scale the keys up or down and not side to side, or the timing will be thrown off.

- Experiment with the scale values while the animation plays until you are happy with the motion.

5   Continue animating

Continue animating Meeper until you are satisfied with his animation. Animate secondary animation on the eyes, fingers and antennae.

Refined Meeper animation

Cleaning up

Although Meeper was set up carefully, and his character set contains no unnecessary attributes, *static channels* (animation curves that represent no change in value) have been generated. Any attribute that is included in the character set but has not been manipulated thus far will have static channels.

Now that Meeper's walk is basically done, it's a good time to delete these channels. Deleting the channels will have no effect on Meeper's walk, but it will reduce the size of the scene file.

1   Delete the static channels

- Select **Edit** → **Delete All By Type** → **Static Channels**.

  All the static animation curves in the scene are now deleted.

2   Save your work

- Save the scene as *28-simple walk_13.ma*.

Conclusion

Animation is a key part of character rigging because a rig must be tested and qualified as it is being put together. You will want to have a high degree of confidence in a rig before you go too far down the path of skinning and building higher orders of control. Understanding the animator's needs is also an important function of the character rigger.

In this lesson, you learned how to animate a simple walk cycle. Animation here was done in a rudimentary fashion using low resolution geometry, but it is a good method for streamlining the performance. You also learned about character sets, the best friend of any animator.

In the next lesson, you will learn about file referencing.

Lesson 29   References

In this lesson, you will learn the basics of scene references. References are very useful in a production since you can have several files referencing the same character. Then, if you update the referenced file, you automatically update the rest of the scenes.

In this lesson you will learn the following:

- About file referencing;

- How to create references;

- How to load and unload a reference;

- How to use a temporary reference scene;

- How to update a reference;

- How to replace a reference;

- How to switch references through a Text Editor.

File referencing

File referencing allows users to assemble multiple objects, shading materials and animation into a scene without importing the files into the scene. That is, the contents that appear in the scene are read or referenced from pre-existing files that remain separate and unopened. File referencing empowers users for collaborative production in situations where multiple users need to work concurrently and share various assets in complex scenes.

For instance, in a production context you might have several scenes for accessories, background and character (ABCs). Those scenes are usually assembled into shots, scenes, or sequences. Without using references, all the ABCs would be duplicated, and depending on how many shots you have in the project, it could result in lots of wasted disk space and a lot of work in order to replace or update one of the ABCs.

A scene file that references other files lower in the hierarchy is known as a *parent scene*. A parent scene reads or references other files that make up a scene from where they reside on disk (or on a network). These files are known as referenced *child scenes*.

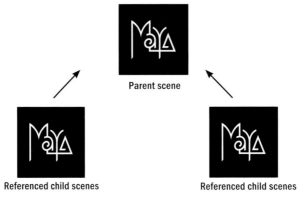

Parent scene

Referenced child scenes   Referenced child scenes

Logic of file referencing

Even though the referenced child scenes appear within the currently open parent scene, they remain separate from the currently open parent scene at all times. When the currently open parent scene file is saved, all the connections to the child scene are saved, but any referenced scene data is not saved within it.

> **Note:** *In the case of a parent scene referencing a character that was animated, only the animation data is saved with the parent scene. That way, the parent scene size remains very small.*

Create references

In the following exercise, you will prepare the animation scene file to be used all along this project. To do so, you will reference the required ABCs.

1   Scene file

- Create a new scene.

2   Create a reference

- Select **File** → **Create Reference** → ◻.

- In the option window, set the following:

    Use Namespaces to **Off**;

    Resolve all nodes with this string: *meeper*.

- Click the **Reference** button.

A browse dialog box will appear, letting you choose the file to reference.

- Select the scene named *meeper_lores.ma*.

- Click the **Reference** button.

Meeper is loaded into memory and displayed in the current scene.

3   Outliner

- Open the Outliner.

Notice that the Meeper nodes were prefixed with meeper_ (that prefix was defined in the previous step).

- Select a Meeper node in the Outliner and press the **Delete** key.

An error message will be displayed specifying that objects from a reference file are read-only and thus cannot be deleted.

Note: *In the Outliner, an* **R** *on the object icon tells you that this node is part of a reference. In the Hypergraph, the name of the node is read when it is part of a reference.*

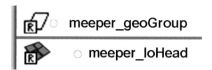

The R icon in the Outliner

4 Create a deferred reference

- Select **File** → **Create Reference** → ❐.

- In the option window, set the following:

    Deferred to **On**;

    Resolve all nodes with this string: *diva*.

- Browse for the scene called *diva_lores.ma*.

The reference is added to the scene, but is not loaded.

5 Reference Editor

- Select **File** → **Reference Editor...**

The Reference Editor is the place where you can see all references in the current scene.

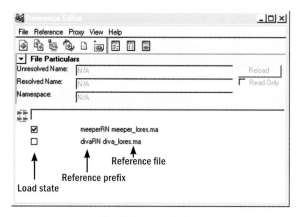

The Reference Editor

- Load the *Diva* reference by turning **On** its checkbox.

The Diva is loaded in the current scene.

> **Note:** *By checking* **On** *and* **Off** *the checkboxes, you can load and unload references.*

6   Stage reference

- Select **File** → **Create Reference** → ☐.

- In the option window, set the following:

    Deferred to **Off**;

    Resolve all nodes with this string: *stage*.

- Browse for the scene called *stage.ma*.

The stage background is now loaded to the scene.

7   Microphone reference

- Select **File** → **Create Reference** → ☐.

- In the option window, set **Resolve all nodes with this string**: *microphone*.

- Browse for the scene called *microphone.ma*.

8   Stool reference

- Select **File** → **Create Reference** → ☐.

- In the option window, set **Resolve all nodes with this string**: *stool*.

- Browse for the scene called *stool.ma*.

9 Save your work

- Save the scene as *29-references_01.ma*.

Temporary references

You will now create a temporary reference file with only a simple cube in it. Doing so will let you create a scene with all the references needed, but with stand-ins for objects that are not yet modeled.

1 Scene file

- Create a new scene.

2 Create the stand

- Create a primitive cube.

- Rename the cube as *stand*.

Later in this exercise, you will come back and model a stand for the microphone.

3 Save the scene

- Save the scene as *stand.ma*.

4 Open the parent scene file

- Open the scene called *29-references_01.ma*.

Notice that each child reference is getting loaded at this time.

5 Stand reference

- Select **File** → **Create Reference** → ❑.

- In the option window, set **Resolve all nodes with this string**: *stand*.

- Browse for the scene called *stand.ma*.

6 Select the reference's contents

- Select **File** → **Reference Editor…**

- Highlight the *stand* reference.

- In the Reference Editor, select **File** → **Select File Contents**.

The reference objects created earlier are now selected.

Note: *Now the cube and nodes that come from that file are selected.*

7 Place the objects

- Move the *stand* cube at the front of the stage.

- Move the *Diva's Master* node behind the *stand*.

- Move the *microphone* in front of *Diva*.

- Move the *stool* behind *Diva*.

- Move *Meeper* to stage left.

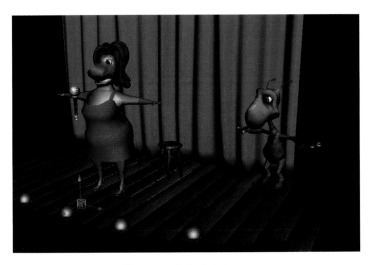

The scene is taking shape

8   Save your work

- Save the scene as *29-references_02.ma*.

Update a reference

You have placed the various ABCs in the parent scene, but it would be nice to have the microphone stand modeled. You will now model the stand and save its scene, so that the next time you open the parent scene, the stand will be loaded.

1   Scene file

- Open the scene called *stand.ma*.

2   Model the stand

- Draw a profile curve in the *side* view.

- Select **Surface** → **Revolve** to generate the surface.

- Create a microphone holder.

- Refine the geometry and assign materials.

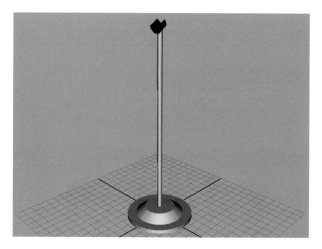

The stand model

3 Clean up

- Select **Edit** → **Delete All by Type** → **History**.

- Open the Outliner and delete obsolete nodes, such as the curve and the stand-in cube.

- Rename the surfaces to *shaft* and *holder*.

- Group the surfaces together.

4 Stand hierarchy

When you created the stand-in file, you named the temporary cube *stand*. Since you moved the cube in the parent scene, if you want the new stand to be moved to the same location, you must call the stand group *stand*.

- Rename the group *stand*.

Note: *It is an important concept to understand that a parent scene saves only the names and attribute connections. When you update a reference, it is important to keep the names and attributes of the reference identical. If Maya doesn't find certain nodes or attributes, it will not be able to connect their related data and you might end up losing information.*

5 Layer

It would be nice to have the stand on a layer so that you can set its visibility in the parent scene.

- Create a new layer and rename it *standLayer*.

- Add the *stand* group to the new layer.

6 Save your work

7 Open the parent scene

Now that the reference has been modified, the next time the parent scene referencing that scene is loaded, the new objects will be updated correctly.

- Open the scene called *29-references_02.ma*.

The stand is in the same position as the stand-in cube because it has the same name and attributes.

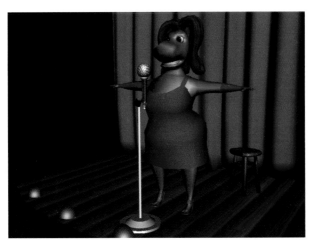

The stand is now updated in the parent scene

Note: *If the parent scene is already open, you can also reload the reference through the Reference Editor.*

Replace references

When you created the Meeper and Diva setups, you created a low resolution file and a high resolution file. Later in this project, when you have animated the characters, you will want to see the animation on the high resolution models. Since the high and low resolution files have the same rig names and attributes, you will be able to switch the references seamlessly.

The following example will show you how to replace a reference.

1   Reference Editor

- Still in the parent scene, select **File** → **Reference Editor...**

- Highlight the *Diva* reference.

- Select **Reference** → **Replace Reference**.

A file browser is now displayed where you can specify the file to replace the current Diva reference.

- Select the file called *diva_hires.ma*.

- Click on the **Reference** button.

The high resolution Diva is now loaded and correctly placed in the scene. Also notice that the Diva reference scene has changed to diva_hires.ma in the Reference Editor.

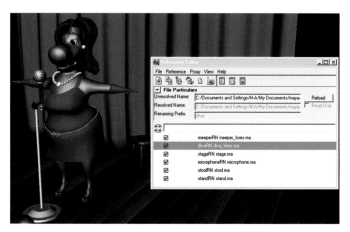

The high resolution Diva reference

2   Save your work

- Save the scene as *29-references_03.ma*.

Switch references in a Text Editor

It is nice that you can switch references within Maya, but sometimes it can be a long and tedious job. For instance, you would have to open the parent scene (and load all of its references), replace the reference (which loads the new reference), and then save the parent scene.

By using the Maya ASCII format, which saves the scene in plain text, you can replace a reference file by editing the parent scene in a Text Editor.

The following example shows how to replace the current Diva with her low resolution scene without even opening Maya.

1 Scene file in a Text Editor

- Open the scene called *29-references_03.ma* in a Text Editor.

2 Locate the reference lines

- At the top of the file content, locate the following lines:

```
file -rdi 1 -rpr "diva" -rfn "divaRN" "./scenes/diva_hires.ma";

file -r -rpr "diva" -dr 1 -rfn "divaRN" "./scenes/diva_hires.ma";
```

Note: *The path of the Diva file might be different so that it points to the file on your computer or network.*

3 Replace the reference lines

- Replace the scene name from *diva_hires.ma* to *diva_lores.ma* as follows:

```
file -rdi 1 -rpr "diva" -rfn "divaRN" "./scenes/diva_lores.ma";

file -r -rpr "diva" -dr 1 -rfn "divaRN" "./scenes/diva_lores.ma";
```

4 Save your changes

5 Open the scene in Maya

- Open the scene called *29-references_03.ma*.

Tip: *If you have the scene already open in Maya, reopen it but do not save. That would overwrite the edits made in the Text Editor.*

Conclusion

Using references in a production environment or even to build a simple scene is a great workflow that can save you quite some time. In this lesson, you learned the different ways of using file references and you now understand their purpose and usage.

In the next lesson, you will set up some constraints between Diva, the microphone and the microphone stand.

Point	❐
Aim	❐
Orient	❐
Scale	❐
Parent	❐
Geometry	❐
Normal	❐
Tangent	❐
Pole Vector	❐
Remove Target	❐
Set Rest Position	
Modify Constrained Axis...	

Lesson 30   Constraints

In this lesson, you will use constraints to have one object follow another one. Constraints are used often in animations and a user must understand their purpose and set up in order to control them successfully.

In this lesson you will learn the following:

- About the different constraint types;

- How to constrain objects;

- How to maintain object offset while constraining;

- How to change the weight of a constraint;

- How to change the interpolation type of a constraint.

Constraint types

The numerous constraint types in Maya are outlined here:

Point constraint

A point constraint causes an object to move to and follow the position of an object, or the average position of several objects. This is useful for having an object match the motion of other objects.

Aim constraint

An aim constraint keeps an object aimed toward another object.

Orient constraint

An orient constraint matches the orientation of one object to one or more other objects. Orient constraints are useful for keeping objects aligned.

Scale constraint

A scale constraint matches the scale of one object to one or more other objects. Scale constraints are useful for keeping objects the same size.

Parent constraint

A parent constraint relates the position (translation and rotation) of one object to another object, so that they behave as if part of a parent-child relationship.

Geometry constraint

A geometry constraint restricts an object's pivot to a NURBS surface, NURBS curve, subdivision surface or polygonal surface.

Normal constraint

A normal constraint keeps an object's orientation so that it aligns with the normal vectors of a NURBS or polygonal surface.

Tangent constraint

A tangent constraint keeps an object moving along, and oriented to a curve. The curve provides the path of the object's motion, and the object orients itself to point along the curve.

Pole vector constraint

A pole vector constraint causes the end of a pole vector to move to and follow the position of an object, or the average position of several objects.

Note: *Most of these constraints were already used in the rigging lessons, but were not intended for animation.*

Constrain the microphone

You will now constrain the microphone to keep it in Diva's hand as you animate her.

1   Scene file

- Open the scene from the last lesson called *29-references_03.ma*.

2   Create a point constraint

- Select the *diva_RightHand* joint, then **Shift-select** the *microphone_geometry*.

Tip: *The object you want to be constrained must always be selected last.*

- Select **Constrain** → **Point Constraint** → ❑.
- Reset the options, then click on the **Add** button.

The microphone will move to fit its pivot to the pivot of the hand joint.

3   Test the constraint

- Move Diva's right hand manipulator.

You will notice that the microphone is obeying the position of the hand, but not its rotations.

Point constraint

4   Undo the constraint

- Undo until the microphone goes back to its original position.

5   Create a parent constraint using Maintain Offset

In the previous steps, you could clearly see that you would need to constrain the microphone both in position and rotation. Instead of creating two constraints, you will use the parent constraint, which simulates a parent-child relationship. You will also use the Maintain Offset option, which will prevent the pivot of the microphone from snapping to the pivot of the hand joint.

- Move and rotate the *microphone_geometry* group so it is correctly placed in the palm of Diva's right hand.

Correct position of the microphone in Diva's hand

- Select the *diva_RightHand* joint, then **Shift-select** the *microphone_geometry*.

- Select **Constrain** → **Parent Constraint** → ❑.

- Reset the options, then set **Maintain Offset** to **On**.

- Click on the **Add** button.

The microphone now maintains its offset to the hand joint.

6   Test the constraint

- Close Diva's fingers on the microphone.

- Move and **rotate** Diva's right hand manipulator in front of her.

The microphone now follows the hand perfectly.

Diva is getting ready to sing

7   Save your work

- Save the scene as *30-constraints_01.ma*.

Constrain Diva's hand to the stand

As another constraint setup, you will now constrain Diva's left hand to the microphone stand. Using the following setup, you will be able to slide her hand along the stand.

1   Scene file

- Continue with your own scene.

Or

- Open the scene called *30-constraints_01.ma*.

2   Create a locator

- Create a locator and rename it *slideControl*.

- Move the *slideControl* where you want the hand to hold the stand.

- Parent the *slideControl* to the *stand*.

- Freeze the *slideControl* attributes.

- Lock and hide all the attributes of the *slideControl* except the **Translate Y**.

3   Move the hand into position

- Move and rotate the *diva_LeftArmManip* so it is placed on the shaft of the microphone stand, over the *slideControl*.

- Place Diva's fingers appropriately.

4   Parent constraint

- Select the *slideControl*, then **Shift-select** the *diva_LeftArmManip*.

- Select **Constrain** → **Parent Constraint**.

Diva's left hand is now constrained to the slideControl, which is in turn parented to the microphone stand.

5   Test the constraint

- Move and rotate the stand to see if Diva's hand follows correctly.

- Move the *slideControl* on its **Y-axis** to see if Diva's hand slides along the stand.

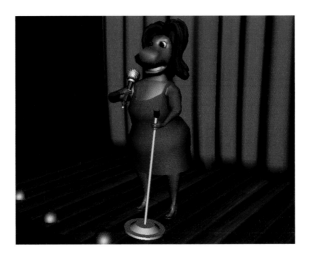

Diva's hand follows the stand's motion

Constraint weight

Every constraint has at least one weight attribute. There can be multiple weight attributes if you define multiple targets on a single constrained object. These attributes determine the percentage of weight coming from a target object.

When the weight is set to **0**, that specific object target is said to be disabled. When the weight is set to **1**, that specific object target is said to be fully enabled.

To see a constraint's weight attribute, select the constrained object, then highlight the constraint node in the **Inputs** section of the Channel Box. The weight attribute is usually labeled with the name of the target object, followed by the weight index (**W0** for instance).

In this exercise, you will add the microphone as a target object to the parent constraint on Diva's left hand. Doing so will allow you to blend her hand from holding the stand to holding the microphone.

Note: *Constraints' weights are to be used to blend between target objects and not between constraint and animation. You will be blending constraints and animation in the next lesson.*

1 Disable the parent constraint

- Select the *diva_LeftHandManip*.

- In the Channel Box, under the **Inputs** section, highlight the *parentConstraint* node.

- Set the **Slide Control W0** attribute to **0.0**.

Doing so turns off the constraint on the slideControl object.

2 Position the hand

- Move and rotate the *diva_LeftArmManip* so it holds the microphone.

3 Parent constraint

- Select the *microphone* group, then **Shift-select** the *diva_LeftArmManip*.

- Select **Constrain → Parent Constraint**.

In the Channel Box, you can now see a second target weight on the parentConstraint node called **Microphone_geometry W1**.

4 Tweak the weights' attributes

- Set the **Slide Control W0** attribute to **1.0** and the **Microphone_geometry W1** attribute to **0.0**.

Diva's hand is now on the microphone stand.

- Set the **Slide Control W0** attribute to **0.0** and the **Microphone_geometry W1** attribute to **1.0**.

Diva's hand is now on the microphone.

Diva can now hold either the stand or the microphone

5   Constraint interpolation type

Blending between targets can sometimes be tricky because the constraint node might interpolate the rotations of the constrained object in an inappropriate way (flipping). If you notice this while changing the weight attributes, the following should help solve the problem:

- Set the **Slide Control W0** attribute to **0.5** and the **Microphone_geometry W1** attribute to **0.5**.

The hand might be all twisted up.

- In the Channel Box with the constraint highlighted, change the **Interp Type** attribute to either **Shortest**, **Longest** or **No Flip**.

The hand flip problem should now be fixed.

6   Save your work

- Save the scene as *30-constraints_02.ma*.

Conclusion

In this lesson, you experimented with a few constraints that will be used throughout this project. Key concepts such as the constraint types, the Maintain Offset option and the weight attributes were covered.

In the next lesson, you will animate a simple walk with Meeper.

Lesson 31   Character animation

In this lesson, you will animate Meeper and Diva on a stage fighting for the microphone. This exercise makes use of several actions that are common with character animation such as walking, interaction with another object, anticipation and follow through.

In this lesson you will learn the following:

- About the animation workflow;

- How to study motion as a guideline for the animation;

- How to block your animation;

- How to switch and animate constrained objects;

- How to playblast your animation;

- How to optimize playback refresh.

Animation workflow

This is an outline of a suggested animation workflow that you can follow - or you can take this any direction you choose. Whichever workflow you use, there are several helpful animation tools and techniques that you might want to keep in mind.

Storyboarding

The storyboard is where you hope to find as many problem areas and special requirements as possible. Here is where you note and plan for timing issues that may occur.

For the particular animation created here, following is a short text description of the motion you will attempt to achieve:

> As Diva is singing onstage, Meeper comes in with a determined walk. Diva turns her head to figure out why Meeper is approaching her. Meeper pushes her away from the center of the stage. Diva, unbalanced, throws the microphone in the air and falls out of frame. Meeper grabs the microphone and gets ready to sing his favorite song.

Motion study

Once you have completed the storyboard to assess the basic timing and actions of the character, you need to evaluate how the characters need to move.

"When in doubt, go to the motion study," is a refrain of professionals at leading production companies. There is no substitute for learning character animation from real live examples. To do this, there is no better example than your own body.

Throughout this lesson, try to stand up and move the way you would like your character to. As you are moving and repeating the movement, concentrate on the different parts of your body and the timing of your motion.

You can also use digitized video of a performance as flipbooks and bring them into Maya as image planes. Fcheck serves as a great method for quickly viewing the reference motion. While not as fast, image planes work very well as frame-by-frame placement guides.

Blocking

Before setting keys for the detailed motion, you will block the shot. Blocking a shot consists of setting key poses every 5-10 frames to rough out the animation. Working with character sets is a good way to set general keyframes on all of your characters' attributes.

For scenes where the motion is not repetitive, it is important to study the extreme positions the character gets into. These are the poses that really define the feel of the animation.

After blocking, you will review the motion asking the following questions:

- Does the motion and timing work in this scene?

- Is the motion too fast/slow?

- Is there continuity with other shots?

Don't worry about the motion details until you are comfortable with the generalized motion.

In-betweens and breakdowns

Once you have finalized the blocked motion, it's time to start rounding out the motions. The in-between is responsible for creating the interpolations from one blocked key to the next. It shapes the motion away from the linear point to point motion you have established.

In-betweens can occur every 3 to 5 frames, or as needed. When your character is moving very fast, the in-betweens could occur on every frame. At this stage, you are not concerned with perfect motion. The resulting motion will look better than the blocked motion, but it will still need some fine-tuning. Study your own movement or a reference video; you may be surprised where and when these keys occur.

Consider using breakdown keys for your in-between keyframes. Breakdown keys are designed to be placed between blocked poses so they can later be moved in the timeline to maintain the relationship between the standard keyframes. Although adjusting overall timing may not be used as much if you are working straight from a motion test, it is still a good idea to get in the habit of using breakdown keys. It will also be useful if you decide to change the timing of your animation later on.

straight from a motion test, it is still a good idea to get in the habit of using breakdown keys. It will also be useful if you decide to change the timing of your animation later on.

Also, consider using sub-characters for your in-between poses so you don't key all of the attributes in the entire character set. A main character set can be created to block out the animation, while sub-characters can be used to key specific parts of the character. For example, the legs and hips can be their own sub-character that controls all of the lower body motion.

Try to avoid keying all of the attributes on an object like you did when you blocked out the motion for the animation. In some places, you may still want to set a key on all the keyable attributes. However, in other more focused places, you will want to key only the selected object. Use the **RMB** in the Channel Box to key individual attributes by selecting **Key Selected** or **Breakdown Selected**. This will result in linear curves in the Graph Editor. The fewer keys you set in this phase, the easier it is to make major changes later.

After you have completed a cursory in-between, save this file as your rough in-between. If you need to make major changes to the animation, this is where you will most likely start.

After the in-betweens are finished, you will go back through and address the rough edges and start working on the details that make the animation interesting.

Adding in-betweens

The motion study is the chief guide for adding in-betweens. Some of the main movements that may escape the casual observer have been pointed out. This is a largely self-guided exercise based on motion study and your creative interpretation. Decide for yourself whether to use standard keyframes or breakdown keys.

Working with the characters

Once you have animation ideas and a basic storyboard done, it is time to start working with the characters in 3D. Following are some guidelines for your animation:

- Frame 1 – Everyone is in position and ready for action.

- Frame 15 – Meeper comes in, Diva turns her head.

- Frame 30 – Meeper anticipates getting the microphone from Diva.

- Frame 45 – Meeper pushes her.

- Frame 55 – The microphone flies off and Diva falls.

- Frame 65 – Meeper grabs the microphone.

- Frame 75 – Meeper gets ready to sing.

Note: *This is only a guide of where the extreme poses could be. If you want, set up a list of the poses you wish to block.*

1   Scene file

- Open the scene file from the last lesson called *30-constraints_02.ma*.

2   Create character sets

- Create a character set for Meeper like you did in Lesson 28.

- Create a character set for Diva with all the relevant nodes to be used for animation.

Note: *You might get warnings about nodes not being evaluated as expected. This is normal and can be ignored.*

3   First frame

Meeper is getting ready to walk toward Diva. Diva is posed as if she was singing.

- Go to frame **1**.

- Pose both characters appropriately using the different nodes and manipulators.

Note: *Pose Diva's left hand to hold the microphone stand by switching its constraint appropriately.*

- Set a **key** for both characters by making their character sets active and hitting the **s** key.

Frame 1

 Tip: Don't bother at this point to place fingers, antennae, tail, blend shapes, etc. Those are subject to change as you continue animating the scene and should be done last.

4   Meeper comes in

As Meeper gets closer, Diva turns her head toward him.

- Go to frame **15**.

- Pose both characters appropriately.

- Set a **key** for both character sets.

Frame 15

5 Meeper gets ready to push Diva

Meeper is now anticipating jumping on the microphone by moving downwards. At the same time, Diva anticipates a surprise motion and also moves down.

- Go to frame **30**.
- Pose both characters appropriately.
- Set a **key** for both character sets.

Frame 30

6 Meeper jumps on the microphone

Meeper will now jump on the microphone, but Diva will do a move that will prevent him from getting it.

- Go to frame **45**.
- Pose both characters appropriately.
- Set a **key** for both character sets.

Lesson 31

Frame 45

7 Diva falls

Diva is now falling, totally unbalanced. Meeper lands, looking at the microphone, which is now flying in the air.

This step will require some constraint animation because Diva lets the microphone go. You will first place the characters, and then concentrate on the microphone.

- Go to frame **55**.

- Pose both characters appropriately.

- Set a **key** for both character sets.

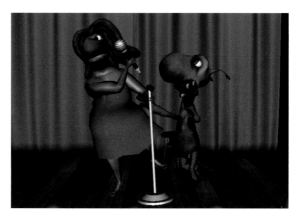

Frame 55

- Select the *microphone_geometry* group, which is constrained to Diva's hand.

- Go to frame **45**.

- Set a keyframe on the microphone in translation and rotation.

Tip: *The microphone is not part of any character set and, therefore, will have to be animated separately.*

This is the last good position of the microphone in Diva's hand.

- Go to frame **55**.

- Move the microphone up in the air and set a keyframe in translation and rotation.

*The microphone has now been animated to fly off between frame **45** and **55**, but the constraint seems to be off prior to frame **45**. This is because Maya has created a special setup to let you use both constraints and animation on the microphone.*

- Locate the **Blend Parent1** attribute on the *microphone_geometry* group.

*This attribute specifies blending between the animation and constraint. When this attribute is at **0**, the animation will prevail and when it's at **1**, the constraint takes over.*

- Go to frame **45**.

- Set a keyframe on **Blend Parent1** to **1**.

- Go to frame **55**.

- Set a keyframe on **Blend Parent1** to **0**.

*The animation on the microphone is now correct up to frame **55**.*

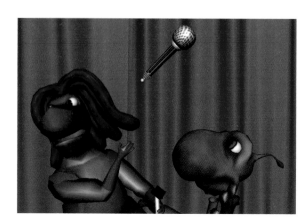

Microphone at frame 55

8 Meeper grabs the microphone

Meeper grabs the microphone as it is falling down. Diva goes completely outside the camera frame and brings the microphone stand with her.

- Go to frame **65**.

- Pose both characters appropriately.

- Set a **key** for both character sets.

- Pose the microphone in Meeper's right hand and key it.

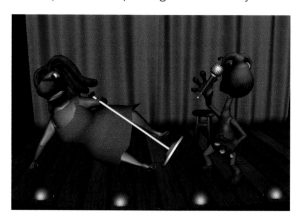

Frame 65

- Select Meeper's *rightHandManip*, then **Shift-select** the *microphone_geometry* group.

- Select **Constrain** → **Parent**.

There is now a new target weight on the microphone's parent constraint. You will animate the weights to switch from Diva to Meeper.

- Set a key at frame **55** on the *Diva_RightArmW0* weight to **1**.

- Set a key at frame **55** on the *Meeper_RightArmW1* weight to **0**.

- Set a key at frame **56** on the *Diva_RightArmW0* weight to **0**.

- Set a key at frame **56** on the *Meeper_RightArmW1* weight to **1**.

Doing so switches the weight of the constraint in a single frame. You must now blend the microphone's animation back to the constraint.

- Set a keyframe on *Blend Parent1* to **0** at frame **56**.

- Go to frame **65**.

- Set a keyframe on *Blend Parent1* to **1**.

*The microphone's constraint now blends back to its active constraint state for frame **65**.*

9   Fixing the microphone's rotations

If the microphone is flipping in an inappropriate way while in the air, it is usually due to a bad rotation interpolation between the constraints and the animation. The following should fix this problem:

- Select the *microphone_geometry* group.

- In the **Inputs** section of the Channel Box, highlight the *pairBlend1* node.

A pairBlend blends between two sources of animation and was created automatically when you keyed the microphone.

- Set its **Rot Interpolation** attribute to **Quaternions**.

Note: *Quaternions are explained in Lesson 38.*

- With the *microphone_geometry* group still selected, go to frame **45**.

- Set a keyframe in rotation.

Doing so updates the keyframes on the microphone using Quaternions.

- Go to frame **65**.

- Set a keyframe in rotation again.

Note: *You might have to repeat the above steps in order for the rotations to be well evaluated.*

10 Meeper gets ready to sing

Now that you have gone through the task of switching the microphone between characters, you can establish a last pose before Meeper starts singing. Also, you will set another pose for Diva, as she lays on the planks of the stage.

- Go to frame **75**.

- Pose both characters appropriately.

- Set a **key** for both character sets.

Frame 75

11 Save your work

- Save your scene as *31-characteranimation_01.ma*.

Playblast

A *playblast* is a way to view and evaluate your animation quickly. It is a very fast screen grab that captures the animation of the current camera as it is currently displayed. Thus, you can see your animation in wireframe mode, shaded mode or shaded with texture mode (which may take a little longer to calculate). The purpose of this tool is to get realtime playback by using a compressed movie file.

At each stage of creating the animation, you should playblast your animation to create motion tests and to evaluate your work in real time.

The following step will create a playblast of your scene.

1 Playblast the animation

- Position the view to an advantageous position to see all the action.

- Set the playback range to go from frame **1** to frame **75**.

- Select **Window** → **Playblast**.

- Wait for the playblast to be complete.

Once the playblast is over, the movie it created will be played for you.

Tip: *Be careful to not put other windows in front of the Maya interface. Since the playblast is a screen capture, that would stop the playblast of your scene.*

- View the playblast, scrub through and note areas that need work.

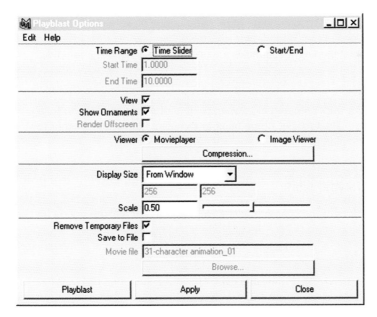

Playblast options

Fine-tune the motion

Once you are comfortable with the in-betweens, you can start to fine-tune the motion. This is the stage that never ends. This is where you can find yourself tweaking and adding keys on every frame. You want to avoid doing that as much as possible. Here are some things to keep in mind that will hopefully keep you on target.

Work on major keys and in-betweens first, then secondary and tertiary keys next, working in layers of refinement.

Get your main keyframes looking as good as possible first, then breakdown into the next layer of in-betweens. Once this layer looks good, go to the next layer. You will find you have intimate knowledge of these milestone keys, instead of having random keys scattered all over the timeline.

Adjust the animation curves in the Graph Editor

In the Graph Editor, you can get a lot of mileage out of a key by working with the tangency or method of interpolation. Keeping keys on whole frames makes for much cleaner curve management and editing.

Remove superfluous keys

Remove keys that don't seem to be contributing or were made ineffective. This is best done in the Graph Editor where you can see the direct result on the curve by removing the key. If you make a mistake, simply undo the removal.

Testing

Test in the work area and in playblasts. It is often a good idea to take a break while you build a movie. Come back to the computer a little fresher to view the movie and plan the changes you will make.

Add subtle motions to major and minor joints and control points

You will often find that after the basic in-betweens are completed, it is time to look at parts of the character you have not keyed at all. The hands and head are very important, as are the shoulders and hip joints that will contribute to the motion of the attached joints. Rotations and translations in all dimensions are what make the subtleties of realistic movement.

Offset the motion of joints to achieve secondary motion

Offsetting is the act of delaying a joint's motion in relation to the surrounding joints. This is often seen as a breaking movement. When an arm, for example, moves toward an object that it wants to pick up, it does not move in unison at once toward its target. Rather, it will break at the main joint (elbow) first, then at the wrist, then the fingers.

Consider another example - the hand. When you make a fist, all of your fingers do not close at once. Some fingers may begin to close ahead of others while some may start late but finish first. These subtle movements and accelerations are at the heart of realistic motion.

High resolution models

When your animation is quite refined, you might want to look at the high resolution characters in order to track final modifications to be done.

Utilizing what you learned in Lesson 29, use the Reference Editor to replace the low resolution characters with the high resolution characters. You can then playblast your animation and see if there are places on the characters that behave differently than the low resolution models.

Once that is done, you can call the animation final and try rendering the scene to see the final results.

Optimization

There are several options for optimizing feedback when setting up the animation of a character.

Display optimization

Geometry can be viewed at many levels of accuracy. By selecting the geometry and then pressing **1**, **2**, or **3** on the keyboard, you can select between coarse, medium, and fine display accuracy. This will not affect how the geometry is rendered, only how it will display. There are several options under the **Display** menu that affect the performance of the Maya display.

NURBS smoothness

Under the **Display** menu you will find a sub-menu for **NURBS Smoothness**. These options control how NURBS surfaces are displayed.

- ·Selecting **Display** → **NURBS Smoothness** → **Hull** displays the selected geometry in the crudest form. From the option box you can adjust the coarseness of the hull display.

- Selecting **Display** → **NURBS Smoothness** → **Rough**, **Medium**, and **Fine** are as you would expect and are selected by pressing the **1**, **2** or **3** key on the keyboard. The option box for each of these allows you to decide whether you want this mode to affect the selected object or all objects.

- Selecting **Display** → **NURBS Smoothness** → **Custom** is a user defined setting for display smoothness. There are many customizable settings in the options box allowing for almost infinite combinations to suit your needs.

Fast interaction

- Selecting **Display** → **Fast Interaction** enables the user to interact with the scene more quickly by temporarily changing the resolution of the geometry while the scene is being manipulated, then switching back to the higher resolution after the scene has settled. This setting will also improve playback of animation in the timeline, but be prepared for some degraded looking geometry.

Animation preferences

In **Window** → **Settings/Preferences** → **Preferences**, the **Timeline** section has a few settings that will influence the way Maya plays your animation. In the **Playback** section you have options to change:

Update view

Update the Active panel or All panels.

Looping

Determines the Looping method.

Playback speed

Play every frame – Maya will play every frame regardless of frame rate settings.

Real-time – This setting forces Maya to playback at the frame rate that is set in **Time** in the **Settings** section. Video frame rate is 30fps and film is 24fps.

Half/Twice – Maya plays back at half or twice the specified frame rate.

Other – Maya will playback at a user defined percentage of the specified frame rate.

▪ In the **Settings** section you also have options to change: **Time** - Maya can playback at a wide range of frame rates.

Performance settings

Under **Window** → **Settings/Preferences** → **Performance Settings**, there are several other options that you can set to improve playback speed.

Conclusion

In this lesson, you animated characters interacting. Understanding the animation process and the animation toolset is a must for every animator. The animation process usually will involve a blocking course and then cycles of refinement until the performance is as good as the schedule permits.

Your characters also used character sets to aid keyframing their attributes. A typical fully articulated character can contain hundreds of attributes that will need to be keyed.

Optimization is also important for maintaining an animatable environment. Work to keep the interface light so there is not too much waiting time for the application to refresh.

The next lesson will be a quick overview about importing audio in your scene.

Lesson 32   Lip-synch

In this lesson, you will import an audio file and have Diva lip-synch to it. Even though this lesson is quite short, there is a lot of experience to gain in lip-synching.

In this lesson you will learn the following:

- How to import an audio file;

- How to create a lip-synching workflow;

- How to drag keyframes in the Time Slider;

- How to copy and paste keyframes through the Time Slider.

Animating Diva

You will now use Diva's blend shapes to lip-synch over a simple recorded audio file. Work through the following steps to create the lip-synch animation, but keep in mind that experimentation is the key to good lip-synching.

1 Scene file

- Create a new scene.

- Reference the file *diva_lores.ma*.

2 Import an audio file

In the *sound* directory of the current project's support files, you will find a simple audio track of a female talking.

- Select **File** → **Import**.

- Select *funky.aiff* from the *sound* directory.

- Click the **Import** button.

The sound file is imported into the scene but is not currently active.

- Load the sound file by **RMB-clicking** in the timeline and selecting **Sound** → **funky.aiff**.

The waveform will appear in the timeline. To hear this in playback, you must set the **Playback Speed** *to* **Real Time** *in your animation preferences. You can also scrub in the timeline to hear the audio.*

Audio in the Timeline

> **Note:** *Interactive performance is critical when doing lip-synching. If the computer is sluggish while you scrub through the Time Slider, it will be difficult to judge the timing of the sound.*

3 Timeline option

In order to better see the waveforms in the timeline, you will now change its height.

- Select **Window** → **Settings/Preferences** → **Preferences**.

- Highlight the **Timeline** category.

- Set the **Timeline Height** to **4x**.

Doing so will change the timeline height in the main interface.

- Click the **Save** button.

- Set the Time Slider to go from frame **0** to frame **38**.

4   Keyframe a blink

When doing lip-synch animation, it is generally a good idea to do the actual lip movement last. Animating the eyes and head movement first helps to set the context for the lip movement, which reduces the likelihood of over-animated, or *chattery* mouth action.

- Select the Diva's *blendShapesManip* node.

- Go to frame **1**.

- Keyframe the **Left** and **Right Blink** attributes.

Tip: *It is better to set keyframes directly on the affected attributes in order to prevent the creation of static channels.*

- Go to frame **3**.

- Set the **Left** and **Right Blink** to **1.0** and set a key.

- Go to frame **5**.

- Set the **Left** and **Right Blink** to **0.0** and set a key.

You have just keyframed a full blink over 5 frames.

5   Dragging keys

When settings keys, you might want to offset certain keyframes in the Time Slider without having to go to the Graph Editor. It is possible to drag keyframes directly in the Time Slider.

- Hold down **Shift**, then **click+drag** from frame **1** to **5** in the Time Sider.

A red manipulator should display.

- **Click+drag** in the middle of the manipulator to offset the keyframes.

- **Click+drag** the arrows of the manipulator to scale the keyframes.

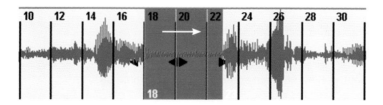

Dragging keys in the Time Slider

6 Duplicate blinks

The red manipulator in the Time Slider can also be used to copy keyframes.

- With the manipulator still active over the blink keyframes, **RMB-click** in the Time Slider and select **Copy**.

- Move the current time to another location, then **RMB-click** and select **Paste → Paste**.

A new eye blink has been pasted at the current time.

7 Head animation

Take some time to animate the head moving along with the audio.

Tip: *Base your animation on the waveform to know where a certain word is spoken.*

8 Preview your animation

Tip: *If the playback is not quite realtime, it might be a better idea to playblast the sequence.*

9 General facial expression

- Select the Diva's *blendShapesManip* node.

- Go to frame **1**.

- Set **Smile** to **1**.

- Set **M** to **1**.

- Set a keyframe on those two attributes.

- Keyframe the other facial blend shapes based on your own ideas.

10 Save your work

- Save your scene as *32-lipsynch_01.ma*.

Phonemes

It is now time to keyframe the phonemes of the audio track onto Diva. Just like other types of animation, you want to first block the animation, then refine the in-betweens and finish by fine-tuning the overall lip-synch.

1 Blocking

Following is a breakdown of Diva's phonemes to use for this specific audio file. It should give you an idea about the timing and which phonemes to use, but you should experiment with different values to shape the mouth properly.

Frame 0: **M**;

Frame 3: **A, Jaw Down**;

Frame 6: **F**;

Frame 8: **E**;

Frame 11: **all Off**;

Frame 14: **U**;

Frame 16: **O**;

Frame 20: **U**;

Frame 23: **F, Blow Cheeks**;

Frame 26: **A, Jaw Down**;

Frame 29: **M**;

Frame 30: **E**;

Frame 38: **M**.

Tip: *Mix multiple shapes to achieve more precise mouth shapes.*

2 Playblast the animation

3 Save your work

- Save your scene as *32-lipsynch_02.ma*.

Refinement

At this point, you might want to double check the animation tangents to make sure that the shapes blend well together. You might also want to start refining the overall animation.

If your computer is powerful enough to playback the high resolution Diva model, you should consider switching Diva's reference.

Tip: *You might want to temporarily disable the jiggle animation.*

High resolution animated Diva

Continue experimenting with the curves in the Graph Editor and playblasting the animation. As you work with the character, it is advisable to make playblasts frequently and early on. This feedback is necessary to anticipate how the flow of the motion is occurring. Avoid the temptation to apply keys on every frame in an effort to pronounce every little nuance and syllable. A good rule in facial animation is *less is more*. Try to animate with as few keys as possible.

Conclusion

In this lesson, you experienced a lip-synching workflow. You also learned a couple of tricks with keyframes in the Time Slider. The key to good lip-synching is to practice a lot to get your brain used to timing and motion. You should now have the confidence to animate Diva and Meeper singing in the scene from the last lesson.

In the next project, you will overview Alias MotionBuilder, which offers realtime animation and non-linear editing.

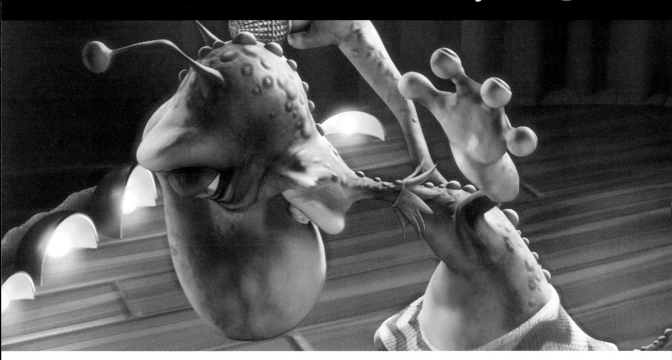

Lessons

In Project Eight, you are going to operate a pipeline that uses Maya software and Alias MotionBuilder software together. MotionBuilder allows real-time playback, powerful animation tools and even animation retargeting. You will learn how to export and set up a character in MotionBuilder, use the animation capabilities of the software and import the final results back into Maya.

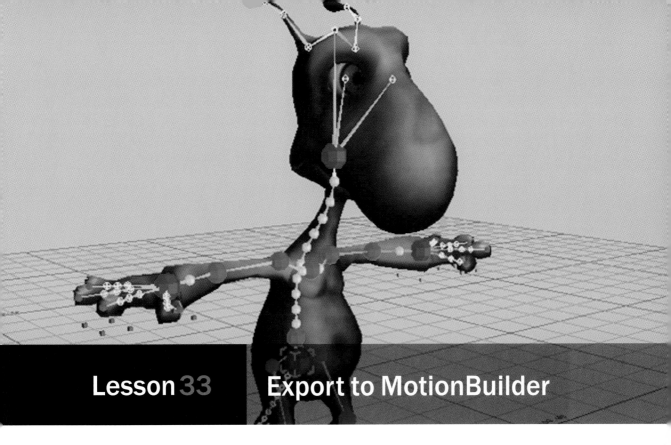

Lesson 33   Export to MotionBuilder

In this lesson, you will learn how to export a character from Maya to MotionBuilder. You will start by changing Meeper's setup to a simple FK skeleton. Then you will alter a few things to make some aspects of the scene more compatible with MotionBuilder. Finally, you will export Meeper to MotionBuilder.

In this lesson you will learn the following:

- How to set up a simple FK character for MotionBuilder in Maya;

- How to convert shading networks to simple textures;

- How to extract blend shape targets;

- How to export a character to MotionBuilder;

- How to characterize a character.

- How to create a control rig.

FK rig

MotionBuilder works well with biped or quadruped characters using only FK skeletons. This means that if you want to use Meeper's rig in MotionBuilder, you will need to either convert it to work only with FK, or attempt to convert the entire rig and make it compatible using advanced techniques. For this lesson, you will simply convert Meeper to use a FK skeleton.

1 Scene file

- Open the scene file called *33-meeperFK_00.ma*.

Note: *This scene is the same scene you created at the end of Lesson 21, which is Meeper bound with blend shapes.*

2 Strip the rig to simple FK

- Select **Edit → Delete All by Type → IK Handles**.

- Select **Edit → Delete All by Type → Clusters**.

- Select **Edit → Delete All by Type → Constraints**.

3 Delete obsolete nodes

- Select **Edit → Select All by Type → NURBS Curves**, and press the **Delete** key.

- In the Outliner, under the *rig* group, keep only the *Hips* root node; delete all the other *rig* children.

- Delete the *multiplyDivide1* utility node controlling both forearm roll bones.

You should now have a simple FK skeleton with its geometry.

4 Make the attributes unlocked and keyable

- Select **Edit → Select All by Type → Joints**.

- Through the **Channel Control** window, make all the **Rotation** attributes unlocked and keyable.

5 Reset the joints' rotations

- Select the *Hips* joint, then **RMB-click** and select **Assume Preferred Angle**.

Doing so will reset the skeleton into its original position.

6   Convert the textures

- In the Hypershade, select the *lambert2* shader used to texture Meeper's body, then **Shift-select** the *Meeper* geometry.

- Select **Edit** → **Convert to File Texture** → ☐.

- In the option window, set the following:

    X and **Y Resolution** to **512**;

    File Format to **TIFF**.

- Press the **Convert** button.

- Repeat to convert the eye material and make both eyes use the same texture.

- Make sure none of the old materials are connected to the new materials in the work area, then select **File** → **Optimize Scene Size**.

Doing so will remove any unwanted nodes.

Tip: *It might be a good idea to rename the converted file textures in the current sourceImages folder with meaningful names. If you do so, don't forget to set the new texture names in Maya to make them easy to find.*

---

7   Save your work

- Save the scene as *33-meeperFK_01.ma*.

Meeper for MotionBuilder

Since the beginning of this book, you have been giving specific names to your nodes. Your process for naming the joints that are part of Meeper's skeleton is very important since MotionBuilder can automate some tasks when using those specific names.

Note: *The following name convention can be somewhat confusing. Remember, the names represent the limb and not the articulations.*

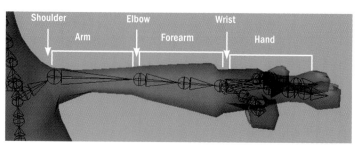

Naming convention

1   Naming convention

- Following is a list of base nodes that are required to properly create a character in MotionBuilder. Make sure your joint names follow this list:

Head

LeftArm	*RightArm*
LeftForeArm	*RightForeArm*
LeftHand	*RightHand*

Spine

Hips

LeftUpLeg	*RightUpLeg*
LeftLeg	*RightLeg*
LeftFoot	*RightFoot*

- Following is a list of auxiliary nodes that can be used if needed. Make sure your joint names follow this list:

Neck

LeftShoulder	*RightShoulder*
LeftFingerBase	*RightFingerBase*
LeftToeBase	*RightToeBase*

Project Eight

- Any other spine joints should be named as follows:

    Spine1

    Spine2

    ...

    Spine9

- Any other neck joints should be named as follows:

    Neck1

    Neck2

    ...

    Neck9

- Any roll joints should be named as follows:

LeftUpLegRoll	*RightUpLegRoll*
LeftLegRoll	*RightLegRoll*
LeftArmRoll	*RightArmRoll*
LeftForeArmRoll	*RightForeArmRoll*

- Any finger and toe joints should start with the following:

LeftHand	*RightHand*
LeftFoot	*RightFoot*

    and end with the following:

    Thumb1, 2, 3, 4

    Index1, 2, 3, 4

    Middle1, 2, 3, 4

    Ring1, 2, 3, 4

    Pinky1, 2, 3, 4

    ExtraFinger1, 2, 3, 4

Note: *Other nodes can be named any other way.*

2 Blend shapes

In order for MotionBuilder to understand your character's blend shapes, you must have the actual targets in the scene. If you don't have the targets in the scene, the attributes will be listed in MotionBuilder, but the geometry will not update. Following is a way to extract the blend shapes and recreate the blend shape deformer.

- Select the *Hips* joint, then select **Skin** → **Go to Bind Pose**.

- Following is a short MEL script that will duplicate each blend shape target:

```
for($i = 0; $i < `blendShape -q -wc blendShape1`; $i++)

{

    blendShape -e -w $i 1 blendShape1;

    string $name = `aliasAttr -q ("blendShape1.weight[" +
$i + "]")`;

    rename `duplicate -rr meeper` $name;

    blendShape -e -w $i 0 blendShape1;

}
```

Note: *MotionBuilder does not support in-between target shapes. The MEL script will only extract the targets defined at a weight of 1.*

You must now recreate the blend shape deformer using those targets.

Note: *Hide the extracted blend shapes if you want to speed up your scene.*

- Delete the *blendShape1* node.

- Select all the blend shape targets in order through the Outliner, then **Shift-select** the *Meeper* geometry.

- Select **Deform** → **Create Blend Shape** → ❑.

- In the option window, select **Edit** → **Reset Settings**.

- In the **Advanced** tab, set the **Deformation Order** to **Front of Chain**.

- Click the **Create** button.

3 Save your work

- Save the scene as *33-meeperFK_02.ma*.

Export to MotionBuilder

To be able to export to MotionBuilder, you must make sure the *FBX* plug-in is loaded. The FBX plug-in exports FBX files, which is a file format specific to MotionBuilder. By loading this plug-in, you allow Maya to export that kind of file, which can then be opened directly in MotionBuilder.

1 Load the FBX plug-in

- Select **Window** → **Settings/Preferences** → **Plug-in Manager**.

- In the Plug-in Manager window, find the *fbxmayaXX.mll*.

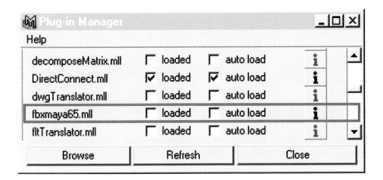

Plug-in Manager

- Turn **On** both **loaded** and **auto load** checkboxes.

- Click the **Close** button.

2 Export FBX file

- Select **File** → **Export All**.

- At the bottom of the **Export** window, set **File of type** to **Fbx** (*.*).

- Enter the **File name** as *33-meeperFK_03.fbx*.

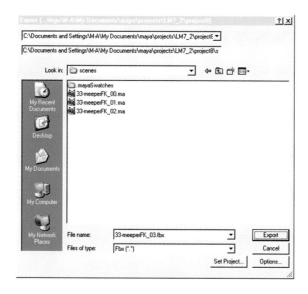

Export window

- Click the **Export** button.

3   Export FBX options

When you export an FBX file, an option window is displayed allowing you to set some simple options upon the creation of the FBX file.

FBX option window

- Leave the options as they are and click the **Export** button.

  The file will be exported in the location you specified earlier.

Note: *If any error occurs as the file is being exported, a message will appear explaining the problem.*

Meeper in MotionBuilder

You can now open Meeper in MotionBuilder.

Note: *The following exercise explains the basics of MotionBuilder, but it is recommended that you read and experiment with MotionBuilder in order to reap the maximum benefits out of the rest of this project.*

1   Open MotionBuilder

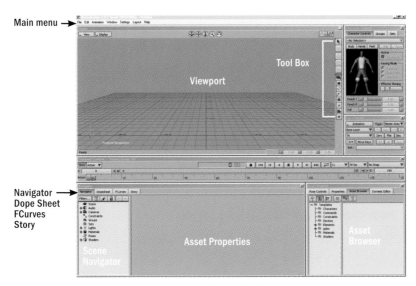

MotionBuilder

2 Open Meeper

- Select **File** → **Open**.

- Browse to the *33-meeperFK_03.fbx* file created in the last exercise.

- Click the **Open** button.

*The **Open** options will be displayed. Leave them as they are for now.*

- Click the **Open** button again.

Note: *Alias MotionBuilder will create the blend shape deformer and will delete the targets automatically.*

3 Change the background color

- In the Navigator window, under the **Navigator** tab, click on the **+** sign next to **Cameras** to expand the group.

- **Double-click** on the **Producer Perspective** to display its properties in the right side of the window.

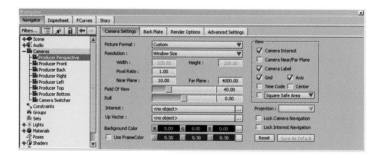

Perspective properties

- Set the **Background Color RGB** to **0.6**, **0.6** and **0.6**.

4 Navigate in the viewport

- Select **Settings** → **Keyboard Configuration** → **Maya**.

You will now be able to navigate in the viewport using **Alt** *and the three mouse buttons, just like in Maya.*

> **Alt+LMB** to **Tumble**;
>
> **Alt+MMB** to **Track**;
>
> **Alt+RMB** to **Dolly**.

Meeper in MotionBuilder

> **Note:** *Changing the keyboard layout also changes various hotkeys to better suit Maya. For instance, the classic MotionBuilder layout* **Undo** *is* **u** *and the Maya layout* **Undo** *is* **z**.

5 Change joint size

- In the **Navigator** window, click on the **+** sign next to **Scene** to expand the group.

- Click on the **+** sign next to the *rig* group to expand it.

- **RMB-click** on the *Hips* node and select **Select Branches**.

Doing so will select the entire skeleton hierarchy.

- In the **Asset Browser** window, click on the **Properties** tab.

- Expand the **Skeleton Node Settings** section.

- Change the **Size** attribute to **10**.

- **Double-click** in an empty space in the viewport to clear the selection.

6 Change the display

- In the viewport window, enable **Display** → **X-ray**.

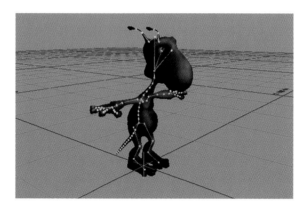

X-Ray view

7 Save your work

- Select **File** → **Save As**.

*The **Save As** dialog box will appear.*

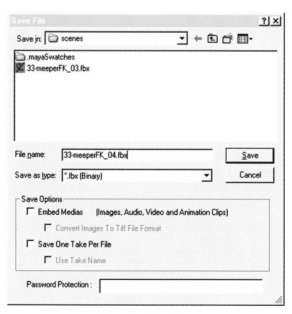

Save As dialog box

- Turn **Off** the **Embed Medias** checkbox.

- Enter the name *33-meeperFK_04.fbx*, then click the **Save** button.

The Save options will be displayed. Leave them as they are.

- Click the **Save** button again.

Create a character

MotionBuilder has an asset called a *Character*. Adding a Character asset to your character will allow you to use several powerful features, such as motion capture, character retargeting and many more. Next, you will add a Character asset to Meeper.

1 Scale up Meeper

MotionBuilder's units are in centimeters and some tools' default settings are meant to be on human sized characters. Since Meeper is currently about 25 centimeters high, you will scale him up.

- In the **Navigator** window, select the *rig* node located underneath the **Scene** group.

- In the **Tool Box** on the right side of the viewport, select the **Scale Tool**.

- **Click+drag** the center of the **Scale Tool** to scale Meeper up.

Note: *You can see the currently selected node, the active manipulator and the global scaling value at the bottom right of the viewport.*

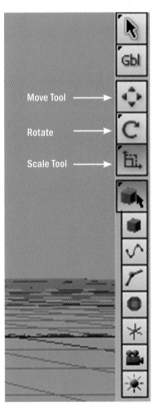

Move Tool

Rotate

Scale Tool

Tool Box

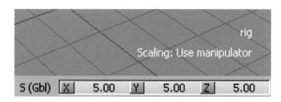

Info on scaling values

- Scale Meeper uniformly to **5** in **XYZ**.

2   Create the character automatically

- In the **Asset Browser** window, select the **Asset Browser** tab.

- Under the **Templates** section on the left side of the window, highlight the **Characters** group.

The different character assets that can be created are loaded on the right side of the window.

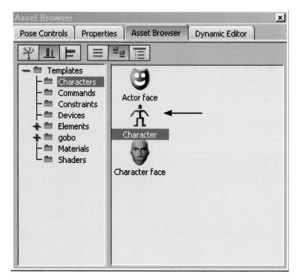

The Character asset

- **Click+drag** a **Character** asset onto any parts of Meeper's skeleton in the viewport, then release the mouse button.

A Characterize pop-up will be displayed.

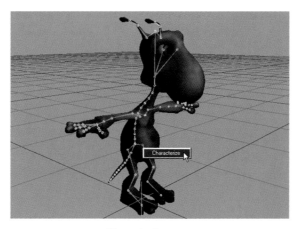

Characterize pop-up

- Select **Characterize**.

Another dialog box appears to let you specify the character type.

- Select **Biped**.

Doing so tells Alias MotionBuilder to automatically look into Meeper's hierarchy and find all the names that match the naming convention outlined earlier in this lesson. If the tool does find the appropriate nodes, a biped character asset will be created successfully.

Note: *If a problem occurred, the character will be created regardless, but you will have to specify each node manually. This topic is explained in the next step.*

3   Character name

- In the **Navigator** window, click on the **+** sign next to **Characters** to expand the group.

- **RMB-click** on *Character* and select **Rename**.

- Enter *MeeperCharacter*, then press **Enter**.

4 Character definition

- **Double-click** on *MeeperCharacter* to display its properties in the right side of the window.

- Select the **Character Definition** tab.

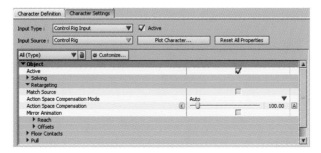

Character Definition tab

> **Note:** *If the automatic characterization from* **Step 1** *failed for your character, you will have to manually specify all the nodes of your character in this window. You can do this by dragging nodes from the hierarchy in the left side of the Navigator into each slot of the Character Definition tab. Once that is done, simply turn* **On** *the* **Characterize** *checkbox.*

5 Control rig

Now that MotionBuilder knows the structure of your biped character, you must create the *control rig* that goes with your character. A control rig is a predefined setup that gives you all the character animation power of Alias MotionBuilder.

> **Note:** *The Full Body IK in Maya is similar to the MotionBuilder control rig.*

To create the control rig, do the following:

- Click on the **Create** button on the left of the **Character Definition** tab.

- Select the **FK/IK** button.

The FK/IK control rig will allow you to use both IK and FK to animate your character.

6   Character settings

- Click on the **Character Settings** tab and set the following:

  Input Type to **Control Rig Input**;

  Active to **On**.

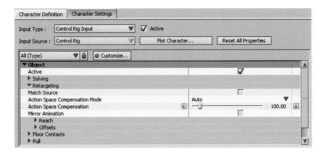

Make the character active

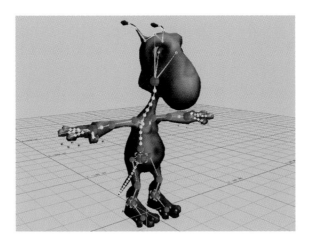

Meeper with control rig

7   Save your work

- Save the file as *33-meeperFK_05.fbx*.

Conclusion

You have now exported Meeper to MotionBuilder and set him up so he can be animated using a standardized control rig.

In the next lesson, you will experiment with the control rig and keyframe simple animations.

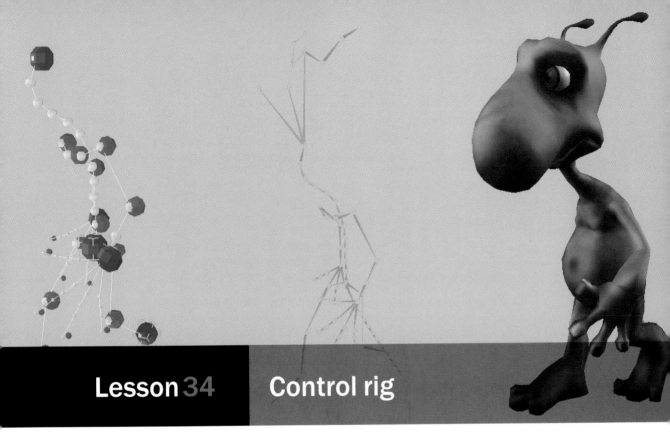

Lesson 34   Control rig

In this lesson, you will experiment with the control rig of Alias MotionBuilder. You will begin by setting up some general behavior and then move on to keyframe an animation. You will also learn about layers and takes.

In this lesson you will learn the following:

- How to set up floor contact settings;

- How to keyframe the control rig;

- How to save, load and mirror poses;

- How to keyframe on a layer;

- How to create auxiliaries;

- How to use and keyframe auxiliaries;

- How to plot animation to the skeleton.

Floor contact

A nice character rig feature is the ability to define floor contacts. In this exercise, you will define contact between the feet and the floor. By doing so, Meeper will not be able to move his feet or toes below the floor. When calculating the feet/floor contact, note that if the toes go through the floor but the heel does not, the toes will bend automatically.

1   Scene file

- Open the scene file called *33-meeperFK_05.fbx* from the last lesson.

2   Character settings

- In the Navigator, **double-click** on the *MeeperCharacter* to display its properties.

- In the **Character Settings** tab, open the **Floor Contacts** section.

- Turn **On** the **Feet Floor Contact** checkbox.

This option will prevent you from animating the feet below the floor surface.

3   Adjusting the floor contact markers

When the character rig was created, feet/floor contact markers were also created and displayed in the viewport.

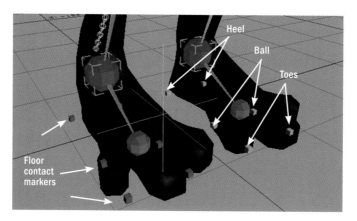

Feet floor contact markers

Note: *Hand/floor contact markers were also created, but you will not use them at this time.*

- **Double-click** on any toes/floor contact marker.

- Select the **Move Tool** in the tool box.

- Move the marker on the **Z-axis** in front of the toe geometry.

Note: *Updating one floor contact marker will also update the other markers.*

- Move the marker on the **Y-axis** to align it with the foot/sole geometry.

- **Double-click** on any ball/floor contact marker.

- Adjust the marker to be in line with the toe bone.

- **Double-click** on any heel/floor contact marker.

- Adjust the marker to be in line with the heel of the geometry.

The Character Controls

The Character Controls window is an all-in-one window that allows you to select handles and define their behavior. You can determine if a limb is controlled by IK or FK, if it is pinned into position or translation and also how you want to keyframe your character.

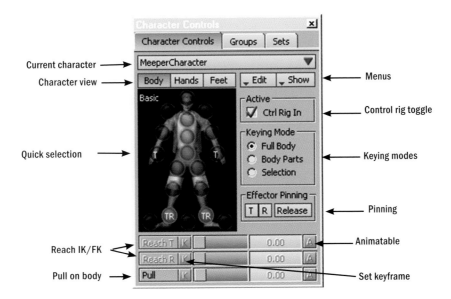

Character Controls window

1   Hide the control rig

Since you will be using only the Character Controls window to animate Meeper, you will now hide the control rig.

- In the **Character Controls** window, make sure the current character is set to *MeeperCharacter*.

- Select **Show** and turn **Off** all options.

- In the viewport, select **Display** → **Models Only**.

You should now see only the Meeper geometry in the viewport.

Tip: Press **Ctrl+a** to cycle between **Normal**, **X-Ray** and **Models Only**.

2   Quick selection

The quick selection diagram represents a biped with circles on the various body parts. Clicking in those circles will select the corresponding marker in the control rig. You can use **Shift** and **Control** to select and deselect markers. If you click in an area where there are no circles, toggle the selection between all selected and none selected.

You can change between the body, hands and feet diagrams by clicking on the buttons at the top of the quick selection diagram.

- Select the *Left Hand* circle.

The circle will change to yellow, specifying that it is currently selected.

3   Keying modes

Just like in Maya with character and sub-character sets, you can specify which part you want to keyframe with the control rig. If **Full Body** is selected, a keyframe will be set on the entire character. If **Body Parts** is selected, a keyframe will be set on only the body parts that are currectly selected. If **Selection** is selected, only the selected marker will be keyframed.

- Select **Body Part,** as the current **Keying Mode**.

Notice the other circles that are part of the left arm are highlighted to specify that keyframes would also be set on those.

Body Parts keying mode

4   Pinning

Pinning defines how a limb reacts as you move the control rig. Pinning a marker in translation will prevent it from moving if any other body part is moved. Pinning a marker in rotation will keep its rotation if any other body part is moved.

If a marker does not have pinning, it will move with the rest of the body. If it is pinning both in translation and rotation, it will be locked in space.

- With the *Left Hand* still selected, turn **On** pinning for both translation and rotation by clicking on the **T** and **R** in the **Pinning** section.

- Repeat for the other hand.

5   Reach Translation and Reach Rotation

When Reach T and Reach R are enabled, the character's skeleton will follow the control rig IK system rather than following the control rig FK system. Set those attributes depending on what you intend to do with the character.

Tip: *For instance, enable Reach T and Reach R for the hands when you need them to interact with the environment. Keep Reach T and Reach R off for the hands if the arms will be left dangling.*

6 Save your work

- Save the scene as *34-meeperAnim_01.fbx*.

Posing Meeper

You have now set up the control rig in a way that will make it easy to pose and animate Meeper. In this exercise you will pose and set keyframes on Meeper.

1 Scene file

- Continue with your own scene.

Or

- Open the scene file called *34-meeperAnim_01.fbx*.

2 Switch layouts

Alias MotionBuilder has the ability to set and save window layouts. When animating a character, it is recommended to switch to the **Animation** layout.

- Select **Layout → Animation**.

The different windows will be reorganized in a way that help for animation tasks.

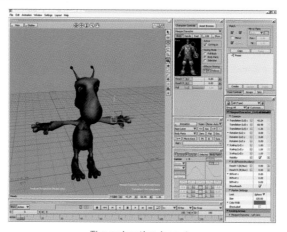

The animation layout

3   Pose Meeper

Using the quick selection diagram along with the **Move** and **Rotate Tools**, pose Meeper as if he would be walking like the following:

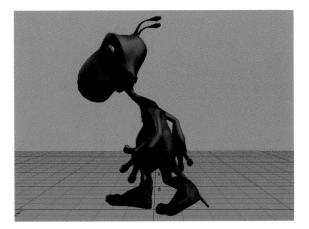

Meeper first pose

> **Tip:**   *Switch between the tools using the* **w** *and* **e** *hotkeys. Switch between local and global manipulators by pressing the* **F5** *and* **F6** *hotkeys.*

4   Keyframe Meeper

- Select **Full Body** as the current **Keying Mode** in the **Character Controls** window.

- With any control rig marker selected, press **s** to set a keyframe.

A keyframe marker should appear in the Time Slider.

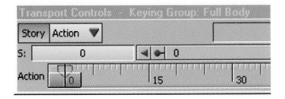

Keyframe in Time Slider

5 Save pose

When using a character rig, you can save and load poses through the **Pose Controls** window. The **Pose Tool** can even let you mirror a pose in a single click.

- In the **Pose Controls** window, click the **Create** button.

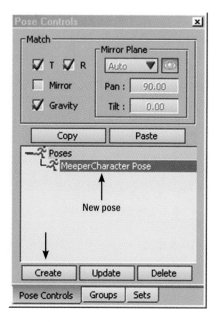

Create a pose for Meeper

6 Move current time

- Move the current time indicator to frame **15**.

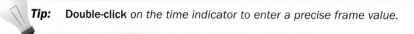

Tip: **Double-click** *on the time indicator to enter a precise frame value.*

7   Load and mirror a pose

- Turn **On** the **Mirror** checkbox.

- **Double-click** on the *MeeperCharacter Pose* item.

Doing so will load the pose on Meeper and mirror it.

- Press **s** to set a keyframe.

8   Key another pose

- Move the current time indicator to frame **30**.

- Turn **Off** the **Mirror** checkbox.

- **Double-click** on the *MeeperCharacter Pose* item.

- Press **s** to set a keyframe.

9   More keyframing

- Repeat the previous step to set keyframes at frames **45** and **60**.

10 Test the results

- **RMB-click** in the Time Slider, then select **Time** → **Frame Take**.

- Press **Play** in the Time Slider or scroll using the time indicator.

Meeper should be walking, but without moving forward.

11 Save your work

Animating Meeper

You can now set keyframes to move Meeper forward. You will do so by releasing the pinning of the control rig.

1   Scene file

- Continue with your own scene.

Or

- Open the scene file called *34-meeperAnim_02.fbx*.

2   Release pinning

When you move the hips, the feet and hands will stay behind since they are pinned in translation. One quick way to prevent this is by enabling the **Release Pinning** button.

- Go to frame **15**.

- Attempt moving the hips to see if the hands and feet are locked in position.

Cannot move the hips forward because of the pinning

- Undo the last move.

- Turn **On** the **Release** button in the **Pinning** section of the Character Controls window.

- Move the hips forward on the **Z-axis** by about **25** units.

Now Meeper is moving appropriately.

Tip: *The current value can be seen in the lower-right corner of the viewer window.*

- Press **s** to set a keyframe.

3 Translate the other poses

- Translate the other poses forward at frame **30**, **45** and **60** and set keyframes.

- Turn **Off** the **Release** pinning button.

FCurves

The **FCurves** window in Alias MotionBuilder is very similar to the Graph Editor in Maya. You will use the **Fcurves** window to edit the walk you just keyframed.

1 Select the foot markers

- In the **Character Controls** window, select the two *foot* markers by holding down the **Ctrl** key.

2 Open the FCurves window

- Select **Window → FCurves**.

3 View the translation curves

- On the left side of the FCurves window, highlight the **Translation** item.

Doing so will display only the translation curves for the selected models.

- Press **a** to frame all.

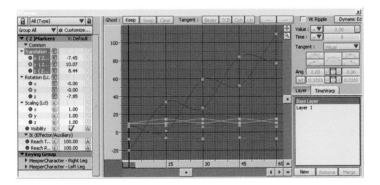

The FCurves window

4 Fix the sliding feet

- **Click+drag** to select all keyframes.

- Click the **Set Flat Left** button in the **Tangent** section.

Since the tangency of the keyframes is not broken, all the keyframes will be made flat.

- **Double-click** in an empty space to clear the keyframe selection.

- Flatten every set of two keyframes on the **Z-axis** to plant the feet as Meeper moves forward.

Note: *Don't worry about fixing the feet perfectly; you will experiment with another tool to help with this task later in the lesson.*

5 Close the FCurves window

6 Save your work

Layers

Alias MotionBuilder has the ability to layer animation quite simply.

It is important to understand what is happening when you keyframe on a layer. A layer keyframe keeps the difference between the base layer and the new position of an object. In order to get the final position, Alias Motionbuilder will add layer values to the base layer for the specific time.

For instance, if you set a single layer keyframe to offset a hand, that offset would be kept for the entire animation because of a constant curve infinity. In order to prevent that, you must set keyframes with values of zero before and after the portion of the animation that you want to modify.

Tip: *Keyframing on a layer will create curves that are Bezier by default, so make sure to set the keyframes tangency in order to prevent bad overshooting animation.*

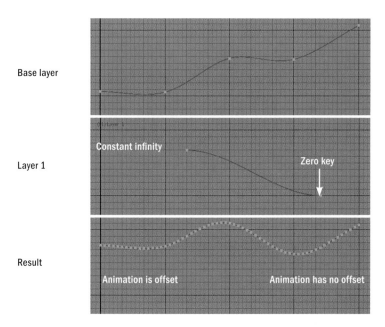

Layers logic

You will set keyframes on a new layer of animation to refine Meeper so he lifts his feet as he walks. Any changes will be made in that layer, making it easy to fine-tune them.

1 Scene file

- Continue with your own scene.

Or

- Open the scene file called *34-meeperAnim_03.fbx*.

2 Add a layer

- In the **Key Controls** window, change the **Layers** combo box from **Base Layer** to **Layer 1**.

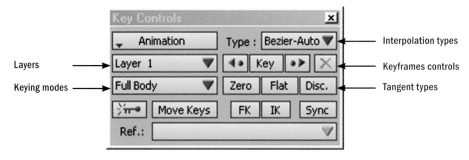

The Key Controls window

Note: *Notice the keyframes that were in the Time Slider have disappeared. This is because you will now keyframe on the new Layer 1, which is empty.*

3 Zero key

- Go at frame **1**.

- Select the *Left Ankle*.

- Change the **Keying Mode** to **Body Parts**.

Any new keyframes will now be set only on the leg.

- Press the **Zero Key** button in the **Key Controls** window.

*You have now set a zero keyframe at frame **1**.*

- Press the **Flat Key** button in the Key Controls window.

This will make the tangent of the new keyframe flat.

4 Second zero key

You must now isolate the section of animation that you want to modify by setting a second zero key.

- Go at frame **15**.

- Press the **Zero Key** button.

- Press the **Flat Key** button.

5 Modify the foot position

It is now safe to modify the foot any way you want between those
two zero keys.

- Go to frame **8**.

- Move the foot up and forward and rotate it as needed.

- Press **s** to set a keyframe.

6 Playback the results

You can now see the effect of the layer keyframes on the base animation.

7 Continue keyframing

Continue keyframing the feet rising between steps by repeating
steps **3** to **5**.

Improve the walk cycle

Tip: *Since layer keyframes are offsets and not positions, you can easily copy and*
paste them in the Time Slider. To do so, simply click on a keyframe marker
to highlight it, then **RMB-click** *and select* **Copy**. *Move the time indicator*
to a new time and **RMB-click** *and choose* **Paste**.

8   New layer

▪ In the **Key Controls** window, change the **Layers** combo box from **Layer 1** to (**New Layer**).

Doing so will create a second layer.

9   Secondary animation

Add secondary animation on Meeper's *Hips* and *Head* on the second layer.

Tip: *Pin the head in rotation to make it easier to move it while keeping it straight.*

Note: *Body parts that are not part of the control rig, such as the tail and antennae, must be animated using their joints. Display the joints by selecting* **Show** → **Skeleton** *in the* **Character Controls** *window.*

10 Save your work

Auxiliaries

The ability to create *auxiliaries* is a powerful control rig tool. Auxiliaries are override nodes that can control the character's animation. For instance, you can create auxiliaries to plant a character's feet, even though the control rig animation is not planted. You could also parent a hand auxiliary to the hips so the hand stays on the hips as the character walks.

You will now use an auxiliary to place Meeper's hand on his head. You will also plant Meeper's feet using auxiliaries.

1   Scene file

▪ Continue with your own scene.

Or

▪ Open the scene file called *34-meeperAnim_04.fbx*.

2   Display settings

▪ Select **Display** → **X-Ray** in the viewport window.

▪ In the **Character Controls** window, select **Show** → **Auxiliaries**.

3   Create a hand auxiliary

- Go to frame **1**.

- In the **Character Controls** window, **RMB-click** in the *Left Wrist circle* to pop the contextual menu and select **Create Aux Effector.**

The auxiliary is created at the current wrist position.

Left wrist auxiliary

- Select **Show** → **FK** to display the FK control rig.

You can now see the yellow markers of the FK control rig.

- With the auxiliary selected, select **Edit** → **Parent**.

- **Click+drag** the auxiliary node on the head FK marker.

The head FK marker will highlight to specify it will be the parent.

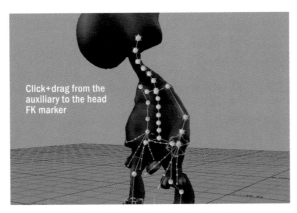

Parent the auxiliary to the head

- **Release** the mouse button.

The auxiliary is now parented to the head.

4 Position the auxiliary

- Move and rotate the *auxiliary* so Meeper's hand touches his face.

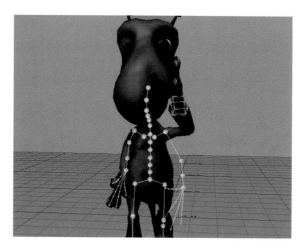

Hand on the face

Note: *You can clearly see the offset created between the auxiliary and the arm's FK rig. The arm FK keeps it animation, but the wrist is constrained to the auxiliary.*

- Select **Show** → **FK** to hide the FK control rig.

5 Play the scene

Since the auxiliary fully controls the wrist at this time, you can playback the scene and see the hand locked to Meeper's face.

6 Create an auxiliary

- Go to frame **15**, where Meeper's foot should begin in the planted position.

- In the **Character Controls** window, **RMB-click** in the *Left Ankle circle* to pop the contextual menu and select **Create Aux Effector**.

The auxiliary is created at the current location of the ankle.

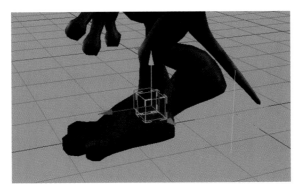

Left ankle auxiliary

7 Key the auxiliary

You must now keyframe the auxiliary *on* for the time the foot needs to be planted.

- In the **Character Controls** window, click on the **k** button to keyframe both the **Reach T** and **Reach R** attributes at **100** for the currently selected auxiliaries.

The auxiliary is now keyframed **On**.

Tip: To reselect an auxiliary, either click on it in the viewport or **RMB-click** in the circle in the **Character Controls** window.

- Go to frame **12**.

- Set the **Reach T** and **Reach R** attributes to **0** and click their **k** buttons to set a keyframe.

The auxiliary is now keyframed **Off** *from the beginning of the take up to frame 13.*

- Go to frame **30**.

- Set the **Reach T** and **Reach R** attributes to **100** and click their **k** buttons to set a keyframe.

This keyframe is only to maintain the auxiliary **On** *to this point.*

- Go to frame **35**.

- Set the **Reach T** and **Reach R** attributes to **0** and click their **k** buttons to set a keyframe.

This keyframe turns the auxiliary **Off** gradually over 5 frames.

Note: *Don't forget to set your tangents to flat. You can do this quickly by selecting the keyframes in the Time Slider, then pressing* **RMB-click** *and selecting* Interpolation → **Flat**.

8   Key the foot

At this time, Meeper's foot is trying to reach both the control rig IK and the auxiliary. As a result, the foot is not yet planted. You must turn off the reach attributes on the control rig marker opposite the auxiliary.

Note: *You only have to do the following when the IK control rig* **Reach T** *and* **R** *are turned on.*

- In the **Character Controls** window, **RMB-click** in the *Left Ankle* circle and select the *LeftAnkleEffector*.
- Go to frame **12**.
- Keyframe both **Reach T** and **Reach R** attributes at **100**.
- Go to frame **15**.
- Keyframe both **Reach T** and **Reach R** attributes at **0**.
- Go to frame **30**.
- Keyframe both **Reach T** and **Reach R** attributes at **0**.
- Go to frame **35**.
- Keyframe both **Reach T** and **Reach R** attributes at **100**.

Tip: *Use the [,] and [.] hotkeys to browse between keys.*

9   Test the results

- Playback the scene to confirm that the left foot stays planted while it's on the ground.

10 Plant the other steps

- Repeat steps **3** to **5** to create other auxiliaries and plant all of Meeper's steps.

Note: *Creating multiple auxiliaries for each control rig node is the easiest solution. Advanced users might animate the auxiliary nodes for the different steps.*

11 Delete animation on the toes

When you keyframed different poses for Meeper, you also keyframed the toes in a bent position. This is why Meeper's toes appear animated. To correct this, you must delete the FK toes' animation.

- Select **Show** → **FK** to display the FK control rig.

- Select the yellow marker *LeftToeBase* and *RightToeBase*.

- Change the **Keying Mode** to **Selection**.

- Change the current layer to **Base Layer**.

- Select all the keyframe markers in the Time Slider.

- **RMB-click** and select **Delete**.

The toes should now be animated correctly.

12 Save your work

Plot animation

When an animation is on the control rig, it is not yet on the character's skeleton. The character's skeleton is only driven by the control rig. In order to have the actual animation on Meeper's skeleton, you will need to *plot* the animation to the skeleton. Plot animation is similar to *bake* animation in Maya. By doing so, MotionBuilder will set a key per frame in order to have the skeleton as accurate as the control rig.

1 Scene file

- Continue with your own scene.

Or

- Open the scene file called *34-meeperAnim_05.fbx*.

2 Switch layout

- Select **Layout** → **Editing** to go back to the original layout of the windows.

3 Plot the animation

- In the Navigator, **double-click** on the *MeeperCharacter* node to display its properties.

- Under the **Character Settings** tab, click on the **Plot Character** button.

A message box will appear asking if you want to plot the control rig to the skeleton.

- Click on the **Skeleton** button.

The plot options will be displayed. This window offers you choices such as the frame rate to be used, or if you want to use filters on the animation curves to simplify them.

Plot options

- Leave the options as they are and click the plot button.

Alias MotionBuilder will take a second to plot the animation. Once it is done, it automatically deactivates the control rig and shows you the animation on the skeleton.

4   Test the results

5   Save your work

- The final scene file is called *34-meeperAnim_06.fbx*.

Conclusion

You have now been introduced to the basics of the control rig keyframing workflow. You were taught how to set up floor contact and how to save, load and mirror poses. As well, you learned pinning, keyframing, editing fcurves and creating auxiliaries. Lastly, you plotted the animation from the control rig to the character's skeleton. This is a lot of information for a beginner in MotionBuilder, but being able to use the power of MotionBuilder's control rig and real-time display will greatly speed up any animation tasks.

In the next lesson, you will learn about takes and how to blend motions together.

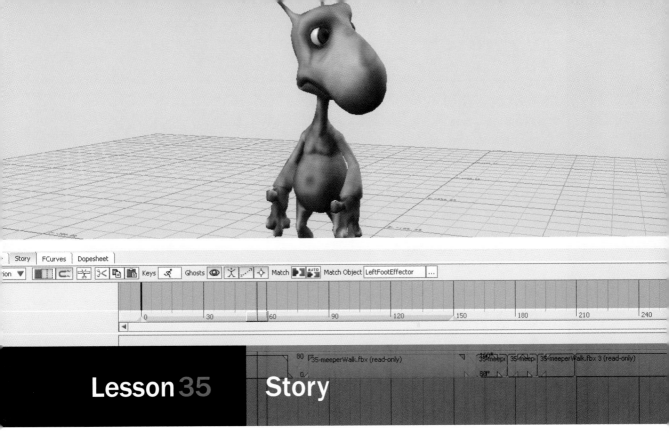

Keys   Ghosts   Match   Match Object   LeftFootEffector

0   30   60   90   120   150   180   210   240

80   35-meeperWalk.fbx (read-only)   35-meep 35-meep 35-meeperWalk.fbx 3 (read-only)

0/

Lesson 35   Story

In this lesson, you will use some of MotionBuilder's Story Tool features to blend two Meeper motions together. The Story Tool is similar to Trax in Maya.

In this lesson you will learn the following:

- How to use the Story Tool;

- How to add a favorite path to the Asset Browser;

- How to blend two animations together;

- How to display ghosts;

- How to use the Razor Tool to cut a clip;

- How to plot the animation.

Story Tool

The Story Tool is a non-linear editor that gives you unprecedented control over characters, models, cameras, audio and video. It allows you to build a story using clips containing animation, sound, video, models, cameras, commands and constraints, which you place on tracks along a timeline.

In the following exercise, Meeper will be animated using two different takes: the walk cycle done in the previous lesson and an idle animation.

1   Scene file

- Select **File** → **New**.

You will start from an empty scene.

- Select **Layout** → **Editing**.

2   Add a favorite path

- In the **Asset Browser**, under the **Asset Browser** tab, **RMB-click** and select **Add favorite path**.

A browser window will be displayed, asking you for the folder.

- Browse in the *support_files* directory and select the *scenes* folder for *project 8*, then click on the **OK** button.

The folder will be added as a favorite on the left side of the Asset Browser.

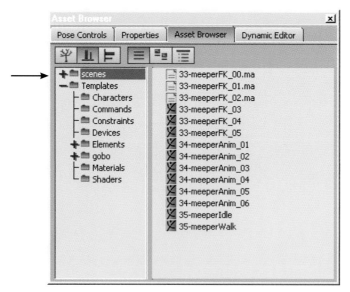

Motion blending

- Highlight the *scenes* folder to load its content into the right side of the window.

3   Add Meeper to the scene

- **Click+drag** the scene file called *33-meeperFK_05* from the Asset Browser to the viewport.

As you release the mouse button, a pop-up menu will be displayed allowing you to open the dragged file.

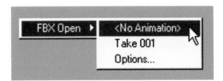

Drag file pop-up menu

- Select **FBX Open** → **<No Animation>**.

Meeper and its animation will be loaded.

4   Open the Story Tool

- In the **Navigator** window, select the **Story** tab.

*The **Story** window is divided into two sections, the top section, which is used for camera cuts, and the bottom section, which holds animation tracks where you can blend animations together.*

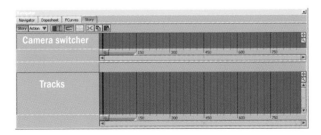

The Story Tool

5   Import animations

You will now import animations for Meeper by dragging additional files from the Asset Browser into the story's track section.

- **Click+drag** the file *35-meeperIdle* from the Asset Browser to the story's track section.

The animation contained in the dragged file will be loaded as a clip onto the models of the current scene.

Note: *The start of the loaded animation will be placed at the position of the mouse cursor.*

- **LMB-click** on the clip in the **Character Track** to highlight it.

The clip in the Story Tool

- **Click+drag** the clip until it snaps to frame **0**.
- **Click+drag** the file *35-meeperWalk* from the Asset Browser to the Story Tool, on the same track as the first clip.

The two clips should now be side by side.

Note: *Dragging the new file to another track will not blend the two animations together.*

- Press **a** to frame the clips in the Story window.

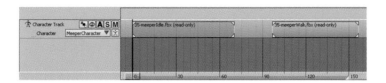

The two clips side by side

- **Click+drag** the clip around frame **80**.

6 Match clips

At this time, if you playback the scene, the two animations will play one after the other without being aligned together. It is easy for the tool to align the characters using a pivot.

- Highlight the *meeperWalk* clip.

- At the top of the **Story** window, click on the **Match Options** button.

The **Match Options** *window will be displayed.*

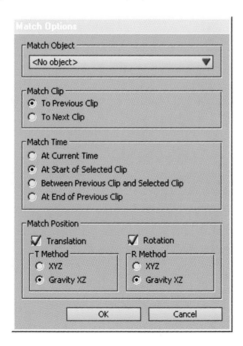

The two clips side by side

- Open the **Match Object** list box and select *MeeperCharacter_Ctrl: LeftFootEffector* from the list.

- Leave the other options as they are, then click the **OK** button.

Doing so will match the left foot effector of the two clips together. If you playback the scene, you will see that the two clips are now aligned based on the position of the left foot.

7   Create a blend

- **Click+drag** the lower right blend arrow of the first clip to the start of the second clip.

Doing so extrapolates the end of the first clip.

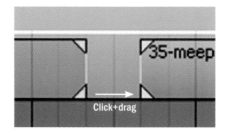

Drag the first clip's blend arrow

- **Click+drag** the lower left blend arrow of the second clip to the start of the first clip.

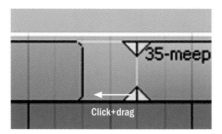

Drag the second clip's blend arrow

Doing this actually creates a blend area.

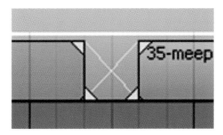

The blend area

8   Smooth interpolation

At this time, the blending area is linear. In order to give a more natural look to the blend, you will change the blending interpolation to be smooth.

- **RMB-click** in the **Story** window and select **Select Clips** → **All**.

- In the **Asset Browser** window, select the **Properties** tab.

- In the **Fade In-Out** section, set the following:

> **Fade In Interpolation** to **Smooth**;

> **Fade Out Interpolation** to **Smooth**.

The curves in the blend area between the clips will now ease in and ease out.

9   Playback the results

Play the scene to see how the clips are blending together and to see how Meeper reacts.

10 Save your work

- Select **File** → **Save As** and call the file *35-meeperStory_01.fbx*.

Ghosts

In order to ease the task of blending motions, the Story Tool can display ghosts of the different clip animations. Ghosts are a wireframe representation of the character and its animation. They can be used to preview more precisely how animations blend. Through the Story Tool, you can select a clip and position and reorient it to suit your needs.

Next, you will make Meeper turn while he is walking.

1   Scene file

- Continue with the scene file called *35-meeperStory_01.fbx*.

2   Display the ghosts

- In the viewport window, select **Display** → **X-Ray**.

- In the Story window, enable the **Show/Hide Ghost** button which is represented by an eye icon.

The ghosts are displayed in the viewport.

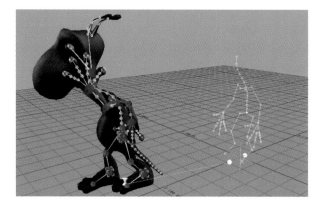

The animation ghosts

3   Offset a clip's position

- Click on the *meeperWalk* clip in the Story window to highlight it.

- Select the **Rotate Tool**.

- In the viewport, rotate the clip's pivot point to reorient the whole clip motion.

- Playback the scene to see the effect of reorienting the clip animation.

4   Clip cycling

- **Click+drag** the end of the *meeperWalk* clip toward the right.

Doing so will cause the clip to be repeated. Since the walk was already cycled, the resulting animation is seamless.

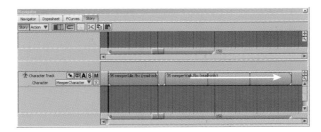

Cycling the clip

5 Razor Tool

- Move the time indicator in the **Story** window toward the middle of the new cycled *meeperWalk* clip.

- With the *meeperWalk* clip selected, select **RMB** → **Razor**.

Doing so will cut the clip at the time indicator's position.

6 Ghost offset

Attempt to select the last portion of the clip and have Meeper do a 45-degree turn. In order to improve the quality of the transition, you will have to create a blend area.

Tip: *You will achieve better blending if the blend occurs when one of the feet stays planted. You should also consider gradually turning the animation by making several cuts and blends rather than doing the turn in one single blend.*

7 Playback the animation

- **RMB-click** in an empty space of the **Story** window and select **Frame Start/End**.

- Play the animation.

8 Save your work

- Select **File** → **Save As** and call the file *35-meeperStory_02.fbx*.

Plot animation

When you are finished creating and editing animation using the Story Tool, you can save the entire result by plotting it to the character. Until you plot, a scene built in the Story window is separate from the animation outside the Story window.

1 Scene file

- Continue with the scene file called *35-meeperStory_02.fbx*.

2 Plot the animation

- **RMB-click** in an empty space of the **Story** window and select **Plot Whole Scene To Current Take**.

The plot options will be displayed.

- Keep the options as they are and click the **Plot** button.

3 Clean up

- Select the **Character Track** in the **Story** window.

When selected, the whole track becomes green.

- **RMB-click** and select **Delete**.

The selected track will get deleted.

4 Play the scene

- Play the scene to make sure Meeper has the appropriate animation.

5 Tweak the animation

At this time, all the animation is on Meeper's control rig. If needed, you can now plant Meeper's feet as he is walking and turning. You can also keyframe some secondary motion to refine the motion further.

6 Plot the animation on the skeleton

In order to be able to get the animation back into Maya, you must plot the animation on Meeper's skeleton.

- Select the **Navigator** tab in the **Navigator** window.

- **Double-click** on the *MeeperCharacter* to display its properties.

- Under the **Character Settings** tab, press the **Plot Character** button.

- Select the **Skeleton** button and keep the options as they are in the plot options.

- Click the **Plot** button.

The animation is now on Meeper's skeleton

7   Save your work

- Select **File** → **Save As** and call the file *35-meeperStory_03.fbx*.

Conclusion

In this lesson, you used the Story Tool of MotionBuilder to blend motions together. For the interests of this project, you only used the motion blending capabilities of the tool, but it has much more advanced features that go beyond the scope of this lesson.

In the next lesson, you will import the animation you just created on Meeper back in Maya.

Meeper:LeftArm
          Rotate X 39.3
          Rotate Y 20.161
          Rotate Z -49.767
          Radius 0.595
INPUTS
  Meeper:rigLayer
OUTPUTS
  Meeper:bindPose1
  Meeper:skinCluster1

⊙ Display ○ Render
Layers Options

V   Meeper:rigLayer
V   Meeper:geometryLayer

Lesson 36

Import in Maya

In this lesson, you will import the animation that was created in the last lesson back into Maya. This process is seamless and allows you to bring back animations that were made using the power of Alias MotionBuilder's tools, such as the control rig, story blending and motion capture.

In this lesson you will learn the following:

- How to import the animation from Alias MotionBuilder in Maya;

- How to use animExport to work around characters with different names.

Import FBX files

Once you have animated the character in Alias MotionBuilder, you can bring the animation back into Maya. There are two ways to import the animation; either you import the whole MotionBuilder scene directly into Maya, or you import only the animation on the character file you used to export to MotionBuilder.

In this lesson, you will import the animation on the existing Meeper rig that you used to export to MotionBuilder.

1   Scene file

- Open the scene file called *33-meeperFK_01.ma*.

Note: *This is the same scene you used to export Meeper in MotionBuilder, except that the blend shape targets are not in the scene.*

2   Import the FBX scene file

- In Maya, select **File** → **Import**.

- Make sure to set the **File of type** to **Fbx** (*.*).

- Select the file called *36-meeperRefined_01.fbx*, then click the **Import** button.

Note: *This FBX scene file's animation was refined to have secondary animation on the hands, eyes, antennae and blend shapes.*

3   Import options

- In the **Import** options, make sure to set the following:

  Animation take to import to **Take 001**;

  Exclusive Merge to **On**.

- Click the **Import** button.

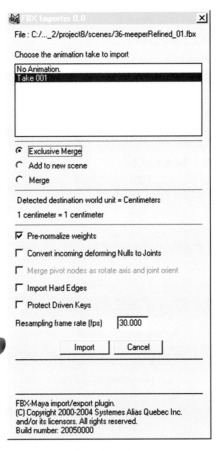

Note: *If you are warned that some attributes are locked and cannot receive animation data, just click the* **Keep All Locked** *button. For instance, if the rig node's scaling is locked, the plug-in will not be able to scale it up by five like you did while setting up Meeper in Alias MotionBuilder. Since attributes that should be animated are unlocked, you can keep them locked without losing any valuable animation.*

Import options

4 Playback the scene

- Play the scene to see if Meeper is animated correctly.

5 Save the scene

- Select **File → Save As**, and name the file *36-meeperRefined_ 02.ma*.

Meeper is animated back in Maya

Workaround

One general issue encountered when bringing the animation back from Alias MotionBuilder into Maya, is that when using namespaces or prefixes on the character's hierarchy, the importer will not be able to find the corresponding nodes to import the animation data.

As a workaround, you can use the same technique outlined in the previous exercise, but then export the animation using *animExport* and re-import it on another Meeper with a different name. This is possible because the *animImport* plug-in can ignore node names and base itself only on the hierarchy of the character.

1 Scene file

- Open the scene file called *36-meeperRefined_02.ma* from the previous exercise.

2 Export the animation

- Select Meeper's *rig* node.

- Select **File** → **Export Selection** → ❏, and set the following:

     File Type to **animExport**;

     Hierarchy to **Below**;

     Channels to **All Keyable**;

     Shapes to **On**;

     Time Range to **All**.

- Click on the **Export Selection** button.

- Export the file as *36-meeperRefined_03.anim* in the current *scenes* folder.

3 Create a reference

In order to simulate a shot where Meeper would be using namespaces, you will create a new scene and reference Meeper.

- Select **File** → **New**.

- Select **File** → **Create Reference** → ❏.

- In the option window, set the following:

     Use Namespace to **On**;

     Resolve all nodes with **this string**: *Meeper*.

- Click the **Reference** button and choose the file *33-meeperFK_01.ma*.

Meeper is now referenced in the current scene using the Meeper namespace prefix.

4   Import the animation

- Select the *Meeper:rig* node.

- Select **File** → **Import** → ❐, and set the following:

     File Type to **animImport**;

     Time Range to **Clipboard**;

     Clipboard Adjustment to **Preserve**;

     Paste Method to **Replace**;

     Replace Region to **Entire Curve**.

- Click on the **Import** button.

- **Import** the file *36-meeperRefined_03.anim* from the current *scenes* folder.

Meeper should now have the proper animation, despite the fact that he had different node names.

5   Playback the scene

- Play the scene to see if Meeper is animated correctly.

6   Save the scene

- Select **File** → **Save As**, and name the file *36-meeperRefined_04.ma*.

Conclusion

You have now correctly imported the animation generated in Alias MotionBuilder onto Meeper in Maya. You also resolved potential problems due to mismatching names.

In the next lesson, you will go back into Alias MotionBuilder to experiment with its character retargeting feature.

Lesson 37 Retargeting

In this lesson, you will experiment with the character retargeting of Alias MotionBuilder. Character retargeting allows you to apply the animation of one character to another character in a few mouse clicks. Doing so will speed up any animating tasks since you will not have to create two identical animations for two different characters.

In this lesson you will learn the following:

- How to prefix a hierarchy;

- How to import a second character into your scene;

- How to set the character for animation retargeting;

- How to copy and paste animation.

Import Diva

You will now open the last MotionBuilder scene where Meeper's animation was refined and merge the Diva character into the scene.

1 Scene file

▪ In MotionBuilder, open the scene file called *36-meeperRefined_01.fbx*.

2 Make sure Meeper is driven by its control rig

In order to be able to use the character retargeting ability of Alias MotionBuilder, you must make sure that the animation from the source character is on its control rig.

▪ In the **Navigator** window, **double-click** on the *MeeperCharacter* to display its properties.

▪ Under the **Character Settings** tab, change the **Input Type** to **Control Rig Output**.

Doing so specifies that you want the control rig to follow the skeleton.

▪ Click on the **Plot Character** button.

▪ In the **Character** window, specify that you want to plot to the **Control Rig**.

▪ Leave the plot options as they are and click the **Plot** button.

The control rig has been plotted following Meeper's skeleton and has now been made active.

Note: *One thing that could go from the skeleton to the control rig is the animation of the tail and the blend shapes. You will see how to copy the secondary animation later in the lesson.*

3 Prefix Meeper's hierarchy

Before being able to import Diva into the scene, it is a good idea to prefix Meeper's setup to not confuse the two characters. This will also prevent MotionBuilder from putting a suffix to every single Diva node.

▪ In the **Navigator** window, open the *Scene* group.

▪ Highlight the *geoGroup*, then **RMB-click** and select **Rename**.

▪ **Rename** the group using the prefix *MeeperGeo*, then add a *column* [:] character.

Note: *The namespace column [:] character is very important in the above step since it tells Alias MotionBuilder to prefix the entire hierarchy with MeeperGeo:.*

- Highlight the *rig*, then **RMB-click** and select **Rename**.
- Rename the group with *MeeperRig:*.

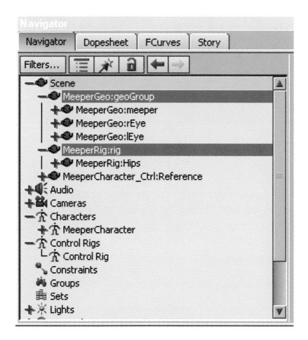

Hierarchy prefixes

4   Merge the Diva scene file

The Diva file was already exported from Maya and set up in Alias MotionBuilder.

- Select **File → Merge**, then select the file called *37-DivaFK_01.fbx*.
- In the **Merge** options, **RMB-click** in the **Element** column of the **Scene** section and select **Append All Elements**.

All the scene element boxes should display a checkmark with a + sign, meaning that the merged scene will append to the current scene.

Merge options

> **Note:** *If the merge options are set to merge, some of the Diva scene objects could be merged with those from Meeper and create an unwanted result.*

- Click on the **Merge** button.

The scene now contains Meeper and Diva.

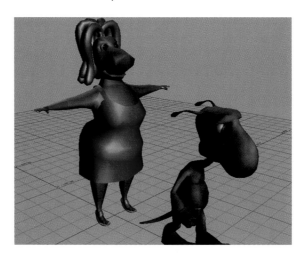

Meeper and Diva

Character retargeting

You will now feed the animation coming from Meeper's control rig to Diva's control rig. Once that is done, you will copy the secondary animation of Meeper's tail and blend shapes to Diva using the *Paste Special* command.

1 Retargeting

- In the **Navigator** window, **double-click** on the *DivaCharacter* to display its properties.

- Under the **Character Settings** tab, change the **Input Type** to **Character Input**.

- Set the **Input Source** to **MeeperCharacter** and make sure the *DivaCharacter* is **Active**.

The Diva character is now animated proportionately to her scale.

Diva is animated like Meeper

2 Plot the Diva animation

- Click on the **Plot Character** button for the *DivaCharacter*.

- In the **Character** window, specify that you want to plot to the **Control Rig**.

- Leave the plot options as they are and click the **Plot** button.

Diva's control rig has been plotted following Meeper's control rig.

3 Move Meeper aside

- In the **Character Controls** window, select the *MeeperCharacter*.

- Click in an empty area in the quick selection diagram to select Meeper's entire control rig.

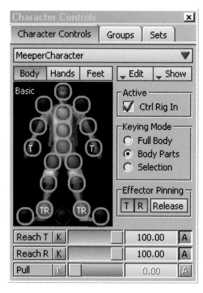

Meeper's control rig selected

- Select the **Move Tool**, and move *Meeper* on the **X-axis**, beside *Diva*.

- Select the **Layer 1** in the **Key Controls** window, then click the **Key** button.

4 Copy the blend shape animation

The following steps will copy the blend shape animation of Meeper to Diva.

- Select *Meeper*'s geometry.

- Select **Edit → Copy**, or press **Ctrl+c**.

This will copy the selected nodes and their animation.

- Select *Diva*'s geometry.

- Select **Edit → Paste Special**, or press **Ctrl+b**.

*Doing so will display the **Paste Onto** options.*

- In the **Paste Onto** options, turn **On** only the **Shape** checkbox.

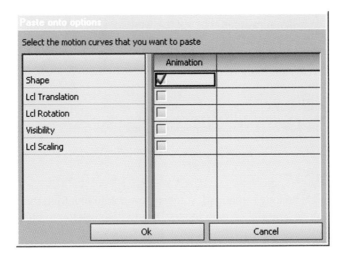

The Paste Onto options

- Click the **OK** button.

The facial expressions of Meeper are now copied onto Diva.

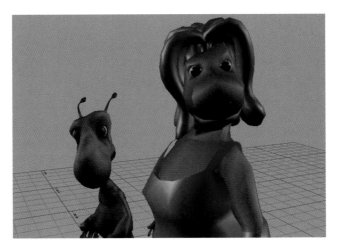

Both blend shapes are animated alike

Note: **Paste Onto** *also works for multiple selections, as long as the objects have the same names and attributes.*

5 Tweak the animation

Animation retargeting does most of the work for you, but you will still need to tweak the animation to fit the proportions of the character. Take some time to refine the Diva animation using the control rig, so the Meeper animation fits her proportions.

6 Save your work

- Save the scene as *37-divaAnimation_01.fbx*.

Clean up

Since Meeper is no longer required, you can now delete him from the scene. Once that is done, you will be able to plot Diva to her skeleton to bring her back into Maya.

1 Scene file

- Continue with your own scene file.

Or

- Open the scene called *37-divaAnimation_01.fbx*.

2 Delete Meeper

- In the **Navigator** window, under the **Navigator** tab, **RMB-click** on *MeeperGeo:geoGroup* from the *Scene* group and select **Select Branch**.

- **RMB-click** on *MeeperRig:rig* and select **Select Branch**.

You should now have all of Meeper's hierarchy selected.

- **RMB-click** on one of the selected nodes and select **Delete**.

- You will be prompted to keep or delete the *MeeperCharacter*; select **Delete Character**.

Meeper is now completely deleted from the scene.

3 Plot Diva

- In the **Navigator** window, **double-click** on the *DivaCharacter* to display its properties.

- Under the **Character Settings** tab, click on the **Plot Character** button.

- In the **Character** window, specify that you want to plot to **Skeleton**.

- Leave the plot options as they are and click the **Plot** button.

Diva's animation has now been plotted to her skeleton.

4 Save your work

- Save the scene as *37-divaAnimation_02.fbx*.

You can now import this file back in Maya.

Note: *You will be able to import the file in Maya easily since you took the time to prefix Meeper before merging the Diva models. If you had not prefixed Meeper, all of Diva's nodes would have been renamed, thus compounding the process of importing the animation back in Maya.*

Conclusion

You have now been able to use the powerful character retargeting ability of MotionBuilder. You also used the Paste Special command, which can simplify animation copying. Lastly, you prefixed hierarchies to prevent clashing of names, which conserved the appropriate node names in order to come back into Maya easily.

In the next lesson, you will go back into Maya and learn about Euler and Quaternion rotation interpolation.

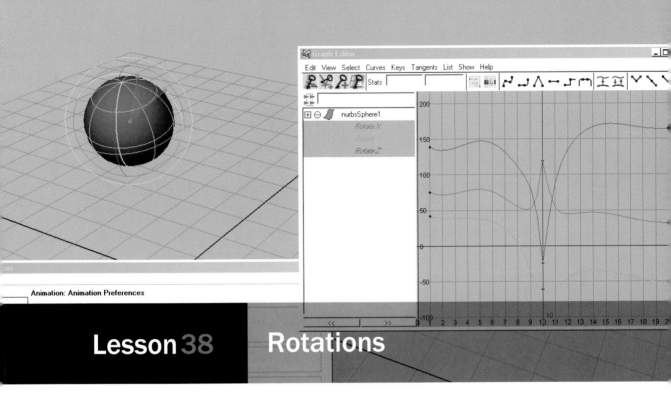

Lesson 38 | Rotations

In this lesson you will gain some insights into the Maya implementation of Euler and Quaternion rotation

interpolation.

In this lesson you will learn the following:

- What rotations are;

- What Euler angles are;

- What Quaternions are;

- What flipping is;

- What gimbal lock is;

- How to set the desired rotation type.

What are rotations?

When you keyframe an object's rotations, Maya calculates the object's orientations between keys by interpolating the rotation values from one key to the next. In Maya, there are two methods of rotation interpolation: Euler and Quaternion. For each animated rotation in your scene, you can specify a rotation interpolation method. The rotation interpolation method you choose for an animated object determines how Maya calculates its rotations.

By default, Maya uses Euler rotations unless otherwise specified.

Note: *Euler and Quaternions are also used in Alias MotionBuilder.*

Euler angles

When interpolating the animated rotations of an object using the Euler method, Maya uses Euler angles to determine the object's axis-specific orientations over time. Euler rotations are calculated using three separate angles representing rotations about the X, Y and Z axes, and an order of rotation.

The rotation order specifies the order in which an animated object is rotated about its X, Y and Z axes. Changing an animated object's rotation order changes its final orientation. For example, if you set an animated object's Rotate Order to YZX, the object will first rotate in Y, then Z and finally X. You can use the Rotate Order attribute to match the rotation order of imported, animated objects to the coordinate systems (for example, XZY opposed to the Maya default XYZ) of the 3D software packages from which they came. This is important if you want the animated rotations of your imported objects to appear as intended.

Note: *You can change the **Rotate Order** of an object through the Attribute Editor. Default **Rotation Order** is **XYZ**.*

There are two kinds of Euler rotation interpolation in Maya: *Independent* and *Synchronized*.

For independent Euler curves, interpolation is calculated from key to key on each individual curve, independent of their neighboring rotation curves. Use independent Euler curves when you want to keyframe a single rotation channel, or when you need to add additional keyframes (and thus detail) to a single rotation curve.
Independent Euler curves are ideal for simple, animated rotations.

All the keyframes on synchronized Euler curves are locked together in time. This means that if an object has synchronized Euler rotation curves, interpolation is calculated from key to key on all of its rotation curves simultaneously. Use synchronized Euler curves when you want to keyframe multiple rotation channels (X, Y and Z) or when you need to add additional keyframes (and thus detail) to all the rotation curves of an animated object. Synchronized Euler curves are ideal for more complex animated rotations.

The main difference between independent and synchronized Euler curves are their keyframes. For example, moving a key in time on an independent Euler Rotate X curve moves only the key on the Rotate X curve, whereas moving a key in time on a synchronized Euler Rotate X curve will also move the corresponding keys on the Y and Z curves. Similarly, if you key only the Rotate X channel for an animated object, and the rotation interpolation type is set to independent Euler, then only the Rotate X channel is keyed. However, if the rotation interpolation type is set to synchronized Euler, then all three (X, Y, and Z) Rotate channels are keyed.

When Euler angles are used to interpolate the animated rotations of an object, the object's orientation about its individual axes is evaluated one axis at a time. This is why Euler-angled rotation is prone to artifacts, such as gimbal lock and flipping. *Gimbal lock* occurs when rotations about a single axis cause unwanted rotations about complementary axes or when axes become coincident. *Flipping* occurs when angles unexpectedly wrap around positive or negative 180 degrees during Euler-angled rotation interpolation between keyframes.

Quaternions

Quaternions provide smooth interpolation of animated rotations and always produce the most efficient path between keyframes, in comparison to Euler angles. Quaternions store the overall orientation of an object, rather than a series of individual rotations. This means that a single Quaternion stores the same amount of rotation data as three Euler angles. Since Quaternions store only orientation values, they can be used to calculate the shortest rotation from one orientation to another.

When animating an object's rotations with Quaternions, Maya first stores the keyed orientation values for the object as Euler angles, converts them to Quaternions for interpolation, and then converts the interpolated Quaternion rotation values back to Euler angles for display in the Channel Box and Graph Editor.

In Maya, Quaternions are displayed as synchronized Euler curves and values. When an object's rotation curves are synchronized, the keyframes on its X,Y and Z Rotate curves are locked together in time. When you add, delete, or move a keyframe on one of the object's rotation curves, the corresponding keys are also updated on the related rotation curves. This eliminates unexpected interpolation problems that can occur when keyframes are deleted from one of the axes, or when keys are moved independently in time.

Flipping

With Euler based evaluation of rotational values, Maya internally calculates the rotational path without respect to the shortest possible solution in world or local space. Often, the shorter path is the correct or logical path for an object to rotate, especially for character or animal movement. This can create the case where an object's rotation is calculated to take the long way around. This can appear as a *flip* in the object's rotation.

Imagine a sphere that was keyframed at **frame 10** with rotational values of **<< 300, 0, 0 >>**.

The sphere is then rotated to **<< 10, 350, 0 >>** and keyframed at **frame 20**.

There are several ways to get to this target value:

It could **rotate -390 degrees** on the **X-axis** and **+350 degrees** on the **Y-axis**. These are large rotations, however. It could also achieve the same ultimate position by **rotating +70 degrees** on the **X-axis** and **-10 degrees** on the **Y-axis**.

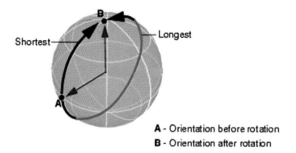

A - Orientation before rotation
B - Orientation after rotation

Rotation possibilities

Which solution is intended? Did the user intend for such a large rotation or were they more interested in the most natural possible solution? Typically in nature (as in muscle driven bone rotations in animals), the shortest path or easiest solution requiring the least amount of energy is preferred. Quaternions follow this type of interpolation - the shorter path by default.

Quaternion evaluation works in ±180 degree values. It does not directly keep track of an object's spin or revolutions. (0, 360, 720...) values are kept normalized to a 360 degree range. -180 to +180, and a solution that involves the shortest path is invoked. Think of a path or arc along the surface of a sphere, which represents the intended rotation of an object.

Gimbal lock

Also with Euler angles, interpolation for each angular curve (X,Y, Z) is calculated separately and the result is combined to form the ultimate angular orientation. This can lead to a logical, yet undesirable path of rotation. Gimbal lock is such a side effect, where an axis appears to not be involved in the rotation because the Euler angle based interpolation has established an alignment between two complementary axes.

Note: *If gimbal lock or flipping occurs, you may be able to correct this behavior using the* **Euler Filter** *found in the Graph Editor.*

If you rotate to a position where the X-axis overlaps the Z-axis, a subsequent X rotation can appear to be the same as Z rotation. These can fight against each other and result in a loss of degree of freedom during interpolation and interaction, cancelling out an axis' role in the Rotate Tool manipulation of the object.

Note: *You can view the gimbal by opening the* **Rotate Tool** *options and selecting* **Gimbal**.

 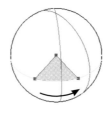 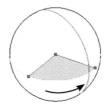

X and Z-axis overlap

XYZ gimbal lock

Quaternion interpolation can alleviate these problems, but also has its own limitations. Because Quaternion interpolation is achieved by calculating from all three axes, you are prevented from editing or manipulating a single axis or degree of freedom independently.

The display of Quaternion curves is also different in the Graph Editor. Euler space uses an open range of values, which appear logically in the Graph Editor. The Graph Editor has an open range as well (0 to very large positive and negative numbers). Quaternion curves, which have only values normalized between -180 and +180, do not fit the Graph Editor's format as well. For this reason, you may see display of Quaternion value and tangent in this context.

Changing the rotation type

You have three ways to work with rotation curves in Maya:

- Independent Euler-Angle Curves;

- Synchronized Euler-Angle Curves;

- Synchronized Quaternion Curves.

Each rotation evaluation can be used by either establishing the certain rotation type as the default manner for Maya to handle rotational evaluation, or it can be selected and changed to the other types from the Graph Editor menu using the **Curves → Change Rotation Interp** menu.

Tip: *When changing curve interpolation type, be sure to select the curves in the* **Outliner** *portion of the* **Graph Editor***. Also, note that if you change from Euler to Quaternion and then back to Euler, the original Euler tangency is maintained.*

To set the different interpolation types as the default:

- Under **Window** → **Settings/Preferences** → **Preferences...**
- Select the **Animation** category.
- Set the **New Curve Default** type as desired.

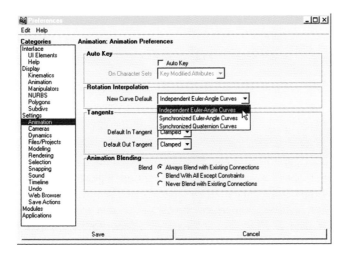

General preferences

Note: *Quaternion curves do not have tangency control. They are created as linear or step type interpolations only.*

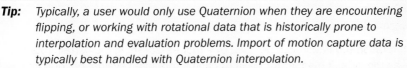

Tip: *Typically, a user would only use Quaternion when they are encountering flipping, or working with rotational data that is historically prone to interpolation and evaluation problems. Import of motion capture data is typically best handled with Quaternion interpolation.*

Constrained animation and camera animation are other areas that are vulnerable to the effects of Euler angle interpolation flipping and gimbal lock. Rigid body and dynamic simulation animation can also lead to flipping and rotational problems that can benefit from Quaternion interpolation.

Index

Notes

Notes

Silver Membership

EVE – Online © CCP2005

GET MORE OUT OF MAYA®
with the Maya Silver Membership program!

As award-winning software, Maya® is the most comprehensive 3D and 2D graphics and animation solution on the market. And whether you're using Maya Personal Learning edition to learn more about computer graphics and animation, or you have a full Maya license that you're using to produce professional content, the Maya Silver Membership program helps you take your Maya skill to the next level.

What is Maya Silver Membership?

Your Maya Silver Membership program gives you quick, online access to a wide range of Maya learning resources. These educational tools – in-depth tutorials; real-life, project-based learning materials; the Maya Mentor learning environment plug-in; Weblogs from experienced Maya users – are available for a fixed monthly, or cost-saving annual, subscription fee.

Silver Membership also keeps you abreast of the latest computer graphics industry developments and puts you in touch with other Maya users and industry experts. Plus, you get 30 days of personal help to orient you around the site.

© TEAM 17 LTD. 2005

Key Benefits

- **Unbeatable Value**
- **Faster Learning**
- **Competitive Advantage**
- **Industry Contacts**

For more information visit www.alias.com/silver